D0646753

Mary Gilliatt's

DICTIONARY

OF ARCHITECTURE AND INTERIOR DESIGN

PLUS ESSENTIAL TERMS FOR THE HOME

Mary Gilliatt's

DICTIONARY

OF ARCHITECTURE AND INTERIOR DESIGN

PLUS ESSENTIAL TERMS FOR THE HOME

Watson-Guptill Publications / New York

A Note on the Life Dates: Every effort was made to find the birth and death dates for the architect, designer, and decorator entries included in this dictionary. Question marks, in place of a death date, indicate that the exact date of death could not be found; entries that have neither birth nor death dates indicate that neither could be found.

First published in 2004 by Watson-Guptill Publications, a division of VNU Business Media, Inc., 770 Broadway, New York, NY 10003

Library of Congress Cataloging-in-Publication Data

Gilliatt, Mary.
  Mary Gilliatt's dictionary of architecture and interior design : essential terms for the home / Mary Gilliatt.
      p. cm.
  Includes bibliographical references and index.
  ISBN 0-8230-1339-1 (hardcover : alk. paper)
  1. Interior decoration—Dictionaries. 2. Architecture—Dictionaries. I. Title: Dictionary of architecture and interior design : essential terms for the home. II. Title.
  NK1704.G54 2004
  729'.03—dc22
                                                    2004012624

SENIOR EDITOR: Victoria Craven
EDITOR: Holly Jennings
DESIGNER: Margo Mooney
PRODUCTION MANAGER: Ellen Greene

Printed in the United States of America

First printing 2004

2 3 4 5 6 7 8 9/12 11 10 09 08 07 06 05 04

Text set in Hoefler and Syntax

For Kate Coughlan,
who has taught me so much

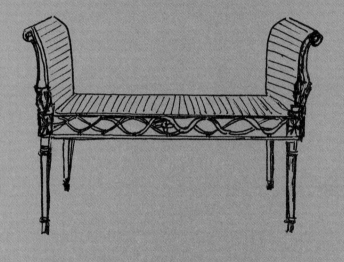

CONTENTS

PREFACE

In my very long career as a writer and decorator, I have often wished for some sort of guide that not only gives as much information as possible on the various terms used in architecture and interior design and on the significant protagonists, but which also demystifies and somehow organizes the whole unwieldy subject in one easy-to-use resource. What's needed, I've often thought, is a reader-friendly dictionary, reference book, and *Who's Who* all rolled into one. Most of us, whether architecture or interior design students, confused home owners, or even the most assured of gifted amateurs, suffer at one time or another from a lack of confidence when it comes to designing, decorating, or renovating our own homes. Money, or lack of it, and worry about putting our tastes on show—or being unsure about what is good design and what is not— can add to our insecurity. But a large part of a home owner's hesitancy comes from what could be termed "option paralysis." Yes, we want choice and knowledge, but we do not want to be overwhelmed by it. If knowledge is power and power begets confidence, then we clearly have to come to terms with somehow organizing that knowledge and putting it into its most logical and useful context.

There are, of course, some excellent, helpful, and magnificently researched dictionaries of architecture, interior design, furniture, and furnishings in existence—some of them date back several decades and are still being updated and reprinted today. The invaluable *Penguin Dictionary of Architecture* (now *The Penguin Dictionary of Architecture and Landscape Architecture*) comes to mind—I've used it so often over the years that it has literally disintegrated into crisp, yellowed little pieces, forcing me to buy the new (and even better and weightier) fifth edition.

Rarely, however, are *all* the different aspects of architecture and interior design combined in one easily comprehensible volume, even though they often become jumbled in an anxious home owner's mind. In my ongoing attempt to make these confusing and interwoven topics as simple as possible, I thought it might be useful to produce just such a one-stop guide. It should be divided, I decided, into relevant sections on architects, designers, and decorators, including their work and influence; the wealth of different architectural, decorating, and related terms; and various styles and movements. Ultimately, I hope that the entries in this *Dictionary of Architecture and Interior Design* will not only help the reader to flesh out a name or term, but will also give a comforting sense of context and connection as design influences and cross-fertilizations are discovered and recognized by the reader.

A Guide that Works on Many Levels

Along with creating an all-in-one guide, I was also anxious to create something that could work on many levels. I have made every effort to define or identify each term or name I use in its correct alphabetical placement and section. However, on occasion the reader will be referred to another term or section, though this type of cross-referencing has been kept to a minimum. Terms that have multiple applications may appear in more than one section.

All terms are organized into twelve practical subject areas, such as Flooring, Furniture and Upholstery, Lighting, Windows and Window Treatments, and so on. For those who simply wish to look up an unfamiliar term—or for that matter a particular architect, designer, or decorator—but have no idea of its context, there is a keyed A–Z index at the end of the book. And for those who want to delve deeper into a particular subject, I've suggested several books for further reading in a selected bibliography.

Finally, since the subject of this dictionary is a visual one, and because many of us learn more easily through visual aids, my publisher asked me to provide sketches to illustrate occasional terms here and there. One word about the sketches, which are just that and no more. Though they do serve to enliven the page and lighten the monotony of so very many words, I apologize for their somewhat casual nature and often wonky perspective. I am in no way a professional illustrator, as can be seen all too clearly. But I can, at least, say that this dictionary is literally all my own work.

Different Audiences Have Different Needs

This book contains the sort of information that will not only help inform decisions, but also impart confidence when home owners must work with architects, interior designers, or builders. When professionals such as these, along with contractors and lighting experts, present ideas, schemes, bids, or quotes, they are sometimes apt to forget that their clients are not necessarily conversant with their specific vocabulary and references. Equally, their clients are sometimes embarrassed to admit any ignorance. This can lead to miscommunication and expensive mistakes on both sides. The same difficulties often apply to antique dealers or furniture salespeople, Oriental rug or other flooring dealers, curtain and shade suppliers, or upholsterers. This dictionary's logical organization allows home owners to easily and quickly brush-up their knowledge in relevant areas before meeting with a professional; or, at minimum, a pertinent section can be consulted (sometimes, perhaps, surreptitiously) whenever an unfamiliar term, name, or reference is used.

Travelers, too, and aficionados of old buildings from the Renaissance to the early Modern period, and iconic new buildings, too, for that matter, will find the notes on architects, designers, and decorators useful. And most new students of architecture and interior design, whether professional or amateur, will be helped by the short descriptions of

Architects, Designers, Decorators, and Their Roles

styles and movements, who influenced who, and how one thing led to another.

There is often some confusion among the general public about the various, sometimes interconnecting roles played by architects, designers, and decorators or interior designers. In short, architects design a building and if they are interested in the *total* building and in every aspect of the interior, they may well design them, too. (In the eighteenth century, for example, Robert Adam insisted on designing everything down to the last doorknob.) I use the word *designer* in the first section of the dictionary to include furniture, lighting, and product or industrial designers who design objects and, more ambitiously, projects like bridges, rather than interiors. I use the word *decorator* as an umbrella term for the shared and sometimes identical roles of decorators and interior designers. There is generally, however, some controversy about the use of the two terms and, not least, as it relates to professional pride. I would say that people who take the title of the interior designer have qualified at a design school and are well versed in schematics, lighting, and even simple furniture design, as well as all sorts of design and architectural theories. Some are even hired by architectural firms to keep the entire job under the firm's roof, so to speak. *Decorators*, on the other hand, are mostly gifted but more *intuitively* than *professionally* qualified. However, there are some well-qualified interior designers who are actually proud to call themselves decorators and find nothing wrong with the term.

The section on architects, designers, and decorators was especially hard to tackle and finalize, particularly for the later twentieth and twenty-first centuries. However appealing, original, and important contemporary work may seem, it is mostly too early to judge its long-term impact. Therefore, deciding whom to include and whom to omit was a difficult task. Although there is currently an unprecedented number of gifted architects, designers, and decorators from which to choose, the sad fact is that a household name of one generation—or a name revered by a professional peer group, the critics, and cognoscenti and fashionistas—rarely makes it to the next.

In the end, I was forced to include only those who I, as an interested amateur and writer on design, think have a particular relevance to or influence on the development of various styles in the past as well as the present. I've included those whose major buildings or designs have stood the test of time, and those whose work has somehow added to today's architectural and design ideas and ways of living in areas as far reaching as Europe, the Far East and the antipodes, the United States, and Central and South America. I have included very few current interior designers or decorators, much as I am an admirer of so many, partly for reasons of space, partly because it is they who are today's synthesizers of all the various threads from both the past and present, and partly because they deserve a book of their own.

Any glaring omissions are my fault and my fault alone, and I apologize, if from unwitting ignorance, I have caused hurt or offense. I do not, however, make any apology for going into some detail about figures from the past. I am a very firm believer that to understand any subject, and to put it into context, one needs to have some sort of knowledge of its history. In any event, my guiding motive was to make this guide as all-embracing as possible for the vast group of interested self-taught home-decorating amateurs and students just at the threshold of professional knowledge, as well as for those interested in architecture and design in general. All-embracing, I should say, but in no way do I claim that it is totally comprehensive. What I have aimed to do is to give as much brief *initial* information as I can on as many relevant subjects as possible.

ACKNOWLEDGMENTS

This has been the toughest, most mind-stretching and most time- and life-consuming book that I have ever written, which, since I have now written almost forty of them, is quite something—at least for me. It has also been the most enlightening because defining so many different facets of such a vast and complicated subject has led me to all sorts of fascinating connections and an absolute verification of the fact that there is very rarely anything new, just new versions. And it has been the most pleasurable because in spite of the mega number of hours this whole project has taken, I have felt so supported in so many different ways by the various people who have helped me, like Baudelaire's *Compagnons des Mauvais Jours*, except that the days though exceptionally long were not so very *mauvais*.

On the book front, first and foremost should come my friends at Watson-Guptill Publications. And first and foremost among these is my editor, Holly Jennings. She has ceaselessly plagued me with all sorts of questions, as well she should with such a complicated reference book. But Holly has been with me every step of the way with charm, tact, and humor, so I think of this dictionary as *our* project. She is, I feel, every bit as responsible for it as I am, and I thank her so much. I am very grateful to Bob Ferro and Victoria Craven who let me do this book (which has, after all, grown like Topsy) and who have put up so patiently with my many *cris de coeur*. Lee Wiggins is always a sympathetic and faithful support, and I have been lucky with the design and production prowess of Margo Mooney and Ellen Greene, respectively. I would also like to mention Alison Cathie, who was my publisher in England for so many productive years and who thoughtfully put me back in touch with Fiona Lindsey of Limelight, now my talented agent.

Of necessity, writing, and for that matter drawing, needs to be done alone. These tasks are not so much lonely—there is no time for that—as people and talk depriving. I have been so lucky then to have had the chance of unwinding—in what have inevitably been the small hours—by chatting away or e-mailing to friends in the antipodes when friends and family this side of the world have long gone to bed. I particularly want to mention my good friend, Jane Turner, who, most valuably, is always there for me (and, I suspect, for a good many other people) and who always both cheers me up and calms me down; Judith Tucker, the most subtle of sub-editors; and Sybille Hetet, Rosemarie White, Ursula and Woody Woodhouse, and Molly Coughlan who, along with my dear and admired friend of so many years, Judy Lance, are two of the world's best *maters familiae*. In America, too, I have always had the support and valued criticism of Barbara Plumb, my first American editor and most stalwart of friends, and I have been helped, sustained, and stimulated by Virginia Cooper, Francis Finlay, Sharon Nathan, Steve Udem, and Angela Thompson—not least for introducing me to her son, Charles Thompson, such a gifted photographer, and to Olya, his wife.

In Europe, I always have to thank my dear Annie and Christopher Cruice Goodall, David Gough and Jan Kern, George and Joy McWatters (my first and best newspaper editor), and Virginia Bredin, who has long outstripped me in decorating—all of whom one can always come home to, so to speak. Also, of course, Helen Preston and Oliver Prenn, Vicky Ellerton (as talented in friendship as she is in decorative painting), Katrina Power (most imaginative of publicists and loyal friend), Carmel and John Jones, Anthony and Sarah Green, Ursula Klocke, and the late Elizabeth Gilliatt. Linda Cohen and Philippe, Jill and Lucy Sublet have been so understanding and companionable in spite of my enforced reclusiveness, quite apart from feeding me so deliciously now and again. Mike Adams has helped me over many ups and downs, as have Christopher Elletson, Marie-Therese Silvia, William Ledward, and Frederique Flory. On the technical front, John Murphy has unfailingly sorted out my overworked computer from its all too frequent collapses. Finally, as always, I want to thank my beloved children, their partners, and my five special grandchildren (Annie and David Constantine; Olivia, Georgia, and Iona Constantine; Sophia Gilliatt and Tori Winn; Tom and Sophie Gilliatt; and Freddie and Rosie Gilliatt) for putting up with their errant mother and grandmother. No one deserves to be so lucky. I am fully aware of that.

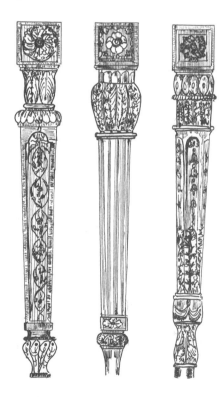

ARCHITECTS, DESIGNERS, AND DECORATORS

No person who is not a great sculptor or painter can be an architect. If he is not a sculptor or painter, he can only be a builder.

John Ruskin (1819–1900), from
Lectures on Architecture and Painting

The comment on the overleaf by John Ruskin—that great nineteenth-century art and architecture critic—may seem a little harsh on architects who are not so diversely gifted, not to mention builders, but as can be seen in this section, many of the world's great architects, particularly during the Renaissance, were indeed sculptors and painters of distinction. Right up until the mid-nineteenth century in America and Europe, when architectural training was finally formalized, most architecture was not practiced as a business but as an art by gifted but untrained amateurs or dilettantes. It is true that there were exceptions. There were architects who called themselves professionals and who were exceedingly busy, but they had learned from observation and theory and were primarily imaginative artists and draftsmen who prepared drawings to be carried out by skilled craftsmen. In France, however, J-F Blondel established the first French school of architecture in the 1730s, which spawned many other such schools. This is presumably why that country took the lead in domestic comforts and sophisticated interiors for so many decades.

In the rest of the world, the majority of architects took little heed of the furnishing and decoration of interiors. A smaller number of architects—such as the English Palladian William Kent and the Neoclassicists Thomas Jefferson, Robert Adam, William Chambers, and James Wyatt—went in the opposite direction, busying themselves with designing every facet of their rooms as well as the furniture. Although early-twentieth-century ladies like Elsie de Wolfe and Syrie Maugham used to call themselves the first interior decorators, they had certainly been preceded by these great Neo-classicists of the late eighteenth and early nineteenth centuries. And architectural members of the Bauhaus School, as well as many of the founders of Modernism in the late nineteenth and early twentieth centuries, certainly occupied themselves with furnishings and interiors as much as the manipulation of space and the general aesthetics of buildings.

In general though and for many hundreds of years, the design of furniture and interiors was left open to gifted cabinetmakers who had enormous influence, and to upholsterers who, recognizing the business opportunities, enlarged their scope to coordinate all aspects of the interior. In eras besotted by fashion, they created trends in furnishing and decorating quite as much as today's fashionistas. They thus took on the role that segued, in the twentieth century, into the separate profession of interior designer, which, in turn, split up into specialties such as lighting and textiles.

AALTO, ALVAR (1898–1976)

Legendary Finnish architect and furniture designer who, after designing many distinguished Modernist buildings for his native country, was commissioned after World War II to design several buildings in the United States. They were Baker House, a residence hall at the Massachusetts Institute of Technology, Cambridge, Massachusetts (1947–49) and the Mount Angel Abbey Library, St. Benedict, Oregon (1970). But his best building may well have been his last, the Finlandia Hall, Helsinki, (1967–75). Architecturally, he is particularly known for his individual style, with its play of brick and timber, curved walls, and single-pitched roofs. However, to the general public he is probably most famous for his exploitation of the natural spring in birchwood and his subsequent use of bent plywood and laminated wood (which he used in the early 1930s, much as Marcel Breuer and Ludwig Mies van der Rohe had used the spring of steel in the 1920s). These techniques were applied to the production of his cantilevered chairs and the Aalto Stool, made by the Helsinki firm of Artek, with which he developed a whole range of laminated birch furniture. His eponymous stool was designed in the 1930s from birch with three separately glued legs that were sliced and bent to form a radius curve extending beyond the seat. Numerous cheaper copies made of plywood exist.

Baker Dormitory (1947–48), Massachusetts Institute of Technology, by Alvar Aalto

ADAM, ROBERT (1728–1792)

The most famous of four Scottish brothers—sons of William Adam, the leading Scots architect of his day—who all became architects and designers in their turn. Robert, however, was arguably the most famous British architect of the second half of the eighteenth century, particularly for his interiors and furniture designs—so much so that he has been frequently described as an interior designer who also created architecture. In fact, his light, elegant, and colorful brand of Neoclassicism has passed into the language as "Adam Style." (This style fully utilizes motifs learned from his studies of Imperial Roman architecture under the French architect Charles-Louis Clérisseau and the then-recently discovered ruins of ancient Herculaneum and Pompeii, cities destroyed by the eruption of Mount Vesuvius in A.D. 79) At a period when there were many arguments about the relative merits of Greek versus Roman classicism, Adam's allegiance to the latter (and later, "Etruscan" decoration) caused him to be nicknamed "Bob the Roman." But there can be little doubt that his light-hearted approach to colors and details in interiors and furnishings was both subtler and more charming than the Anglo-Palladianism that preceded him or the Greek Revival fashion that followed on both sides of the Atlantic. All the same, he was not immediately acclaimed. Some of his early interiors were described by those more used to the austere nobility of Palladianism as "snippets of embroidery." Nevertheless,

he proved to be brilliant at fitting new and exquisite interiors into the shells of existing great houses like Syon House just outside London, Kedleston Hall in Derbyshire, Saltram House in Devon, and Osterley Park, also outside London, as well as creating the famous Kenwood House in North London, Harewood House in West Yorkshire, Home House in Portman Square, London, and many others. Adam was also known for his "classicizing" of the Neo-Gothic: adding comfortably classical interiors to massive Neo-Gothic castles. His influence spread as far afield as America and Russia. He was joined in his London practice by his brother James (1730–1794) in 1758, and the brothers used the name Adelphi (Greek for "brothers") as their trademark. It was therefore particularly ironic that their eponymous speculative building, a palatial group of houses on the banks of the Thames (now destroyed), was a massive failure, and they were saved from bankruptcy only through a lottery and by loans from their elder brother, John.

ADLER, DAVID (1882–1949)

American architect, educated at Princeton and the École des Beaux-Arts in Paris. After traveling widely in Europe he set up practice in Chicago (like his namesake Dankmar Adler of Adler and Sullivan, who died in 1900). He was the brother of the much-admired Californian designer Frances Elkins, who had an influence on subsequent generations. Adler was known particularly for his meticulous modern reinterpretations of eighteenth- and early-nineteenth-century European designs. As an admirer commented: "Adler was brilliant at small-scale interpretations of grand European architecture, but in a totally modern, simplified, and updated way."

ALBERTI, LEONE BATTISTA (1404–1472)

Italian architect, architectural theorist, mathematician, scientist, and writer of the first book on architecture published during the Renaissance—*De re Aedificatoria*. Alberti's book was based on Vitruvius's ten books called *De Architectura* (published in full in 1485 in Latin, but not until 1546 in Italian). In his scholarly study, Alberti discussed contemporary ideas on proportion, the classical orders, and various precepts for ideal urban planning. As if this were not enough, he was also an athlete, a musician, a painter, a playwright, and a student of law—the ideal well-rounded Renaissance man. He wrote other noted books on architecture, perspective, and painting that greatly influenced later architects, artists, and craftspeople down the centuries. And he made every effort to practice what he preached, although he had nothing to do with the actual building of his designs and was, in fact, the first great dilettante architect. His new facade for the originally Gothic church of Santa Maria Novella in Florence (1456–70) was based on a complex system of squares and was thus the first instance of the use of harmonic proportions—a system of proportions first perpetrated in ancient Rome that

related architecture to music—in the Renaissance period. Alberti was convinced that this proportion system was the key to the beauty of Roman architecture and even to the harmony of the universe. He defined architectural beauty as "the harmony and concord of all the parts achieved in such a manner that nothing could be added or taken away, or altered except for the worse." (Not a cheery message for future decorators.) And he considered ornament (which, in his mind, was the classical vocabulary of orders—columns, pilasters, and architraves—adapted to the wall architecture of the Renaissance) to be "a kind of additional brightness and improvement of Beauty."

ANDO, TADAO (B. 1941)

Distinguished both for his beautiful minimalist buildings (many of them in his native Japan), which seem so often to rise out of water, and for the fact that he is self-taught. His latest building is the new Modern Art Museum in Fort Worth, Texas (opened 2002), which finalized the Fort Worth triumvirate of Louis I. Kahn's Kimbell Art Museum and Philip Johnson's Amon Carter Museum. He won the distinguished Pritzker Architecture Prize, considered to be the equivalent in stature of the Nobel Prize, in 1995. (See also *Pritzker Architecture Prize*.)

ANDREWS, JOHN (B. 1933)

Sydney-trained Australian architect who also worked under José Luis Sert, after Sert took over Walter Gropius's position at Harvard University. Much of Andrews's work has been done in

Canada and the United States, including Scarborough College, University of Toronto (1962–69) and the CN Tower, Toronto (1976); the Seaport Passenger Terminal, Miami (1967); and the Gund Hall Graduate School of Design, Harvard University (1968), which so appealed to the now-iconic Philip Johnson that he named it "one of the six great buildings of the twentieth century." Buildings in Andrews's native Australia include the American Express Tower, Sydney (1976) and the Merlin Hotel, Perth (1984).

ARCHER, THOMAS (1668–1743)

English Baroque architect who designed the imposing north front of Chatsworth, Derbyshire, as well as three distinguished churches: Church of St. John, Smith Square, Westminster, London (1713–28); St. Paul's Church, Deptford, London (1713–30); and Birmingham Cathedral (1710–15). He was quite unusual for an English architect of his period in that he showed a fine appreciation of European Baroque— as opposed to the usual British reinterpretation that was either imperfectly understood or more classical than flamboyant—and that he was much influenced by the great Italian architects Gian Lorenzo Bernini and Francesco Borromini, whose buildings he came across on his four-year grand tour between 1689 and 1693.

ARCHIGRAM

Every now and then in the history of architecture there arise individuals or groups who have an inverse reputation and influence either through their writings or imaginative sketches, or through their actual buildings. Archigram, a cutting-edge English group started in 1961 by Peter Cook, Michael Webb, and David Green, all born in the mid-1930s, was one such group. Their spot-on, for the time, Pop Art designs for a Plug-In City (1964), an Instant City (1968), and Urban Mark (1972)— with their visions of candy-colored, flexible, and disposable buildings with clip-on technology—were all considered brilliantly innovative in the climate of the Swinging Sixties, although they were never, of course, actually built. The group did, however, realize a much-praised project for Expo '70 in Osaka, Japan—their "Capsule." The group disbanded in 1975. Nevertheless, they created what must have been at least a gratifying amount of favorable publicity in the decade and a half of their existence.

ARISS, JOHN

Very little is known about the early life (or even death) of this eighteenth-century British-born architect, except that he emigrated to America from England about 1751 and was said to be America's first professional architect. He may even have worked in England for James Gibbs, who was one of the most influential British architects of his day. In any event, he reputedly designed some of the finest English Palladian-style houses in Virginia—such as Mount Airy in Richmond County (1755–58)— in the style of Gibbs, who was well known in America through his *Book of Architecture* (published 1728). Gibbs had died in 1754, only a couple of years after Ariss's arrival on American shores. Clearly enterprising and, some might say, opportunistic, Ariss advertised himself as "lately from Great Britain and ready to undertake buildings of all Sorts and Dimensions...either of the Ancient or Modern Order of Gibbs, Architect."

ARQUITECTONICA

A uniquely American partnership started in Florida in 1977 by Bernardo Fort-Brescia (b. 1951); his wife, Laurinda Hope-Spear (b. 1950); and Hervin A. Romney (who left the partnership in 1984). They came to public attention with the colorful Atlantis Condominium, Miami residential apartments (1980–82), subsequentially featured in the television series *Miami Vice*. Two buildings in Lima, Peru, followed: Mulder House (1983–85) and Banco di Crédito (1983–88). Further buildings in the United States for quite disparate clients included: the North Dade Justice Center, Miami (1984–87); the Center for Innovative Technology, Herndon, Virginia, (1985–88); the Rio Shopping Center, Atlanta, Georgia (1987–88); and their greatly publicized Walt Disney's All-Star Resort in Orlando, Florida (1994). They had a somewhat more solemn-sounding commission for the Banque de Luxembourg, Luxembourg (1989–94), but went back to their quirky entertainment architecture with their winning entry for the Westin Hotel New York at Times Square, a hotel and entertainment complex at Forty-second Street and Eighth Avenue in New York, with the theme of converting Times Square to a symbolized rocket crashing down on Disneyland.

ARUP, OVE (1895–1988)

British architect and structural engineer who trained in engineering in Denmark and in Germany. Arup Associates was formed in 1963 as a partnership of architects and engineers with Peter Rice and was responsible for various university buildings, including new buildings in Great Britain for Corpus Christi College, Cambridge and Somerville College, Oxford. The associates gained a fine reputation for overcoming difficult structural problems, most notably with Jørn Utzon's Sydney Opera House, and as consultants for a great many other notable late-twentieth-century buildings including Norman Foster's Hong Kong and Shanghai Bank, Hong Kong; Renzo Piano and Richard Rogers's Centre Pompidou in Paris; and Nicholas Grimshaw's International Railway Terminal at Waterloo Station, London. Arup only became involved in architecture between 1936–39 when he worked with Berthold Lubetkin's Tecton Group, pioneering a new approach with freely molded concrete for the much-lauded Penguin Pool at London Zoo. Arup's own works include a series of bridges in the 1960s and '70s.

ASHBEE, CHARLES ROBERT (1863–1942)

An architect, craftsman-designer, and one of the founders of the British Arts and Crafts movement along with the poet and artist William Morris, the architects Charles F. A. Voysey and W. R. Letharby, and the cabinetmakers Ernest Grimson and the Barnsley brothers. A "medievalist" enamored with the Gothic style, in 1888 Ashbee founded his own Guild and School of Handicrafts numbering about 150 working men, women, and boys.

ASPLUND, ERIK GUNNAR (1885–1940)

Considered the most important Swedish architect of the twentieth century, though he actually started off working in the manner of the Scandinavian classicism developed by Denmark. In 1930 he began to work more in the Central European Modern style, but substituted a distinctive lightness of form for the rather massive work then current. Probably his most famous works were the extension to the Town Hall of Göteborg (1934–37) and the Woodland Crematorium, Stockholm (1935–40), for which he also designed the interiors and furniture.

AULENTI, GAE (B. 1927)

Versatile and innovative Italian architect and furniture and lighting designer. Although one of her major jobs between 1980 and 1986 was the radical transformation of the 1900 Parisian train station Gare d'Orsay into the Musée d'Orsay, she had already achieved a widely diverse and impressive body of work. In the 1960s she produced the "Pipistrello" telescoping lamp for Martinello Luce, the

Woodland Crematorium (1935–40), Stockholm, Sweden, by Erik Gunnar Asplund

"Jumbo" coffee table for Knoll, the Olivetti showrooms in Paris and Buenos Aires, a showroom for Knoll in New York, and showrooms in Turin and Brussels for Fiat. In the 1970s she designed the "Aulenti" collection for Knoll, the "Gaetano" glass table for Zanotta, and the "Patrocio" table map for Artemide. In the 1980s, while supervising the dauntingly large Gare d'Orsay transformation, she managed to design the interiors for the Musée d'Art Moderne in Paris, the "Cardine" and "Sanmarco" tables for Zanotta, and a "Jumbo" full-sized table for Knoll, as well as convert the Palazzo Grassi in Venice into a museum. In the 1990s she designed her well-known "Tour" glass-topped table on wheels for Fontana Arte and the Italian Pavilion for Expo '92 in Seville.

BAILLIE SCOTT, MACKAY HUGH (1865–1945)

English architect who went on to become, like his contemporary Charles Rennie Mackintosh, much admired and emulated in Europe. In fact, at the turn of the twentieth century, one of the first indications of the spread of a whole new train of thought in design was the publication of rooms designed by Baillie Scott and C. R. Ashbee for the Grand Ducal Palace at Darmstadt in the German design periodical *Innendekoration*. Baillie Scott, like Mackintosh, integrated built-in furniture into his wall patterns, unified by innovative, mainly pastel color schemes of great delicacy.

BAKER, SIR HERBERT (1862–1946)

Born in Kent, England, Baker went to work in South Africa for Cecil Rhodes, and is primarily known for his work in that country. His projects included private houses in Johannesburg in the Arts and Crafts manner and the Government House and Union Buildings in Pretoria (the capital), on which he worked on and off from 1905 until 1913. With Edwin Lutyens, he also worked on government buildings in New Delhi, India and was responsible for the Secretariat and Legislative Buildings there (1912). He was, however, less original than Lutyens, as is evident in his later public buildings in London: The Bank of England (1921), India House (1925), and South Africa House (1930). His best building in England is thought to be the considerably less grand War Memorial Cloister at Winchester College (1922–24).

BALDWIN, BILLY (1903–1983)

American decorator who has been extremely influential on other decorators; in his turn he managed to synthesize ideas he most admired from those who influenced him (not least of which included his ultrastylish and glamorous clients). He turned these influences into a fresh, comfortable, and simple but luxurious and instantly recognizable style of his own, which was never vulgar or pretentious but always looked new, crisply modern, and well maintained, even if the room was mainly full of antique furniture—an admirable feat. He began his career in

Baltimore where he was born, before coming to New York to work for the equally legendary decorator Ruby Ross Wood, who herself came from the South, but more so, one might say, being from Georgia. He had several other distinguished mentors, among them Van Day Truex—one-time head of the Parsons School of Design in New York City and brilliant designer for Tiffany's—who kept him in touch with European and specifically Parisian design trends; the Parisian Jean Michel Frank, whose woven straw chair became a Baldwin staple; the famously stylish fellow citizen from Baltimore, Pauline Potter, who became the Baroness Philippe de Rothschild; the redoubtable Elsie de Wolfe, grand decorator between World War I and World War II; Syrie Maugham, who always quite erroneously described herself as the "first decorator"; and Frances Elkins, who was the first great Californian decorator, though she came from the Midwest.

BARNES, EDWARD LARRABEE (B. 1915)

Environmentally concerned American architect who trained under both Walter Gropius and Marcel Breuer at Harvard University. His sensitivity to community concerns has ranged from the rural and charmingly low-key Haystack Mountain School of Crafts (1958–62) on Deer Isle, Maine, to his creation of one of the best appreciated urban public spaces—the spectacular atrium he included in his IBM Building (1973–83) at 590 Madison Avenue, New York. Other notable buildings are the New England Merchants National Bank, Boston (1963–70); the Walker Art Center, Minneapolis (1971–74); the Dallas Museum of Art (1983–84); and another of his Manhattan skyscrapers, 599 Lexington Avenue (1981–86).

BARNSLEY, ERNEST (1863–1926) AND SYDNEY, (1865–1926)

Brothers who started off as British architects of the Arts and Crafts movement and formed the firm of Kenton & Co. with Ernest Grimson and W. R. Letharby. In 1893 the Barnsley Brothers moved to the Cotswolds with Grimson and ten years later to the village of Sapperton, where they concentrated on cabinet and furniture making, particularly in unstained oak. They became the most accomplished of the so-called Cotswold Group of Furniture Makers.

BARRAGÁN, LUIS (1902–1988)

Mexico City architect and landscape architect who combined the spare geometric forms of Le Corbusier (whom he much admired) with lush landscaping, distinctly local Mexican elements, and painted walls singing with sizzling colors, to create a highly individual style of his own. His vivid "wall architecture" has encouraged imitators around the world. The Museum of Modern Art in New York showed his work in 1976 and, in 1980, he was the second winner of the prestigious Pritzker Architecture Prize, first awarded in 1979 to Philip Johnson.

San Cristobal stable and house in Mexico City built by Luis Barragán in 1968.
The pavilion with the fountain to the left is painted a deep orange.
The stucco work to the right of the white main building is candy pink.

BARRY, SIR CHARLES (1795–1860)

Early Victorian eclectic British architect, principally known for winning the important competition to design the Houses of Parliament in 1835–36. (Work actually started on the buildings in 1839, although they were not formerly opened until 1852.) He started off as a Gothic Revival architect designing what he termed "pre-archeological" Gothic churches that owed little to a correct interpretation of the style and much to his own fanciful invention. Nevertheless, his Travellers' Club in London, modeled after an Italian quattrocento *palazetto*, marked the beginning of the English neo-Renaissance style, while his elegant Reform Club owed more to the Italian cinquecento.

BASEVI, GEORGE (1794–1845)

A pupil of Sir John Soane and architect of the Fitzwilliam Museum in Cambridge, England (1836–45). Basevi's elegantly prosperous Belgrave Square (less the corner houses), solidly handsome Thurloe Square, and various other graceful stuccoed terraces and crescents in South Kensington, London are all examples of a variety of gracious urban planning that have been much emulated.

BASSETT, FLORENCE KNOLL
(B. 1917)

Legendary American architect, space planner, furniture designer, and founder—with her first husband Hans Knoll (killed in 1954 in an auto accident)—of Knoll International, the world-renowned office design and furniture company. She trained with Eliel Saarinen (father of Eero) and Ludwig Mies van der Rohe, and her first commission was to design the Rockefeller brothers' Manhattan offices. Other notable commissions were the interiors for the Connecticut General Life Insurance headquarters near Hartford, designed by Gordon Bunshaft of Skidmore, Owings & Merrill, and the interiors of Eero Saarinen's CBS Building in Manhattan. In her capacity as head of the Knoll Planning Unit, she was responsible for the production of many of the twentieth-century furniture classics like the Mies van der Rohe Barcelona chairs, the Saarinen Womb and Tulip tables and chairs, and furniture by Harry Bertoia, Gae Aulenti, and Richard Schultz, as well as the designs she produced herself.

BAUDOT, ANATOLE DE
(1834–1915)

A follower and pupil of Eugène-Emmanuel Viollet-le-Duc, scholar, medievalist, and restorer. Baudot's Saint-Jean de Montmartre in Paris (1894–1902) was actually the first nineteenth-century Gothic building that successfully combined old and new as advocated by his old master in his two-volume work *Entretiens* (published 1863–72). All the structural members, including the vaulting ribs, were made of reinforced concrete, which was most unusual at that time.

BEHRENS, PETER (1868–1940)

German architect and industrial and typeface designer who could be said to have run a training camp of sorts for great architects, since he had Walter Gropius, Ludwig Mies van der Rohe, and Le Corbusier all working for short periods in his office. One of the founders of the determinedly Modernist Vereinigte Werkstatten at Munich, for whom he designed table glass and other domestic products, he had actually started off as a painter and in the 1890s was much attracted to the teaching of William Morris and the Arts and Crafts movement. This may well explain why, in 1907, he was also one of the founders of the Deutscher Werkbund, an association of avant-garde manufacturers, artists, and writers trying to create a new national art based on the cooperation of architects, artists, and artisans. Possibly as a result of this cooperation, Behrens was appointed that same year to A.E.G. (General Electric Company), for whom he also designed shops, products, and stationery as well as factories, the latter being the first wholly modern factories to be taken seriously architecturally. After World War I (1914–18) his style changed radically first to the current Expressionism and then to International Modern.

BELLINI, MARIO (B. 1935)

Italian architect and furniture designer for C&B Italia, Cassina, Artemide, and Heller among others. As early as 1961, he won the first of several Italian Compasso d'Oro awards and in 1966 was designing the first of his furniture for C&B Italia (now B&B Italia), the company set up by the Cassina brothers and Piero Busnelli to produce contemporary furniture. The *Pianeta Ufficio* office systems furniture he set up in 1974 became very well known. He designed a Tokyo showroom for Cassina in 1991 (in a building designed by Tadeo Ando), the stylish Design Centre, Tokyo (1992), and the Presidential complex and tower for the Citadel in Moscow (1995).

BENJAMIN, ASHER (1773–1845)

A carpenter-builder who, through his enormously successful books, was probably one of the greatest influences on American nineteenth-century colonial architecture and design. He synthesized the works of both Charles Bulfinch and Benjamin Henry Latrobe in his widely read *The Country Builder's Assistant: Containing a Collection of New Designs of Carpentry and Architecture* (1797) and went on to produce an even more successful work. His hardly succinctly titled *The American Builder's Companion: or a New System of Architecture Particularly Adapted to the Present Style of Building in the United States of America (1806)* went though six editions during the succeeding years.

BELTER, JOHN HENRY (1804–1863)

A German immigrant craftsman who remains well known for his extraordinarily elaborate nineteenth-century Rococo Revival furniture, which are today considered collectors' pieces. Some one hundred years before it reached its real commercial success, Belter was also one of the pioneer originators of what is now called plywood, or laminated plywood, which consists of a number of veneers glued or laminated over each other, usually at right angles.

BENNISON, GEOFFREY (1921–1985)

London antique dealer and decorator who had—and still has—a great influence on international fellow designers with what he called his "New-Trad" style, a look often thought of as the new "style Rothschild" since he did so much work for the Rothschild family on both sides of the Atlantic. All through the 1960s and '70s a visit to Bennison's shop was like a sensitively edited trip through the centuries. In those two crowded floors painted with his favorite warm scarlet paint, upholstered pieces in their original leather or velvet jostled with old tapestries, needlework, and faded fabrics. Nineteenth-century Persian carpets flanked overscale eighteenth- and nineteenth-century French mirrors and armoires. Elaborately decorated consoles and side tables combined with often eccentric but useful incidental furniture of any century or country.

There were handsome examples of marquetry and *pietra dure* (the Italian term for a mosaic of semiprecious stones embedded in stone and often used for tabletops, altar fronts, and so on); inlaid ebony and boulle; Imari jars and blue and white porcelain; and bronze and marble classical sculpture, not to mention the plaster casts and busts either perched on pedestals or crowded on the tops of huge old bookcases. All of this ever-expanding stock went to achieve rooms of a moody, nostalgic comfort that many relate to the world-popular Ralph Lauren look of instant ancestry that followed a decade or so later.

BERNINI, GIOVANNI LORENZO (1598–1680)

Great Roman Baroque architect who was equally famous as a sculptor and painter. Although he was born in Naples, his family settled in Rome in 1605, and it is said that no other city is as full of one man's vision, grandeur, and flamboyance—including Baron Haussmann's nineteenth-century grand boulevards for Paris and John Nash's Regency London. Bernini was appointed architect to St. Peter's in 1624 at the age of twenty-six, and it was he who really rediscovered the genius of Michelangelo's earlier grand conception. But although the amazing baldacchino he erected under Michelangelo's dome at St Peter's is considered a wonderfully showy masterpiece, with its enormous bronze barley sugar twist columns, the majority of his most important ecclesiastical buildings were achieved in his middle age and after.

Later Roman works, mostly from 1650 onward, included the extraordinary oval Piazza of St. Peter's, with its surrounding colonnades of freestanding columns with a straight entablature above; the facade and imposing staircase of the Palazzo Barberini; the Cornaro Chapel in the Church of Santa Maria della Vittoria, with its stunning lighting and scenic illusions; and Sant'Andrea al Quirinale, with its sculptural decoration and the Palazzo di Montecitorio and Palazzo Odescalchi, this last a model for subsequent European palaces. His fame became so prodigious that Louis XIV of France, the great "Sun King," was said to have begged him to come to Paris to help complete the east front of the Louvre, although the subsequent very grand designs were never used; they were discarded in favor of the amateur architect Claude Perrault's much lighter and more elegant facade, with its pairs of slender columns. It is said, however, that Perrault, a former doctor turned architect, used Bernini's designs as a basis for his work.

BERTOIA, HARRY (1915–1978)

American furniture designer who is particularly known for the wire-mesh and wire-shell "Diamond" chair he designed for Knoll, which is now a twentieth-century classic.

BLONDEL, JACQUES-FRANÇOIS (1705–1774)

More influential as a writer and teacher than as a practicing architect, Blondel ran his own school of architecture in Paris during the Louis XV Rococo period.

**The colonnade in the Piazza di San Pietro, Rome,
by Giovanni Lorenzo Bernini, begun 1656**

His publications included *L'Architecture Française* (1752–56) and *Cours d'Architecture* (1771–77). He taught that the
walls, furnishings, and furniture in a room
should be designed as a single entity and
result in a homogenous whole. This idea
became a guiding principle of the Rococo
movement, though Blondel, who equally
extolled the great classical traditions of
Mansart and Perrault, also laid down
the foundations for the Neoclassicism
that was to follow. In 1756, he gave up
his school to become professor at the
Académie Royale d'Architecture.

BOFFRAND, GABRIEL-GERMAIN (1667–1754)

Like Bernini, Boffrand—the greatest
French Rococo architect, who in the
Rococo manner, included the decoration and furnishing of interiors as
part of the whole building project—
began as a sculptor before he became
first pupil and then collaborator with
Jules Hardouin-Mansart, the then-
official architect to the court of King
Louis XIV. He specialized in sophisticated but simple and elegant elevations with luxurious interiors and

made a fortune with the speculative building of large Parisian *hôtels particulières*, but lost most of it in the infamous Mississippi Bubble of 1720. He had great influence abroad, particularly in Germany, whose enthusiasm for the Rococo in the eighteenth century continued in the face of the growing taste for the Neoclassical (mostly because Germany at that time was dotted with principalities all vying with each other for the best and most sumptuous architecture). The cogniscenti appear to think that his most striking and elegantly informal building is in his Château de Saint-Ouen, consisting of a small Trianon-like pavilion of three rooms set in a spacious courtyard formed by the guest's apartments, stable, and domestic offices—small, as they say, but perfectly formed.

BOFILL, RICARDO (LEVI)
(B. 1939)

Spanish architect and founder of the Barcelona architectectural workshop Taller de Arquitectura in 1962. His first vividly painted and quirky low-cost housing complexes were a little reminiscent of Luis Barragán's equally vivid "wall architecture" in Mexico. But Bofill is particularly known for his huge French Postmodernist housing and commercial developments, most of them around Paris. He also designed the Alice Pratt Brown Hall, home for the Shepherd School of Music at Rice University, Houston, Texas.

BORROMINI, FRANCESCO
(1599–1677)

Particularly gifted but unconventional Roman Baroque architect. He was a contemporary of and, for a time, an assistant to Bernini (of whom he was said to be neurotically jealous); nevertheless, unlike Bernini, he started as a stonecutter rather than as a sculptor and painter. He progressed to being a stone carver at St. Peter's and from there became chief assistant to Bernini, both working on St. Peter's and on the Palazzo Barberini. Borromini, however, abhorred what he considered to be Bernini's lack of technical knowledge, and when he was offered the job of designing the miniature San Carlo alle Quattro Fontane (1637–41), he seized the opportunity to produce, in effect, one of the most ingenious spatial compositions in existence. He went on to design San Ivo della Sapienza (1643–60), famous for its vertical star-hexagon shape and ziggurat-like spiral dome. Later buildings, however, were either left unfinished, or for various reasons, were less of a success.

BOTTA, MARIO (B. 1943)

Leading Swiss architect who had the inimitable advantage of working under both Le Corbusier and Louis I. Kahn. He started his career fairly modestly with a series of small houses gently worked into their surrounding landscape. He then proceeded to create some highly individual major buildings notable for their relaxed but innovative use of modern construction techniques, for their arresting shapes, and for

Ceiling of a small room in the Palazzo
Falconieri (ca. 1640), Rome, by
Francesco Borromini

their boldly colored and patterned
facades. These include the triangular
Watari-um, Tokyo (1990); the
Commercial and Residential Building,
Lugano, Switzerland (1991); the
Museum of Modern Art San Francisco
(1994); the Cathedral at Evry, near
Paris (1995); and the Tinguely
Museum, Basel, Switzerland (1996).

BOUDIN, STÉPHANE (1888–1967)

French interior designer who worked
for the House of Jansen, a Parisian
decorating firm, for the first sixty or
so years of the twentieth century.
Representing for many the apotheosis
of refined French taste and grandeur, he
designed rooms for royalty (the Duke
and Duchess of Windsor), for presi-
dents (the Kennedy White House),
for the aristocracy, and for the international super-rich.

BRAMANTE, DONATO
(1444–1514)

Great High Renaissance architect,
much influenced by Alberti, Michelozzo,
and Leonardo da Vinci, who was
described flatteringly by the great
architect Palladio as "the first who
brought good architecture to light."
Certainly, his monumental classical
buildings in Rome, which approximated
the spirit of antiquity, were to have a
lasting influence on the development
of Italian architecture. He was born
and grew up near Urbino, where he
met leading painters of the day—such
as Piero della Francesca and Francesco
di Giorgio—who may have fueled his
abiding interest in perspective and its
problems. In fact, in 1481 Bramante
made a drawing that was subsequently
engraved as a model of perspective
for painters. In the meantime, he was
employed by Duke Ludovico Sforza,
for whom he worked as a decorative
painter as well as an architect. His first
building of any note was Santa Maria
presso San Satiro in Milan. Begun in
1482, it elegantly wrapped around the
very small ninth-century Capella della
Pietà. He designed or worked on different parts of various other Milanese
churches, until the French invasion of
Lombardy in 1499 and the consequent
fall of the Sforza family made it advisable to leave Milan for Rome. Apparent
in his circular Tempietto of San Pietro
in Montorio (commissioned 1502; built
1504–after 1510) in Rome, his style
changed out of all recognition, assuming
a gravitas more appropriate to that city.
Raphael, who inherited his mantle as

the first architect of Rome, eventually acquired the Palazzo Caprini, which Bramante had envisaged and had only just begun at the time of his death. Its design, with a heavily rusticated basement and five pedimented windows between coupled half columns on the upper floor, was widely imitated over the next century.

BREUER, MARCEL (1902–1981)

Born in Hungary and one of the chief Bauhaus architects and furniture designers. He studied at the Bauhaus School in Weimer with Walter Gropius from 1920, at the age of eighteen, until he resigned in 1928 to start his own practice in Berlin. In 1925 he had became head of the joinery and cabinet workshop at the Bauhaus and that same year, inspired, it was said, by the handlebars of his bicycle, designed the first tubular steel and cantilevered chair called the "Wassily" chair. In 1928, he produced his most famous chair, called the "Cesna," consisting of one continuous steel frame acting as a cantilever with a cane seat and back in a black bentwood frame. "The most up-to-date material—chrome steel," he explained, "contrasts with the oldest material— cane seating and wood." Both chairs are considered icons of twentieth-century furniture designs. His first two architectural commissions in the early 1930s (the Harnischmacher House I in Wiesbaden, Germany, and the Mehrfamilienhäuser Doldertal, a residential complex in Zürich, designed with Alfred and Emil Roth) also showed an unmistakable talent. In 1935 he was forced by the rise of Nazism to move to London, which he apparently found less than hospitable—although his famous laminated wood "long chair" was first made by a British firm, the Isokon Furniture Company, in 1936 and his "Civic Center for the Future" project evoked great interest. In 1937, his old mentor Gropius invited him to teach at Harvard. Breuer worked in association with Gropius from 1937–40 before starting once more on his own. Many of America's most outstanding architects—including Philip Johnson, Paul Rudolph, I. M. Pei, Edward Barnes, and John Johansen—were students of Breuer. He was commissioned to design some private houses in New England, including one for himself (the first of four he designed at different times), which had considerable influence on American residential architecture, as did the "Butterfly" house that he designed for the Museum of Modern Art in New York in 1949 after he had moved his practice to New York in 1946. There, although he always liked to have some houses to design, he moved on to designing larger domestic and more international buildings, such as the Ferry Cooperative House, a dormitory for Vassar College in Poughkeepsie, New York; the De Bijenkorf Department Store in Rotterdam, Holland; and the new UNESCO headquarters in Paris (with Bernard-Louis Zehrfuss of France and Pier Luigi Nervi of Italy), all in the early 1950s. These were followed, among others, by the Lecture Hall, New York University Heights campus, Bronx (now part of the City University of

New York); the IBM Research Center building in La Gaude, France, near Nice; the mountain resort town of Flaine, France; the IBM complex at Boca Raton, Florida; and the 1966 Whitney Museum of American Art, New York.

BROSSE, SALOMON DE
(1571–1626)

Early French classical architect and the most distinguished precursor of François Mansart, who was believed to have been Brosse's pupil when he worked on the Château de Coulommiers (1613). The Château de Luxembourg (1615; enlarged and altered in the nineteenth century) and the Château de Blérancourt (1612–19), along with the Palais du Parlement at Rennes (1618), were his most notable works. They conveyrd his sense of plasticity and his ability to view architecture in terms of mass—in contrast to the emphasis of the Mannerists of the previous generation on complex and often ambiguous surface decoration.

BROWN, "CAPABILITY"
(CHRISTENED LANCELOT, 1716–1783)

British architect of some elegant, landscape-accessory buildings, like temples, ornamental bridges, and gateways in the frivolous—as opposed to the more serious—Gothic taste, and one or two extensions to country houses, as well as a few new houses, including Croome Court, Worcestershire. Brown actually started off as a gardener, which he parlayed into fame as an outstanding landscape architect. He often talked of his work in terms of exploiting the "capability" of a site, hence his nickname. In 1741 he was appointed head gardener and supervisor of building works at Stowe, in Buckinghamshire, working there with William Kent on his great master plans for the park. After that outstanding success, he set himself up, nine years later, as a consultant landscape architect. Of his work it was said that his numerous artfully informal parks were less an alternative to formal gardens than an alternative to nature in the raw. The results of his landscaping plans can still be seen today, most notably at Warwick Castle (1750); his own Croome Court (1751–53) in Worcestershire; Bowood House (1761) in Wiltshire; Dodington Park (1764), South Glou-cestershire; Blenheim in Oxfordshire (1765)—though it is now much altered; Ashburnham (1767) in Sussex; and Nuneham Park, Nuneham Courtenay (1778), again in Oxfordshire. His work and philosophy came to be appreciated as much in America and continental Europe as in England, although he was criticized toward the end of his life for making his landscapes look *too* much like common pastureland and for their lack of variety and somewhat sleepy tranquility.

BROWN, ELEANOR McMILLEN
(1890–1990) & McMILLEN, INC.

One of the first American "lady decorators" of the early twentieth century to found, in 1924, a proper, full-scale, professional design business that has flourished ever since. She studied the history of decorating under William Odom (known as "Mr. Taste"), then principal of the New York School of Fine and Applied Arts, which became Parsons School of Design in 1940. McMillen, with the help of William Odom, who shipped beautiful furniture to the firm from Europe, established a fine reputation for correct period detailing and the highest quality work allied to a deep and relaxed comfort. In short, the firm established a set of standards for the best of American decorating; subsequently many of America's most famous interior designers have passed through its portals.

BRUNEL, ISAMBARD KINGDOM
(1806–1859)

The great British bridge-and-tunnel man, as well as ship and docks builder, was educated in Paris and trained in his father's office. (His father, Sir Mark Isambard Kingdom Brunel, designer of the Thames Tunnel from Wapping to Rotherhithe, 1824–43, was born in Normandy and had worked in the French navy and as the city engineer for New York State before settling in England in 1799.) The son's triumphs ranged from the noble Clifton Suspension Bridge at Bristol (1829), which he designed when he was only twenty-three, to the Royal Albert Bridge at Saltash (opened in 1859); the Great Western Railway line from London to Bristol, which included the Box Tunnel; and *The Great Western* ship that took only fifteen days to get to America, an astonishing feat in those days, and the even larger *Great Eastern*, as well as the Bristol and Monkwearmouth docks.

BRUNELLESCHI, FILIPPO
(1377–1446)

Although he began as a goldsmith and sculptor, he ended up—almost by accident after a visit to Rome with Donatello to study antique sculpture—as the first and one of the greatest Italian Renaissance architects. He was considerably less dogmatic than his immediate successors, Alberti and Michelozzo, being much less concerned with antiquity than with the practical problems of construction and space management. Although his interiors were exquisitely pure and simple, he seemed to have been drawn toward ancient Rome for its engineering prowess rather than for aesthetic reasons. Importantly, he was also the prime formulator of the laws on linear perspective, a subject that often confused early painters and architects. His first architectural project seems to have been to give advice on one of the buttresses for Florence Cathedral in 1404. In fact, most of his great buildings were subsequently erected in Florence, his native city, from 1418 onward, and his masterpieces were the dome of the Cathedral in Florence begun in 1420, and the Ospedale degli Innocenti, also in Florence, designed in 1419 and built between 1421 and 1444, which is often declared the first real Renaissance building.

BUGATTI, CARLO (1856–1940)

Extraordinarily inventive and eclectic late-nineteenth-century and early-twentieth-century Italian designer who created part oriental, part

Clifton Suspension Bridge, spanning 702 feet across the Avon Gorge near Bristol, England, by I. K. Brunel. Begun in 1836 and completed in 1864, five years after Brunel's death.

machine-inspired, and nearly always exotic entities from jewelry and silver to whole rooms (his son, Ettore Bugatti, later became well known for his racing cars). He won the Diploma of Honor at the 1902 Turin exhibition for his Snail Room, which was furnished with his own eccentric furniture and whose walls were finished in a mixture of wood veneers, pewter, and vellum painted in red and gold. In 1904 he moved from Milan to Paris to concentrate on his silver designs, but his extraordinary furniture continued being produced by the Milanese firm De Vecchi.

Pazzi Chapel, set in the cloister of Santa Croce, Florence, by Filippo Brunelleschi, begun 1429

BULFINCH, CHARLES (1763–1844)

A distinguished late-eighteenth-century and early-nineteenth-century American architect from Boston who, after graduating from Harvard, embarked on a prolonged two-year visit to Europe, where he met with and was advised by Thomas Jefferson. Other abiding influences were Sir Christopher Wren, Robert Adam, and Sir William Chambers. On his return to the States he started work on some of the most outstanding public buildings of his time, including, between 1789 and 1817, a sixty-foot-high Doric column called the Beacon Monument in Boston; the Old State House at Hartford, Connecticut; and the Massachusetts State House and the Court House, both in Boston, as well as some particularly pleasant and unified terraces of town houses in that city. His career culminated with the Capitol in Washington, D.C., where he was in charge of the ongoing work from 1818 to 1830.

BUNSHAFT, GORDON
(1909–1990)

American architect with a long career as a partner and chief designer for Skidmore, Owings & Merrill, one of the iconic architectural partnerships for twentieth-century commercial buildings. Bunshaft designed many of Manhattan's towering landmarks of the 1950s and '60s: Lever House (1952), the Manufacturers Trust Building (1954), and 140 Broadway (1967). He also designed the National Commercial Bank building in Jeddah, Saudi Arabia (1977–84). In 1988, he was the tenth winner of the Pritzker Prize for Architecture.

BURGES, WILLIAM (1827–1881)

Widely traveled nineteenth-century Gothic Revivalist architect known for his highly decorative designs and decoration as well as his particular renditions of both English and French Gothic forms. He was originally trained as an engineer but then switched to designing both the exteriors and interiors of buildings. In 1856 he won, with fellow architect Henry Clutton (1819–1893), the competition for the Cathedral at Lille, France, but, as all too often happens with the winners of architectural competitions, he did not actually get to do the work. Three years later he added the east end of Waltham Abbey, in Essex, England, and went on to design additional buidings: Cork Cathedral in Ireland (1862–76); a substantial and resplendent addition to Cardiff Castle in Wales (1868–85); Harrow School Speech Room (1872); Hartford College, Connecticut (1873–80); and his own elaborately decorated house in Melbury Road, Kensington, London (1875–80).

BURLINGTON, RICHARD BOYLE, THIRD EARL OF BURLINGTON AND FOURTH EARL OF CORK
(1694–1753)

The leading apologist for English Palladianism, as well as being a brilliant amateur architect in his own right. He first visited Italy in 1714–15, but his overwhelming conversion to Palladianism did not manifest itself fully until his return to London, which happened to coincide with the publication of Colen Campbell's *Vitruvius Britannicus* as well as Leoni's edition of Andrea Palladio's *Four Books of Architecture*. Deeply impressed by the designs in these publications, he replaced James Gibbs—whom he had formerly commissioned to design his own Burlington House off Piccadilly, London (now housing the Royal Academy but, since its restoration, still containing a splendid room fully furnished and decorated by William Kent)—with Campbell. He then set out for Italy once again to study Palladio's buildings more thoroughly and at first hand, returning in 1719 with the talented young protégé William Kent, whom he had met on his travels. For the next three decades Burlington, aided and abetted by Kent, virtually held sway over the British architectural scene, as well as its landscape, spreading the fashion for unadulterated English Palladianism, which, according to the satirist Alexander Pope, filled "half the land with imitating fools." And, indeed, houses designed for the sun in Italy did not necessarily sit well in the colder and rainier climate of the British Isles. Burlington's own best-known works were Chiswick House, his villa based on Palladio's Villa Rotonda (1723–29)—one of several around the world; the Dormitory at Westminster School, London (1722–30; rebuilt in 1947); and the Assembly Rooms building in York (1732; refronted in 1828), an exact copy of Palladio's Egyptian Hall, which in turn was based on one of Vitruvius's designs.

BURTON, DECIMUS (1800–1881)

Prolific and precocious nineteenth-century British architect, who at twenty-three designed the Colosseum in Regent's Park, London with a Greek Doric portico, including what must have been one of the first elevators and a dome larger than St. Paul's Cathedral. The building was destroyed in 1875. At twenty-five he had already started work on the improvements to Hyde Park, including the Hyde Park Corner screen and Constitution Arch (1827–28). By the age of thirty he had designed and built the grand Athenaeum Club, looking over Carlton House Terrace. Other considerable achievements were the great Palm House at the Royal Botanic Gardens, Kew and Chatsworth estate in Derbyshire (with Sir Joseph Paxton, 1801–1865), as well as a number of villas in Regent's Park, various country houses, and a development of handsome villas (many of them presciently designed with an arcade of bow-windowed shops underneath) in Tunbridge Wells, Kent. Sadly, an entire Burton terrace in Tunbridge was torn down in the first half of the twentieth century to make way for a new town hall, which, ironically, is now itself preserved.

BUTTERFIELD, WILLIAM (1814–1900)

Well-known British High-Church Gothic Revivalist architect, responsible for a large number of Victorian ecclesiastical and scholastic buildings including St. Augustine's College, Canterbury, Kent (the 1840s); the red-brick All Saints Church, Margaret Street, London (1849–59); Keble College, Oxford (1867–75); Rugby School buildings (1870–86); and, an exception to his ecclesiastical and scholastic work, the sturdy and utilitarian County Hospital at Winchester, Hampshire (1863).

CALATRAVA, SANTIAGO (B. 1951)

Highly original Spanish architect and concrete engineer who has designed a series of bridges, railway stations, and telecommunications towers in France, Switzerland, and Spain, respectively. (His work has all the fizzing vitality yearned over in the futuristic drawings of the young Italian Sant'Elia, who was killed in World War I before he could build a thing.) Calatrava's stunning City of Arts & Sciences in Valencia, Spain, and auditorium for the Tenerife Opera House on the waterfront in the Los Llanos area of Santa Cruz, the capital of Tenerife, Spain, are both generating new tourist trade in themselves. In its way, the form of the Santa Cruz auditorium takes over where the Sydney Opera House leaves off. His addition to the Cathedral of St. John the Divine in New York was a comparatively recent commission, but his latest job in that city was the new station at the revived World Trade Center site (the master plan for rebuilding the 16-acre site of the former World Trade Center was designed by Daniel Libeskind). Another fairly recent commission was the expansion of the museum complex for the Milwaukee Art Museum (1994–2001).

CALLICRATES

Not much is known about his personal dates and details, except that he was the ancient Greek Athenian architect, who, together with Ictinus, designed the Parthenon (448–432 B.C.). He was thought to have built the little Ionic temple of Nike on the Acropolis as well as the south and central portions of the Long Walls from Athens to Piraeus.

The Parthenon (temple to Athena) (448–432 B.C.), Acropolis, Athens, by Callicrates and Ictinus

CAMERON, CHARLES (CA. 1745–1812)

Scottish-born architect, designer of interiors, and follower of Robert Adam, who visited Rome in 1768 and was inspired to publish in 1772 *The Baths of the Romans Explained and Illustrated, with the Restorations of Palladio Corrected and Improved.* The book may have caught the imagination of Catherine the Great of Russia because in 1773 she apparently fired the French architect Charles-Louis Clérisseau, whom she had invited to submit designs for a new building to be built on the grounds of Tsarskoe Selo, her Palace near St. Petersburg, and summoned Cameron to her court. Seven years after the book's publication she appointed him chief architect in charge of designing various interiors for her within some of her palatial residences, including the marvelously inventive and fanciful interiors at Tsarskoe Selo, started in 1779, and the adjacent Cold Baths, Agate Pavilion, and Cameron Gallery (1779–85). He also built the enormous palace at Pavlovsk (1782–85) for Grand Duke Paul (Catherine's son).

The Temple of Friendship (1780) was the first Greek Revival monument in Russia. Cameron was dismissed from royal service when Catherine died in 1796 but stayed on in Russia working for private patrons. In 1805 he also designed the naval hospital and barracks at Kronstadt.

CAMPBELL, COLEN (1676–1729)

Although he built Wanstead House, now demolished, which became the model for the English Palladian country house, little is known about Campbell's early life until 1715, when he published the first volume of *Vitruvius Britannicus*, his treatise on the Roman Vitruvius's work *De Architectura*, which had had such an enormous influence on Italian Renaissance architecture and in turn on Andrea Palladio, English Palladianism, and finally on Neoclassicism. After he had remodeled James Gibbs's designs for Burlington House, London (1718–19) for Lord Burlington, he designed the imposing Houghton Hall, Norfolk (1721, executed by Ripley with modifications by Gibbs), Mereworth Castle (1722–25)—considered the best variation of the various English versions of Palladio's Rotunda design (Lord Burlington's Chiswick House was another)—as well as the elegant Compton Place in Eastbourne, Sussex (1726–27).

CAMPEN, JACOB VAN (1595–1657)

One of Holland's leading Palladian architects, known for his simple and economic form of classicism and his use—most unusual at the time—of brick mixed with stone. His style was expressed particularly well at the Mauritshuis in The Hague (1633–35); his huge Town Hall in Amsterdam (1648–55), which now serves as the Royal Palace, is entirely built in stone and is a much-heavier-looking building.

CANDELA, FELIX (1910–1997)

Spanish-born, Mexican concrete engineer and architect, important as a mid-twentieth-century Expressionist. Some of his most interesting earlier works are considered to be the midcentury Expressionist Church of Our Lady of Miracles (1953–55), the very small Cosmic-Ray Pavilion, University City (1951–52), and the Radiation Institute (1954), all in Mexico City. Later buildings included a 1958 restaurant at Xochimilco (which he designed with Joaquin Alvarez Ordóñez and is reported to be skillfully perched in "water gardens like an eight-petaled flower of paraboloids"), as well as the Olympic Stadium, Mexico City (1968).

CANDELA, ROSARIO (1884 –1966)

American architect and a transformer of the Upper East Side of Manhattan. He was the architect who replaced so many of the nineteenth-century single-family mansions with the stately limestone-fronted Beaux Arts style apartment buildings that now line Fifth and Park Avenues. He managed to convert the prosperity of the time into the feel of the structures and instill a sense of stability and luxury that are as endemic to the beautifully detailed buildings as their sense of substance.

CASTAING, MADELEINE (1894–1992)

Another French decorator of great individuality and idiosyncrasy, who worked until she was almost one hundred and had, through her shop on the corner of the Rue Jacob and Rue Bonaparte in Paris, an enormous influence on American and British designers and decorators. In her shop, opened in the 1940s and not shut until the 1990s, she pioneered the idea of furnishing its various spaces like rooms in a house. In her decorating she pursued, like Proust, the results of her own *Recherche du Temps Perdus*, basing her work on a kind of nineteenth-century literary fantasy. Although her style was always based on some sort of dreamlike invented past, she was—like her contemporary and another great international influence, Jean Michel Frank—a Modernist who, nevertheless, was also inspired by the past. In the decoration world she is considered to be one of the true twentieth-century design originals.

CHAMBERS, SIR WILLIAM (1723–1796)

Important eighteenth-century British architect born in Göteborg, Sweden, where his Scots father was a merchant. He joined the Swedish East India Company at the age of sixteen and for the next nine years traveled back and forth to India and China. His travels would later inform his treatise on oriental architecture and play a role in his subsequent architectural success. However, his training at the architectural school in Paris, run by Jacques-François Blondel (1705–1774), did not start until he was twenty-six and was then continued in Italy until 1755, when he went to live in London. Within a year he had been appointed architectural tutor to the then Prince of Wales. He published his influential *Designs of Chinese Buildings* in 1757, and shortly after that he was appointed architect to King George III, along with Robert Adam. He was then appointed Comptroller and finally Surveyor-General for the King, during which time he wrote his standard work, *A Treatise on Civil Architecture*. His style was based on a rather academic Palladianism overlaid with the eclecticism and finesse imparted by his various travels. The Pagoda at Kew Gardens, London, is one of his most famous works. Another is Somerset House, off the Strand, London, with its front facade—a deliberate imitation of a Palladian composition originally carried out on the same site by Inigo Jones—shielding a splendidly spacious courtyard, and an interesting rear facade facing onto the river Thames.

CHIPPENDALE, THOMAS, II (1718–1779)

Enormously influential eighteenth-century furniture designer on both sides of the Atlantic. He was the middle and most distinguished of three generations of eighteenth-

The Pagoda (1757–63) at
Kew Gardens, near London,
by Sir William Chambers

Chippendale Gothic chair

century English furniture designers, all called Thomas, which can lead to some confusion. He worked with Robert Adam in the 1770s, producing some beautiful inlaid, Neoclassical pieces, but he also worked in a number of other styles including Gothic, Rococo, and Chinoiserie. His name and influence became particularly widespread after the publication of his trade catalog *Gentleman and Cabinet-Maker's Director* in 1754. Although it was intended as an advertisement, the *Director* was actually the first complete and comprehensive pattern book for furniture to appear and was duly seized upon by lesser American and British cabinetmakers for its inspiration. Apparently, most of the designs were actually the work of Matthias Lock and Henry Copeland, who were employed by Chippendale at that time. Nevertheless, it was Chippendale who—according to J. T. Smith, the nineteenth-century writer—gained the reputation of being "the most famous Upholsterer and Cabinet-maker of his day, to whose folio work on household furniture the trade formerly made constant reference." The *Director* was reprinted in 1755, and in 1762 a third and much enlarged edition was produced. In America, a group of furniture designers on the East Coast started to work in the Chippendale fashion and were consequently called American Chippendales. Their work, whenever one comes across it, is now highly prized. The group included such names as William Savery, Jonathan Gostelowe, Thomas Tufts, and Benjamin Randolph from Philadelphia; John Goddard and his relatives Christopher and John Townsend of Newport; Benjamin Frothingham of Charlestown, Massachusetts; Marinus Willett and Andrew Gautier of New York; Aaron Chapin of Hartford, Connecticut; and Webb and Scott of Providence. Of these works it is mostly the chairs and highboys—of William Savery (ca. 1721–1787) and John Goddard (ca. 1750)—and the fine secretary desks formerly known as Rhode Island desks that are the best known.

CLÉRISSEAU, CHARLES-LOUIS (1721–1820)

French Neoclassical draftsman and architect who, paradoxically, widely inspired his peer group both in Europe and the United States by his teaching and his deep knowledge of Roman architecture, although his own buildings were undistinguished. Thomas Jefferson became one of his patrons, as did his former pupils Robert and James Adam and William Chambers in England. Catherine the Great of Russia also commissioned designs from him, but like so many designs planned with high hopes for royalty, they were never built.

COATES, WELLS WINDEMUT (1895–1958)

A British pioneer of the International Modern Style as early as the 1930s. His pioneering Lawn Road Flats (apartment complexes) in Hampstead, London, built in concrete in the Modernist style in 1932–34, were one of the first developments of their kind in Britain.

COLOMBO, JO (1930–1971)

One of the most conspicuously original of the Italian architects and furniture and lighting designers of the 1960s who, for a decade or so, turned furniture, product, interior, and industrial design on its head. In 1948, Colombo founded the Movimento Arte Concreta along with Tawny Munari and Gillo Dorfles. In the productive and sizzling-colored 1960s, before his early death at forty-one, he designed the "Colombo" lamp for O-Luce, his "Mini-kitchen" for Boffi, his "4801" plywood chair for Kartell, the "Additional System" seating group of self-assembly furniture for Sormani, his "Tube" chair for Flexform (made from four plastic tubes covered in polyurethane foam and stretch fabric) and the "Roto-Living" unit for Sormani. In 1971, the year he died, Bayer, the German manufacturer, honored Colombo, the American designer Verner Panton, and the French designer Olivier Mourgue with a tripart exhibition of their work.

CONRAN, SIR TERENCE (B. 1931)

Prescient British furniture designer who virtually revolutionized furniture selling around the world with the opening of his groundbreaking store, Habitat, in 1964, that made high design available at lower prices for the young. Stores were subsequently opened in major cities all around the world. The Conran name, through his design group, has become synonymous with sympathetic, clean-lined public and office spaces as well as with a whole raft of restaurants as far apart as New York and Tokyo, and Paris and London, not to mention his various books on so many different aspects of design for the home.

CORTONA, PIETRO BERRETTINA DA (1596–1669)

Great Italian Baroque painter and apparently natural-born architect with very little, if any, training who announced that he only regarded architecture as a pastime. In fact, the villa (now destroyed) he designed for his first patrons, the Sacchetti family, was said to be a landmark in villa design, and his first church, S. S. Martina e Luca in Rome (1634–69), was the first entirely homogenous Baroque church. Born in Cortona in Tuscany, the son of a stonemason, he moved to Rome at the age of eighteen to apprentice with an undistinguished Florentine painter. Happily for him, he was taken up by the highly cultivated Francesco Barberini and his circle, who ensured that Cortona had as many architectural as painting commissions. Particularly interesting are S. Maria della Pace in Rome (1656–59), which was treated rather like a theater, S. Maria in Via

Lata in the same city (1658–62), and the dome of S. Carlo al Corso (begun 1668).

COSTA, LUCIO (1902–1998)

French-born Brazilian architect, planner, and distinguished architectural historian on the International Commission for Ancient Monuments. He led the team working on the new building for the Ministry of Education in Rio de Janeiro (1937–43), one of whose members was Oscar Niemeyer, who also worked in his office. Le Corbusier was the consultant on the project. Costa also built the Brazilian Pavilion at the New York World's Fair of 1939 with Niemeyer. In 1957, he won the competition to plan the city of Brasilia, then scheduled to become the new capital of Brazil, and Niemeyer became the chief architect. All the results of this long collaboration between the two men have been impressive, but both the general planning and the extraordinarily original buildings of Brasilia have been particularly memorable.

CUVILLIÉS, FRANÇOIS (1695–1768)

Leading French Rococo architect and, like Sir William Chambers, a pupil of Jacques-François Blondel. His masterpiece is the wonderfully delicate and exotically silvered interior of Amalienburg (1734–39) in the park of Nymphenburg, near Munich, Germany. The little Amalienburg Pavilion is considered by many to be the apotheosis of secular Rococo architecture.

DANCE, GEORGE, THE YOUNGER (1741–1825)

Reputedly, one of the most innovative British Neoclassical architects of his age, although many of his buildings—such as Newgate Prison (1770–80) and the Council Chamber of Guildhall, London (built in 1777, with a parachute-like dome and fine lines radiating from the glazed opening in the center—were sadly destroyed. His father, George Dance senior, also an architect, designed the Mansion House, London (1739–42), home to the Lord Mayor. George Dance junior, together with his brother, Nathaniel Dance, the painter, were sent to study in Italy for seven clearly profitable years. Dance started his career by winning a gold medal in Parma in 1763 for some impressive Neoclassical designs and went on to design the pure and beautiful All Hallows Church on London Wall (1765–67). He became a founder member of the Royal Academy in 1768, and some of his subsequent work still extant in London includes the Library of Lansdowne House (1788–91) and the College of Surgeons (1806–13), as well as the austere Stratton Park (1803–06) in Hampshire, these last two with early Greek Revival influence. The manipulation of light at Landsdowne House, through concealed windows set in the exedrae (semidomed, semicircular recesses) at either end of the long flat-vaulted room, recalls the work of Sir John Soane, who was actually a pupil of Dance, and perhaps his best legacy.

DAVIS, ALEXANDER JACKSON (1803–1892)

Versatile American nineteenth-century architect and one of the founders of the American Institute of Architects. With his partner Ithiel Town (1784–1844)—who had already designed the Connecticut State Capitol with a Greek Doric portico in 1827—he designed the state capitols of Indiana (1831), North Carolina (also 1831), Illinois (1837), and Ohio (1839). Although Davis was talented at designing grandly Greek Revivalist buildings, he was equally adept at collegiate Gothic, as can be seen, for example, in New York University, Washington Square (1832 onward). But he was also interested in using the latest contemporary materials, designing an iron storefront as early as 1835 when metals of any sort were not yet fully accepted as building materials.

DAY, ROBIN (B. 1915) AND LUCIENNE (B. 1917)

British husband and wife design partnership for furniture (mainly by Robin) and textile, wallpaper, and ceramic (mainly by Lucienne). They designed, among other furniture, the best-selling polypropylene "Mark II" stacking chairs (more than 12 million sold) in 1963 and the "Hadrian" seating series in 1981 for the British furniture manufacturer Hille, the latter of which was chosen as the seating for the lobbies at the then new Barbican Center in London. One of their earliest successes as a couple was the Homes and Gardens Pavilion at the

State Capitol (1839–61), Columbus, Ohio, by
Alexander Jackson Davis with Henry Walter

Festival of Britain in 1951; Robin designed the actual pavilion and furniture, and Lucienne designed the upholstery. In 1954 Lucienne was awarded the Grand Prize at the 10th Milan Triennale, along with Gio Ponti, for their *One Room Apartment* (she designed the textiles). The couple had a much-heralded resurgence in the early part of the twenty-first century with an exhibition of their work at the Victoria and Albert Museum, London.

DE SANCTIS, FRANCESCO (1693–1740)

Best known as the designer of the wonderful curvilinear Baroque Spanish Steps in Rome, leading from the Piazza di Spagna to S. Trinità dei Monti.

DEINOCRATES (4TH CENTURY B.C.)

Greek architect and a contemporary of Alexander the Great who was apparently one of the architects, along with Paeonius, of the Temple of Artemis at Ephesus (ca. 356 B.C.). He is also credited with having designed the town plan for Alexandria.

DOWNING, ANDREW JACKSON (1815–1852)

Nineteenth-century American architect in partnership with Calvert Vaux

(1824–1895) but much better known as a writer on landscape gardening and country houses who is often called America's Humphry Repton or John Loudon. Publications include the following: *A Treatise on the Theory and Practice of Landscape Gardening* (1841), *Cottage Residences* (1842), *Notes about Buildings in the Country* (1849), and *The Architecture of Country Houses* (1850).

EAMES, CHARLES (1907–1978) AND KAISER, RAY (1912–1988)

Influential Californian architects and furniture designers. As husband and wife working together, they produced some of the most interesting and ubiquitous twentieth-century furniture, now considered design classics. During the 1940s they started experimenting with molded plywood and fiberglass-reinforced plastic shapes and developed a curved molding process based on aviation technology, as well as criss-crossed wire chairs, some with snap-on upholstery, and an elegant elliptical table, all constructed on thin metal legs. Their "LCW" molded-plywood stacking chair was produced by Herman Miller in 1946 after the company's new design director, George Nelson, had insisted that Miller take on the Eames as designers. (In 1999 this chair was named "the chair of the century" by *Time* magazine.) In the mid-1950s they produced the famous Eames laminated rosewood "Lounge" chair and ottoman on metal swivel bases with comfortable black leather cushions and headrest separated from the back support by an air space. They also produced a fiberglass swivel desk chair, among many other forms. Their own Californian house was one of the most publicized of the Case Study Houses program, set up in the 1940s by John Entenza, then editor of *Art & Architecture*, to encourage the propagation of good design. Although the house was unique and not meant as a prototype, nevertheless, it served as an inspiration for the imaginative results that could be obtained by the intelligent use of generally available factory-produced components.

EASTLAKE, CHARLES LOCKE (1836–1906)

Author of *Hints on Household Taste in Furniture, Upholstery, and Other Details* (1867), which had almost as big an influence on design reform in the late nineteenth century as the work and writings of William Morris. Eastlake expounded on the virtues of lighter, less eclectic styles of furnishing, emphasized the personal elements that should always be found in home decoration, and expanded on the tradition of handicrafts (rejecting most mass-produced furniture in favor of individually made pieces). Above all, he declared very sensibly, each home should be thought of as an individual work of art, assembled slowly and lovingly rather than thrown together as quickly as possible for the sake of convenience. The first British edition of the book was followed by four further editions and by six editions in the United States.

EFFNER, JOSEPH (1687–1745)

Munich-born German architect who was sent by the Elector of Bavaria to be trained in Paris by Gabriel Germain Boffrand. He was made Court Architect to the Elector in 1715, whereupon he industriously completed the Palace at Schleissheim, designed the splendid Treppenhaus, turned the then Italianate Schloss Nymphenburg outside Munich into a German Baroque palace over twelve years (1716–28), and built several fanciful pavilions in the park, ranging from the half-Classical, half-Chinoiserie Pagodenburg to the very Roman Badenburg and the fantasy Magdalenenklause. The last is a very early example of Picturesque architecture.

EIFFEL, GUSTAV (1832–1923)

French engineer, chiefly known for his famous Eiffel Tower, erected, apparently temporarily, for the Paris World's Fair of 1889. The structure, of course, remained rooted, and became the preeminent symbol of Paris. It also marked the acceptance of metal— in this case iron—as a respected building material.

EISENMAN, PETER (B. 1932)

American avant-garde architect, theorist, and teacher who, like other members of the so-called 1970s New York Five group (now disbanded) thought, basically, that function should follow form and not the reverse. Reflected in his first houses, which were considered to be more akin to live-in sculptures than "machines for living," Eisenman took this precept very literally. In this the New York Five (the other four members were Michael Graves, Charles Gwathmey, John

Hejduk, and Richard Meier) were not so much being Neomodernists and revolutionary as following, in many ways, the original classicists of the Italian Renaissance, who mainly started out as sculptors, or at least stonemasons, and thought very little of domestic comfort. The classicists, however, did apply the measured and balanced framework of the Classical orders and a sense of perspective, whereas many of Eisenman's buildings are deliberately created to look as if they are lurching, leaning, or even toppling. Eisenman taught at Harvard, Princeton, and Yale, as well as at the Institute for Architecture and Urban Studies in New York, which he started in 1967. In 1988, he exhibited at the exhibition for Deconstructivists organized by Philip Johnson at the Museum of Modern Art, New York. His buildings include the Wexner Center for the Visual Arts, Columbus, Ohio (1983–86); the Koizumi Lighting Theater/IZM, with Kojiro Kitayama (1990) and the NC Building (1992), both in Tokyo; and the Aronoff Center, New York (1991–96).

ELKINS, FRANCES (1888–1953)

The first well-known 1930s Californian decorator who, although widely traveled in Europe and well versed in European architecture and design, was renowned for the clean, crisp, fresh clarity of her interiors—a look that at that time was uniquely Californian. She was born in Milwaukee but went to live in Monterey at the beginning of World War II and soon became known for her easy mixture of old-fashioned luxury and contemporary chic. This is readily seen in the house she bought in 1918, which is now a United States Historic Trust Landmark. Just as Coco Chanel and Jean Michel Frank (whose furniture and accessories she used a great deal) were great influences on her, she became the muse to another great California decorator, Michael Taylor, as well as Billy Baldwin in New York. She also had a great influence on her older brother, the extremely successful Chicago architect David Adler, as did he on her. Many of the decorating ploys that we see today—such as geometric Moroccan rugs or kelims used both as hall rugs and stair carpet; all the books in a bookcase bound in creamy vellum or parchment, or variations of one color (like the late David Hicks's plethora of reds); the repetition of colors in various weights from room to room; white-painted plaster palm tree pilasters; white shaggy cotton carpeting, and white fur throws on beds—originated with her or as the result of her friendship with Jean Michel Frank and Syrie Maugham.

FONTAINE, PIERRE-FRANÇOIS-LEONARD (1762–1853)

Reputedly Napoleon I's favorite architect and more or less responsible, with his partner Charles Percier (1764–1838)—with whom he worked from 1794 to 1814—for a revolution in interior decoration and indeed the creation of the French Empire style, as well as for their achievements in urban planning and architecture. The two had spent the years 1786 to 1790 in Rome, absorbing the ancient classical vocabulary as well as that of the Renaissance, and first caught the public eye with the publication of their *Palais, Maisons, etc., à Rome*. Fontaine and Percier's body of work was outstanding. Their first big commission was to design the furnishings for the Salle de la Convention at the Tuileries. They went on to design the Rue de Rivoli in 1801, the fountain in the Place Dauphine in 1802, and starting in 1802 they worked for Napoleon on Malmaison, where they paid particular attention to the Empress Josephine's private quarters. In fact, the empress's tented bedroom, with its painted "open" sky ceiling, set a fashion for bedrooms that still exists. After the Malmaison project the pair extended the north wing of the Louvre to the Tuileries and built the Arc du Carrousel between the Tuileries and the Louvre's Grand Gallery in 1806–07. They also designed the Salle des Cariatides at the Louvre, and busied themselves with a great deal of renovation, restoration, and decoration at the various royal residences of Fontainebleu, Saint-Cloud, Compiègne, Rambouillet, and Versailles. Fontaine and Percier influenced architects and designers all over Europe and America with their book *Receuil de decorations intérieures*, which was published in installments from 1801 and in one volume in 1812 and was full of fetching line drawings showing their various designs for interiors and details of their furnishings. The two declared that "furniture is too much part of interior decoration for the architect to remain indifferent to it"—a precept that many modern architects might do well to note.

**Arc de Triomphe du Carrousel (1806–08), Paris, by
Pierre-François-Leonard Fontaine and Charles Percier**

When the partnership split up, Fontaine went on to restore the Palais Royal in Paris between 1814 and 1831.

FONTANA, CARLO (1638–1714)

An assistant to Bernini for ten years—he finished Bernini's Palazzo di Montecitorio in Rome, including the main entrance (1694–97)—Fontana eventually became the leader of his profession in that city, but more by diligence and hard work than for his originality. Nevertheless, like Blondel and Clérisseau in Paris in the eighteenth century, he had widespread influence throughout Europe and eventually America through his many distinguished pupils, who included James Gibbs.

FORNASETTI, ENRICO

Distinctive twentieth-century Italian designer whose furniture and ceramics, with their unique lacquered black-and-white and often stylized architectural designs, are instantly recognizable. His work has a cult following.

FOSTER, SIR NORMAN (B. 1935)

Prolific and distinguished British architect who has fulfilled distinctive commissions all around the world. They are distinctive because of their exposed structure and services that in no way detract from his buildings' cool, precise looks or their general flexibility. Foster formed his High-Tech, sophisticated engineering approach to buildings in the 1970s, together with his contemporary and former partner Richard (now Lord) Rogers. The style is, in its way, a continuation of some of the late-nineteenth-century thoughts on the aesthetics of glass and metal fused with the centralized or "plug-in" essential services of the late visionary Buckminster Fuller, as well as the 1960s Archigram Group. These appealing ideas have led him to design buildings as diverse as his 1970s suspended, tinted solar glass structure for the Willis-Faber-Dumas Insurance Offices in Ipswich, Suffolk and his somewhat aeronautical-looking building that houses the Sainsbury Center for the Visual Arts in Norwich, both on the east coast of England. Those projects, in turn, led to several more: the painted metal-and-glass Distribution Center for Renault cars in Swindon, Wiltshire (1980–83); the Hong Kong and Shanghai Bank Headquarters, Hong Kong (1979–86); the Stansted Airport Terminal, Essex (1989–91);

ITN Headquarters, London (1989); the Century Tower, Tokyo (1992); the glamorous Chek Lap Koh Airport Terminal in Hong Kong; and various other equally impressive bank, university, and commercial buildings. In 1999, he was the twenty-first recipient of the Pritzker Prize for Architecture and in 2004, Foster finished the Swiss Re Headquarters, his newer, softer-lined building in the City of London, nicknamed "the gherkin" and based in many ways on the visionary controlled environmental theories and geodesic domes of Fuller.

FOWLER, JOHN (1906–?)

Partner with first Sibyl Colefax and then the American-born Nancy Lancaster (her mother was one of the famously beautiful and glamorous members of the Langhorne family of Virginia) in Colefax & Fowler, he promulgated a brand of elegant and beautifully detailed English, and particularly English Country, style. Fowler's early experience as a decorative painter, and in particular his ability to achieve the effects of age on almost any surface, stood him in marvelous stead when he became a full-time decorator, as did his superb sense and knowledge of color, his constant absorption and regurgitation of ideas from the past, and the legendary lightness of his touch. Both his work and his teaching (leading United States decorating practitioners such as Mario Buatta and Georgina Fairholme passed, as they say, through his portals) have inspired legions of other decorators all over the world.

FRANK, JEAN MICHEL (1895–1941)

A Modernist, yet thoroughly conversant with the past and one of the great French early-twentieth-century influences on designers and decorators all over the world. Like Madeleine Castaing, another true French original though in quite a different style, he had his own shop in Paris (in the Rue du Faubourg St.-Honoré) with the decorator Adolphe Chanaux, who had worked with the great Art Deco cabinetmaker or *ébéniste*, Jacques-Emile Ruhlmann, in the Art Moderne movement. It was from this shop that Frank not only sold inspired furniture and objects designed by himself and his circle but also radiated his talent for a kind of exotic chasteness. He could also be described as one of the first spatial and neutral minimalists, since he managed to make his rooms look almost empty (he rarely, if ever, allowed paintings to be hung on walls). And his color palette hardly ever proceeded beyond a creamy white to a pale, tawny brown. He managed to effect a peaceful truce between simplicity and luxury, as well as informality and glamour, by using materials associated with informality for his upholstery and unadorned curtains: linens, tweeds, corduroy, and men's suiting, in combination with beautifully detailed leather (often made up especially by Hermès). He allied these materials to the hard surfaces of walls, furniture, and doors that also *looked* simple but were actually covered in vellum or parchment, shagreen, lacquer, bronze, or straw to create rougher textures. He was the decorator embodiment of Mies van der Rohe's aphorism that "simplicity is not simple." Some of his regular pre–World War II customers, Syrie Maugham from London and Frances Elkins—the first great Californian decorator—together with Elkins's influential architect brother David Adler from Chicago, introduced Frank's designs to their respective countries. It was to the United States that he fled from the Nazis and where, a curiously diffident character in spite of his obvious talent, he killed himself.

FRY, MAXWELL (1899–1987)

Another British pioneer of the International Style of the 1930s who was distinguished for his brief partnership with Walter Gropius from 1934 to 1936 and his specialized tropical design and architectural work. This partnership included various important university and government buildings for Nigeria after World War II, as well as housing at Chandigarh in India in conjunction with Le Corbusier. All through this period he worked with his wife, Dame Jane Drew (1911–1996) under the name of Fry, Drew, and Partners.

FULLER, RICHARD BUCKMINSTER (1895–1983)

Modern Renaissance American, who described himself as "someone engaged in comprehensive anticipatory design science." Others, however, have styled him more simply, if diversely, as an engineer, visionary thinker, mathematician, chemist, philosopher, scientific idealist, eccentric, prophet, and, as

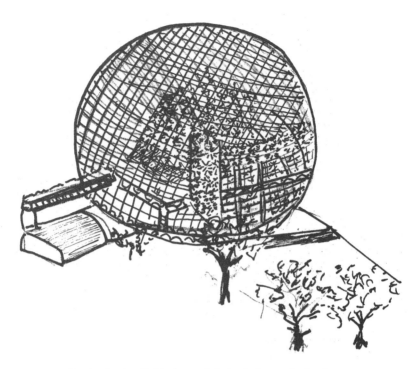

**Buckminster Fuller's prefabricated geodesic dome
at the United States pavilion at Expo '67**

a result of his inventions, on a par with Leonardo da Vinci. His inventive designs in so many areas seem to have tripped off his drawing board as words off the tongue of a masterful gossip. Among the many were his Dymaxion house (1927), followed by his Dymaxion car (1937), which was the essence of simplicity compared with car production today. (The term "dymaxion" is a Fuller amalgam of dynamic and maximum, by which he meant maximum gain of advantages for minimal energy output.) Fuller was frustrated by the time lag between so many really useful inventions and improvements and their commercial realization. During that period, the late 1920s and '30s, he found an average four-year gap in the aircraft industry, a fifteen-year gap on the railways, and "approximately forty-two years" in the building industry. Moreover, he was convinced that traditional building techniques, already inadequate, as he thought, for current problems, would be totally inadequate for the future housing needs that he anticipated. Unfortunately for Fuller, his ideal housing prototype for industrial production consisted of a finished house that could be repeated on demand. The industry, on the other hand, preferred the more flexible approach of supplying various standardized elements of a house that could then be assembled together (rather like

Geodesic dome by Buckminster Fuller with an interior diameter of
over 375 feet. Built near Baton Rouge, Louisiana, this all-welded
steel dome is made up of bright yellow hexagonal units supported by
a skeleton frame of blue pipes.

the Charles and Ray Eames Californian Case Study House; see also *Eames, Charles and Kaiser Ray*) according to needs, imagination, and geographical location. Fuller's preassembled Dymaxion house, therefore, was not welcomed with much enthusiasm, although it demonstrated sophisticated technical advances for the creation of a controlled environment. For example, it contained a double-glazed enclosed area with a living room, two bedrooms, a bathroom, a study, and a utility room, the whole area fitted with a number of visionary mechanical labor-saving devices. Above, there was an open relaxation area shaded by a roof and, below, an open, sheltered services space and parking area. The structure was supported by a radial system in which tension cables extended from a central mast containing a centralized mechanical system for lighting, plumbing, and air-conditioning. In 1946, Fuller designed and built a second, more handsome, more refined, and stronger prototype in Wichita, Kansas. With limited mass production the house would have cost, at that time, only $6,500 (that's equivalent to about $53,575 in today's money), and less still as demand and production increased. As it happened, he received 37,000 unsolicited requests for reproductions of his prototype, but alas, a combination of postwar lethargy, lack of funds, and most of all a suitable service industry for distribution and installation meant that the idea went no further—although the idea could surely be realized now with greater success. Fuller began to understand that just as the aircraft industry had separated the manufacture of the air frame or body of a plane from the power-producing units or engine, so, too, his mass-produced house prototype might benefit by separating the manufacture of its energy and environment-controlling shell (or main body of the house) from the self-contained mechanical services package (the heating, air-conditioning, electrical wiring, and plumbing). Unfortunately, while the solution for the mechanical services seemed quite easy to provide, the structural solutions were not. This set him in a new, ultimately successful, and certainly more profitable direction for his research—this time into geodesic structures ("geodesic" being the shortest distance between points on a curved or spherical surface)—to try to provide cheap, light, and effective shelter that could cover large spans and be erected with speed. The Ford Motor Company commissioned a ninety-three-foot-diameter dome for its Detroit plant. The United States Marine Corps then asked Fuller to advise on mobile, flexible shelter systems, resulting in various ideas from a dome fifty-five feet in diameter, to be delivered where needed by helicopter, to the "Kleenex House"—a disposable paperboard shelter, fifteen feet in diameter for six men, "one third the weight of a tent, which cost one-

fifteenth as much, used less than $10 worth of material, and packed into a small box." After these early successes, Fuller built others on the space-frame principle in materials as diverse as plywood, timber, cardboard, aluminum, prestressed concrete, and bamboo. He also did a good deal of work as well on Tensegrity (Fuller's term, an amalgam of tension integrity) structures to provide alternative means for environmental control.

GABRIEL, ANGE-JACQUES (1698–1782)

In 1742, Gabriel succeeded his father, Jacques Gabriel (1667–1742), as *premier architecte* and Director of the Academy, to King Louis XV. Many consider the son to have been the greatest eighteenth-century architect in France, if not all of Europe. Unlike many of his contemporaries, Gabriel never visited Rome; nevertheless, he was the creator of some of the greatest French eighteenth-century classical architectural icons. These included the École Militaire, Paris (1750–68); the layout of the Place de la Concorde—then called the Place Louis XV—together with the Rue Royale (worked on from 1755); the Hôtel de Crillon; the Ministère de la Marine, Paris (1757–75) that flanks both sides of his Rue Royale; and the Château at Choisy (1754–56), of which nothing remains. He was equally busily employed making extensive additions and alterations to the various royal residences of Fontainebleu, Compiègne, and Versailles. And finally, during the 1750s and '60s, he occupied himself with some exquisite small buildings, combining elegance with the requisite classical severity for Madame de Pompadour (Louis XV's mistress of acclaimed taste and discernement)—such as her Pavillon Français on the grounds of the Petit Trianon in the Park of Versailles; her Hermitage at Fontainebleu; several other hunting lodges and pavilions dotted about the forests around Versailles; and his masterpiece, the perfectly proportioned Petit Trianon, which was commissioned by Louis XV in 1761 so that he and Madame de Pompadour could occasionally enjoy some simple pastoral pleasures and be alone together without the pomp and circumstance of the court. The plans for the Petit Trianon are worth describing because they show such concern for the ease of running the house and its consequent enjoyment. By designing the house with three floors, which was unusual in a comparatively modest building of the time, Gabriel was able to provide for various household services at the most convenient points. Interestingly, the original plans for the dining room and neighboring servery, or buffet, show two mechanical "flying" tables, which, having been laid by the servants in the basement, could be made to rise through the floor to the rooms above, and eventually brought down again once a meal had been eaten, thus allowing for meals to be eaten with the minimum of servants present. Moreover, the absence of more conventional dining tables meant that people sitting in the room could enjoy an uninterrupted view across the balustraded terrace to the King's Garden. Sadly, Madame de Pompadour died in 1764 when only the walls of the Trianon had been completed. The "flying" tables were never built, and the interiors were not finished until 1769, when the king dined there for the first time. Still, after Louis XV's own death five years later, the rather maligned Marie-Antoinette, wife of Louis XVI, continued the royal search for naturalness and simplicity, by replacing the formal gardens with a more romantic English-style landscaping—complete with undulating lawns, rocky grottoes, and irregular lakes—and added her famous *hameau*, or Normandy-like village, which included a rustic farm and dairy.

GARNIER, JEAN-LOUIS-CHARLES (1825–1898)

French winner of the competition for designing the Paris Opéra House in 1861. The very splendid Second Empire building, with its glamorous foyer and staircase, was completed in 1875. In fact, in today's parlance, one could say that Garnier "did" glamour, since he also designed the famous Casino at Monte Carlo (1879–85), which was such a subsequent influence on grand resort architecture in general.

GAROUSTE, ÉLIZABETH (B. 1949) AND BONETTI, MATTIA (B. 1952)

Lively and original French architectural, furniture, and interior-design partnership especially popular in the 1980s and early '90s. Their work includes the interior and furnishing for the couturier Christian Lacroix's Paris *salon*, restaurants, and furniture collections made variously of twigs, wood, and canvas.

GAUDÍ, ANTONÍ (1852–1926)

Extraordinary Spanish exponent of Art Nouveau at its most extravagantly original and sometimes, one could say, deliberately nightmarish, who worked mainly in and around Barcelona. Like his Scottish contemporary, Charles Rennie Mackintosh (1868–1928), he used many elements from local traditions in his work, in his case Moorish, Moroccan, and Gothic. And because his father was a coppersmith and a pot and kettle maker, he grew up with a thorough knowledge of metals, which he put to inventive use in his metal railings, ornamental grilles, and gates. The Art Nouveau use of iron in so many domestic interiors was a real breakthrough at the time—metal such as iron had never been considered as an integral building material in the past. Gaudí designed several innovative houses that owed little or nothing to any known historical style, before he was commissioned in 1883 to continue the designs for the up to then conventional Neo-Gothic church, the Sagrada Familia, now with cathedral status. He had finished the crypt and begun the transept facade when he was commissioned to design a town house for an industrialist, the Count Güell, who remained Gaudí's patron for the rest of his life. The town house, the Palacio Güell, was built in 1885–89 and was the start of Gaudí's penchant for parabolic arches and outrageous roof excrescences. From then on, Gaudí's buildings grew ever more consciously wild. Construction for the asymmetric and jagged-looking chapel of Sta. Coloma de Cervelló, with its slanting pillars, for one of Count Güell's estates was begun in 1889 but was never finished. After designing the Parque Güell, with its distinctive long and undulating bench faced with bits of broken tile and crockery, he borrowed the same sort of finish for the turrets of the Sagrada Familia, which he had begun, along with the upper parts of the transept, in 1903. The effect, like oversized crustaceans crouched on the roof, had never been seen on any building before, ecclesiastical or otherwise. In spite of these eccentricities, or maybe because they suited a certain bravado in the Spanish character, Gaudí was commissioned in 1905 to design two buildings of luxury apartments, the Casa Battló and the Casa Milá. In both there appear to be no straight walls. The facades rise and fall and undulate; there are sharp, aggressive-looking wrought iron balconies; and both buildings are topped with more bizarre excrescences. Strangest of all, however, in an age of fairly general conformity, was the fact that Gaudí's clients, and indeed *their* clients—those who lived in the apartment buildings—were more than happy with the vigorous but eccentric results. Tragically, Gaudí was hit by a tram as he was leaving the Sagrada Familia in June of 1926, and he died three days later. His body was

La Sagrada Familia Cathedral (1882–1926), Barcelona, Spain, by Antoní Gaudí

buried in the crypt of the Sagrada Familia, the building on which he had worked for the last forty-three years of his life, and which is still under construction. When he died, it was said that he was mourned almost as a saint.

GEHRY, FRANK O. (B. 1929)

Avant-garde Californian architect, educated in California and at Harvard, but actually born in Canada. He came to his architectural maturity rather late but has had a radical influence on aesthetic thought and possibilities in the last few decades. An appropriate analogy for Frank Gehry might be to think of him as the Gaudí of the twenty-first century: someone who throws almost every previous architectural concept up in the air, then jumbles all the (sometimes quite deliberately homely) pieces together in a subtly controlled, often humorous—and, particularly lately— rather beautiful way. It is not hard to admire his complicated compositions of curving and slanting, softly rounded and sharply angular forms, often clad in various metals. They take forms that one can hardly imagine the human brain slotting together and interlocking with any sort of ease. Nevertheless, his interiors, which work surprisingly effectively, show a skillful control of light. His own house at Santa Monica, California (1978–79), is an early example of his thought processes, although it makes great play with cheap industrial materials. There have been numerous innovative buildings since: the Vitra Design Museum, Basel, Switzerland (1987–89); the University of Toledo Arts Building, Ohio (1990–93); the stainless steel Frederick R. Weisma Art Museum, Minneapolis (1990–91); the American Center, Paris (1993–94); the Nationale-Nederlanden Building, Prague (1994–96); the glorious titanium-clad Guggenheim Museum, Bilbao, Spain (1994–97); the steel-enveloped Walt Disney Concert Hall in Los Angeles (1989–2003); the Vontz Center for Molecular Studies in Cincinnati (1997–99); the plans for the then-projected new Guggenheim Museum to be built off the island of Manhattan (2000); and, not least, the dramatic staff cafeteria for the new Conde Nast Building in New York. In 2000, too, he received the first Lifetime Achievement Award from the first Annual National Design Awards instituted by the Cooper-Hewitt National Design Museum, having already won the Pritzker Architecture Award in 1989.

GIBBERD, SIR FREDERICK ERNEST (1908–1984)

British pioneer of the International Style and the designer of the original buildings for Heathrow Airport, London (1950–69), as well as some of the more important buildings for Harlow New Town in Essex, begun in 1946. His earliest well-known building was Pulman Court in Streatham, London (1934–36).

GIBBONS, GRINLING (1648–1721)

Dutch-born immigrant to Britain and outstandingly accomplished sculptor and wood and plaster carver in the Restoration. He worked in close association with Sir Christopher Wren on both the choir and the stalls of St. Paul's Cathedral, London. Horace Walpole, the English essayist and son of Sir Robert Walpole, the prime minister, was a great fan and wrote that he "admired the loose and airy lightness of flowers…the various productions of the elements with free disorder natural to each species" evident in Gibbons's carving. He also described the wonderful wood musical instruments Gibbons carved entirely in the round for Petworth House, Sussex "as worthy of the Grecian age of cameos." One of Gibbons's great staircases, now on display in the Metropolitan Museum of Art, New York, is believed to have been made originally for Cassiobury House, Watford, Hertfordshire, in 1674, and shows the kind of openwork and naturalistic carving that replaced the old strapwork for balustrade decoration in the 1630s. For the staircase at Ham House, Richmond, near London, he filled the panels with military trophies. Gibbons also did very handsome work at Windsor Castle; Sudbury Hall; Derbyshire, Badminton House, and Ramsbury Manor in Wiltshire; and Burleigh House.

GIBBS, JAMES (1682–1754)

Scottish-born architect whose work became widely popular in America. He studied first for the priesthood in Rome in 1703, then left to study painting in the same city, and finally ended up as an architectural student with Carlo Fontana. His first building after setting up practice in London was the church of St. Mary-le-Strand (1714–17), which he followed with the then ground-breaking St. Martin-in-the-Fields by Trafalgar Square. Its combination of a noble temple portico with a steeple rising from the pitch of the roof was widely copied; the recessed oversized columns and pilasters on the side elevations frame were much admired, along with his eponymous Gibbs windows. (Gibbs's typical windows have surrounds of alternating large and small blocks of stone, or of inter-mittent large blocks, sometimes with a narrow raised band connecting up the verticals and running along the face of the arch. These surrounds became so popular with other archi-tects and builders that they are now known as Gibbs surrounds.) Distinguished secular Gibbs buildings include several large country houses (including Ditchley House, 1720–25, Oxfordshire, one-time home of the fabled Nancy Lancaster, owner of Colefax & Fowler, when she was Mrs. Herbert Tree); the Senate House (1722–30) and King's College Fellows' Building in Cambridge (1724–49); and the unique Radcliffe Library in Oxford (1737–49), with its Italian Mannerist influence, rarely seen in Britain. His *Book of Architecture* (1728) had a great influence in America through the architects and builders who emulated his designs. In fact, the White House in Washington (or Executive Mansion as it was then called) started in 1792 from plans by the Irish-born architect James Hoban, is thought to have been inspired by one of Gibbs's plates.

GILLOW, ROBERT (1704–1772)

English furniture designer who founded, in 1730, one of the most successful eighteenth-century furniture companies, Gillows of Lancaster and London. Until its demise in 1932, the company had stamped every one of its pieces of furniture. From their inception the Gillow designs were so good that they soon had an appreciable European following. They were active in the West Indies trade, bringing large supplies of mahogany to England in their own ships in the eighteenth century as well as importing darker mahogany from Cuba and all sorts of rare woods for inlays. The London branch was opened in 1771. George Hepplewhite is thought to have been one of their apprentices.

GILLY, FRIEDRICH (1772–1800)

Neoclassical first-generation German architect of French Huguenot origin who died young but had many followers in America and Britain, as well as in his homeland. In a way, he provided the only real link between late-eighteenth-century thought and the seeds of twentieth-century Modernism. Interestingly, Gilly started his brief career with an enthusiasm for the Gothic, yet deeply inspired the next-generation German architects such as Karl Friedrich Schinkel with his massive Greek Doric temple memorial to Frederick the Great (1796), which was set on a high podium and approached through a solemn arched gateway. His work was similar to the Parisian *barriers*, or customs buildings (they were part of an unpopular new wall built to encircle Paris to try to suppress smuggling), designed by his contemporary Claude-Nicholas Ledoux. Gilly's Monument, which he designed when he was only twenty-four-years old, won a competition set up by King Frederick William II to encourage a uniquely German architecture, or at least one not so dependent on French taste. In 1798, just before he died at the age of twenty-eight, Gilly was made Professor of Optics and Perspective at the newly started German Academy of Architecture and at the same time designed the forward-looking, almost purely geometric Berlin National Theater—a style of building that was not seen again until the very end of the nineteenth century.

GIRARD, ALEXANDER
(1907–1993)

An architect and an early progenitor (in 1958) of the Postmodernist movement of the 1970s and '80s, Girard was an arbiter of twentieth-century taste and an éminence grise of twentieth-century furniture and textiles (mostly for Herman Miller); interiors for Billy Wilder, Herman Miller, Hallmark, and Braniff; and some influential and legendary exhibitions. He was the color consultant for the General Motors Research Center and an influential aficionado of Santa Fe, New Mexico. One way or another, from the late 1920s onward, he was almost always in the design forefront. In 1929, at the age of twenty-two, he received a gold medal for design at the International Exposition in Barcelona, Spain. He moved to New York in 1932 (opening his architecture and interior design office there) and, in 1949, curated "An Exhibition for Modern Living" at the Detroit Institute of Arts. In 1950 he designed a traveling exhibition called "Europe. Design for Modern Use: Made in the USA" for the Museum of Modern Art (MoMA) in New York City and, in 1953 and 1954, designed the "Good Design" exhibitions for MoMA and the Merchandise Mart in Chicago. In 1955 he designed the sumptuous "Textiles and Ornamental Arts of India" exhibit for MoMA. In 1966 he made airline news as design director for Braniff Airlines, for whom he designed everything from airline lounges to airplane interiors, and staff uniforms to graphics. In 1982 he installed his own folk-art collection in the Museum of Folk Art, Santa Fe, New Mexico. And in 2000, very fittingly, the Cooper-Hewitt National Design Museum in New York presented its exhibition "The Opulant Eye of Alexander Girard."

GODDARD, JOHN (1723–1785)

Outstanding American cabinetmaker from Newport, Rhode Island, who was a disciple of Chippendale and became particularly well known for his fine secretary desks known as Rhode Island desks until it was realized that they were all the work of one man. Made of mahogany, the desks all had drawers with block fronts and shell carving on the front of the writing leaf as well as on the doors of the bookcase compartment above and on the pigeon holes and drawers of the interior. Most, too, had broken pediment bonnet tops with flame finials.

GODWIN, EDWARD WILLIAM (1833–1886)

British architect and designer and a chief exponent of the Aesthetic movement, a uniquely British/American late-nineteenth-century style. Max Beerbohm, the theatrical entrepreneur and writer, once called Godwin "the greatest Aesthetic of them all," and certainly he produced many beautiful rooms in which structure was simplified to its essential elements and decoration limited to the minimum. As early as 1862, when most homes on both sides of the Atlantic were sporting over-crowded rooms with rich, dark walls and layers of curtains, Godwin's own house had, according to Nikolaus Pevsner in his *Pioneers of the Modern Movement* (1960), "bare floors, pale walls, a few Persian rugs, a few Japanese prints, a few pieces of antique furniture." It sounds familiar, but at the time it was quite revolutionary. The houses he designed in London for James McNeill Whistler—then the most interesting house in England, according to Pevsner—and for Oscar Wilde, whose rooms were white on white with the palest of possible gray contrasts, were forerunners of the white-on-white style of Syrie Maugham from the 1920s to the '40s.

GRAVES, MICHAEL (B. 1934)

One of the leaders of the American Postmodern movement and another member of the late New York Five. He developed an easily recognizable style as a reaction to Modernism in which he juxtaposed classical details and historical references with purely American Pop idioms; the result is buildings with an idiosyncratic elegance. His Public Services Building in Portland, Oregon (1980–83) was the structure that first drew international attention to his particular style. His Humana Tower, Louisville, Kentucky (1982–86); the Environmental Education Center, Liberty State Park, New Jersey City (1981–83); and the San Juan Capistrano Library (also 1983) all moved on somewhat from the original whimsicality of the Portland building. He nevertheless shows a certain relish for the deft use of Americana in his many recent buildings for Disney World in Florida, Disneyland in California, and Euro-Disney France. (See example on the next page.)

GRAY, EILEEN (1879–1976)

British Modernist designer who settled in Paris in the early 1920s and worked with the French interior designer Jean Badovici. She was

**The Portland Public Service Building (1972–82),
Portland, Oregon, by Michael Graves**

**Eileen Gray "Bibendum" armchair,
designed for J. Suzanne Talbot, 1926–29**

supposed to have been the originator of the new craze for lacquered surfaces of the kind exemplified in the walls of the chic, luxurious apartment she designed for the Paris milliner and couturier J. Suzanne Talbot. Its floor was built entirely out of silvered glass, lit from below, and rugged with leopard skins. Although this was typical Jazz Moderne 1920s style, some of her now-classic furniture designs

and rugs (which are still being reproduced), with her taste for dark colors
and simplified forms, were forerunners
of the International Style to come.

GREENE BROTHERS: CHARLES SUMNER (1868–1957) AND HENRY MATHER (1870–1954)

Two of the first Eastern architects
(Massachusetts Institute of Technology
trained) who came west to California
at the turn of the twentieth century.
There they developed a strong regional
idiom, a relaxed but sensitive style,
and an indoor–outdoor relationship with
gardens or yards that had a great
influence on subsequent Californian
architecture and, indeed, on architecture
for the sun in general. They were particularly inspired by nature and the numerous
possibilities inherent in timber, as well as
the simple wood buildings of Japan and
Scandinavia. Their own houses were
boldly expressed timber structures with
broad overhanging eaves, sheltered
terraces, and sleeping porches that were
considered quite radical at the time.

GRIMSHAW, SIR NICHOLAS (B. 1939)

British High-Tech architect of the
handsome glass-and-steel Waterloo
International Railway Terminal
(1988–93) for the Channel Tunnel. In
fact, for many overseas travelers
arriving in England, his are the first, or
at least some of the first, buildings to
be seen, since he also designed the
Compass Center at Heathrow Airport
(1994) as well as many other British and
European buildings of some elegance.

GROPIUS, WALTER (1883–1969)

German-born founder, in 1919, of the
Bauhaus (meaning "house of building"),
an extension of the Weimer School of
Arts and Crafts and the single most
powerful influence on the development
and acceptance of what was then a
totally new kind of design. Gropius
started his studies at the Colleges of
Technology of Berlin and Munich.
Then, for three years, he joined the
office of Peter Behrens, who was a firm
believer in good design both for the
workplace and for everyday objects.
Inspired by this attitude (as he was
inspired by Frank Lloyd Wright's work
in America), Gropius started his own
architectural practice in 1910 and wrote
a detailed memorandum on the possibilities inherent in the standardization
and mass production of housing and
equipment. In 1911, he and a colleague,
Adolph Meyer (1881–1929), designed the
Fagus factory at Alfield in unadorned
cubic blocks with revolutionary glass
curtain-walling and corners with no
visible supports; in short, he incorporated some of the main ingredients of
the Modernist movement that segued
into the International Modern style.
In 1914, again with Meyer, he com-
pounded this early Modernist success
with a design for a model factory
and office building for the Werkbund
Exhibition in Cologne. It was this
radical departure from the norm that
prompted Henry van de Velde, the
retiring head of the School of Arts and
Crafts at Weimar, to suggest Gropius as
his successor. After World War I,
Gropius took up the appointment, and
running with the ideas of William

Morris and the Arts and Crafts movement on the one hand and the Expressionists on the other, proceeded to transform the place, rechristening it the Bauhaus to suggest that the school should be the meeting and training place of all proponents of the arts and crafts; the initial training for all should be an introduction to color, form, and the nature of material. In the early 1920s, somewhat influenced by his contacts with the Dutch De Stijl group, Gropius returned to his earlier ideals and reorientated the school to an emphasis on industrial design rather than on craft—an emphasis that took physical form in the school's new premises at Dessau. When Hitler assumed power, Gropius went to London, where he worked for a short time in partnership with Maxwell Fry, designing Impington Village College near Cambridge, before moving to the United States and Harvard University. There he started to teach again, joined (for the second time) with Marcel Breuer for a few years, and started his own firm, full of younger men each generously given a great deal of independence, called The Architects' Collaborative. The firm produced the Harvard Graduate Center. Gropius also designed the United States Embassy in Athens, but probably his greatest contribution, apart from his inspired teaching and his enormous contribution to the International Style, was to the field of medium-priced domestic architecture and his early thoughts on the standardization of mass housing.

GUIMARD, HECTOR (1867–1942)

French Art Nouveau architect, best known for his Paris Metro stations (1899–1904), which consisted of a series of high metal arches that decorate various entrances. His most interesting building is the Castel Bérenger (1894–1912), a Paris apartment building with an interior of glass bricks, metal, and faience and room shapes as offbeat as those in Gaudí's buildings in Spain.

GWATHMEY, CHARLES (B. 1938)

Prolific, much-publicized American architect and another member of the New York Five. He started Gwathmey, Siegel & Associates with Robert Siegel (b. 1939) in 1968, and since then the two have designed university buildings for Columbia University, New York; Princeton University, Princeton, New Jersey; and Harvard University, Cambridge, Massachusetts. Other projects have included the American Museum of the Moving Image, Astoria, New York and the Science, Industry and Business Library of the New York Public Library. The firm has also designed much-photographed private houses, done work for Disney in Florida, and shouldered the extremely sensitive job of adding on an extension to Frank Lloyd Wright's Solomon R. Guggenheim Museum in Manhattan.

HADFIELD, GEORGE (1764–1826)

British-born Greek Revival architect who studied at the Royal Academy

Schools in London, won his Gold Medal in 1784, went on to study in Italy, and emigrated to America in 1795. There he was rapidly appointed as yet another construction supervisor of the new Capitol in Washington, D.C., but he made it very clear that he disapproved of the design and suggested radical alterations that were neither appreciated nor approved, so he lost the job. Undeterred, he continued to work industriously in the new city, producing designs (which were accepted) for City Hall (1820), the United States Bank (1824), Fuller's and Gadsby's Hotels, Van Ness's mausoleum (1826), and the splendid Arlington House (1818), considered one of the best Greek Revival buildings in the United States.

HADID, ZAHA (B. 1950)

Gifted and especially innovative Iraqi-born architect, trained in London, and now a British citizen, who in 2004 was the first woman and the twenty-eighth architect to have been voted a laureate of the Pritzker Architecture Prize. She worked with Rem Koolhaas at the Office of Metropolitan Architecture (OMA) until the early 1980s. After winning a competition for a Club House in Hong Kong with an extraordinary "fragmented" design (the plans for which were later shown at the 1988 Deconstructivist Exhibition at the Museum of Modern Art in New York), she left to work on her own and has produced other significant designs for projects, including the Cardiff Bay

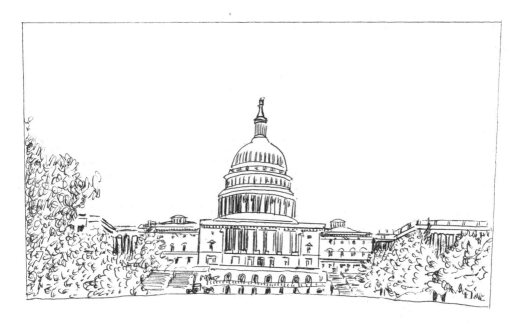

The Capitol (1792–1827), Washington, D.C., designed and redesigned or added to by William Thornton, Etienne (Stephen) Hallett, George Hadfield, Bejamin Latrobe, and Charles Bullfinch

Opera House in Wales and an office building in Berlin. Neither were realized; this is the disappointing fate of so many original designs, remarkable though they may be. However, she subsequently produced a distinguished body of work that *has* been built in Japan and Germany (including, in 1989, a fire station for Frank O. Gehry's Vitra Design Museum, Weil-am-Rhein, Germany); some equally original interiors for restaurants and other commercial buildings; the stunning, somewhat Russian Constructivist–style Rosenthal Center for Contemporary Arts in Cincinnati, Ohio (opened 2003), which was dubbed by *The New York Times* as "the most important American building to be completed since the end of the Cold War"; and the Price Tower Arts center in Bartlesville, Oklahoma, to coexist with a Frank Lloyd Wright building. She now has a stupefying list of international commissions, including a masterplan for the City of Bilbao in Spain; a National Center of Contemporary Art in Rome, Italy; another Guggenheim Museum in Taichung, Taiwan; and a high-speed train station just outside Naples, Italy.

HADLEY, ALBERT (B. 1921)

Unconventional, deeply versed in the classical, but anticlassical American decorator's decorator. Albert Hadley's career has had a broad range, going from design workrooms to teaching at Parsons School of Design, New York, not to mention working with two of the grandes dames of American twentieth-century decorating. He joined Eleanor McMillen Brown, founder of McMillen Inc.—one of the oldest decorating firms in the United States—in 1957; in 1962, Hadley left McMillen Inc. to work with Mrs. Henry "Sister" Parrish II (reputedly because Brown remarked that women made better decorators than men). After six years, Parrish invited Hadley to be a partner in what became Parish-Hadley, Inc., and finally, in 2000, Albert Hadley Inc. "The chic of suitability" is reputedly his motto, and few decorators are as capable of combining the past with the present with such aplomb.

HALFPENNY, WILLIAM (D. 1755)

British architect who is best known for his score or so of influential pamphlets created to assist country gentlemen and provincial builders in America as much as in Britain. These pamphlets illustrated mainly Palladian-inspired designs that could be copied successfully for new buildings. He also helped to popularize the taste for chinoiserie. Halfpenny's books, some of which he wrote with his son, include *A New and Compleat System of Architecture* (1749); *The Modern Builder's Assistant* (1757); *New designs for chinese temples, triumphal arches, garden seats, palings, etc.* (1750–52); and *Rural Architecture in the Chinese Taste* (1750–52)—although the last seems something of an oxymoron since these Chinese buildings were follies, sophisticated and highly fanciful structures introduced as decorative elements to gardens and parks, and were not at all pastoral or rural.

HARDOUIN-MANSART, JULES (1646–1708)

Architect of the spectacular Place Vendôme in Paris (1698 onward), Hardouin-Mansart was royal architect to Louis XIV (whose extravagant needs he exceled in anticipating) in 1675, premier architect in 1685, and suprintendent des bâtiments in 1699. He may well have been trained by his great uncle François Mansart, although he was considerably more reliable and adaptable. But he certainly owed a good deal to Louis Le Vau, whose grand manner he perfected and, together with Charles Lebrun, brought to summation in the marvelous Galerie des Glaces, or "Hall of Mirrors," in Versailles. The circumstances are not known, but it seems sad that Hardouin-Mansart, when put in charge of all the new extensions to Versailles from 1678 onward, managed to ruin Le Vau's beautifully proportioned garden facade for the palace by filling in the central terrace and tripling its length. His new Grand Trianon (1678–89)—replacing Le Vau's Trianon de Porcelaine—was considerably more successful, as were his orangery, chapel, and stables for Versailles. In the 1690s, his style became lighter, losing most, if not all, reference to what some considered the straitjacket of the Classical orders. Heavy paneling gave way to pale-painted panels and the lightest of moldings; indeed, some of the rooms he designed for Versailles, as well as for the Grand Trianon and for the king's residence at Marly, give a foretaste of the *Régence* and Rococo style that was to come.

HARDWICK, PHILIP (1792–1870)

Eclectic nineteenth-century British architect of mainly London public buildings of interesting stylistic diversity. One such was Euston Station (1836–39), whose Greek Doric propylaeum (entrance gateway) was wantonly destroyed—in spite of public protest—by the British Rail Company. He also designed the classically inspired warehouses for St. Katharine Docks (1827–28)—now also used as "loft" apartments; the Baroque-inspired Goldsmith's Hall (1829–35); and the Tudor-inspired Lincoln's Inn Hall and Library (1842–45), which, with its finesse of period detail, is far removed from the usual nineteenth- and twentieth-century Tudor imitations.

HARRISON, PETER (1716–1776)

One of the best-known pre-Revolutionary amateur American architects who, though born in England, immigrated to America in 1740, ten years or so before John Ariss (reputed to be America's first *professional* architect). He started as a trader of wines, rum, molasses, and mahogany in Newport, Rhode Island, but taught himself architecture in his spare time. He quickly became competent in first the English Palladian style and then—like Ariss—came somewhat under the influence of the redoubtable James Gibbs. His first commission was the Redwood Library in Newport (1749–50); it was followed by the Newport Synagogue (1759–63), known as Touro Synagogue, which is the oldest in the United States. These buildings and others, such as those in the town of Brick Market (1761–62), gave Newport the reputation of being the center of architectural art in New England, a design reputation that continues to this day with the Rhode Island School of Design. Harrison also designed Christ Church, Cambridge, Massachusetts (1760).

HARRISON, WALLACE KIRKMAN (1895–1981)

American architect who designed a roll call of iconic American buildings in Manhattan with his partner, Max Abramovitz. He designed Rockefeller Center (1931–40) with Raymond Hood, who had previously designed the Daily News Building and did the centerpiece of Rockefeller Center, the RCA Building; the United Nations Head-quarters with a team that counted Le Corbusier among its members (1947–53); and Lincoln Center (1962–68), including the new Metro-politan Opera House and Philhar-monic (now Avery Fisher) Hall. Outside of Manhattan, he designed the massive New York State Center at Albany (1962–78) and the domed University of Illinois Assembly Hall, Champagne-Urbana (1963).

HAUSSMANN, BARON GEORGES-EUGÈNE (1809–1891)

Born in Alsace, and first of all a lawyer and civil servant of a somewhat ruthless disposition, he was appointed Prefect of the Seine Department in 1853 by Napoleon III and entrusted to carry out the Emperor's grand plans for the improvement of Paris, much of which had been destroyed during the Revolution, the Siege of Paris, and the Commune. This he did for almost twenty years, achieving perhaps more than even the Emperor had envisioned with his series of peerless boulevards, *ronds-points*, and dramatic vistas radiating off the Arc de Triomphe. Probably with good reason, many people thought that Haussmann's long, straight boulevards were conceived not from aesthetic considerations but to obtain good firing lines in the case of another revolution; yet he was also guided by finding solutions to traffic problems and by providing good connections to the new railway stations.

HAWKSMOOR, NICHOLAS (1661–1736)

Great English Baroque architect who was employed by Sir Christopher Wren and Sir John Vanbrugh. He worked with the former as an amanuensis—a kind of literary and research assistant—as well as on Wren's plans for Greenwich Hospital and other buildings. For Sir John Vanbrugh he worked on Blenheim Palace in Oxfordshire and on Castle Howard in Yorkshire, where his most recognized contribution was the austere and circular Doric mausoleum that forms such a landmark in the Park. Subsequently, he designed six original and slightly eccentric London churches, including St. Anne's, Lime-house (1714–30); St. Mary Woolnoth, London (1716–24); St. George's,

Bloomsbury (1716–30); and Christ-church, Spitalfields (1714–29). He also designed the quadrangle, hall, and Codrington Library at All Souls' College, Oxford (1716–35) and the west towers (1729) of Westminster Abbey.

HEAL, SIR AMBROSE (1872–1959)

Like William Morris before him and the Scandinavian firm Ikea and Terence Conran with his Habitat shops after, Heal wanted to prove that progressive, well-designed furniture could be sold at reasonable prices to the general public. He joined the family firm of Heal & Son in 1893 and issued his first *Plain Oak Bedroom Furniture Catalogue* in 1898, which popularized the simple wood bedstead in England for the next thirty years. But he was also capable of producing individual pieces in the same bright and airy style as Charles F. A. Voysey's wallpapers. For example, a decorative and original wardrobe that he showed at the Paris Exhibition Universelle of 1900 was made of slightly fumed and waxed oak and decorated with small inlaid panels of pewter and ebony that were juxtaposed with gracefully drawn little flowers.

HENNEBIQUE, FRANÇOIS (1842–1921)

French architect who was not only one of the great pioneers of concrete architecture but who also engineered the spectacular glass-and-metal roofs for both the Grand Palais and Petit Palais (1900), which now seem such a characteristic part of Paris. He built the first-ever reinforced-concrete bridge in Viggen, Switzerland in 1894 and began his first concrete-and-glass factory buildings that same year. The following year he went on to install the first grain elevator in France (in Roubaix). In 1896 he built a cantilevered concrete staircase for an exhibition in Geneva, and, in 1899, he designed some cantilevered galleries for a small theater in Morges, France. He built his own eccentric concrete house at Bourg-la-Reine in 1904 and the reinforced-concrete Ponte Risorgimento over the river Tiber in Rome for Rome's Esposizione Internazionale d'Arte of 1911.

HEPPLEWHITE, GEORGE (D. 1786)

English furniture designer, thought to have been an apprentice of Thomas Gillow. He was not particularly known in his lifetime but became famous through his *Cabinet-Maker and Upholsterer's Guide*, published by his loyal and enterprising widow in 1788, two years after his death. It was sold as a "Repository of Designs for every article of Household Furniture—near Three Hundred different Designs." One of the most immediately popular of these designs was a comfortably upholstered gout stool, "being so easily raised or lowered at either end," Hepplewhite explained, "that it is particularly useful for the afflicted." By 1794, the book had gone into three editions and the "Hepplewhite" heart-shaped or shield-back chairs carved with ferns, Prince of Wales feathers, swags, and wheatears were widely copied in America. (See examples on the next page.)

Shield back chairs, from *The Cabinet-Maker and Upholsterer's Guide* (1788–94) by George Hepplewhite

HERRERA, JUAN DE (CA. 1530–1597)

Spanish architect whose only partly executed designs for the Cathedral at Valladolid (1585) had, nevertheless, an important influence on the designs of the Salamanca, Puebla, Mexico City and Lima cathedrals. He also designed the Royal Gardens of Aranjuez (1569), the Exchange in Seville (1582), and some additions to the Escorial in Madrid, including the infirmary and chapel (1574–82).

HERZOG, JACQUES (B. 1950) AND DE MEURON, PIERRE (B. 1950)

Swiss partners since 1978 in the architectural firm of Herzog & de Meuron, best known, so far, for their transformation of a former Bankside power station into the Gallery of Modern Art for the Tate Museum, London (1998–2000). Previous work over the last decade or so includes the Dominus Winery, near Yountville, California (1996–98); their fanciful copper-clad signal box for Basel Railway Station (1995); their Caramel Factory and Storage Building for Ricola in France's Mulhouse (1993); and their minimalist private gallery for the Goetz Collection in Munich, Germany (1992). In 2001, they were joint winners of the Pritzker Architecture Prize.

HICKS, DAVID (1929–1998)

British decorator who came to the fore in the 1960s with his courageous juxtapositions of vivid colors (especially red, pink, and eggplant), clean lines, distinctive geometric carpets, dramatic lighting, and genius for arranging disparate objects. He was hugely successful and had as big an effect on American decorators of the period (and, for that matter, French decorators like François Catroux) as Jean Michel Frank and Madeleine Castaing had in the 1930s. Certainly, like Terence Conran, though in entirely different mode, he was instrumental in contributing an entirely different feel to trans-Atlantic interior design.

HITCHCOCK, LAMBERT (1795–1852)

Connecticut designer and manufacturer of one of the best-known American "Fancy" chairs, as they were then called—an alternative to the ubiquitous nineteenth-century Windsor chairs. These chairs, like the Windsor, were also based on an English design, in this case a Sheraton style combined with a French Napoleonic chair with "pillow" backs or an oval-turned top rail. (See also *Hitchcock chair* in Furniture and Upholstery).

HOBAN, JAMES (CA. 1762–1831)

Irish-born architect who emigrated to America after the Revolution and is chiefly known for his designs for the White House in Washington, D.C., the facade of which was supposedly based on an illustration in James Gibbs's *Book of Architecture*, although it also bears a resemblance to Leinster House in Dublin. The presidential domicile was built between 1793 and 1801, and

Hoban also supervised its rebuilding after the British burned it down in 1814, a construction that was not finished until 1829. Other Hoban buildings in the District of Columbia are the Grand Hotel (1793–95) and the State and War Offices, begun in 1818. An earlier building was the South Carolina State Capitol at Columbia, which was completed in 1791 but burned down in 1865, during the Civil War, like so many of Columbia's buildings.

HOFFMANN, JOSEF (1870–1956)

Austrian architect and furniture designer, and one of the founders in 1903 of the Wiener Werkstätte (along with Otto Wagner and Joseph Maria Olbrich), premised on the William Morris ideal of a unity between architecture and the crafts. Hoffmann

Stoclet House (1905–11), Brussels, with fountain and pool, by Joseph Hoffmann

was a pupil of Otto Wagner's in Vienna, but, influenced by the mixture of elegance and austerity in the furniture and other work of Charles Rennie Mackintosh, which had been included in the Vienna Secession exhibit (from the German term *Sezession*) in 1900, he moved away from the Art Nouveau style to unrelieved square or rectangular forms. He first used such embellishment, but with a typical Viennese refinement, in the Convalescent Home at Purkersdorf (1903–11) outside Vienna. His most famous work, however, is the Stoclet House (1905–11) in Brussels, Belgium, with an exterior in bronze-framed white marble and interiors lined with jewel-like mosaics by his contemporary Gustav Klimt. This was unmistakable proof that his simple shapes could be made to look both monumental and luxurious when built with lavish materials.

HOLL, ELIAS (1573–1646)

German Renaissance architect, and one of the first advocates of Classical design in Prussia. He traveled in Italy, where he is thought to have studied the work of Andrea Palladio and other Renaissance architects. He visited Venice at the beginning of the seventeenth century and holds a position in his own country's architectural history equivalent to his exact contemporary Inigo Jones, who first brought Classical architecture to England. On his return from Italy he became city architect of Augsberg and built its exquisite Town Hall between 1615 and 1620.

HOLL, STEVEN (B.1947)

Versatile American architect, internationally trained (in Washington, Rome, and London) who first received particular attention for some relatively small but distinguished commissions: a vernacular, free-spirited, all-wood house he designed on Martha's Vineyard, Massachusetts (1984–88); a shop and showroom for the Pace Collection (1985); the Giada shop, a women's clothing store (1987); an apartment in Metropolitan Towers (1987); the very minimalist offices for D. E. Shaw and Company, the investment firm (1991); and, with Vito Acconci, the Storefront Gallery (1992–93)—all in New York. In the meantime, however, he started to expand first by writing his book *Anchoring: Selected Projects, 1975–1988* (Princeton Architectural Press) in 1989 and then, in the same year, by producing his interesting Void Space/Hinged Space Housing, Nexus World Kashii, Fukuoka, Japan. In 1999 he won the National AIA Design award for KIASMA, the Museum of Contemporary Art in Helsinki, and, in 2000, he was commissioned to do a new addition for the Nelson Atkins Museum of Art, Kansas City, Missouri.

HOLLAND, HENRY (1745–1806)

One of the first English Neoclassical architects, known for the refined simplicity of his interiors as well as his knowledge of French Classicism. He added strains of the lighter and more esoteric Louis XVI style to the more solemn underlay of antiquity. His talent was said to be most apparent at Carlton

House, London, that he enlarged and altered for the Prince of Wales (1783–85), but which is now sadly demolished, in spite of its allegedly beautiful rooms. However, there are at least illustrations of Holland's splendid Chinese Room at Carlton House in Thomas Sheraton's *The Cabinet-Maker and Upholsterer's Drawing Book* (1791–1802) and in William Pyne's *Royal Residences* (1819). He also designed Brooks' Club, London (1776–78), and the Marine Pavilion at Brighton (1786–87), which was later transformed into the Royal Pavilion by architect John Nash. Holland had worked as an assistant to "Capability" Brown and had married Brown's daughter before starting out on his own. He had good "connections" with the Whig aristocracy of the day and received many commissions. He was as popular for his meticulous attention to aesthetic detail, creating devices such as a gilded pelmet box with eagles to support curtains, as he was for his sense of comfort. One of his most thoughtful inventions was heated window seats.

HOLLEIN, HANS (B. 1934)

Austrian architect and winner of the 1985 Pritzker Architecture Prize. He is considered to be just as much an artist as an architect, teacher, author, and designer of furniture and silverware and, as one of the judges of the Pritzker put it: "An architect who is also an artist who has the good fortune to design museums that are as eager to place within their walls works of art from his hand, whether in the form of drawings, collages, or sculpture." After graduating from the School of Architecture in Vienna in 1956, he was awarded a Harkness Fellowship for Travel in the United States and took advantage of it to do graduate work at the Illinois Institute of Technology in Chicago and to finish his masters in architecture at the University of California in Berkeley. In 1960 he met and worked with Mies van der Rohe, Frank Lloyd Wright, and Richard Neutra. After working for a time in Sweden, he settled back in Vienna in 1965 and became, as he has been called, a kind of "architectural Fabergé," combining an architect's sense of space with a goldsmith's sense of craft. His work includes the 1970 Richard Feiger Gallery in New York City (1970) and the Abteiberg Museum in Monchengladbach, near Dusseldorf, Germany (1972–82). In 1985 he won the competition for the Museum of Modern Art in Frankfurt and the Cultural Forum in Berlin.

HOPE, THOMAS (1770–1831)

Early-nineteenth-century British furniture designer, dilettante, and transitional figure between the old aristocratic patronage and the aspiring middle classes. In a way, he epitomized the Regency style, the British version of the French Empire style, with its restless eclecticism contained in a Neoclassical framework. Originally a banker, he was seriously interested in Classical and Egyptian archeology and was also a great admirer of the designs of Charles Percier and Pierre-François-Leonard

Fontaine, the Emperor Napoleon's favored designers. Yet, most of all he had a burning desire to improve the public taste at whatever cost. To this end he set about decorating and commissioning furniture for both his London and country houses with Egyptian, Turkish, Indian, and Greco-Roman references, which he then let selected members of the public see—much as people are given guided tours of various homes today. He also wrote the influential *Household Furniture and Interior Decoration* (1807), which was as widely admired in America as it was in Britain.

HOPKINS, SIR MICHAEL (B. 1935) AND LADY PATTY (B. 1942)

British High-Tech architects popular with the design cognoscenti who have been in partnership since 1976, after Sir Michael left the offices of Sir Norman Foster to set up on his own. Part of the Canary Wharf Development in London uses their successful Patera Building System. Other refined but relaxed public buildings include the new opera house at Glyndebourne, Sussex (1988–94) and the new Parliamentary Building, Westminster, London (1989).

HORTA, BARON VICTOR (1861–1947)

Belgian Art Nouveau architect and designer who was the first to understand that, as in the Rococo period, the essence of the movement was to synthesize architecture, room decoration, and furnishings into one indivisible whole. Like Robert Adam in the eighteenth century, Horta designed every part of that whole himself, from the hardware and light fittings to the furniture, furnishings, and stained glass—this last is a commodity he used a great deal, not only in window and door panes but for whole ceilings. A good example is the Hotel Van Eetvelde in Brussels, finished in 1896. Like Gaudí in Spain, Horta was excited by Eugène-Emmanuel Viollet-le-Duc's two-volume *Entretiens sur l'architecture* (published in France from 1858 to 1872, and in English, in Boston, from 1875 to 1881). In particular, he was inspired by Viollet-le-Duc's writings on the possibilities of iron sculpture; he flew with this idea, as it were, in his balustrades, columns, and girders, which curved, weaved, and twisted in tendril-like forms that were often repeated in the painting on walls and ceilings and in mosaic patterns on the floors (just as Adam had repeated the intricate designs of his plaster ceilings in his specially woven carpets). Horta used his sculptural ingenuity to great effect in his first house, the Tassel House (1892) in Brussels, the sight of which is supposed to have moved his former master and teacher, Alphonse Balat, to tears. Other splendid Horta projects were the Hôtel Solvay (1895–1900; the "hôtel" prefix is used here in the original sense, in France and Belgium, to denote a large town house); the Maison du Peuple (1895–99), with its curved glass and iron facade; and the Brussels store called L'Innovation (1901).

HUNT, RICHARD MORRIS (1827–1895)

The first American neo-Renaissance architect, as well as a painter and sculptor, who came from a prosperous early Colonial family and moved to Paris in 1843. There he attended the École des Beaux-Arts and worked with Hector Lefuel, Napoleon III's chief architect to the Louvre, which at that time was being extended. Having received firsthand knowledge of the French Renaissance Revival, he took the fashion back to New York, from where he commuted back and forth to France until he finally settled back in New York in 1868. He designed the Tribune building (1873), one of the first New York buildings with an elevator; various "cottages" for the Vanderbilts and the Astors in Newport, Rhode Island; as well as the impressive Biltmore Castle, in Ashville, North Carolina in the 1890s, with its particularly handsome library. At the beginning of the same decade, he also designed the facade of the Metropolitan Museum of Art (1894–1902). He was one of the founders of the American Institute of Architects.

ICTINUS

One of the greatest of ancient architects in Periclean Athens who designed and built the Parthenon with Callicrates (447/6–438 B.C.). He was reputedly the architect of the Doric temple of Apollo Epicurius at Bassae, begun around 430 B.C. after the Great Greek Plague.

INCE, WILLIAM (1738–1804)
AND MAYHEW, JOHN (1736–1811)

Successful partnership of Neoclassical cabinetmakers who published an equally successful folio design book—*The Universal System of Household Furniture* (1762)—somewhat modeled on Chippendale's *Gentlemen and Cabinet-Maker's Director*.

ISOZAKI, ARATA (B. 1931)

An extremely versatile leader of the post–World War II generation of Japanese architects who first worked with Kenzo Tange before designing his much-praised Space City Project in Japan in 1962. In the mid-1960s he developed an East–West fusion style for several of his buildings until, in the late 1970s, he veered off into a whole new phase that he called "schizoid," apparently quite aptly, which led to a commission to design the Museum of Contemporary Art in Los Angeles (1984–86). Afterward he changed direction again, this time to Postmodernism, the result of which was an extraordinarily successful building—or perhaps monument would be a better word—The Art Tower, Mito, Japan (1990). (The Art Tower is topped by an endless column of "titanium-paneled tetrahedrons," the edges of which create a DNA-like double helix, which sounds considerably more complicated than it looks.) On he went again, this time to work with that commissioning genius Disney (which often seems like a casting agency for architects) to design its Team Disney Building at Lake Buena Vista, Florida, in quite another sort of fusion—this time between European Rationalism and Pop Disneyland. At present he has moved on to a whole new dynamic international style, with buildings in Spain and Poland, as well as Japan.

ITO, TOYO (B. 1941)

Korean-born, but trained and working in Japan, Ito is one of the most experimental and innovative architects working today. He juxtaposes shapes and various, often transparent, materials in wholly ingenious ways, and since he is reported to have wanted to create architecture that is "as light as the wind," he evidently succeeds as well as anyone can. In his own spatially ambiguous house, the Silver Hut, Nakano (1984), he experimented with layers of perforated, semitransparent screens of industrial materials. In his Tower of Winds, Yokohama (built in 1986 and taken—not blown—down in 1995), he used 1,300 flickering lamps, twenty-four floodlights, and twelve neo-rings within its perforated outer skin, all computer programmed to produce shimmering patterns that shifted and transmuted according to the direction of the winds. For the Municipal Museum at Yatsushiro (1991), he created a bubble-shaped repository to "float" above vaulted stainless steel roofs and perforated metal screens. The UFO-shaped Egg of Winds, Tokyo (1991) was hotly followed by the floating UFOs for the Nagayama Amusement Complex, Tama, Tokyo (1993), and that same year Ito pulled off an almost completely transparent building for ITM in Matsuyama, using every possible kind of glass, whether it was clear, wire-meshed, opaque, or frosted. Even his fire station at Yatsushiro floats some

twenty feet above the ground—good practice, one supposes, for the firemen.

JACOBSEN, ARNE (1902–1971)

Danish architect and furniture designer who built many meticulously designed and elegant private houses in the 1930s before he started being commissioned to design various, equally meticulous Town Halls and other public buildings in Denmark. He also designed St. Catherine's College, Oxford, England, finished in the 1960s, and during the 1950s designed his well-known laminated plywood and steel stacking chairs and the famous Egg pivoting chair, as well as some simple but handsome tableware.

JEFFERSON, THOMAS (1743–1826)

Not just the third President of the United States, but also an undoubtedly influential architect and educator who looked back to antiquity and to ancient Roman villa architecture for his architectural theory and inspiration; yet he seemed happy to use the writings and buildings of architects he admired from the present as well. He used several sources for his own meticulously well-thought-out house, Monticello, in Albemarle County, Virginia, begun in 1768. He selected the plan originally from Robert Morris's *Select Architecture* (1755), adapting it to some of James Gibbs's ideas as well as incorporating some Palladian elements culled from Giacomo Leoni's English edition of Palladio's work (1715). When he was the United States Ambassador to France, he was asked in 1785 to design the Virginia State Capitol in Richmond. This he did with the help of the French architect and teacher Charles-Louis Clérisseau, with whom he studied architecture (and later with Benjamin Latrobe), producing a templelike design with Ionic pillars and pilasters on the sides and rear of the building. Finished in 1796, the building set the pattern for official buildings in the United States. From 1792 onward, as Secretary of State to George Washington, he made a substantial contribution to the planning of the new Federal Capitol in Washington. And when he became President he called in Latrobe in 1803 to complete what turned out to be a very long job. The new Capitol was almost entirely burned down in 1814 and had to be rebuilt. Latrobe also assisted Jefferson with the planning of the impressive University of Virginia at Charlottesville (1817–26).

Jefferson Library (1817–26) of the University of Virginia, Charlottesville, by Thomas Jefferson

JOHNSON, PHILIP (B. 1906)

One of the American twentieth-century architectural icons who came to the actual practice of architecture rather late, although he had been an energetic critic and protagonist of the new modern architecture of the time for some years. While studying Greek and philosophy at Harvard, Johnson somehow became aware of the groundbreaking work of the De Stijl group, Walter Gropius, Le Corbusier, and Mies van der Rohe, and from then on "Nothing," he said, "existed but architecture." After traveling through Europe in 1930 with Henry-Russell Hitchcock, the historian and critic, looking at Modern architecture for their book *The International Style: Architecture Since 1922* (1932)—which is said to have given that style its name—he became a convinced devotee of Mies for his classic approach and his devotion to beautiful materials. On his return, Johnson was offered and accepted the job of starting the Department of Architecture at the Museum of Modern Art (MoMA) in New York, curating the museum's landmark exhibition introducing the new European architecture in the same year as the publication of his book on the same subject. Seven years later, Johnson returned to Harvard to study architecture for himself and was given the chance to build his thesis project in Cambridge. These were the years when Gropius was teaching, but still a convinced Miesian, Johnson worked on a project Mies had designed but had not built: "a house designed as a walled court where the rectangular living volume opened onto a paved court through a glass wall." It is a prototype for so many urban houses today. After Harvard, he returned to MoMA, where he published his book *Mies van der Rohe* in 1947. During his many talks with Mies for the preparation of the book they discussed the idea of completely glazed buildings. Johnson thought it could not be done. Mies thought it could. They both worked on the idea: Mies produced his Farnsworth house and Johnson built his own Glass House on a fabulous site in New Canaan, Connecticut, in 1949. They are now considered to be two of the most famous houses in America. Many more houses followed. Then, as associate architect with Mies for the Seagram Building, he designed the stunning interior for the building's Four Seasons Restaurant, though the building also marked his divergence from the Mies single-mindedness. Whereas the architects who came to fame in the 1920s denounced history as an influence on their respective designs, Johnson has done as much as any modern architect to reinstate it. "We cannot *not* know history," he is reported to have said in an interview, and, "I do not think there is such a thing as originality." To prove it, his many divergent buildings—including the Kneses Tifereth Israel Synagogue in Port Chester, New York; the Amon Carter Museum in Fort Worth, Texas; the Art Gallery for the University of Nebraska, the New York State Theater at Lincoln Center; the Roofless Church in New Harmony, Indiana; the Munson-Williams-Proctor Arts Institute in Utica, New York; the

outdoor terracing for MoMA in New York; and the Nuclear Reactor at Rehovot, Israel—all show certain erudite but lighthearted references to nineteenth-century Classicism, whether derived from the German Karl Friedrich Schinkel, the British Sir John Soane, or the French Claude-Nicolas Ledoux. But, as Johnson has also said: "Professionalism—how you approach a building, how you get into it, and how you feel when you are there—has carried right through, as a main concern in my work, from Mies to today." He could have added the well-known Mies aphorism: "I do not want to be original. I want to be good." Johnson's lifetime achievement was honored in 1979 when he was the first architect to be awarded the Pritzker Architecture Prize, set up by the Hyatt Trust and now the leading international award for architecture.

JONES, INIGO (1573–1652)

Great English Renaissance architect who was ahead of his time and, in his way, as much of a genius as his slightly older contemporary, William Shakespeare. The son of a cloth worker, he somehow managed to visit Italy before 1603 in the role of "picture-maker" and returned to England to become a popular figure at the royal court of James I as a stage designer for masks in the Italian manner. (Some of his beautifully executed and quite fantastic designs for Baroque costumes and architectural sets still survive.) At the same time he seems to have picked up architectural skills for, in 1608, he created designs for the New Exchange in London. In 1613 he visited Italy again, this time in the company of the well-known collector Lord Arundel. He stayed there for nineteen months while making extensive sketches of antique Roman details as well as of villas in the Veneto designed by Andrea Palladio; when he returned to England he became the first English architect to have a firsthand knowledge of not just the Italian Renaissance master, but of his Classical sources. In 1615, he was made Surveyor of the King's Works and was continuously employed at the various royal palaces until 1642. In that period he built three outstandingly original classical houses that were the first buildings to break with the Elizabethan and Jacobean building traditions, even though they were erected almost a century after the Classical ideal had spread from Italy to France. Nor were they in any ways slavish copies of Palladio: correct in detail, those details were subtly transmuted to an essential solid Englishness. These original houses were the Queen's House, Greenwich (1616–18, continued 1629–38); the Prince's Lodging, Newmarket, Suffolk (1619–22, now destroyed); and Jones's masterpiece, the Banqueting Hall, Whitehall, London (1619–22). Nearly all his buildings for the next monarch, Charles I, have been destroyed, except for the continuation of the Queen's House,

The Queen's House, Greenwich, near London, begun by Inigo Jones in 1616 (extended by John Webb in 1661)

Greenwich; the great Corinthian portico for the Old St. Paul's Cathedral, which transformed a medieval structure into a Roman one; and Covent Garden, the first London Square, thought to be somewhat based on the Place des Vosges in Paris, although only the church and a fragment of the original square now survive. The famous double-cube room at Wilton House, Wiltshire, for Lord Pembroke, often cited as the most beautiful room in England, was actually completed in Jones's old age by his nephew by marriage, John Webb, but it bears every sign of his style. In his lifetime, Jones's influence was mostly in court circles. Nevertheless, a century later, his was the greatest influence on the Palladian Revival engineered by Lord Burlington and William Kent.

KAHN, LOUIS I. (1901–1974)

Although his followers from the so-called Philadelphia School, and many others, think of him as one of the finest American architects of the twentieth century and second only to Frank Lloyd Wright, Kahn did not get much international attention until quite late in his career. An Estonian by birth, who emigrated to Philadelphia with his parents in 1905, he had a gift for both painting and music, but at sixteen was inspired by his prescient high school art teacher to choose architecture. After a Beaux Arts–style education at the University of Pennsylvania, he went to Europe for a year in 1928, where he was as impressed by Greek and Roman antiquity as he was by the new work and teaching of Le

Corbusier. In 1947, he became visiting design critic at Yale and soon became a professor; a few years later he was commissioned to design the university's first Modern building, the extension to the Yale University Art Gallery. In 1957, Kahn returned to the University of Pennsylvania as a teacher and was invited to design its Richards Medical Research Building, considered by many to be one of the world's most important buildings of the 1960s. This led to commissions to design the National Assembly in Dhaka, Bangladesh, the second capital (the first capital being in Islamabad), where he was given a brief (a client's instructions and list of needs) to design the Assembly and the Supreme Court as well as hostels, schools, a stadium, and a hotel for ministers, their secretaries, and members of the Assembly; the diplomatic enclave; the living sector; and the market. All of this, plus a mosque, was to be designed within one thousand acres of flat land prone to flooding. Other projects included the Salk Institute for Biological Studies, La Jolla, California (1959–65); the United States Consulate in Luanda, Angola; Erdman Hall Dormitories at Bryn Mawr College, Pennsylvania; the library for the Phillips Exeter Academy, Exeter, New Hampshire (1965–72); the Trenton Bath House, Trenton, New Jersey; and the Institute for Public Administration, Ahmedabad, India. The Sher-e-Bangla Nagara Dakar (1962–87), built in Bangladesh over a span of twenty-five years, but unfinished at the time of Kahn's death, is considered one of the great post-war buildings on a grand scale. Another distinguished commission back in the United States was the Kimbell Art Museum, Fort Worth,

Texas (1966–72). All of Kahn's buildings, whatever their geographical location, are buildings of some drama with an exquisite exploitation of natural light combined with a feeling of solid permanence, and a tough, unyielding urbanity, although they are always subtly detailed.

KENT, WILLIAM (1685–1748)

Naturally gifted eighteenth-century furniture designer, landscape gardener, painter, and architect. Although he came from poor parentage, he somehow managed to get to Rome to study painting for ten years, where he met his future and lifelong patron, Lord Burlington, who brought him back to London in 1719, where he corralled him into becoming another advocate for English Palladianism. However, since Palladio had failed to provide any ideas for furniture among his many illustrations of buildings, Kent had to look to other sources for inspiration. The result was sumptuous, somewhat architectural, and richly carved and gilded furniture and interiors that were partly influenced by the Italian Baroque of Rome and Florence and partly by Inigo Jones, whose designs Kent published in 1727 with the financial assistance of Lord Burlington. Kent's own designs, published in America as well as England, influenced the design of American furniture for some years thereafter. Interestingly, Kent did not actually turn to the study and practice of architecture until he was already in his forties. Nevertheless he managed to design some notable buildings, interiors, and gardens, revolutionizing the relationship of house to landscape. From Kent's time on, country houses were built to harmonize with their surroundings rather than to dominate them. His masterpiece, Holkham Hall in Norfolk (1734 onward), was almost certainly designed in conjunction with Lord Burlington. Its extraordinary entrance hall, which is considered to be one of the grandest eighteenth-century rooms in Britain, is half based on a Roman basilica and half on Vitruvius's illustrations of the Egyptian Hall (the latter taken from Colen Campbell's edition of Vitruvius's work published about fifteen years before Kent's design). Kent's spatially ingenious staircase in 44 Berkeley Square, London (1742–44) is also well worth seeing, as are his interiors and furniture for Lord Burlington's Chiswick House on the outskirts of London. One of his rooms, complete with furniture, has recently been beautifully restored at Burlington House, Piccadilly, now the Royal Academy.

KIKUTAKE, KIYONORI (B. 1928)

Japanese architect and a leading member of the Metabolism movement. Founded by Kenzo Tange, Kikutake, Kisho Noriaki Kurakawa, Fumihiko Maki, and Masato Otaka, the movement sought to promulgate a completely different kind of flexible, organic architecture that would concentrate much more on interior space—and on the flexibility to completely change function whenever necessary—than on form. The group was set up as a reaction to what they thought of as the rigidity of western Modernism.

KOOLHAAS, REM (B. 1944)

Dutch architect, theorist, product designer, urban designer, design visionary, teacher, image-maker, and writer—in short, a modern equivalent of a Renaissance man. He trained in London and New York and has had a major influence on modern architectural thinking, as much from his books and teaching as for his architecture (he has won the Progressive Architecture Prize in New York as well as the prestigious Royal Gold Medal from the Royal Institute of British Architects and the 2000 Pritzker Architecture Prize). The various construction elements in Koolhaas buildings, like those of Frank Gehry and Toyo Ito and his ex-colleague Zaha Hadid are usually combined in totally innovative and thought-provoking ways. Former projects of note include the Netherlands Dance Theater in the Hague (1984–87); Nexus World Kashii Condominium, Fukuoka, Japan (1991); and the Eurolille project and Grand Palais Convention Center (1990–94), for which he was the head architect. Some of his latest buildings include the Educatorium in Utrecht, Holland; the Netherlands Embassy in Berlin; the Campus Center for the Illinois Institute of Technology in Chicago; the Kunsthal Rotterdam in Rotterdam, Netherlands; the Seattle Public Library in Seattle, Washington; the Casa de Musica, a concert hall in Porto, Portugal; and CCTV, the enormous headquarters he is designing for China Central Television in Beijing, a city for which he is proposing a new conservation policy. He has also designed the new European Union flag, the Prada shop in Soho in New York City, and some Condé Nast magazines. His books include *Delirious New York* (first published 1978; reissued 1996) and *S.M.L.XL.* (1996) as well as various works in conjunction with architectural students at Harvard, where he also teaches. His company, OMA (Office for Metropolitan Architecture), has locations in London and Rotterdam.

KURAKAWA, KISHO NORIAKI (B. 1934)

Another Japanese architect and Metabolist who publicized the group's philosophy as much with his writings as with his various projects like Wall Cluster (1960); Helix City (1961); and his capsule buildings (like the 1960's English Archigram's wishful living pods) for Takara Beautillion Expo '70, Osaka; and the Nagakin Capsule Tower in Tokyo (1972). This last was designed as a solution for the need for mobile urban residential buildings and was formed from 144 prefabricated capsules bolted to reinforced concrete shafts. Many other buildings followed, combining a fusion of tradition and modernism as well as East and West. (See also *Kiyonori Kikutake*.)

KJAERHOLM, POUL (1929–1980)

Danish furniture and interior designer. Probably best known for his elegant leather-and-steel daybed, designed in the 1950s, although he designed a whole series of good-looking chairs and tables including his last in 1980—a steam-bent wood and cane chair.

LANGLEY, BATTY (1696–1751)

One of the best-known and influential compilers of architectural books, meant mainly for country builders, carpenters, and artisans. He built hardly anything himself, and what he did is now destroyed, but his works were studied avidly in eighteenth- and early-nineteenth-century America and Britain and used as blueprints for both buildings and details. Some of the best-known titles are *A Sure Guide to Builders* (1729); *The Builder's Compleat Chest-Book* (1727 and 1739); *Ancient Masonry* (1736; particularly popular in Colonial America); and *Gothic Architecture Restored, Improved by Rules and Proportion in Many Grand Designs* (1747), which was instrumental in creating the American interest in Gothic Revival.

LANNUIER, CHARLES HONORE (1779–1819)

Leading New York cabinetmaker in the Federal style and an immigrant from France, just as his New York contemporary Duncan Phyfe immigrated from Scotland.

LARSEN, JACK LENOR

Architect, interior designer, and noted and innovative textile designer and weaver who founded Jack Lenor Larsen, Inc. Textile House in the early 1950s. He managed to achieve a fine amalgam of interesting style, craftsmanship, and high standard of technical production so sought after by William Morris and his contemporaries—a yardstick that many have emulated and few have achieved.

LATROBE, BENJAMIN HENRY (1764–1820)

An architect and engineer, much influenced by Sir John Soane, who spent his youth between England and Germany and emigrated to America in 1795. After some years he was noticed by Thomas Jefferson, who asked his help with the exterior of the Capitol in Richmond, Virginia, the start of what would become as fruitful an American partnership as that of Lord Burlington and William Kent in England. Latrobe's Philadelphia buildings—the Bank of Pennsylvania (1799–1801) and the Water Works (1800)—were the first fine examples of Greek Revival architecture in the United States—the first in the simpler Greek Doric style and the second in the more decorative Ionic; yet at much the same time he built Sedgeley, the earliest Gothic-Revival house in America. From 1803 to 1811, he again went to help Jefferson, this time with the Capitol in Washington, where he executed some splendid vaulted stone interiors, which almost all had to be redone after the disastrous fire of 1814. The Neoclassical Baltimore Cathedral (1804–18) designed over the same period was also a triumph, and he was instrumental with Jefferson in designing the University of Virginia in Charlottesville. (See example on the next page.)

LE BLOND, JEAN-BAPTISTE ALEXANDRE (1679–1719)

French architect notable for his introduction of the Rococo to Russia, most especially with his designs for the Peterhof Palace in Saint Petersburg (1716).

The Supreme Court chamber (1815–17), The Capitol,
Washington, D.C., by Benjamin Latrobe

LEBRUN, CHARLES (1619–1690)

The most important painter and decorator in the court of Louis XIV of France. He worked on the grandly formal interiors of Vaux-le-Vicomte, the excessively lavish house built by the foremost Baroque architect, Louis Le Vau, for the king's finance minister, Nicholas Fouquet. After Fouquet was arrested in 1661 by his great rival, Jean-Baptiste Colbert (ostensibly for embezzlement, but also, one suspects, for daring to outdo the Sun King himself), Lebrun became, as did Le Vau, one of the elite team working on the interiors of the Palace of Versailles, as well as other royal residences. When Jules Hardouin-Mansart took over from Le Vau at Versailles, Lebrun went on working on the interiors in his capacity as director and chief designer for Le Manufacture Royale des Meubles des Couronne (The Royal Factory for the Crown Furnishings), which was a sort of royal cooperative started rather cleverly by Louis XIII to concentrate and control France's decorative arts. It was also known as the Manufacture des Gobelins, and its purpose was to provide furnishings for the royal residences as well as to help instigate a national style. Lebrun produced some extraordinary work in the grandiose style of the day, but one of his best achievements was the staggeringly sumptuous semicircular vaulted arch and panels for Mansart's Galerie des Glaces (Hall of Mirrors) in Versailles.

LE CORBUSIER (1887–1966)

One of the leaders of the International style, a semiabstract painter, possibly the most influential architect of the twentieth century, and one of the great masters—along with the Frenchman Auguste Perret (1874–1954), with whom he worked from 1908 to 1909—of the use of reinforced concrete. Born in French Switzerland as Charles-Édouard Jeanneret (he took the pseudonym of Le Corbusier from a Monsieur Le Corbezier, his Belgian great-grandfather), he traveled to the Balkans and Asia Minor, met Josef Hoffmann, worked for a short time with Peter Behrens in Berlin, and settled in Paris in 1917. He made his main contribution to the International style between the two World Wars, using huge strip windows, simple columns, glass bricks, and metal as fundamental ingredients of both his interior and exterior compositions. His "total" plans for cities, with a center of identical skyscrapers symmetrically arranged in a park setting with lower buildings, and complex traffic routes between, were brilliant, if not particularly practical, but were never taken up. Years later, however, his layout for the town of Chandigarh in India and his powerful Law Courts and Secretariat buildings (1951–56) would have a major influence in Japan. Le Corbusier's other major interests were in the mass production of housing as well as developing a whole new concept of the villa—a white, cubist private house perched on cylindrical stilts or pillars with rooms flowing into one another.

Ideas for the latter were first shown publicly in his Esprit Nouveau exhibit at the Paris Exhibition of 1925, which had a tree growing through the building. And his subsequent villas, particularly the Villa Stein at Garches (1927) and the Villa Savoye at Poissy (1929–31), were profoundly influential on domestic building as much for the clever melding of the inside with the outside as for the innovative molding of walls and staircases. Another major desire—to reform furniture and furnishings in general—was shared by his cousin Pierre Jeanneret (1896–1966) and Charlotte Perriand (1903–1999). Their combined design for furnishing a *unité d'habitation* (living unit), exhibited at the Salon d'Automne des Artistes-Décorateurs in Paris in 1929, was a conscious and uncompromising effort to make people come to terms with "modern living" along with the advent of new technology—to create a "machine for living" that matched the age with built-in furniture, laminated surfaces, concealed lighting, and chromium-plated steel-tube furniture. Though scorned by many at the time, the fact is that decades later, few contemporary architects designing a modern home would even consider doing an interior without incorporating some of Le Corbusier's ideas and, for that matter, some of his furniture such as his Grand Confort chair designed in the 1930s. Around the same time, Le Corbusier designed the Salvation Army Hostel in Paris (begun 1929) that had far-reaching influence; a plan for the League of Nations in Geneva (1927; not executed); the Centrosojus in Moscow (1928); and the Swiss House in the Paris Cité Universitaire (1930–32). In the late 1930s, he went to Rio de Janeiro to advise on the new Ministry of Education building being built by Lucio Costa and Oscar Niemeyer and subsequently worked with Niemeyer as advisor on his buildings for Brasilia. In 1947, he worked with others on the United Nations Headquarters and the Secretariat building in New York, which was, as it turned out, his last glass and steel building. After this, Le Corbusier's work took an entirely different direction—one that became just as influential on progressive architects as his earlier work. Where his buildings had been rational, they were now antirational; where they had been smooth they were now Brutalist and aggressively sculptural, often exposing heavy concrete members. The first such building was the Unité d'Habitation at Marseilles (1947–52); its proportions were worked out based on a complicated system that he invented called Modulor. The system, which was based upon the human figure (as was Palladio's system four centuries earlier), was used to determine the proportions of each building unit, and was first propounded by Le Corbusier in his book *Le Modulor* (1951). Other such *unités* were built in Nantes and Berlin, but his most revolutionary building in this style is the pilgrimage chapel of Ronchamp (1950–54). This last was followed by some hard, heavy-looking houses at Ahmedabad in India (1954–56); the Museum of Modern Art in Tokyo (1957); and the Dominican friary of La Tourette at Eveux-sur-l'Arbresle near Lyon (1953–57).

LEDOUX, CLAUDE-NICOLAS (1736–1806)

Another of J-F Blondel's gifted students and a major disciple of Ange-Jacques Gabriel. Ledoux started off as a Louis XVI, early-Neoclassical architect who, though apparently somewhat eccentric and quarrelsome, managed to design a number of seemingly effortlessly glamorous Parisian *hôtels particulières* that held the same cachet for the prevailing taste in the eighteenth century as had earlier Italian palazzi and the great English country houses. As Robert Adam wrote: "To understand thoroughly the art of living, it is necessary, perhaps, to have passed some time among the French." Ledoux also designed the witty interior of the Café Militaire in the Palais Royal (now in the Musée Carnavalet); the extraordinarily elegant Pavillon de Louveciennes for the king's mistress, Madame du Barry (now mostly removed, but recorded in *le Jeune*, a watercolor by Moreau); the minute

Le Corbusier chaise longue, 1928

boudoir for Madame de Serilly, now to be seen in the Victoria and Albert Museum, London (the word *boudoir* is derived from the French verb *bouder*, meaning "to pout," and appropriately the boudoir became the private getaway or sulks rooms for fashionable ladies); and finally, for this phase of his career, the dazzling Hôtel Thelusson in Paris, which was surrounded by an (unusually for France) informal English-style garden approached through an enormous triumphal arch. After all these undoubted successes, Ledoux precipitously dispensed with his elegant Neoclassical simplicity and geometric forms, did a complete about-face, and became the most extreme and original interpreter of a quite elemental Romanticism.

LE NÔTRE, ANDRÉ (1613–1700)

The designer of the Park at Versailles (1662–90) for Louis XIV that is famous for its radiating avenues, huge parterres, stretches of water, and grand fountains. The overall plan sensitively extended the symmetry of Le Vau's designs for the new garden at the front of the Palace to the surrounding countryside. Generally thought of as the most distinguished designer of formal gardens and parks in the French manner, Le Nôtre was trained in architecture and painting as well as in landscape. He was appointed controller general of the king's buildings in 1657 while he was working on the gardens at the magnificent Vaux-le-Vicomte (1656–61) for Louis XIV's overly ambitious finance minister, Nicholas Fouquet. He later

worked on the royal parks of St. Cloud, Fontainebleau, Clagny, and Marly.

LE VAU, LOUIS (1612–1670)

Leading French Baroque architect, remodeler of the Palace of Versailles for Louis XIV, and the designer of the even more magnificent Vaux-le-Vicomte for Louis XIV's finance minister Nicholas Fouquet, who was arrested in 1661 by his great rival, the statesman and churchman Jean-Baptiste Colbert, ostensibly for embezzlement, but also, one suspects, for daring to outdo the Sun King himself. A great organizer, Le Vau had assembled a talented team of sculptors, painters, decorators, furniture makers, masons, carpenters, gardeners, and so on who had astonishingly managed to complete Fouquet's house in just one year. As a result of Fouquet's fall from glory, the king was able to take advantage of Le Vau and his team for the further enriching of his own palaces, including Versailles, as well as the Galerie d'Apollon in the Louvre (1661–62) with interiors decorated by both Le Vau and Charles Lebrun. Unfortunately, Le Vau's purportedly beautiful garden front for Versailles was ruined a few years later by the alterations and extensions made by Jules Hardouin-Mansart (Louis XIV's new royal architect and superintendent of buildings). Nor, sadly, does anything now remain of the interiors Le Vau worked on, again with Lebrun, including his famous Escalier des Ambassadeurs, though this had nothing to do with Mansart, who also replaced Le Vau's nearby Trianon de Porcelaine with his own Grand Trianon. Fortunately for lovers of the Baroque, Le Vau's other great building in Paris, now the Institut de France but formerly called the Collège des Quatre Nations and begun in 1661, was paid for by Cardinal Jules Mazarin and is still intact.

LIBESKIND, DANIEL (B. 1946)

Polish-born American architect who arrived in the United States in 1960 and trained in New York. How fitting, then, that he gives back to this city the new designs for the devastated World Trade Center site. Libeskind exhibited his Lighting Flash zigzag design at Philip Johnson's Deconstructivist Architecture exhibition at the Museum of Modern Art in 1988 and followed with his Osaka Folly Pavilion in Osaka (1989–90) and his Jewish Museum in Berlin (1990–96). At much the same time he won a competition for an extension to the high-Victorian Victoria & Albert Museum in London, just as he won the enormously publicized and emotional competition for the renewal of the World Trade Center.

LONGHENA, BALDASSARE (1597–1682)

Venetian Baroque architect who designed some of the best-known buildings in Venice: Santa Maria della Salute at the entrance to the Grand Canal (first designed 1630 but not finally finished and consecrated until 1687); the monastery of San Giorgio Maggiore (1643–45); the fanciful little church of the Ospedaletto (1670–78); and Palazzo Rezzonico (begun 1667) and Palazzo

Pesaro (1649/52–82; facade begun 1676) on the Grand Canal. His work, most particularly his churches, had a considerable influence on later architects.

LOOS, ADOLF (1870–1933)

Avant-garde early-Modernist Austro-Hungarian architect and designer who was born in Brno, Moravia (which is now the Czech Republic), spent three formative years between 1893 and 1896 in the United States, worked mainly in Vienna and Paris, and achieved a good deal of influence with his somewhat polemical writing. He also designed houses for the so-called intellectual and artistic elite of the time, including Josephine Baker. His austere early-twentieth-century villas were characterized by the total absence of ornament (for example, white walls without any sort of molding) and by the strong cubic shapes that he promulgated in his journalism. However, he *did* like using luxurious materials for his various surfaces, as would Mies van der Rohe a decade or so later. In his celebrated and much disputed article "Ornament and Crime" (1908), he advocated the removal of all ornament, not just from architecture and interiors but from life in general. "Lack of ornament," he wrote, "is a sign of spiritual strength."

LUTYENS, SIR EDWIN LANDSEER (1869–1944)

If you think of that opulent era at the cusp of the nineteenth and twentieth centuries—typified by imposing Edwardian architecture or the grand country houses of the Belle Epoque—it is hard to avoid thinking of Lutyens. He was the architect of most of the "modern" rambling and picturesque country houses of the time, designed with handsome details, many ingenious ideas for greater comfort, and an occasional puckishness. They are, consciously or unconsciously, what most people have in mind when they think of the proverbial "English Country Style" and, for that matter, English gardens. This is because many of them were designed integrally with gardens by Gertrude Jekyll (1843–1932), the garden designer who had revived and expanded the informal cottage garden feel, and to whose lawns and herbaceous borders Lutyens added mellow brick or stone walls, flights of steps, and balustraded terraces—a look much reproduced for early-twentieth-century mansions around the Hamptons, New York State in general, New Jersey, and Connecticut, as well as the antipodes. Lutyens had designed Gertrude Jekyll's own house, Munstead Wood in Surrey, in 1896. But he was most famous for the imperial grandeur and scale of his designs for the layout of New Delhi in India, and for his magnificent Viceroy's House (1912–31), now called Rashtrapati Bhaven, as well as for the four equally grand domed residences (begun in 1920) that surrounded his All-India War Memorial Arch. He also designed the Cenotaph in Whitehall, London (1919–20) and the wrenching Memorial to the Missing of the Somme at Thiepval, near Arras, France (opened in 1932).

MACKINTOSH, CHARLES RENNIE (1868–1928)

A Scottish architect at the more rational end of the Art Nouveau period, who at the age of twenty-eight was commissioned by his clearly admiring old teacher at the Glasgow School of Art to design a new building for the school. The result, some think, is one of the masterpieces of early-Modern architecture. Mackintosh seemed not only to possess an extraordinary sensitivity to spatial relationships but an ability to combine restraint with sensuality, expressed by his use of crisply rectangular shapes with long, languidly delicate Art Nouveau curves. Nikolaus Pevsner, in his absorbing book *Pioneers of Modern Design* (Penguin Books, first published in 1936), thought his early work showed him to be the European counterpart to Frank Lloyd Wright and one of the few forerunners of that most ingenious juggler of space, Le Corbusier. A further influential building took the unlikely form of Glasgow tea shops for Mrs. Cranston (for example, the Cranston Tea Room on Sauchihall Street), with interiors that displayed what have come to be thought of as Mackintosh trademarks: stiff vertical lines contrasted with curvaceous in-fills of rose, deep and pale lilac, and white; almost nonexistent cornices or crown moldings forming paper thin ledges around the room; and elongated ascetic floral forms. Mackintosh was somewhat influenced by the architecture and particularly the interiors of Edward William Godwin, who had almost single-handedly created the Anglo-

Japanese look endemic to the Aesthetic Movement. But like Gaudí in Spain, he also drew inspiration from a number of local sources—in particular, the strains of Celtic and Scottish Baronial, which are evident in his versions of traditional inglenooks and his designs for both freestanding and built-in furniture. This "feel" was translated in diluted form into other furniture, accessories, ceramics, and art glass, which are reproduced still. At the time, Mackintosh's unique mixture of functionalism, austerity, and elegance was much admired in Europe, particularly in Austria, and by the group known as the Vienna Secession, created by Josef Hoffmann, Joseph Maria Olbrich, and Otto Wagner—all precur-

sors of the Modern movement who absorbed many of Mackintosh's ideas into their own work.

MACKMURDO, ARTHUR HEYGATE (1851–1942)

British architect and graphic designer much influenced by the art critic John Ruskin. In 1882 Mackmurdo founded the Century Guild, the first of five societies inspired by the teachings of William Morris to promote artistic craftsmanship. He was also widely credited for creating the impetus of the Art Nouveau movement with his famous design of sinuously weaving forms for the cover page of his book *Wren's City Churches*, published in 1883.

MAGISTRETTI, VICO (B. 1920)

Italian designer, particularly well known from the 1960s to the 1990s for his furniture and lighting for Italian manufacturers such as Cassina, Kartell, Artemide, and O-Luce, and for innovative store designs for companies such as Cerutti. One of his best-known designs for Cassina was the Carimate chair (1959). With its bright-orange frame and rush seat, it has become a classic that is widely emulated by other manufacturers.

MAKI, FUMIHIKO (B. 1928)

Another distinguished "East-West" Japanese architect and the 1993 winner of the Pritzker Architecture Prize, the second Japanese architect to do so. Indeed, he studied with the first winner from Japan, Kenzo Tange, at the

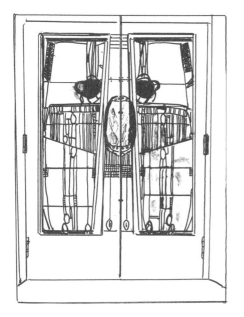

Leaded-glass doors of the "Room de Luxe" (1903), Willow Tea Rooms at 217 Sauchiehall Street, Glasglow, Scotland, by Charles Rennie Mackintosh

University of Tokyo before having a year at Cranbrook Academy of Art in Bloomfield Hills, Michigan, going on to complete his masters of architecture degree at Harvard Graduate School of Design, and working with Skidmore, Owings & Merrill in New York and Sert Jackson and Associates in Cambridge, Massachusetts. He became assistant professor of architecture at Washington University, St. Louis. His first actual design commission was the Steinberg Hall (an art center) on that university's campus. After serving on the faculty of Harvard's Graduate School of Design between 1962 and 1965, he moved back to Tokyo, where he established his own firm, Maki and Associates. There he accomplished some massive commissions, including the gigantic Nippon Cultural Center, the Osaka Prefectural Sports Center, and the Fujisawa Municipal Gymnasium (1984–87). In the meantime he designed a large office complex for Isar Buro Park, near Munich, Germany, and the Yerba Buena Gardens Visual Arts Center, which is part of a large-scale redevelopment in downtown San Francisco involving several prominent architects, including Mario Botta, James Stewart Polshek, and I. M. Pei. The Visual Arts Center is literally on top of the Moscone Convention Center.

MALLET-STEVENS, ROBERT (1886–1945)

The leading European Art Deco architect and furniture designer who segued into the International style in the 1920s as well as to designing early film sets. There is a Parisian street named after him that is filled with his Cubist buildings designed between 1926 and 1927. In 1937 he had the distinction of designing no less than five pavilions at the Exposition Internationale des Arts et Techniques in Paris: the Pavilion of Solidarity, the Pavilion of Hygiene, the Palace of Electricity, the Pavilion of Tobacco, and the Café du Brazil. In 1979, French designer Andrée Putnam included several reproductions of his furniture in her furniture company, Ecart International, which she started in order to present re-editions of classic designs from the 1930s.

MANSART, FRANÇOIS (1598–1666)

The Mansarts, both early French architects but born fifty years apart, are easy to confuse (although Jules—Mansart junior—is always referred to as Hardouin-Mansart). Both were the leading architectural practitioners of their day, but one was great uncle to the other. Mansart senior was the first great French classical architect, treasured for the clarity of his planning and the refinement of his detail, and as famous in France as Nicolas Poussin for his painting or Pierre Corneille for his plays. However, he never traveled out of France, was rarely employed by the king or by any great noble patron (although he was rather abortively consulted in the early 1660s about the Louvre and a royal chapel), and had a hard job, it seems, keeping to deadlines and sometimes finishing a job at all. Nevertheless, he complete a great many beautiful and sophisticated buildings for those members of the newly emerging and prosperous haute bourgeoisie who also happened to possess both ambition and taste, and gave his name to a type of continuous broken roof with a steep lower slope and flatter, shorter upper portion that he invented for the Orléans wing of the château at Blois (1635–38) in the Loire Valley. The château was never fully completed, but the Mansard, or Mansart, roof lives on. When he was halfway through building the Maisons Lafitte, near Paris (1642–51), designed for the very rich René de Longueil, he insisted, to his client's consternation, on pulling down a good chunk during construction so that he could revise his ideas. All the same, it is his most complete work to survive, along

The vestibule in Maison Lafitte
(1642–51), near Paris,
by François Mansart

with his remodeling of the Hôtel Carnavalet (1660–61) in Paris, now the Musée Carnavalet.

MAROT, DANIEL (CA. 1660–1752)

Leading late-seventeenth- and eighteenth-century architect and designer of both furniture and interiors who grew up in France. He fled to the Netherlands in 1685, along with many other Protestant refugees, after Louis XIV's revocation of the Edict of Nantes, which had, since its establishment in 1598, tolerated the Protestant faith. In spite of his refugee status, Marot married the daughter of Pierre Golle, the celebrated *ébéniste* (a cabinetmaker, especially one working in ebony, a favorite Baroque finish for furniture) to Louis XIV, and then took up the position of architect-designer to Prince William of Orange (not unlike the position that Charles Lebrun held at Versailles). In this capacity he designed interiors and furniture—in particular some spectacular four-poster state beds—for the royal palace of Het Loo and the great hall of audience for the States General at the Hague. He thus introduced the flamboyantly luxurious Louis XIV style to the more stolid Dutch who, as the then major sea power with vast colonial possession as well as their trade with the Far East through the Dutch East India Company, were becoming increasingly prosperous. Added to this, the Dutch Prince William of Orange married Mary (daughter of the recently deceased Charles I and, for want of any other heirs, the new Queen of England) and the pair became the joint rulers—known as William and Mary—over what had now become, for the first time, the United Kingdom. Accordingly, Marot accompanied William and Mary to England in 1688 and made several subsequent visits to work on the English royal palaces. He designed, for example, some of the interiors of the old Water Gallery at Hampton Court Palace, Middlesex (1689–98), including some unusual chimney pieces with supports for porcelain and faience vases. The queen had just introduced the fashion for the collecting and display of Oriental porcelain (through the offices of the Dutch East India Company) as well as the Dutch ware known as delft. So it was the Mary half of William and Mary who started the fashion for displaying collections of blue-and-white porcelain, which played such an important role in English, Dutch, and subsequently American interiors of the time—a fashion that has proved amazingly durable.

MAUGHAM, SYRIE (1879–1955)

Famous British decorator of the 1920s, '30s, and '40s, who did much work for the "beautiful people" of the time in the United States. She was the daughter of the famous Dr. Thomas Barnardo of the Barnardo Home for Boys and Girls, and wife and divorcée of the still more famous author Somerset Maugham. Her decoration will always be associated with "white on white on white" (the whites Maugham used were the "old" whites, not new ones, which have become increasingly brighter during the twentieth century with the addition of titanium;

the old ones were much more gentle). For her clients, however, she actually used quite a large palette of delicate colors and an eclectic mixture of old, new, and reproduction furniture, including much Neo-Rococo. Other signature accessories were her ubiquitous shells of all sizes, plaster palm trees, satins and fringes, a good many shiny surfaces, exaggeratedly large dolphin console tables, folding screens, rock crystal, and mirrors, mirrors everywhere. Nevertheless, a smart Modernist mix of whites was the way Maugham decorated the much-photographed, legendary drawing room of her house in London's Chelsea at the beginning of her decorating career (which did not actually begin until her late forties), and it is for her whites that she will always be remembered. Nor, of course, was Maugham the first bold user of whites, though fashionable New York and London clientele might not have guessed it. Whites had been used all through history, most especially in the fifteenth century by Filippo Brunelleschi—with his pure, simple interiors contrasting white or pale-cream plastered surfaces with gray or buff stone moldings and details—and in the nineteenth century by those working in the style of the Aesthetic, Arts and Crafts, and Art Nouveau movements. Architects of these movements—such as Edward William Godwin, Philip Webb, and Charles Rennie Mackintosh—had all produced equally "revolutionary" white interiors, as of course did Maugham's contemporaries Elsie de Wolfe in America and Jean Michel Frank in France. The latter was a great influence on Maugham and many other designers, especially with his signature work of unadorned but exotically covered walls, mirrored screens, white side tables, bamboo, and white palm-tree decoration. Now, once again, these same tonal combinations have become very much de rigueur, leading some decorators better known for their taste than for their historical knowledge to claim the credit for inventing this style.

MAURER, INGO (B. 1932)

Influential German lighting designer and manufacturer who has designed many of the lighting icons of the twentieth and twenty-first centuries, some of them widely imitated—such as his 1981 flexible lighting system strung on a series of taut, low-voltage cables, called YaYaHo and described as the start of the "low-voltage revolution." His first inspiration was his large glass lamp in the shape of a light bulb (1966) simply called Bulb. Later light sculptures, as one might call them, were the flexible angel-winged light bulbs (1992), called Lucellino chandeliers; Zettel'z (1997), made up of sheets of paper that recorded passing thoughts (like an illuminated book of memorabilia); and the bead-filled star shapes surrounding flashing bulbs designed in 2001. In 2004 the Victoria and Albert Museum in London staged a whole homage to Maurer with a lighting show called, quite simply, Brilliant.

McKIM, MEAD & WHITE

Late-nineteenth-century New York architectural partnership whose work was considered to be the "turning point in American architecture." Its first two members—Charles Follen McKim (1847–1909) and William Rutherford Mead (1846–1928)—had worked with the great American original Henry Hobson Richardson. The new firm designed many of the city's nineteenth-century landmark buildings as well as a diversity of magazine and book covers, railway carriages, and yachts. These last were achieved through the talents of the brilliant and seemingly effortless designer, bon vivant, and third partner Stanford White (1853–1906). Some of the firm's buildings in New York City include the group of Villard Houses (1882) on Madison Avenue (now the New York Palace hotel); Madison Square Garden (1891); the Washington Triumphal Arch (1891) in the style of the Étoile in Paris; Columbia University's library rotunda (1893), inspired by the Pantheon in Rome as well as Jefferson's University of Virginia in Charlottesville; the Pierpont Morgan Library (1903–07); and Pennsylvania Railway Station (1904–10), echoing imperial Roman *thermae* (splendid Roman bath complexes often containing libraries and other amenities as well as bathing facilities). Other famous McKim, Mead & White buildings are the stunning, heavily shingled Newport Casino in Newport, Rhode Island and the Boston Public Library (1888–95), with a McKim facade and sumptuous painted interiors by John Singer Sargent and the French painter and decorator Puvis de Chavannes.

MEIER, RICHARD (B. 1934)

Leading American public-building architect with work all around the world, including the Canal Plus Headquarters in Paris (1989–92); City Hall, the Hague, the Netherlands (1994); the Ulm Townhall and Cathedral Square, Germany (1995); the Museum of Contemporary Art, Barcelona (1987–95); and the Getty Center, Santa Monica, California (1985–97). He trained in New York— working with Marcel Breuer in the early 1960s—before starting his own practice, and was the most prolific of the New York Five group. He was also reputedly the most purist of the New York Five; in fact, his work on a group of private houses in the late 1960s/early '70s was one of the reasons the group was also known as "the Whites." His large public buildings have also made clean-lined assertive statements. He was awarded the Pritzker Architecture Prize in 1984, making him the sixth architect to be so honored.

MEISSONIER, JUSTE-AURÈLE (1695–1750)

Though born in Turin, Italy, he was really a native of Provence in southern France, and became one of the leading French promulgators of the Rococo style. He trained as a goldsmith but went on to become "ornament designer" to Louis XV, for whom he perfected the art of rocaille, a form of decoration derived from shellwork in grottoes and one of the chief elements of the Rococo style. Meissonier's S-form and wavelike spiky designs were all published in his very successful book of engravings called *Le Livre d'Ornements*. The book included ideas for fountains, architecture, and decorative ornamentation. Fantastic curved, abstract structures are embellished with gushing water, curling plants and tendrils, animals, and fish. Because the book was so popular, all these motifs entered the contemporary decorators' vocabulary and became known as the *genre pittoresque*. Interestingly, for those who like to make connections, Picturesque is the style that followed the much more severe Neoclassicism of the late eighteenth and early nineteenth centuries, just as the lighthearted and delicate Rococo had followed the formal and massive grandeur of the Baroque. And more interestingly still, although the late-nineteenth/early-twentieth-century Art Nouveau was said to have no historical precedent, many of its vegetal motifs had also been used in the rocaille of the Rococo.

MEMPHIS MOVEMENT (1981–88)

Italian furniture movement, first introduced at the Milan Furniture Fair (the 1981 *Salone di Mobile*) with new-wave furniture by, among others, Ettore Sottsass Jr., Michele De Lucci, Aldo Cibic, Matteo Thun, Mark Zanini, and Javier Mariscal. The group's designs quickly caused a big stir, resulting in a book about their designs called *Memphis* in 1983 (written by Barbara Radice) and an exhibition in 1988 at the International Design Center in New York called "Architects Inside: From Mies to

Memphis," though the latter turned out to be a swan song.

MENDELSOHN, ERICH
(1887–1953)

German-born Modernist architect and visionary with a romantic enthusiasm, not just for the new twentieth-century science, technology, and rational planning, but also for pulsating speed and the roar of machines. Like Antonio Sant'Elia, the Italian Futurist who died at the age of twenty-eight, Mendelson made vigorous, expressive sketches of ideas for buildings that were more like sculpture than architecture. His sketches of buildings were not functionally worked out, but they nevertheless captured the excitement of the new technological age that was unfolding. Unlike Sant'Elia, he did manage to realize his vision in the form of the Einstein Tower at Potsdam (1919–21) and his remodeling of the Mosse building in Berlin (1921), which showed much the same vigorous streamlined curves as his visionary futuristic drawings. In 1921 he met Richard Neutra—who had yet to emigrate to America—and collaborated with him on a competition to design the business center for Haifa in Israel. They won first prize but the project was never built. In 1924 Mendelsohn visited the United States; his excitement about the new skyscrapers he saw there was reflected in later buildings he did in Berlin. Mendelsohn left Germany for London in 1933 and went into brief partnership with Serge Chermayeff, the architect for the much-admired molded-

Einstein Tower (1919–21), Potsdam, Germany, by Erich Mendelsohn

concrete Penguin Pool at the London Zoo. A year later he moved to Israel where he built Hadasah University Medical Center on Mount Scopus in Jerusalem (1936–38). He finally ended up in the United States, building, among other commissions, Maimonides Hospital in San Francisco.

MICHELANGELO (MICHELANGELO BUONARROTI) (1475–1564)

Known famously by his first name only, Michelangelo was not only one of the world's great painters and sculptors but also an extraordinary architect and the so-called "Father of the Baroque." But he was a maverick as well: a restless, single-minded workaholic, apparently almost pathologically proud, and deeply religious but wracked by religious doubts, and as unsociable as he was untidy, he still managed to revolutionize almost everything he touched. He invented a new attitude toward interior spaces, a new vocabulary of ornament, and new principles of composition, and he idiosyncratically made clay models of buildings for builders, rather than the usual detailed perspective drawings. His first major commission was the facade for Filippo Brunelleschi's church of San Lorenzo in Florence, which he conceived as an elaborate framework for greater-than-life-size statues. Just before this plan was abandoned, he was asked to design the Medici family mausoleum in the new sacristy of the same church. His revolutionary plan completely rejected what he thought of as the tyranny of the Classical orders and proposed tapered windows, pilasters without capitals, and walls that he treated as many-layered living organisms as opposed to inanimate surfaces. In 1524 he designed a library for San Lorenzo known as the *Biblioteca Laurenziana* (reading room designed in 1525, vestibule in 1526). The now-famous library linked structure to decoration in a new way. Hitherto decorative pilasters were used only as actual supports for ceilings, just as columns actually supported the roof. However, since Michelangelo placed his columns in niches, like statues, they were made to appear more decorative than supportive. This was Mannerist thinking: A sort of tongue-in-cheek visual joke, when almost nothing was quite as it seemed. Like the Postmodernists more than 450 years later, Michelangelo appeared to be playing with history. Moreover, the crossbeams above the

pilasters were echoed in mosaic on the floor so that the eye was drawn through a perspective of diminished oblongs. This last detail was the kind of thinking that Robert Adam indulged in some two centuries later when he designed carpets to match the intricate plasterwork of his ceilings. In 1534, Michelangelo left Florence for Rome, where his first commission (begun 1539) was to reorganize the capitol to provide a handsome setting for the ancient statue of Marcus Aurelius, as well as a fitting place for outdoor ceremonies. He laid out the space as an oval, the first time this shape had been used in Renaissance architecture, and designed new fronts for the Palazzo dei Conservatori and Palazzo del Senatore using huge columns rising two stories high, a device that had never been used before but that soon became quite commonplace. In 1546, he was commissioned to complete Antonio da Sangallo's Palazzo Farnese, redesigning the upper floors of the inner courtyard and planning a vast garden to link it with the Villa Farnese on the far side of the Tiber River—though the latter was never undertaken. However, the idea for the grand vista that this would have provided, as well as his design for the Porta Pia (1561–65) at the end of a new street from the Quirinal, anticipated the principles of Baroque town planning. In spite of these triumphs, Michelangelo's major work was still the completion of St. Peter's (1546–64), started by Donato Bramante and continued by Antonio da Sangallo, who had also started the Palazzo Farnese. He went back to Bramante's original centralized plan for the cathedral but made it much bolder, and was not in the least hesitant about demolishing a good many of da Sangallo's additions. Even though his work on the interior of the cathedral was entirely covered over in the seventeenth century and his exterior is only visible on the north and south arms of the great building and on the drum of the dome (the dome itself was designed by della Porta and is quite different from Michelangelo's conception), there is no doubt that the cathedral still owes more to his designs than to anyone else's. And the marvelous painted decoration for the ceiling of the papal Sistine Chapel, recently restored, is another monument to his genius. Nevertheless, he must have died a frustrated man. Not one of his other major designs had been completed and, as unbelievable as it now seems, no contemporary seemed to have appreciated his extraordinary feeling for the control of the mass and shape of a building. Nor, for that matter, did anyone else fully appreciate his work until the seventeenth century, and he came in the form of Gian Lorenzo Bernini, another sculptor turned great architect.

MIES VAN DER ROHE, LUDWIG (1886–1969)

One of the great Bauhaus architects, although his earliest designs were inspired by Karl Friedrich Schinkel, considered to be the greatest German architect of the nineteenth century. Presumably, the spare, meticulous, and elegant precision of Mies van der Rohe's lines, and the fact that almost all of his buildings were rooted to podiums of one kind or another (as were most Classical buildings), were founded on early Classical precepts that, after all, denote a stylistic unity into which nothing extraneous is allowed to intrude. But equally, it should not be forgotten that Mies van der Rohe, Sr., was a master stonemason and that the young Mies spent many hours helping him in his workshop, which led to the often repeated Miesian quote: "Architecture starts when you carefully put two bricks together. There it begins." Like Walter Gropius, who was Peter Behrens's chief designer, Mies worked for a time (1908–11) in Behrens's office in Berlin, as he did, for some five months in 1910, with Le Corbusier as well. The dictate "Less is more"—implying the necessity to eliminate all that is irrelevant to function—actually came from Behrens's forward-looking office, not from Mies himself, although this aphorism was always associated with Mies's architecture. Also, like Gropius, Mies became caught up in the enthusiasm of Expressionism and took advantage of the latest technology to design revolutionary and visionary glass skyscrapers between 1919 and 1921 in which the nonstructural glass skin was separated from the structural bones behind it. He made a model with narrow, vertical strips of glass placed at slight angles to one another to make a multifaceted skin. It was at this time that Mies decided that reflections are more important to such buildings than light and shadow. This was clearly an important realization to him, for from that

The Seagram Building (1954–58), New York City, by
Ludwig Mies Van der Rohe and Philip Johnson

time he always kept a framed photo-graph of the design in his office. By 1923, perhaps somewhat inspired by the new concepts of space explored by the painter Piet Mondrian and the Dutch De Stijl group, Mies started to turn toward abstraction. He did not really reveal the huge extent of his true talent, however, until the Barcelona Exhibition (1928–29), when his German Pavilion won enthusiastic accolades not just for its excitingly worked open-plan compo-sition, but also for its exquisite finishes in marble, travertine, polished steel, bottle-green glass, and onyx. And it was there, too, that he introduced his elegant Barcelona chairs and stools that have become such enduring classics. In 1930, he took over from Gropius as director of the Bauhaus but left the position three years later to leave the country. In 1938, having emigrated to the United States, he was made professor of architecture at the Armour

Institute of Technology (now the Illinois Institute of Technology) in Chicago, for which he designed a new campus. After World War II, his output blossomed with a number of private houses, including his Farnsworth House in Piano, Illinois (1946–51), which he undertook to design in glass at nearly the same time Philip Johnson designed his Connecticut version of a glass house. His handsome bronze and marble Seagram Building in New York, off Park Avenue (1954–58), is a Manhattan icon—"The most elegant skyscraper ever built" according to *Architects on Architecture (New Directions in America)* by Paul Heyer (Walker Company, 1966). The Federal Center in Chicago (1959–64) and the new National Gallery in Berlin (1963–68) are also outstanding classics of the twentieth century.

MOHOLY-NAGY, LÁSZLÓ
(1895–1946)

Hungarian architectural theorist, writer, photographer, lighting designer, and Constructivist artist, whose appointment to the Bauhaus in 1923 first steered the school in its new direction toward an amalgam of design and technology. He was appointed the first director of the "New Bauhaus" in Chicago in 1937. His publications include *The New Vision* (1930) and *Vision in Motion* (published in 1947 after his death).

MONEO, JOSÉ RAFAEL (B. 1937)

Spanish architect with tremendous range and the 1996 winner of the Pritzker Architecture Prize as well as of the Spanish government's highest award for architecture, the Gold Medal for Achievement in Fine Arts, the French Academy of Architecture's Gold Medal, and the International Union of Architects Gold Medal. He taught at the Universities of Madrid and Barcelona before a five-year stint as chairman of the Harvard Graduate School of Design, where he is still on the faculty. In spite of this, most of his work has been in Spain, with the exception of the Davis Museum and Cultural Center at Wellesley College in Massachusetts (1989–93) and an addition to Mies van der Rohe's Fine Arts Museum in Houston, Texas. His most admired works in Spain are the National Museum of Roman Art in Mérida (1980–84), the site of the most important city in Spain during the ancient Roman occupation; two minimalist translucent cubes that house the Kursaal Auditorium and Congress Center in San Sebastian; the rehabilitation of the Palacio de Villahermosa in Madrid to house the Thyssen Bornemisa collection of some eight hundred paintings (1989–92); and, on the island of Mallorca, the Pilar and Joan Miró Foundation (1987–92).

MOORE, CHARLES WILLARD
(1925–1993)

Pioneer in environmental architecture with the landscape architect Lawrence Halprin (b. 1916), with whom he worked on the experimental Sea Ranch on the Californian coast—"a place where wild nature and human habitation could interact"—and where his simple, unpainted redwood cabins were integrated seamlessly with the landscape. Subsequently, he took to Postmodernism with various university buildings and the dramatic Piazza d'Italia, New Orleans (1979), among others.

MORRIS, WILLIAM (1834–1896)

Social revolutionary, visionary, poet, decorator, textile designer, and one of the principal influences on the architects and designers of the Arts and Crafts movement. Though not an actual architect, he joined the architectural firm of G. E. Street in 1856, where he met *his* great influence, the architect Philip Webb (who later designed Morris's subsequently famous Red House). Since neither of them could find any contemporary furniture that they liked—"Shoddy is king," Morris is said to have complained, "from the statesman to the shoemaker, everything is shoddy"— they decided to become decorators and furniture designers themselves. In fact, the only bits of furniture that Morris actually made himself were achieved in 1858. It was really in his role as a passionate idealist that he had such influence over the leaders of the Arts and Crafts movement in England, such as C. R. Ashbee, Richard Norman Shaw, and Charles F. A. Voysey; the Secession movement in Vienna; architects such as the Belgian Henry van de Velde and the German Peter Behrens; and subsequently, as it turned out, on twentieth-century design in general. He founded his own company,

Morris, Marshall, Faulkner & Co. in 1861, with a one-hundred-pound loan from his mother and one-pound share contributions from the Pre-Raphaelite painters Sir Edward Burne-Jones, Dante Gabriel Rossetti (who taught Morris to paint), and Ford Madox Brown, as well as the architect Philip Webb. The firm changed its name to Morris & Co. in 1874. The company produced stained glass, textiles, furniture, pottery, and metalwork. Morris's own best contributions, still reproduced, were his clean-colored textile and wallpaper designs, which introduced the desire for new and lighter furnishings and interiors that dominated the last part of the nineteenth century. Although Morris preached so passionately for the return of the medieval craft ethic, his objection was not so much to machine production as to bad workmanship. In fact, ironically, his first registered design was a trellis of marigolds for machine-made linoleum (or corticine floorcloth, as it was then called). And his first carpets were designed to be machine woven, with separate borders of varying widths. The most ironic aspect of Morris's aims, however, was that, although he set out to bring art to the masses, almost all the works of art and furnishings that he produced cost so much in materials and labor that they were unavailable to all but the rich. Happily, his designs were all copied by manufacturers anyway— and *without* shoddiness—so mass-produced emulations of Morris's style appeared in middle class homes everywhere, as they still do.

MUMFORD, LEWIS (1895–1990)

A tremendous influence on American urban planning, regionalism, and ecological equilibrium with his many forcefully argued and widely read books, which include *The Story of Utopias* (1922); *The Culture of Cities* (1938); *The City in History: Its Origins, Its Transformations and Its Prospects* (1961); *City Development: Studies in Disintegration and Renewal* (1961); and *The Urban Prospect* (1968).

MURCUTT, GLEN (B. 1936)

Sensitive Australian architect who has led the way in designing elegant houses and public buildings particularly appropriate to their geographical locations and climate, as well as with his use of vernacular construction materials. A well-known example is the Berowra Waters Inn, near Sydney, designed between 1977 and 1983. He has consistently made the point that he is not interested in designing large-scale projects since it is smaller works that have given him the opportunity for his continual experimentation. The Aboriginal saying "to touch this earth lightly" is his mantra. His particular influences have been Mies van der Rohe and Luis Barragán, and on his first visit to the United States he was particularly taken with Kevin Roche and John Dinkeloo's Ford Foundation Headquarters. He has become greatly in demand for international lectures and teaching, which, he says, have provided wonderful ways to learn more himself. In 2002, he became the twenty-fourth winner of the prestigious Pritzker Architecture Prize and the first Australian to be awarded the prize with the citation that "he has become a living legend, an architect totally focused on shelter and the environment with skills drawn from nature and the most sophisticated design traditions of the Modern movement."

NASH, JOHN (1752–1835)

British Picturesque movement architect and, like Baron Haussmann in Paris, a brilliant urban designer. He was a master of producing large-scale theatrical effect, as in, for example, the transformation of the little marine pavilion—originally designed by Henry Holland for the future George IV—into the amazing Indian and Chinoiserie Brighton Pavilion (1802–21). He was also the first builder of stucco-fronted houses in London. His best work was probably the layout of Regent Street and Regent's Park in London (in progress from 1811), the latter considered to be the forerunner of the twentieth-century garden city since the park is dotted with charming villas (including Winfield House, the residence of the Ambassador of the United States) and surrounded by stunning terraces and crescents of graceful stuccoed houses. In the 1820s, in his energetic seventies, he planned Trafalgar Square, Suffolk Street, and Suffolk Place; built Clarence House (formerly the home of the late Queen Mother and now the London home of Prince Charles) and Carlton House Terrace; and began Buckingham Palace (completed by Edward Blore). His career came to an end with the death of

George IV in 1830, but he was already seventy-eight.

NELSON, GEORGE (1908–1986)

Twentieth-century American design catalyst and prolific designer of furniture, interiors, and exhibitions as well as a respected writer on design. Nelson was also an early fellow of the American Academy in Rome in 1934.

NERVI, PIER LUIGI (1891–1979)

An Italian architect and a civil engineer, an entrepreneur as well as an academic, and considered to be the foremost concrete designer of the twentieth century. His first great concrete building was the stadium in Florence (1930–32), with a cantilevered roof about seventy feet deep and an imaginative, flying spiral staircase. He built his first enormous corrugated-concrete exhibition hall in Turin in 1948 (he subsequently built two others in the same city), and was commissioned to help with the structure of the UNESCO building in Paris (1953–56). And it was his designs that were the underpinnings for the spectacular structure of the Pirelli building in Milan for Gio Ponti (1955–58). One of his last great sculptural buildings was the enormous audience hall for the pope in the Vatican (1970–71).

NEUMANN, JOHANN BALTHASAR (1687–1753)

Most famous German Rococo architect, town planner, and designer of churches and palaces all over Germany, which was at that time divided into various competitive principalities. He was particularly treasured for his extraordinary ceremonial staircases, which were masterpieces of engineering and the single most important element in each of the new palaces he designed. These included the Prince Bishop's new Residenz in Würzburg and the ceremonial staircase leading up to the Kaiseraal (designed 1735, with a ceiling decoration by Giovanni Tiepolo in 1752–53); the staircase at Bruchal (1731–32); and the staircase at Schloss Brühl, near Cologne (1743–48). His masterpiece is considered to be the pilgrimage church of Vierzehnheiligen (designed and worked on from 1742 to 1753, but not actually completed until 1772).

NEUTRA, RICHARD (1892–1970)

American architect, born in Austria, who studied or worked under masters of Modernism like Otto Wagner, Adolf Loos, and Erich Mendelsohn before emigrating to Chicago in 1923 and finally moving to Los Angeles in 1925. With his early experience, he was in an excellent position to promote the new European style of Modernism in America, which he did with immediate success in his exciting Philip Lovell House in Los Angeles (1927–29). Other well-known Neutra houses, always stunningly attuned to their landscape, are the Desert House, Colorado (1946); Kaufmann Desert House, Palm Springs (1947); Tremaine House, Santa Barbara, California (1947–48); and his own house at Silverlake, Los Angeles (1933; redone in 1964).

NEW YORK FIVE

Five influential, and, at the time, young American architects—Peter Eisenman, Robert Graves, Charles Gwathmey, John Hejduk, and Richard Meier—who formed themselves into a New York architectural group. They were also known as the "Whites," mainly because of various houses designed by Richard Meier, the most prolific and ardently purist of the five. They exhibited their work together in New York City in 1969, published a joint book called *Five Architects* in 1972, and disbanded themselves in 1980.

NIEMEYER, OSCAR (B. 1907)

Influential and internationally prolific Brazilian architect who, in 1957, became chief architect for Brasilia, the new inland capital of Brazil, which is remarkable for its various extraordinary buildings and their interplay of the fanciful with the serious, expressed in the sculptural shapes of some of the public buildings and the strictly businesslike office blocks and ministerial headquarters. He joined the office of Lucio Costa, and worked with him, and with Le Corbusier as consultant, on the Ministry of Education Building in Rio (1936–43). He worked with Costa again on the Brazilian Pavilion at the New York World's Fair in 1939. But then, for his first individual commission, he suddenly exploded with a series of completely new and ebullient forms: parabolic vaults, free-flowing double-curves for a porch canopy, and slanting walls for the casino, club, and church of St. Francis at Pampulha, outside Belo Horizonto (1942–43). These dramatically sculptural shapes suited Brazil, with its past of equally dramatic Baroque architecture. His own house built outside Rio ten years later was and is a stunning amalgam of architecture interacting with wilderness. Soon after, Niemeyer was invited to become the

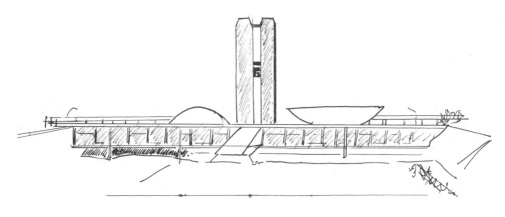

Brasilia (1957–60), Brazil, by Oscar Niemeyer

architectural adviser to Novo Cap, the organization specially started to organize the creation of Brasilia. After he became chief architect for the city (planned by Lucio Costa), on which he lavished a mixture of extreme originality and restraint, he won commissions all around the world, as well as for his landmark Museum of Contemporary Art in Niteroi, near Rio. In 1988 he was the joint winner of the Pritzker Prize for Architecture with Gordon Bunshaft. In his nineties, he still continues to work, evolve, and inspire.

NOGUCHI, ISAMU (1904–1988)

Environmental designer and sculptor, son of a Japanese poet and an American mother, he also designed some classic free-form glass tables, upholstered furniture, and the accordion-pleated Akari paper lanterns that have become classics. He worked for a short while in Constantin Brancusi's studio in Paris, and on a trip back to Japan was immensely inspired by the monastery gardens at Kyoto, which propelled him into various environmental proposals. In the early 1950s he designed two bridges for Kenzo Tange's Peace Center in Hiroshima, and then designed the gardens for Marcel Breuer's UNESCO buildings in Paris, and for Skidmore, Owings & Merrill's Connecticut General Life Insurance Headquarters in Bloomfield, Connecticut. During the same period he also designed the purist, all-white Marble Gardens (without any plants at all) for the Beinecke Rare Book Library at Yale University. His late works, in which he sought "to

create beautiful and disturbing gardens to awaken us to a new awareness of our solitude," were in California; Long Island, New York; and Japan.

OLBRICH, JOSEPH MARIA (1867–1908)

Austrian early-Modernist architect who worked in Otto Wagner's office and designed the building (1897–98) for the Secessionists, a group of young progressive Viennese architects and designers who were determined to change the direction of design. The building attracted much attention, as did hislater projects. Olbrich's chief fame is that he, like his compatriot Josef Hoffmann and Charles Rennie Mackintosh and Mackay Hugh Baillie Scott in Scotland, succeeded in taking most of the vegetal out of Art Nouveau and moving on to a more rational plane.

OMA

The initials of the Rotterdam-based Office for Metropolitan Architecture started by Rem Koolhaas in 1975.

PALLADIO, ANDREA (1508–1580)

One of the greatest and certainly the most influential of Italian architects. He was born Andrea dalla Gondola, and worked as a stonemason before he met Giangiorgio Trissino (1478–1550), his early patron and an intellectual and amateur architect who encouraged him to learn mathematics, music, Latin literature, and to study the works of Vitruvius and the ruins of ancient Rome. Trissino, in fact, also nick-named him Palladio, an allusion to the goddess of wisdom and to a character in a poem he was then writing. The name adhered as, clearly, did his education, for in 1546 the newly named Palladio won a competition to remodel the early Renaissance Palazzo della Ragione in Vicenza. He surrounded the old building with a two-story, airily elegant screen of arches that gave the building such a new and distinctive air that he was inundated with commissions. It is hard to imagine now, but up until the fifteenth century in Europe, the division of a grand villa into rooms, each with its specific function, was quite unknown until the innovations of the Italian Renaissance. In fact, although well-appointed and well-planned villas were commonplace for the rich in ancient Rome and Greece, they became virtually obsolete after the defeat of Rome by the Goths. From then on, at least until the relative prosperity, peace, and calm of the fifthteenth century—when Italy had its fecund rebirth of Classical ideals and interest in all the arts—most dwellings of any size were mainly austere and generally fortified for protection against marauders and warlords looking to increase their properties. Palladio, in the early sixteenth century—at the latter end of the Renaissance period—planned villas with vestibules for receiving visitors; galleries for showing off paintings, sculpture, and the newly fashionable collections of coins and jewels; bedchambers; antechambers; and libraries. Into these interiors he distilled various Renaissance ideas, particularly the revival of ancient Roman symmetrical planning and harmonic proportions, but he was also influenced by predecessors like Bramante, Michelangelo, Raphael, and

Sansovino, as well as by the Byzantine architecture of Venice. In the 1550s he had evolved a formula for the "ideal" villa, which consisted of a strictly symmetrical central block with a distinctive templelike portico front (which Palladio presumed, as it turned out quite erroneously, to be the normal typical Roman entrance) that was sometimes attached, sometimes inset, and sometimes detached, all of which were usually extended by long wings of farm buildings, stretched either horizontally or curved forward in quadrants. He employed numerous variations on this theme from the more elaborate Villa Capra (known as *La Rotonda*, 1566–61), with its porticoes on each of its four sides, to the extreme simplicity of La Malcontenta (1559–61), as well as the severity of Villa Poiana (1549–60), where columns are replaced by undecorated shafts. He also designed churches in Venice: the facade of San Francesco della Vigna (1562); San Giorgio Maggiore (1564–80, and its later facade 1607–11); and Il Redentore (begun 1576). He published several books, but his most famous was his interesting, unstuffy, and unpompous *Quattro Libri dell'Architettura* (1570)—a four-volume set of books on architecture that illustrates his work and discusses his various theories that, although only theories, have been handed down through the centuries as if they were the actual golden rules of Classicism. These were translated into English and published, respectively, by Giacomo Leoni, Colen Campbell, and Isaac Ware between 1715 and 1720, 1728, and 1738. Isaac Ware's 1728 edition remained the standard work until R. Tavenor and R. Schofield published their new work through the M.I.T. Press, Cambridge, Massachusetts, in 1997.

PAXTON, SIR JOSEPH (1803–1865)

Breakthrough designer of the revolutionary Crystal Palace in London (1850–51), notable for being the first really prefabricated, large-scale industrial building and for its glass and metal design. Paxton started off as a gardener for the Duke of Devonshire's house in Chiswick in 1823. The duke, delighted with Paxton's obvious talents, promoted him to be superintendent of the gardens of his enormous country house, Chatsworth, Derbyshire, where the two men developed a steady friendship to the point that they traveled together to Asia Minor as well as to much of Europe. Together with Decimus Burton, the architect of Hyde Park Corner in London, Paxton developed special greenhouses for the estate, one of them as long as three hundred feet. He then went on to lay out plans for the estate village of Edensor (1839–41). With this experience, Paxton, apparently uninvited, was emboldened to submit a design for a glass and iron palace to contain the first-ever international exhibition, called and still known as the Great Exhibition. His design for an 1,800-foot-long, beautifully detailed building, which was worked out in such a way that all its parts could be made in a factory and then assembled on site, was built between 1850 and 1851. It was not only revolutionary for its time, but was a most admirable solution for its purpose and possibly, in its way, the

precursor for some of Buckminster Fuller's geodesic domes. Soon afterward, Paxton evidently developed political skills, in addition to his landscaping and clear-headed architectural talents, and ran as a member of the House of Commons as MP for Coventry, which he secured in 1854 and maintained until his death. In his spare time, he designed some of the earliest public parks in England, notably in Birkenhead, Lancashire (1843–07), and Halifax, West Yorkshire (1856), and worked on two houses, Mentmore and Ferrières in France, for the Rothschild family.

PEI, IEOH MING (B. 1917)

Known simply as I. M. Pei, this Chinese-born, American architect of deserved world fame who trained at the Massachusetts Institute of Technology and Harvard University has achieved a remarkable variety of international buildings. He started work with the developer William Zeckendorf, with whom he designed the Mile High Center in Denver, Colorado (1952–56), as well as the Place Ville-Marie complex in Montreal, Canada (1960). He formed his own firm, I. M. Pei & Partners, New York, in 1956 with Henry Cobb, James Freed, and others, and with them has been responsible for a formidable list of urban buildings and complexes, among them the John Hancock Tower in Boston (1966–76); the OCBC Center in Singapore (1976); the John Fitzgerald Kennedy Library in Boston; the National Airlines Terminal at Kennedy International Airport in New York; the Collins Place develop-

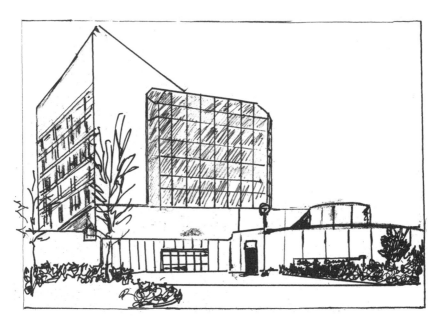

The John Fitzgerald Kennedy Library, Boston, Massachusetts, by I. M. Pei (completed 1979; extension completed 1991)

ment in Melbourne, Australia; the extension to the National Gallery in Washington, D.C. (1968–78); the El Paso Tower, Houston, Texas (1981); the brilliant glass "pyramid" extension and new entrance for the Louvre in Paris (1989); the Miho Museum, near Kyoto, Japan (1990–97); the Bank of China Tower in Hong Kong (1982–90); the Rock & Roll Hall of Fame in Cleveland, Ohio (1993–95); and, with one of his partners, James Freed, the United States Holocaust Museum in Washington, D.C. (1986–93).

PELLI, CESAR (B. 1926)

Argentine-born American architect with some of the world's highest buildings and the changing face of many cities to his credit. He came to America in 1952 to train in Chicago and worked with Eero Saarinen as project manager for the TWA Terminal at Kennedy International Airport, New York. In 1968 he worked with Gruen Associates and designed the Pacific Design Center in Los Angeles (1975) with its blue glazing. The latter was a seminal building for him since it brought him many distinguished commissions, including the residential tower and expansion of the Museum of Modern Art in New York (1977); the Four Leaf Towers, Houston, Texas (1983–85); the World Financial Center Towers and Winter Garden, New York City (1980–88); Canary Wharf Tower, London (1987–91); the Carnegie Hall

Tower, New York City (1987–91); the 777 Tower, Los Angeles (1991); the NTT Headquarters Building, Tokyo (1991–95); and the Petronas Twin Towers in Kuala Lumpur (1991–97), presently the tallest buildings in the world.

PERCIER, CHARLES

(See *Fontaine, Pierre-François-Leonard*.)

PERRAULT, CLAUDE (1613–1688)

French doctor and amateur architect who was mostly responsible for the design of the great east front of the Louvre in Paris, begun in 1667 and chosen by Louis XIV over Bernini's design, which the king had especially commissioned. Perrault went on to design the Paris Observatoire (1667) and translated into French an edition (1674) of Vitruvius's *De Architectura*.

PERRIAND, CHARLOTTE (1903–1999)

Luminary architect and furniture designer who long worked as a collaborator with Le Corbusier—for example, she was just as much the designer of the famous LC1 leather-sling chair and the chaise longue and Grand Confort chair as "Corbu"—yet rarely figures in the leading design reference books. Along with Le Corbusier, she founded the progressive Union des Artistes Modernes in 1929. She was invited to advise the Japanese Ministry of Commerce in 1940 on arts and crafts and a year later, after working in Tokyo, edited *Contact with Japanese Art: Selection, Tradition, Creation* (republished in the United States in 1942 as *Contact with Japan*). In the early 1950s, Perriand collaborated with Jean Prouvé to design furniture, a collaboration that lasted nearly twenty years, during which time she designed the interiors and furniture for the Air France offices in London and Tokyo. In the last twenty years of her life, during her eighties and nineties, she was honored with the Gold Medal of the Académie d'Architecture (1978), made a Chevalier of the French Legion of Honor (1983), and given retrospective exhibitions of her furniture designs at the Musée des Arts Décoratifs in Paris (1985) and the Design Museum in London (1997).

PERRET, AUGUSTE (1874–1954)

An early French experimenter in bold concrete designs who employed the young Le Corbusier for a year (1908–09) before the latter went off to work just as briefly with Peter Behrens in Berlin. Perret's first project was an apartment building with clearly displayed concrete members juxtaposed with Art Nouveau faience infillings (1903–04). His Théâtre de Champs Elysées (1911–14) was originally designed by Henry van de Velde but finalized by Perret, who again took a clear delight in exposing the building's concrete framework, but this time with Classical rather than Art Nouveau details. His later works veered more toward the Classical but were still unapologetically in concrete, or with bold concrete details.

PESCE, GAETANO (B. 1939)

Leading and often controversial Italian architect and designer who—with brilliant contemporaries such as Gae Aulenti, Mario Bellini, the Castiglioni brothers, Vico Magistretti, Richard Sapper, Ettore Sottsass Jr., and Tobia and Afra Scarpa—produced the vibrant, lively, often joyously colorful and sometimes deliberately flippant furniture, lighting, product designs, and interiors that distinguished Italian design for several decades. He started to make his mark in the mid-1960s with the "anti"-design ideas he argued in his *First Manifesto for an Elastic Architecture*. He followed up the manifesto with more provocation in an "environment" called *Habitat for Two People in an Age of great Contaminations* that was included in "Italy: The New Domestic Landscape," a 1972 exhibition curated by Emilio Ambasz at the Museum of Modern Art in New York. Nevertheless, he ended up by being honored with exhibitions in the Musée des Arts Décoratifs, Montreal (1983–84); the Centre Georges Pompidou, Paris (1996); in the show "'Is the Future New?' Gaetano Pesce: Material Exploration" (1997) at the Material Connextion Gallery in New York City; and a retrospective, again at that acme of distinction, the Musée des Arts Décoratifs, in Montreal (1998). His furniture is produced by B&B Italia (formerly C&B Italia), Castelli, and Cassina.

PHYFE, DUNCAN (1768–1854)

Outstanding American furniture designer, born in Scotland and preemi-nent in the first three decades of the Federal Republic. The Fife family emigrated to Albany, New York in 1784 but lost two of their children on the voyage. After serving an apprenticeship either with an unknown cabinetmaker or even a coach-builder—it is not clear which—the young Duncan came to New York City about 1790 and changed his name to Phyfe in 1794. His career, thereafter, was meteoric. He became the protégé of Mrs. Langdon, the daughter of John Jacob Astor, then known as the "fur prince" of New York, and by 1797, it seems, any New Yorker of wealth and position felt it only fitting to have Phyfe design all the furniture for his or her home. (Other distinguished patrons included the Rockefellers, Henry du Pont, and Francis Garvan.) In the three decades of his best work he followed the published designs of Hepplewhite and Sheraton but added touches of ornamentation derived from French cabinetmakers of the Directoire and Consulate periods. The resulting synthesis, far from being a jumble, was always uniquely elegant, although interestingly, extant Phyfe drawings and sketches show that he was much more skillful with his cabinetmaking tools than with his pencil. His earlier work is characterized by the use of reeding, acanthus-leaf carving, and ornamental brass hardware. He was particularly well known for his delicate lyre-back chairs, finely proportioned and delicately carved sofas, and tripod-based tables, or tables with reeded legs. His later work was influenced by the much heavier French Empire style with a liberal use of special bands and panels of grained mahogany veneering with brass-tipped claw-foot table legs, as shown by the three-part banquet table in the Metropolitan Museum of Art in New York.

PIANO, RENZO (B. 1937)

Italian architect whose work in the 1970s with the British architect Richard Rogers on the dashingly colored, exposed structure and mechanisms of the High-Tech Centre Pompidou in Paris (1971–77) made something of a global stir. It was the apotheosis of High-Tech. Piano's subsequent buildings have been both diverse and interesting. Among the most innovative are the Menil Collection and the museum's Cy Twombly addition in Houston, Texas (1980–87); the extraordinary Kansai International Airport in Osaka Bay, Japan (1988–94); the Aurora Place building in Sydney, Australia; the Beyeler Museum in Basel, Switzerland; the Museum of Science and Technology in Amsterdam; the Mercedes Benz Design Center in Stuttgart, Germany; the Pirelli Workshop and factories in Milan; and the Harvard University Art Museums. In 2000 he was commissioned to design a new addition to the Art Institute of Chicago. In 1998 he became the twentieth winner of the Pritzker Architecture Prize.

PIRANESI, GIOVANNI BATTISTA (1720–1778)

Not so much an architect—although he was trained as one—as an architectural

Entrance to Santa Maria del Priorato (1764), Aventine Hill, Rome, a rare building by Giovanni Battista Piranesi

theorist and exquisite engraver. However, his powerful views of ancient Roman ruins and antiquities, together with his own ideas on the form of ancient Roman architecture, had a profound effect on architects of the Neoclassical and Romantic movements. In the eighteenth-century debate over the superiority of Greek as opposed to Roman antiquity, at least as far as architecture was concerned, he was a fierce protagonist for Rome.

POLSHEK, JAMES STEWART (B. 1930)

American architect who trained under Louis Kahn, although his work in no way bears any resemblance to what is often known as the "Philadelphia School." One of his most recent buildings, The Rose Center for Earth and Space at the American Museum of Natural History in New York is extraordinarily beautiful and beautifully planned—confirming the extreme versatility and sensitivity of his range of buildings from the Teijin Research Institutes I and II in Tokyo and Osaka, Japan (1963–71), to the Mashantucket Pequot Museum and Research Center at the Mashantucket Pequot Reserve, Connecticut (1993–97). With Mario Botta, I. M. Pei, and Fumihiko Maki, he worked on the large-scale Center for the Arts Theater, Yerba Buena Gardens redevelopment in San Francisco. Polshek was also chosen as the architect for the William J. Clinton Presidential Library in Little Rock, Arkansas.

PONTI, GIO (1891–1979)

Italian Architect, painter, and brilliant all-round designer who was another twentieth-century "great." Although his best-known building is the slender, tapering Pirelli skyscraper in Milan (1955–58) designed with Pier Luigi Nervi, later neo-Expressionist buildings, such as the Taranto Cathedral and the Denver Art Museum in Colorado, have received much praise. But he is also known for some of his furniture, such as the fragile-looking, rush-seated, black-framed Superleggera side chair designed in 1957 for Cassina as well as for his porcelain, light fittings, ships' interiors, light industrial products, and considerable painting talent. Ponti founded the influential Italian architectural and design magazine *Domus*, which he edited for many years.

PORTZAMPARC CHRISTIAN DE (B. 1944)

The sixth European architect to win the Pritzker Architecture Prize (in 1994) and in the fine Renaissance tradition was a designer who painted and sculpted before he studied architecture. After qualifying as an architect, he spent nine months enjoying the hippiness of Greenwich Village, New York before deciding he might actually be able to help people with his buildings if he practiced what he had learned. Although he has mostly built in France—wonderfully, showy hip reinterpretations of the timeless elements of architecture with a sure sense of scale and proportion allied with irreverent candy colors—he was a finalist in the competition for Chicago's New Museum of Contemporary Art and an art museum for Omaha, Nebraska, as well as for designing apartment buildings in Fukuoka, Japan. His first French building was Château d'Eau (1974), a converted water tower for Marne-la-Vallée, based on the Tower of Babel; his most famous is the Cité de la Musique, finished in 1995, on the edge of Parc de la Villette, a suburban park in Paris. Other buildings are the Dance School of the Paris Opéra in Nanterre (1983–87) and the Café Beaubourg and Ungaro boutiques in Paris.

PRITZKER ARCHITECTURE PRIZE

Since the Pritzker Architecture Prize, sponsored by the Hyatt Foundation, is the highest international award for architecture and now the profession's highest honor, it seems appropriate to explain it in this section on architects and designers. It was started by the Pritzker family in 1979 because of their keen interest in building, due to their involvement with developing the Hyatt Hotels around the world. Architecture was also a creative endeavor not included in the Nobel prizes so the family decided to replicate the Nobel procedures with the final selection being made by an international jury. The purpose of the prize, the foundation says, is to honor annually a living architect whose built work demonstrates a combination of those qualities of talent, vision, and commitment that has produced consistent and significant contributions to humanity and the built environment through the art of architecture.

PUGIN, AUGUSTUS WELBY NORTHMORE (1812–1852)

Nineteenth-century British designer best known for his ardent pursuit of the Gothic and the magnificent detail of his work, not just on the facades of Barry's Houses of Parliament, but for every detail inside down to the inkstands. His handsome wallpaper designs, done around the same time, are still being reproduced. His father, a Frenchman, came to England in the early 1790s and became first a draftsman in the offices of John Nash, the great Regency architect, then a draftsman and editor of books on Gothic architecture, which the young Pugin absorbed as a child. His talent for design was evident at such an early age that he was receiving quite import commissions in his teens. He was only fifteen when he was asked to design some furniture for Windsor Castle and still only nineteen when he designed sets for a stage production of Sir Walter Scott's *Kenilworth*. After his conversion to Catholicism in his early twenties, his naturally fervent nature plunged him into a passion for "the glories of the Catholic past" in the shape of late-thirteenth-century to early-fourteenth-century "Second Pointed" Gothic architecture. No possible building in regular stone or wood could even begin to approach the glory of the designs he drew on paper, and he was as interested in stained glass, metalwork, altars, screens, and general church furnishings as he was in the church buildings he planned. He lost his mind in 1851, having lost two wives within ten years, and died aged only forty.

PUTNAM, ANDRÉE

Much-respected French design icon who started the furniture company Ecart International in 1979 to sell 1930s furniture classics. Among her own varied commissions in the 1980s and '90s are international boutiques for Yves St. Laurent and Karl Lagerfeld; various international restaurants, hair salons, and stores; Morgan's Hotel in New York; Le Lac Hotel near Tokyo; Hotel im Wasserturm in Cologne, Germany; the Sheraton Hotel at Roissy, in France; the French National and Regional Government offices; and the renovation of Le Corbusier's 1916 Villa Schwob in Switzerland.

RAPHAEL (RAFFAELLO SANZIO) (1483–1520)

As a painter, Raphael showed a notable sensitivity to architecture and perspective, as can be seen in many of his backgrounds. Although he produced few buildings himself—most of which have been destroyed—the ones that remain were enough to give him a reputation as the greatest exponent of High Renaissance Classicism through his architectural designs as much as his painting. In fact, his work, along with the ancient Roman remains and the buildings of Donato Bramante, has been the chief inspiration for all later devotees of Classicism. At the age of thirty-two, he was made superintendant of Roman antiquities, and it is supposed that it was either he or his senior, Bramante, who subsequently drew up a plan for measuring all the existing ruins and restoring as many of them possible.

RICHARDSON, HENRY HOBSON (1838–1886)

Louisiana-born American architect who studied at Harvard University and was one of the first American students at the École des Beaux-Arts in Paris, where he studied from 1859 to 1862. Later, while traveling widely in France

and northern Spain, he discovered his passion for Romanesque architecture. His modified, but powerful versions of this style can be seen in his Brattle Square church (1871–73) and Trinity church (1873–77), both in Boston. In Chicago he designed the massive Marshall Field Wholesale Warehouse (1885–87, demolished 1935); in Massachusetts, all in the late 1870s and '80s, he designed the Win Memorial Library in Woburn, the Oaks Ames Free Library with its handsome barrel-vault ceiling, and two original buildings for Harvard University. He is credited with originating the great rise in American architecture by liberating America from its then habit of so closely imitating European revivals as well as by pioneering the "shingle style." This was America's so-called Domestic Revival, influenced by Richard Norman Shaw's domestic housing in Britain, but replacing Shaw's signature tile-hanging with shingles and adding innovative open-planned interiors. Richardson's Watt Sherman House in Newport and Stoughton House in Cambridge, Massachusetts are prime examples of the "shingle style." Louis Sullivan was much influenced by Richardson's work, as were Charles Follen McKim and Stanford White, who were his pupils before forming their own influential firm of McKim, Mead & White.

RIESENER, JEAN-HENRI (1734–1806)

One of the best eighteenth-century French *ébénistes*, or cabinetmakers, who, though trained in the Rococo style during the Louis XV period, produced all his best work in the Classical style of the Louis XVI period that followed. He used all the classic ingredients or details of the style: graceful proportions and lines, exquisitely carved architectural details, and many roses—the latter, because they were a favorite flower of the French queen, Marie Antoinette. He was known for his especially fine marquetry work, for which he made pictorial center panels for the sides of many of his pieces.

RIETVELD, GERRIT THOMAS (1888–1964)

Dutch architect and furniture designer who was a leading member of the young group of artists, architects, and designers called De Stijl (the Style), after the avant-garde magazine of the same name. He was determined to create designs that had absolutely no link with the past and, to achieve this end, used abstract rectangular forms in primary colors. His Red–Blue chair of 1918, with its severe slablike back and seat, was a precursor of the tactile surfaces and strong colors of Art Deco, a good deal of the Italian furniture of the 1960s, and, indeed, some of the buildings of the 1980s and '90s. His groundbreaking architectural masterpiece, the Schroeder House in Utrecht, finished in 1924, inspired many architects, including Mies van der Rohe. Its clean-cut surfaces devoid of moldings and its metal-framed windows in continuous strips running up to the ceiling level were precursors of the International style to come.

ROBSJOHN-GIBBINGS, TERENCE HAROLD (1905–1976)

Popular American (b. England) furniture designer and interior designer who, unusually for the time, worked in the Classic tradition and was inspired by both Greek and Roman antiquities (his 1926 version of the Greek Klismos chair is a classic). His furniture was beautifully made and his interiors equally beautifully detailed—qualities that were clearly appreciated by modern-day Greeks since he designed many interiors for Aristotle Onassis and Nicholas Goulandris. Together with Carlton W. Pullin he wrote *The Furniture of Classical Greece*, published in 1963.

ROCHE, KEVIN (B. 1922)

Irish-born American architect and another creator of familiar New York landmarks. One of his early buildings, however, is equally a Californian landmark: the Oakland Museum (1962) in Oakland, California, is a multilayered building, particularly noticeable for its verdant terraces and roof gardens created on almost every level by the American landscape architect Dan Kiley, who is said to have planted 38,000 trees and enormous numbers of variegated shrubs and vines on the site. Roche worked with Eero Saarinen for ten years, until the latter's death, when he took over the practice with John Dinkeloo (1918–1981). The Ford Foundation Headquarters in Manhattan (1963–08), with its splendid atrium, influenced the design of many office buildings for years to come. Many other commissions all over the United States followed, but the handsome extension to the Metropolitan Museum of Art (1967–78) is especially notable. In 1982, he was awarded the fourth Pritzker Architecture Prize, the second United States architect to be so honored.

ROGERS, RICHARD GEORGE (BARON ROGERS OF RIVERSIDE) (B. 1933)

British architect synonymous with the High-Tech movement, who leaped to fame with his Centre Pompidou, Paris, designed with Renzo Piano (1971–77). He had worked in partnership with Sir Norman Foster up until 1967, after which he worked independently. Although he has designed many buildings of note, the Lloyd's of London headquarters is probably the best known (1978–86), along with the European Court of Human Rights at Strasbourg (1989–95) and his much-praised and imaginative urban renewal schemes for both London and Shanghai. At the time of going to press, the Leadenhall Building, his 737-foot tapered tower with its vertiginous facade-climbing elevators, at 122 Leadenhall Street in London, looks set to be the tallest building—by one hundred feet—in that city.

ROSSI, ALDO (1931–1997)

As much a gifted architect and artist as a stimulating theorist and writer, Aldo's stance was Anti-Modernist/Neo-Rationalist and his book *L'architettura della città* (1966 in Italian, 1982 in English) is considered a valuable

contribution to the study of urbanism is general. His buildings—the San Cataldo Cemetary in Modena, designed between 1971 and 1976 but not built until between 1980 and 1985; his residential apartment building for Aymonino's Gallaratese complex in Milan, built between 1970 and 1973; and his school at Fagnano Olona (1974–77) are all three considered Neo-Rationalist master-pieces. Other notable works are a floating demountable theater for Venice, designed in 1979; his ten-year renovations and additions to the Teatro Carlo Felice in Genoa, carried out starting in 1981; and his Centro Torri in Parma (1985–88). In 1990 he became the first Italian architect to win the Pritzker Architecture Prize.

RUDOLPH, PAUL (1918–1997)

Innovative and experimental American architect, particularly well known in the 1960s, who was trained by Walter Gropius at Harvard. He then went on to become the head of the School of Architecture at Yale in 1957, for which he designed the massive New Brutalist Art and Architecture Building (1958–63) in New Haven, Connecticut—a vast change from the elegant little columned houses in Florida with which he started his career. One of his other major works was the urban renewal project for the Government Center in Boston (1961–63, 1967–72). Interestingly, he did not do much work in America after the end of the 1960s, although he worked a great deal in Indonesia, Japan, Singapore, and Israel.

RUHLMANN, JACQUES-EMILE (1879–1933)

One of the most sought after of the French Art Deco decorators and furniture designers, often compared to great French *ébénistes* of the eighteenth century like Andre-Charles Boulle (1642–1732) and Jean-Henri Riesener (1734–1806). Like these distinguished predecessors, Ruhlmann liked to work with exotic materials; in his case they included tortoiseshell, lapis lazuli, shagreen, lizard skin, and ivory. His pavilion at the 1925 Exhibition of Decorative and Industrial Arts in Paris (an exhibition planned since 1915 but postponed because of World War I, and showcasing all the leading trends of the day) was considered a triumph, unfettered as it was by mundane budgetary considerations.

RUMFORD, SIR BENJAMIN THOMPSON (1753–1814)

American scientist, inventor, social reformer, hospital and workhouse improver, landscape architect, philosopher, politician, soldier, and, not least, the person to find a cause and a cure for "the greatest of all plagues, a smoky fire." He was knighted by the British, made a Count of the Holy Roman Empire, laid out the world's first public park (in Munich, Germany), endowed a Chair and founded the Rumford Professorship of Chemistry at Harvard University, founded the Royal Institution in England, and established the Rumford Medal of the Royal Society.

SAARINEN, EERO (1910–1961)

Pioneering American architect and furniture designer who left as testament to his talent an outstandingly varied body of work in America, including the notable Trans-World Airline (TWA) terminal at Kennedy International Airport, New York (1956–62); Dulles International Airport, Washington, D.C. (1958–63); the CBS Building on Sixth Avenue in Manhattan (1951–05); the United States embassies in London (1955–61) and Oslo, Norway (1959 onward); and furniture that belongs in the firmament of twentieth-century classics. He was the son of Eliel Saarinen, the Finnish architect who designed the famous Finnish railway station in Helsinki (1904, built 1905–14), emigrated to the United States in 1923, and helped establish the influential Cranbrook Academy of Art at Bloomfield Hills, Michigan, with

Eero Saarinen pedestal chairs, manufactured by Knoll Associates, 1955–56

his father and Charles Eames as two of the artists-in-residence.

SANSOVINO, JACOPO D'ANTONIO TATTI (1486–1570)

Called Sansovino after his old master, Andrea Sansovino, he was actually the son of an Antonio Tatti of Florence and started off, as did so many Renaissance and High Renaissance architects, as a sculptor. His name is now synonymous with Venice since he arrived in that city en route to France after escaping the Sack of Rome in 1527. While there, however, he was commissioned to repair the main dome of San Marco, became friends with Titian and other painters, got many more architectural commissions as a result, and decided to stay on. His Venetian buildings included the Library and Mint (1537–45), opposite the Doge's Palace, the former called by Palladio "the richest building erected since Classical times"; the Logetta (1537–42) at the foot of the Campanile di San Marco; the Scuola Grande della Misericordia (begun 1552 but not completed); the church of San Francesco della Vigna (1534; completed by Palladio, who succeeded Sansovino as chief architect of Venice); and the facade of San Giuliano (1553–55).

SANT'ELIA, ANTONIO (1888–1916)

The chief exponent of Italian Futurism, although he died—killed in World War I—before he had a chance to put into practice his fiery theories. Inspired by the designs and forms shown by the Vienna Secession, he left drawings that showed a remarkable prescience for the actual future with skyscrapers, factories, and intersecting highways, and that had great influence on architects to come.

SCARPA, CARLO (1906–1978)

Italian architect much influenced in the beginning by the De Stijl movement as well as by the work of Frank Lloyd Wright. He made his name abroad with his various designs for exhibitions and museums, but his store for Olivetti in Venice (1959) and his Gavina store in Bologna (1960) were as influential to future store design as his Banco Populare (finished 1974) in Verona was to later bank buildings.

SCHAROUN, HANS (1893–1972)

German architect who, although a convinced Expressionist in his youth and a great communicator, was bypassed by the new avant-garde in his middle life and did not really come into his own until his late sixties and seventies, when the style he had always adhered to came back into fashion. Some of his later buildings included the Berlin Philharmonie (1956–63)—having the most wonderful acoustics; the German embassy in Brasilia (1970); and the new National Library in Berlin (finished in 1978, after his death).

SCHINKEL, KARL FRIEDRICH (1781–1841)

The best-known and most influential German architect and interior designer of the nineteenth century, and a great

Greek Revivalist who later segued into the Picturesque. He allied an intensely personal and original interpretation of both styles with interesting spatial interpretations, a caring attention to and knowledge of architectural detail, a daring sense of color, and a keen sense of function. Although he trained as an architect in Berlin, he did not actually start his career in that profession. He traveled in Italy and in Paris for two years from 1803, and when he returned to Berlin, he first earned his living by painting the panoramas and illusionistic dioramas that were so fashionable in the period, as well as highly romanticized landscapes and paintings of various Gothic cathedrals. After this painting stage he moved on to design stage sets, which he worked at for some fifteen years. This last experience stood him in good stead for his later stunningly conceived interiors. While still working for the theater he started to submit various ecclesiastical designs in the hope that he would be noticed (which he was), before swinging into the pure Grecian mode that he subsequently used for so many new public buildings as well as domestic architecture in and around Berlin. After switching to a job as an administrator for Prussian buildings, he was eventually, in 1830 at almost fifty, made head of the new Public Works Department, although he had also managed to design almost all of his chief work over the decade or so before. Although he worked out of his native Prussia, he was respected, and in many cases revered, by later architects and designers in other countries.

SEIDLER, HARRY (B. 1923)

Leading Australian Modernist architect (and brilliant photographer) who was born in Vienna, sent to Britain as a boy to avoid Nazism, and taught by Walter Gropius at Harvard, and who settled in Sydney in 1948, where his first job was a house for his mother, Rose Seidler (now part of the Australian National Trust). Notable achievements are the Australia Square development (1960–71), for which Pier Luigi Nervi served as the engineer; Riverside Center, Brisbane (1983–87); the Australian embassy, Paris (1977–79); and the huge Wohnpark Neue Donau development in his native Vienna; as well as some sensitive private houses that emerge from their respective sites as interestingly as Frank Lloyd Wright's or, in a different vein, Richard Norman Shaw's. Two especially notable examples of his residential work are the Harry and Penelope Seidler House, Kilhara, North Sydney (1966–67) and the Berman House, Joadja, New South Wales, with its stunning, long, and cantilevered terrace (1996). He was a winner of the prestigious Queen's Gold Medal from the Royal Institute of British Architects in 1996 and the winner of the Gold Medal from the Royal Australian Institute of Architects in 1976. In 2003, in time for his eightieth birthday, he published his immensely useful and handsome book for all architectural afficionados, *The Grand Tour* (Taschen), a lifetime's accumulation of his photography of outstanding buildings all around the world.

SERT, JOSÉ LUIS (1902–1983)

Spanish architect who worked with Le Corbusier for three years and eventually emigrated to America in 1939 and succeeded Walter Gropius as professor of architecture at Harvard from 1953 to 1969. His design for the Spanish Republican Pavilion at the Paris International Exhibition of 1937 housed the painting of one of his contemporaries from Barcelona, Picasso's *Guernica*, and it is interesting that some of his best subsequent buildings also housed art: the coolly elegant Fondation Maeght, St. Paul de Vence, France (1959–64) and the Fundación Miró, Barcelona (1972–75).

SHAW, RICHARD NORMAN (1831–1912)

Leading British Arts and Crafts and Queen Anne Revival architect (always known as Richard Norman Shaw), whose work had a profound influence on American houses of the time. He was also the designer of the first garden suburb, Bedford Park, Turnham Green, London. He shared a practice with W. Eden Nesfield, and interestingly, began as a designer of churches in the Gothic style before moving away to various Picturesque country houses, sometimes timber-framed, sometimes stone, and generally more cozy in manner than Edwin Landseer Lutyen's grander versions but notable for their relationship with their landscape. Two of these last—his Glen Andred in Sussex (1868) and Grim's Dyke, Harrow, Middlesex (1870–72; now a hotel), executed in what became known as Shaw's "Old English style"—are said to have been a great influence on the exponents of the new Arts and Crafts movement. His London houses included Lowther Lodge, Kensington (1873), now the Royal Geographical Society; Shaw's own house, 6 Ellerdale Road, Hampstead (1875); and Swan House on the Chelsea Embankment (1876). He was also the architect for the New Scotland Yard building (1887–90) and what is now Bryanston School, Dorset (1889–94). Toward the turn of the century, he changed to a grander Classical style with Baroque details, as in the Piccadilly Hotel, London (1905).

SHERATON, THOMAS (1751–1806)

One of the great names in English eighteenth-century furniture design, although he does not appear to have had a workshop himself or to have played any part in the actual manufacture of any particularly distinguished furniture. Like Hepplewhite, he was known so widely as a result of his books and published patterns, which seem to have been avidly read and followed in America. He was born in Stockon-on-Tees, in the north of England, and worked for several years as a journeyman cabinetmaker. Around 1790, he arrived in London and set himself up as a drawing master and, among other activities, supplied designs to cabinetmakers. This was a sensible idea, since he had design experience as well as practical knowledge of the trade and was an extremely good draftsman. *The Cabinet-Maker and Upholsterer's Drawing Book* was published in four parts between 1791 and 1794 (and in three editions by 1802); it had 113 plates and explanations for all the designs, which were both detailed and practical. As a result, it provided an invaluable guide to the fashions in furniture at the end of the century. Sheraton explained that "finding no one individual equally experienced in every job of work," he had made it his business "to apply to the best workmen in different shops" and had drawn on his own experience as well as that "of other good workmen." His later works, *The Cabinet Dictionary* (1802 and 1803) and the first volume of his *Cabinet Maker Upholsterer and General Artist's Encyclopedia* (1805), were less successful,

Sheraton design for a lady's writing table

although the encyclopedia, if he had lived to complete it, would have been seminal in its sheer scope. It is worth noting that while he was writing that first volume, he employed for a short time Adam Black, the future publisher of the *Encyclopedia Britannica*, to whom he paid a pittance; he could afford no more. For all of Sheraton's future fame and success, the sad fact is that toward the end of his life he could barely make ends meet and died in penury.

SIZA VIEIRA, ALVARO (B.1933)

Portuguese architect and academic who has made enormous strides in low-cost housing among other outstanding building projects, from swimming pools to museums, winning Harvard's Prince of Wales Prize for his Malagueira Quarter Housing Project in Evora, Portugal. He was also the first Portuguese architect to be awarded the Pritzker Architecture Prize, which he won in 1992. He has been professor of architecture at Porto University, and visiting professor at the Graduate School of Design at Harvard, the University of Pennsylvania, the Los Andes University of Bogotá, Columbia, and the École Polytechnique of Lausanne, Switzerland. Other commissions include the new High School of Education at Setubal, Portugal; the Modern Art Museum for Porto, Portugal; the rebuilding of a burned area in Lisbon; an apartment building in Berlin, Germany; and the cultural center of the Ministry of Defense in Madrid, Spain.

SMIRKE, SIR ROBERT (1780–1867)

British Greek Revivalist architect, a pupil of Sir John Soane, and designer of the British Museum (1823–47) with its wonderfully dignified Ionic colonnade. After four years of fruitful traveling around Italy, Sicily, and Greece, sketching and learning all the way, he came back to London in 1805 and, after rather surprisingly designing a couple of medieval-style castles—Lowther Castle, Cumbria (1806–11) and Eastnor Castle, Herefordshire (1810–15)—he designed Covent Garden Theater (1808), the first Greek Doric building in London, which greatly impressed his contemporaries, although it was later destroyed. In 1813, he became one of the triumvirate of great Regency architects appointed to the Board of Works (along with Sir John Soane and John Nash) nearly two decades earlier than his German contemporary Karl Friedrich Schinkel secured much the same appointment in Berlin. Smirke's two greatest buildings, the British Museum and the General Post Office (1824–29) were both designed in the 1820s, although the latter was de-stroyed. Inevitably, since Schinkel designed the Altes Museum in Berlin (1823–30) at much the same time, comparisons are often made between the two museums. Schinkel's design is generally considered to be the more impressive, just as Schinkel is considered to be the more talented. Nevertheless, Smirke's buildings possess gravitas, great presence, and scholarly detailing.

SOANE, SIR JOHN (1753–1837)

Great late-eighteenth- and early-nineteenth-century British architect who was much influenced by the minimalist Greek Revivalism of some of Ledoux's work in Paris (he was said to share Ledoux's somewhat odd temperament). Later, like Karl Friedrich Schinkel in Germany, he became an exponent of the Romantic or Picturesque school and is considered to be one of the most original of all British architects. His work for the Bank of England from 1788 through the 1790s (now destroyed) was immensely advanced for the time, with its emphasis on structural simplicity and a reduction of the classical ornament of the day to mere grooved strips and embryonic moldings. He designed the equally original Dulwich College Art Gallery (1811–14), with its interestingly visually detached elements, and St. Peter's, Walworth, built to his design between 1823 and 1825. But his most idiosyncratic work was his own house—13, Lincoln's Inn Fields, London (1812–13)—with ingenious floor levels and experiments in perspective, Gothicized arches to give the illusion of separating ceilings from walls, extraordinarily original top lighting, and hundreds of mirrors to blur divisions and suggest receding planes. It is now the Sir John Soane Museum. Perhaps, too, in a sense, he was a forerunner of the 1980s Deconstructivists, with his evident delight in the apparent separation of various building elements.

SOTTSASS, ETTORE, JR. (B. 1917)

Italian furniture, interior, and industrial designer well known for his work from the 1960s.

STARCK, PHILIPPE (B. 1949)

Ubiquitous and extraordinarily prolific French architect and interiors, furniture, restaurant, product, lighting, and industrial designer. He seems to have put his hands to almost everything, from French President Mitterrand's offices and apartments in the Elysée Palace to the fashionable Café Costes in Paris (1982 and 1984, respectively); from the Royalton and Paramount hotels in New York (1988 and 1990) to the Sanderson and St. Martins Lane hotels in London (2000); and from other hotels and restaurants in the Far East to a whole raft of furniture, lights, bathroom fittings, and dining accessories.

STERN, ROBERT A. M. (B. 1939)

American architect and architectural historian, as well known for his writings and lively, inspirational television programs on architecture as for his buildings, many of which successfully combine tradition with innovation. This seems appropriate since so many of his commissions have had historic or nostalgic associations, such as the Observatory Hill Dining Hall at Thomas Jefferson and Benjamin Henry Latrobe's University of Virginia (1982–84); Prospect Point, La Jolla, California (1983–85); Copperflagg Development, Staten Island, New York (1983 onward); the Norman Rockwell Museum, Stockbridge, Massachusetts (1987–92); and a good deal of work for those indefatigable commissioners, Disney, in Disney Worlds in both Florida and Paris. His publications include *New Directions in American Architecture* (1969 and 1977); *Modern Classicism* (1988); and, with Thomas Mellins, David Fishman, Gregory Gilmartin, and Raymond W. Gast, a three-volume history of New York architecture and urbanism, *New York 1880, New York 1930,* and *New York 1960* (1983–95).

STIRLING, SIR JAMES FRAZER (1926–1992)

British architect, in partnership with James Gowan (b. 1923), who designed many innovative buildings, first in a fairly low-key New Brutalist style, then early High-Tech, and finally a kind of highly sophisticated Postmodernism. Stirling & Gowan originally became known for its Ham Common Flats in Richmond, London, in the mid-1950s, which were considered to be the best council or project buildings of their time. The firm's late 1950s/early '60s Engineering Department at Leicester University was certainly one of the first High-Tech buildings and, though quite avant-garde for the time, led to a number of university building commissions on both sides of the Atlantic, including the Sackler Gallery for Harvard University (1979–84) and the Performing Arts Center at Cornell University (1983–88). Michael Wilford (b. 1938) became another partner in

1971 and in the late 1970s the firm won the competition for the New Art Gallery at Stuttgart with its imaginative design, which also possessed a certain grandeur. This success led to the Clore Gallery extensions to the Tate Gallery in London (1980–87). Stirlings' last building was a monumental factory complex near Frankfurt, Germany (1986–92). In 1981 Stirling received the Pritzker Architecture Prize. Although all his buildings showed a convinced Modernism and were often somewhat ahead of their time, he was a great aficionado of Regency furniture, which he collected avidly.

STUART, JAMES "ATHENIAN" (1713–1788)

Eighteenth-century architect who, although not particularly dedicated to his own work, could still be called the father of the Greek Revival movement. He was instrumental in steering the Neoclassical movement, hitherto held in thrall by the glories of ancient Rome, toward the glories of ancient Greek architecture, and was the first to publish full scholarly measurements of the surviving monuments to antiquity in Athens (hence his nickname). The publication in 1762 of the first volume of his *Antiquities of Athens*, which he wrote with Nicholas Revett, a fellow Grecian enthusiast, turned Stuart into a temporarily formidable rival to Robert Adam. But only temporarily, since Adam tried—and succeeded—to do everything he could to blacken Stuart's name and to lower his architectural reputation.

SULLIVAN, LOUIS (1856–1924)

Grand old man of American Modernism, a founder of the innovative Chicago School, teacher of Frank Lloyd Wright, and an exponent of Art Nouveau–like decorational motifs before the style had even started in Europe, let alone in the United States. Boston-born, he studied for a short time at the Massachusetts Institute of Technology before moving to Chicago in 1873. He then worked briefly with the engineer and architect William Jenney (1832–1907), whose Home Life Insurance Building—with its iron girders, columns, and steel beams—paved the way for the revolutionary steel skeletons that made possible the first Chicago, and indeed any, skyscrapers. Sullivan next spent a year in Paris working in the studio of Joseph-Auguste-Émile Vaudremer, the first architect in the late nineteenth century to reintroduce the Romanesque style (as opposed to the ubiquitous Gothic style) for ecclesiastical architecture. It is worth mentioning here that Vaudremer (1829–1914) was also a mentor to Henry Richardson, who in his turn also influenced Sullivan. In any event, well prepared for his subsequent brilliant career, Sullivan returned to Chicago, where he went to work for Dankmar Adler (1844–1900), a German who had arrived in America at the age of ten. He became Adler's partner (forming the firm Adler and Sullivan) in 1881, and the two, enamored by the idea of functional expression, produced what must have been at the time an amazing building, an auditorium for over four thousand people (1886–90) with an interior that was embellished with Sullivan's peculiar brand of "feathery, vegetal decoration," thought-up before such vegetal motifs had emerged in Europe. The theater and skyscrapers that followed made use of steel skeleton structures and cellular interior planning. But for a man who begged for an end to decoration in his book *Kindergarten Chats* (1901), Sullivan managed to infuse quite a lot of decoration into his otherwise functional buildings. This was especially true in his and the Chicago School's best-known building, the Carson, Pirie & Scott Store (1899–1904), with its decorated front entrance.

**The Guaranty Building
(1894–95), Buffalo, New York,
by Dankmar Adler and
Louis Sullivan**

TANGE, KENZO (B. 1913)

The most respected of living Japanese architects born before World War I who, in his long and productive career, has had great influence over the younger generation. He first became known in 1949 when he won the competition for the Peace Center in Hiroshima (1950–55). Toward the end of the 1950s he evolved a new kind of style—one that quickly became a trend in Japanese architecture— by merging his strong feelings for Le Corbusier's austere forms with elements from traditional Japanese architecture. In the next decade he set the style somewhat upside down by combining a typical Japanese upswept roof in his Golf Club, Totsuka (1962), with aluminum curtain walls. Working with the Japanese engineer Yoshokatsu Tsuboi, Tange designed the huge sweep of roof that spanned the National Gymnasium, with its capacity for fifteen thousand people, for the Tokyo Olympics in 1964. His prowess in urban planning was first shown in 1960 with his proposal for simplifying or rationalizing the arrangement of streets for the less-than-well-planned city of Tokyo, as well as his idea for extending the city by building it out on piles over Tokyo Bay. Later, in 1965, he won the competition to replan Skopje in former Yugoslavia, and in 1987 he was awarded the Pritzker Architecture Prize, the first Japanese architect to win it. He continues to design various buildings and projects all over Japan with astonishing versatility.

TRUEX, VAN DAY (1904–1979)

Influential twentieth-century American designer who headed the Parsons School of Design in New York before taking over as design director of Tiffany & Co. His sure sense of design and style, which was a complex but unpretentious mix of Classicism and Modernism, had many admiring followers among the American interior design fraternity.

UTZON, JØRN (B. 1918)

Danish architect who is famous for designing the magnificent Sydney Opera House (completed 1973), now as much a symbol of Sydney and Australia as the Eiffel Tower is of Paris and France. Very little in Utzon's early work could have given a clue to the soaring, gleaming white, abstract sail-like structure that now lords over Sydney Harbor. He had designed some housing developments in Denmark based on his exploration of vernacular architecture in Mexico and North Africa, and he had introduced some interesting standardized units to a further project. His winning design—though perhaps *vision* would be a better word—for the Sydney Opera House Competition in 1956 was wholly unlike anything else that he had as yet brought to fruition, and came as a complete surprise, possibly as much to him as to anyone else. It took ten years—from 1963 to 1973—with the help of the engineering skills of Ove Arup to perfect the complicated but beautiful structure; yet even then it was in a somewhat modified form because Utzon had resigned in a welter of bitter argument, recriminations, and controversy about the ever-rising costs. The project was taken over by the young Australian Peter Hall, who courageously brought it to its culmination. Few of Utzon's detractors at the time could possibly have imagined the iconic status the building would achieve. Even so, some critics claim that Utzon's Bagsvaerd Church in Copenhagen (1969–76) is his finest achievement, and that his Muncipal Theater in Zurich, Switzerland (1964) and his National Assembly Building in Kuwait (1972–82) are also distinguished. In 2003, the thirtieth anniversary of the Sydney Opera House, Utzon was asked, as a somewhat belated tribute, to design the reception hall. The same year he was given the prestigious Pritzker Architecture Prize for lifetime achievement.

VANBRUGH, SIR JOHN (1664–1726)

Multitalented playwright and the most original English Baroque architect, who switched his talents from drama to house design "without thought or lecture," said Jonathan Swift rather tartly, when he heard Vanbrugh had been invited by the Earl of Carlisle to try his hand at designing Castle Howard (1699) without any training or qualification. Nevertheless, the house ended up as one of the most famous stately homes in Britain, and Vanbrugh became Christopher Wren's principal colleague. His other great baroque house was

Blenheim Palace (1705–24), but he designed numerous others, including King's Weston (1711–14) and Seaton Deleval (1720–28).

VAN DE VELDE, HENRY
(1863–1957)

Modernist Belgian architect, designer, and early Art Nouveau exponent whose radical theories led to the foundation of the Bauhaus. He started his career as a Pointillist painter but became enamored of the writings of John Ruskin and William Morris and switched first of all to Art Nouveau–inspired book decoration and typography, and then to designing his own house and furnishings. He rapidly became an ardent anti-ornamentalist: "It is dangerous," he said, "to pursue beauty for beauty's sake," and in his own house, the Villa Bloemenwerf (1895–96) at Ucce, near Brussels, he made it his policy to eschew decoration wherever possible. Since Van de Velde was very vocal and avant-garde, he gained the patronage

of the enlightened Grand Duke of Saxony, the art critic Julius Meier-Graefe, and, best for him commercially, the attention and patronage of Siegfried ("Samuel") Bing—the owner of the Parisian shop *Salon de l'Art Nouveau* (opened 1895) that gave Art Nouveau its name—who commissioned him to design interiors (see also *Art*

Villa Bloemenwerf (1895–96), at Ucce, near Brussels (showing an open section), designed by Henry van de Velde for himself

The Werkbund Theater (1914), Cologne, Germany, by Henry van de Velde (Note the dramatic change in style between Villa Bloemenwerf, designed twenty years earlier, and this building.)

Nouveau in Styles and Movements). In 1897 much of his work was shown at an exhibition in Dresden, Germany, where it was received with such great enthusiasm—greater than in Belgium or France—that in 1900 he moved there. Two years later Van de Velde was asked to Weimar by his patron, the Grand Duke Wilhelm, to be a consultant for the coordination of crafts, trades, and design; while there, he rebuilt the art school and eventually became director of the School of Arts & Crafts. When, being Belgian, he was forced to return to Belgium at the beginning of World War I, he suggested that Walter Gropius take over the school as director. And it was under Gropius that, in 1919, the school was renamed the Bauhaus.

VENTURI, ROBERT (B. 1925)

Scholarly American architect and theorist who dared to respond to the familiar Modernist chant of "less is more" with his own quip, "less is a bore." In 1966 he published his articulate polemic *Complexity and Contradiction in Architecture*—his first attack on the simplicity and clean lines of the International style. In 1967, he went into practice with his wife, Denise Scott-Brown (b. 1931), and soon welcomed Steven Izenour (b. 1930) to the firm, which became Venturi, Scott-Brown & Associates. A few years later, in 1972, the three published the equally articulate *Learning from Las Vegas*, which first established the tenets of Postmodernism and brought Venturi international status, though the movement itself did not really establish itself seriously until the mid-1970s. Although his early work concentrated on low-cost buildings, including his mother's house in Chestnut Hill, Philadelphia (many architects' first house designs are for their mothers), Venturi's later work has been a mixture of refinement and provocation, including several art museums: the extension to the Allen Memorial Art Gallery, Oberlin, Ohio (1976); the Seattle Art Museum, Seattle, Washington (1984–91); the Sainsbury Wing extension to the National Gallery in London (1986–91); and the Museum of Contemporary Art, San Diego, California (1996). In 1991 he was awarded the Pritzker Architecture Prize, the seventh American architect to become a Laureate.

VIOLLET-LE-DUC, EUGÈNE-EMMANUEL (1814–1879)

French nineteenth-century architect, scholar, theorist, medievalist, and architectural restorer noted, among other achievements, for his splendid restoration of the Sainte-Chapelle in Paris in conjunction with Felix-Jacques Duban (1797–1870). A combination of having spent a year in Italy studying buildings, having had a chance meeting with Prosper Merimee (1803–70)—the author of *Carmen*, as well as the inspector of the then newly founded Commission for Historical Monuments—plus his enthusiasm for the writings of Victor Hugo launched him on a study of the French Medieval period, of which he rapidly established himself as both scholar and restorer. In addition to Sainte-Chapelle, he restored the cathedral of Vézélay in Burgundy (1840) and Notre Dame in Paris (with Jean-Baptiste-Antoine Lassus, 1807–57), as well as the whole town of Carcassone (1844 onward). He became completely versed in the Gothic style and posited that the rib vaulting of the Gothic era was akin to the iron skeleton of the late nineteenth century. These and other fascinating theories about the Gothic were outlined in his *Dictionnaire raisonné de l'architecture française* (published 1854–68) and, particularly, in his two-volume *Entretiens* (1863 and 1872). In the latter, Viollet-le-Duc the Medieval scholar suddenly deserted the Middle Ages to become an ardent apologist for his own time, passionately promoting recent advances in engineering and the new building components and methods, especially the use of cast iron for supports, framework, and ribs. His writings were a forceful influence on Art Nouveau architects like Victor Horta and Antoní Gaudí, as well as on the early Modernists.

VOYSEY, CHARLES F. A. (1857–1941)

Well-known British Arts and Crafts architect and designer. He set up practice in 1882 and, under the general influence of William Morris, becoming as interested in domestic product design as in architecture. His earliest designs for textiles and wallpapers were in 1883 and his first house commissions date from 1888 to 1889. Like Van de Velde and Adolf Loos in Germany and Austria, he wrote of the importance of "discarding the mass of useless ornament" and set about turning functional features like staircases to decorative effect instead. His many country houses were a great influence on his fellow architects both in Britain and America.

WAGNER, OTTO (1841–1918)

One of the first real Modernists who greatly influenced Josef Hoffmann and Adolf Loos of the Wiener Werkstätte. As early as 1894, as professor of architecture at the Academy in Vienna, he was pleading for a new approach to architecture, for independence from the past, and for Rationalism ("nothing that is not practical can be beautiful"). His most interesting work was the Post Office Savings Bank, Vienna (1904–06). The exterior was faced in marble slabs held in place by aluminum bolts and the interior was topped with a glass barrel vault, not really matched in clarity or economy by any other building at that time.

WEBB, PHILIP SPEAKMAN (1831–1915)

Leading British Arts and Crafts architect, along with Richard Norman Shaw, of single-family houses, and a deeply influential proponent of the movement both through his friendship with William Morris—whose Red House (1859) he designed—and through his designs. The Red House became, in a way, a symbol of the time, at least for the more historically eclectic architects. Rather than referencing Classical tenets, its construction style of exposed brickwork chimneypieces, its haphazard asymmetry, and its lack of refined architectural details reverted back to the ancient, or medieval, English tradition of building. The house rapidly became the pattern for small English country and suburban domestic building and soon found a following in the United States as well.

WHITE, STANFORD

(See *McKim, Mead & White.*)

DE WOLFE, ELSIE (1865–1950)

Renowned American interior decorator who took up the profession at the beginning of the twentieth century, made every effort to do away with Victorian fustiness, and continued to reign more or less supreme in her field for some fifty years. She started by redecorating her own Victorian house in Manhattan; she painted some of her furniture white and gradually lightened, brightened, and softened every room. Her original inspiration was the style of Louis XVI with a good dose of American Colonial that she slowly paled down and down. The effect so impressed the architect Stanford White that in 1905 he suggested De Wolfe as the interior decorator for the building he was designing for the founders of the Colony Club, and she never looked back. The understated femininity of her style became very fashionable and her name (and money) was made when she was employed by Henry Clay Frick to decorate his house on Fifth Avenue, now the much-loved Frick Museum. Ogden Codman, joint author with Edith Wharton of the

influential book *The Decoration of Houses* (1898), became a good mentor for her with his love of eighteenth-century French style. Like Edith Wharton, she spent more and more time in France at her Villa Trianon in Versailles, which she bought together with an apartment in Paris, until she eventually lived there altogether. As famous for her parties as for her work, she eventually married the English Sir Charles Mendl, but they had to go back to the United States when World War II started. There, they moved to Hollywood, California, where Lady Mendl, as she then was, disguised what she called the ugliest house in the area with her by now classic mirrored walls, painted furniture, and masses of flowers. After the war she went back to Villa Trianon, where she died. "Suitability, suitability, suitability" was her message, and an excellent message it was, even if she did not always keep to the mantra herself.

WOOD, JOHN (THE ELDER) (1704–1754)

An English Palladian architect who revolutionized town planning with his scheme for Bath (started in 1727). He died just after the first stone for the exquisite Bath Circus was laid but his work was carried on by his son, John Wood the younger, who took his father's grand design a step further with the open planning for the magnificent Royal Crescent.

WOOD, RUBY ROSS (1880–1950)

Early southern American decorator of influence, as well as a design journalist and writer who actually ghostwrote Elsie de Wolfe's articles in the then *Delineator* magazine, edited by Theodore Dreiser, as well as De Wolfe's *A House in Good Taste* (1913). She wrote her own book, *The Honest House*, in 1914. Her always stylish, sensitively colored, sophisticated rooms had none of the showiness of Elsie de Wolfe's decoration and, in fact, became more understated as she subtly changed her style in the ensuing decades. She employed and enormously influenced that great decorator's decorator, Billy Baldwin, and for the fifteen years before she died, he hardly changed her signature look.

WREN, SIR CHRISTOPHER (1632–1723)

Considered to be the greatest British architect, architect to Charles II, and designer and rebuilder of St. Paul's Cathedral, London. Like Sir John Vanbrugh he started off in an entirely different career. Isaac Newton thought him the best geometrician of the day, and he was made professor of astronomy at the University of London in 1657 and professor of astronomy at Oxford in 1661. Had he died at thirty he would have been remembered only as a distinguished figure in British science. But after the Great Fire of London he was appointed to the commission for the restoration of St. Paul's and one of the surveyors under the Rebuilding of Act, London (1667). In 1669 he became surveyor general of the King's Works. His first buildings, Pembroke College Chapel (1663–65) and the Sheldonian Theater (1664–69), both in Oxford, were

the work of an extraordinarily gifted amateur. But from 1665 to 1666 he spent many months studying French architecture, mostly in Paris, and learned a very great deal from his French contemporaries Louis Le Vau and François Mansart. From then on he was much influenced by both French and Dutch architecture. He built 150 city churches between 1670 and 1686. Apart from St. Paul's, the grandest and most Baroque of all his work is Greenwich Hospital (1696 onward), with its wonderful Painted Hall (1698). Interestingly, although "Wren" houses were tremendously popular in America—as well as the idea of them a central part of the Queen Anne Revival in the late nineteenth century—no town or country house, apart from the Royal Marlborough House off the Mall in London, has ever been definitely attributed to him. Presumably he provided patterns that were subsequently published in America, as did so many of the great architects and furniture designers in the seventeenth, eighteenth, and early nineteenth centuries.

WRIGHT, FRANK LLOYD (1869–1959)

A towering figure among American architects whose work spanned sixty years, most of it decades before the influence of the Bauhaus or Le Corbusier was felt. He influenced both Walter Gropius and the De Stijl group well before 1920, although ironically, since he invariably pursued his own course, he did not really receive full international recognition, if that translates into large and regular commissions, until the last twenty years of his life. In the 1880s Wright took his first job with Joseph Lyman Silsbee (1848–1913), an architect who specialized in the "shingle style" (something like the houses of Charles F. A. Voysey, Philip Webb, and Richard Norman Shaw in England, but hung with shingles rather than tiles). He then moved to work under Louis Sullivan, to whom he was ever grateful as a mentor, working until 1893 on the domestic housing side of the practice. The two of them, as Nikolaus Pevsner pointed out in his classic *Pioneers of Modern Design*, were among the first few architects in the world, along with Otto Wagner, Adolf Loos, and Henry van de Velde in Europe, not only to admire and understand the essential character of the machine but also to realize its consequences to the relation of architecture, design, and ornamentation. Wright and Sullivan were also the pioneers of the innovative Chicago School of Architecture and, in the year after he left Sullivan and started on his own, Wright became a founding member of the Chicago Arts and Crafts Society. He called his first independent houses, built over five or six years in Chicago's outer suburbs such as Oak Park, "Prairie" houses, declaring that he wanted to design "a *natural* building for natural man"—and so they were, being low buildings built of "natural" materials, chosen for the beauty of their pattern and texture,

with projecting roof lines and terraces segueing into gardens just as inside, rooms segued into one another. Wright's Prairie houses were quite unlike the compartmentalized European interiors typical at the time, and indeed, he was sometimes criticized by European architectural contemporaries for not adopting a new attitude in response to the potential of the machine. However, a huge percentage of American houses have followed Wright's idea of rooms flowing into one another ever since. One of the most renowned of the influential Prairie series is the Robie House (1908, also in Chicago). The Larkin Building in Buffalo (1904, demolished 1950), the administrative building for the Larken Mail Order Co. and Wright's first major nonresidential commission, was reputed to possess just the same freshness and innovative use of space. In 1910 he left for Europe and on his return a year later started to build his own house, Taliesin, in Spring Green, Wisconsin—a house to which he kept adding for the rest of his life, and which he twice had to almost completely rebuild because of fires. The rough-textured stone complex was perched on a hill with far views all around, but Wright's building philosophy was fully expressed when he remarked that "No house should ever be 'on' any hill or 'on' anything. It should 'of' the hill, belonging to it, so hill and house could live together each the happier for the other." Certainly Wright's most famous domestic building—Falling Water in Mill Run,

Warren Hickox House (1900), Kankakee, Illinois, by Frank Lloyd Wright

Falling Water (1936), Bear Run, Pennsylvania, by Frank Lloyd Wright

Pennsylvania, designed in 1935 and built between 1936 and 1939 for Edgar J. Kaufmann—rises sheer out of the rock face above a waterfall and has been called variously "One of the most compelling examples of a man-made episode united with the landscape" and "One of the great houses of any architectural period." Wright also designed a circular factory building, the Johnson Wax Building in Racine, Wisconsin (1936–39). And later, still preoccupied with a circular theme "with no sense of enclosure whatever at any angle, top, or sides," he started in 1943 to design his iconic Guggenheim Museum (built between 1959 and 1965) in New York with its continuous spiral ramp used as both gallery, exhibition space, and means of circulation. He died before the structure was complete but with nearly five hundred buildings, an educational endowment, and some dozen books to his name.

WYATT, JAMES (1746–1813)

British late-eighteenth-century architect and contemporary of Robert Adam and William Chambers. He was thought much of in his day—though perhaps, more so now—and designed some beautiful Classical houses and interiors including the prized Heveningham Hall, Suffolk (1780–84) and Dodington, Gloucestershire (1798–1813). Some of his most famous Gothic Revival houses, however—such as Fonthill Abbey (1796–1812) designed for the

eccentric William Beckford, and his evidently exquisite but miniscule Lee Priory (1785–90)—were destroyed (although one room from the Lee Priory can be seen at the Victoria & Albert Museum, London). His apparently heavy-handed and insensitive ecclesiastical restorations of Salisbury Cathedral (1789–92) in Wiltshire, Durham Cathedral in County Durham and Hereford Cathedral (1786–96) in Herefordshire seem to have been deservedly less well received.

WYATVILLE, SIR JEFFRY (1766–1840)

Nephew of James Wyatt who rather grandly added the "ville" to the end of his name when he was knighted in 1828 for his picturesque restoration of Windsor Castle for King George IV. Part of his triumph at Windsor was raising the existing Round Tower 33 feet to make it a dominant feature and surrounding it with newly battlemented additions.

ARCHITECTURAL, BUILDING, AND DECORATING TERMS

The fate of the architect is the strangest of all. How often he expends his whole heart and passion to produce buildings in which he himself may never enter.

Johann Wolfgang von Goethe (1794–1832),
from *Elective Affinities*

No one can pretend that the language of building and buildings is simple. Quite apart from the fact that so many professionals seem to talk a different "building-speak" that can be confusing to laypeople, many architectural and building terms have their roots in Latin, Greek, French, or Italian. Moreover, the language and concepts of the great builders of classical antiquity and of the Italian Renaissance are still applicable today—even if they often have different shades of meaning in different countries. Of course the Classical orders and rules of proportion are sometimes turned on their side, exaggerated and even mocked. But they still act as a foundation to most Western building thought.

Then too, the introduction of new materials and the resulting new architecture has inevitably produced its own vocabulary. The introduction of rolled steel and reinforced concrete well over a century ago (concrete itself was invented by the ancient Romans)—followed by the introduction of plate glass, laminated woods, new tools, aluminum, plastics, and variations of them all—has revolutionized building. New types of buildings for a modern world have also challenged architecture to remake itself time and again—buildings such as skyscrapers, hospitals, factories and industrial plants, public housing projects, sporting facilities, university buildings, schools, opera houses, arts centers, and suspension bridges as well as mass-produced and standardized industrialized housing. Add to the old and new architectural and building terms the language of decoration (excluding the decorative terms that apply specifically to other subjects in this dictionary, such as Fabric and Wallpaper, Windows and Window Treatments, and so on), and the vocabulary can become as confusing as it is enormous. This section aims to disentangle and explain these terms as simply as possible.

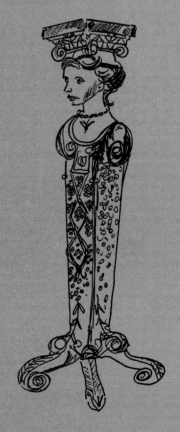

ABACUS

The flat slab of wood or marble on the top of the capital on a column. In the Greek Doric order, the abacus will be an thick unadorned square. If the order is Roman Doric, Roman or Greek Ionic, or Tuscan, the abacus will be a square with a molded lower edge; if Corinthian or Composite, the abacus will have cutoff corners and concave sides. (See also *Classical orders*.)

ABUTMENT

The junction between one building surface and another—as where the roof of one house joins the gable wall of another. Or, in wallpapering, butting one piece of paper up against another.

ACOUSTIC PANELS

Panels—made of sound-absorbing material—used to deaden sound, usually applied directly to hard wall surfaces or suspended from the ceiling, although they can be made to stand independently in, say, open office plans.

ACOUSTIC TILES

Rectangular panels, approximately 12 x 12 inches, normally made of pulped wood, fiberglass, or compressed Styrofoam pellets or mixtures. Like acoustic panels, they are used for deadening sound; they are also used to improve insulation or to disguise a ceiling in poor condition.

ACOUSTICS

The control or reduction of sound transmission and reception, including the reinforcement and implementation of sound.

ACROLITH

A Classic Greek statue—often sheathed in gold in its original form—with the torso made of wood and the limbs and head carved in marble.

ACROTERIA

In Classical architecture, the blocks or plinths at the apex and the lowest end of a pediment, usually used to hold a vase, statue, or bust. The term is sometimes used to describe both a plinth *and* what stands on it.

ADDORSED

Term describing two figures, often animals, placed back to back and found on capitals, thereby forming the head or crowning feature of a column.

ADELPHI

Greek word for *brothers* and the trademark name for the Adam Brothers, who worked in the late eighteenth century.

ADMIXTURE

Additional agent to speed up or slow down the drying time of mortar. Also, a water-repellent or coloring agent added to mortar.

ADOBE

A brick of sun-dried earth and straw used for buildings in Spain, New

Mexico, and Latin America. Also, a building made with adobe bricks.

AEDICULE OR AEDICULA

A small Classical-era shrine framed by two columns supporting an entablature and pediment; or the framing in a similar manner of a window or door; or, more simply, a niche for a statue. Much later, in the nineteenth century, aediculae windows were transformed to look like miniature shrines, framed with two columns, an entablature, and a pediment with, very often, a balcony. A version of this, usually without the columns and the entablature, is seen on the second floor of nineteenth-century town houses throughout France and much of Europe.

AFFRONTED

Term describing two figures, often animals, facing each other and usually found on capitals, thereby forming the head or crowning feature of a column. They are the reverse of *addorsed*.

AGORA

The open space in a Greek or Roman town that was used as a general meeting place or market. It was usually surrounded by porticoes.

AIR BRICK

Perforated brick allowing air to enter and pass through a wall.

AISLE

A walkway in a church (or walkways, if a church is large) parallel to the nave

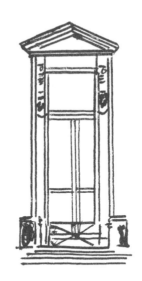

Two aediculae
(the bottom one with
French doors and a balcony)

or central body of the church and the choir stalls, and separated from the nave by an arcade or colonnade. It can also be just the passageway between rows of benches or seats for either a public space or a congregation.

AKROTER

The decoration at the top angle of the pediment on ancient Classical structures. More often than not, it was some sort of variation on a palmette motif, though other devices—such as griffins, various animals, and so on—were also used.

ALABASTER

Semitranslucent, milky white marble-like mineral used for ornaments and sculpture. In Byzantine design it was sometimes used, cut wafer thin, as a window covering to filter and softly whiten daylight.

ALETTE

A small addition to or extra wing on a building. Also, the interior side of a door or window frame, known also as the jamb.

ALKYD

A synthetic resin used instead of oil as a base for paints. Alkyd paints have now largely replaced the oil variety.

ALLOY

A mixture of two or more metals, blending the qualities of both, to create a new metal.

ALMONRY

The room in a monastery from which alms were distributed.

ALTAR

A table or slab on supports consecrated for the celebration of the sacraments.

ALTAR-TOMB

Post-medieval term for a tomb with solid sides that resembles an altar.

ALTO-RILIEVO

Italian term often used for a high-relief sculpture in which the carved area projects beyond the main surface, as in a medallion.

ALUMINUM

Light but strong, hard, corrosion-resistant, silver-colored metal that is also malleable. It is a good heat conductor and can be spun, pressed, or cast. It was first used in the form of duralumin to make zeppelins in World War I, then for architecture, notably for Buckminster Fuller's Dymaxion house (see also *Fuller, Buckminster* in Architects, Designers, and Decorators), for mass-market prefabricated housing after World War II, and for cladding; but it is also used for kitchenware, furniture frames, and outdoor furniture.

AMBIENCE

The overall effect of a room or home.

AMBO

A prominent feature in many Italian early-medieval churches consisting of a stand raised on two or more steps for the reading of the Epistle and the

Gospel. After the fourteenth century the ambo was replaced by the pulpit.

AMORINO

Italian for "little love," a small cupid or cherub used in carved or painted decoration during the Italian Renaissance. It was used again in the Louis XV Rococo period and by the Adam Brothers in ceiling and wall panel decorations. The plural is *amorini*.

AMPHIPROSTYLE

Term applied to a temple with porticoes at either end, but without columns along its sides.

AMPHITHEATER

An elliptical or circular space with rising tiers of seats or steplike structures surrounding a stage or arena. This seating arrangement, first used by the Greeks for plays, was later adopted by the Romans for their gladiatorial contests.

ANAGLYPTA

Greek word for "raised ornament" (a similar word, *anaglypha*, is a metal vase with relief ornamentation). The Adam Brothers invented a technique called *carton-pierre*, or composite ornament, for making anaglyptas in gesso and plaster compounds that were poured into a form and molded. The molded pieces were then used for ceilings and furniture to simulate a carved or bas-relief effect. The word now refers to an especially tough wallpaper with a raised design. (See also *Anaglypta* in Fabric and Wallpaper.)

ANCONES

Brackets or consoles on either side of a doorway to support a cornice.

ANCHOR BOLT

Long metal device used to ensure maximum stability for cornices and pinnacles.

ANGLE IRON

Right-angled or L-shaped bar used for reinforcement and usually made of rolled steel.

ANGLE BRACE OR ANGLE TIE

A timber that joins the wall plates across the corner of a building with a hipped roof. Also, a strip of material that is fixed across a frame to make it rigid.

ANNULET

Similar to a shaft-ring. One of the fillets around a Greek Doric capital, or a band of molding around a Norman column, or a ring of molding holding together a group of column shafts in Gothic architecture. Also, a twelfth- and thirteenth-century motif.

ANTA

A pilaster with a base and capital that do not conform with the order or style of the columns and pilasters used elsewhere in a building. It is usually used in a corner.

ANTEFIX OR ANTEFIXAE

A fanlike ornament, such as a spreading leaf, originally used in Classical decoration to conceal the end of a roof tile.

ANTHEMION

Stylized ornament—common in Classical and Neoclassical architecture—based on the leaves and flower of the honeysuckle.

APEX STONE

The top stone in a gable end, or the triangular upper portion of a wall to carry a pitched roof.

APOPHYGE

The slight concave curve at the top and bottom of a column where the shaft joins the capital. There is no apophyge on a Greek Doric column as opposed to the Roman variety.

APPAREIL EN EPI

French term used for bricks laid in a herringbone pattern.

APPLIED MOLDING

Shaped molding applied to the face of a wall or door (or piece of furniture) to create a paneled effect.

APPLIQUÉ

French term for a wall bracket or a sconce applied to a wall.

APSE

In a Christian church or chapel, a vaulted semicircular or angular termination to a chancel, usually placed at the east end of a nave beyond the transcept.

AQUEDUCT

An artificial channel invented by the Romans for carrying water. It is usually elevated on stone or brick structures.

ARABESQUE

Intricate surface decoration generally based on plant tendrils and leaves, sometimes with the additions of Classical vases, sphinxes, and so on.

ARAEOSTYLE

An arrangement of columns set four diameters apart.

ARCADE

A range of arches either carried on freestanding piers or columns, or attached to a wall.

ARCH

A usually carved structural member spanning an opening that helps to support the wall or weight above the opening. There are many different shapes of arch: A *horseshoe arch*—like a rounded horseshoe—is often found in Islamic buildings. A *lancet arch* is pointed. An *ogee arch*, introduced in the thirteenth century and popular through the fourteenth century, is pointed and usually consists of four arcs: two arcs inside the arch itself, the other two outside. A *pointed* or *equilateral arch* is produced by two curves, each with a radius equal to the span and meeting in a point at the top. A *shouldered arch* consists of a lintel connected with the jambs of a doorway by corbels. A *Tudor arch* is a late-medieval pointed arch with shanks that start with a curve near to a quarter circle and continue on to the apex in a straight line.

ARCHED BRACE ROOF

A roof formed by a pair of curved braces (which are subsidiary timbers set to strengthen the roof frame) in the shape of an arch. The arched braces connect the wall or post below with the tie or collar beam above.

ARCHITECTURAL BRIEF

The detailed instructions given by the client to the architect on his or her needs. These instructions and requirements are what the architect will use as the starting point for his or her building concept and suggested plans. A similar brief should be given to interior designers or decorators.

ARCHITRAVE

Generally, the molded frame surrounding a door or window; specifically, the lowest of the three main parts or moldings of a Classical entablature.

ARCHIVOLT

The continuous architrave molding on the face of an arch, following its contour.

ARENA

The central open space of an amphitheater.

ASHLAR

Hewn or evenly faced or evenly shaped blocks of stone or masonry, as opposed to rubble or unhewn stone brought straight from a quarry.

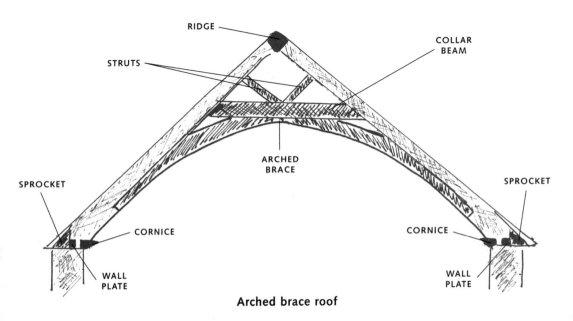

Arched brace roof

ASTRAGAL

A small, rounded beadlike molding. It sometimes includes reel-like or bobbinlike shapes, and then it is called "bead and reel." The term is also used to describe the glazing bars on cabinet doors.

ASTYLAR

A term applied to the plain facade of a building unadorned by columns or pilasters.

ATELIER

French term for a designer's, artist's, or specialist craftsperson's workshop or studio.

ATLANTES

Supports in the form of male figures utilized, instead of columns, to support an entablature, or an architrave, frieze, and cornice. Mostly used in German Baroque architecture. The Roman term was *telamones*.

ATRIUM

An inner court open to the sky and surrounded by the roof, formerly used in Roman domestic architecture. In the context of medieval architecture the term denoted an open space in front of a church, sometimes in the form of a colonnaded quadrangle.

BACK-FILLING

Rough masonry behind the facing material of an arch. Also, brickwork used to fill in between studs in a frame building, which is sometimes called *brick noggin*.

BACKUP

The masonry wall behind the final exterior facing on a building.

BAGUETTE OR BAGNETTE

A small French bread-shaped molding, as the name implies, like an astragal. It is usually part of a string, as in a frame with a small bead molding.

BAILEY

The courtyard of a castle, also known as a *ward*.

BALDACHINO

A canopy supported by columns, usually over an altar in a church. Also, a portable canopy.

BALLOON FRAMING

Method of wood-frame construction in which the studs or uprights are made to run from the sill to the eaves; the horizontal members are then nailed to them.

BANDED DRUM

A column, popular in the French Renaissance period, that has a lower drum, often richly decorated, with a diameter slightly larger than the shaft.

BANDEROLE

A carved or painted ribbonlike motif often used in Renaissance decoration and sometimes filled with an inscription.

BALUSTER

A vertical support in stone or wood for a staircase handrail or landing balustrade.

BALUSTRADE

The assembly of handrail, structural (or newel) post, balusters, and sometimes a bottom rail that flanks a staircase or landing.

BANISTER

A handrail for a staircase. Also, used to refer to the handrail and its supporting posts.

BAPTISTRY

A building, often separate from a church, containing a font for baptisms.

BARGE BOARD

The boards, often decorated, that are fixed to the incline of a gable wall of a building to hide the ends of the horizontal roof timbers.

Barge boarding

BARLEY SUGAR TWIST

Continuous carved twist that is used on some wood columns, chair legs and backs, and side-table legs, and for banisters or balusters.

BARREL VAULT

Made of stone or brick, it is the simplest form of a vaulted or arched ceiling. It consists of a continuous vault of semicircular or pointed sections. Buttressing, dispersed all along the wall beneath, is needed to support the thrust.

BARTISAN

A small turret projecting from the angle or turn on top of a tower or parapet.

BASALT

Dark green or brown stone often used in Egyptian statues and much used in the French Empire period for tabletops because of its Egyptian associations.

BASE

In architectural terms the bottom of the shaft of a column consisting of a series of moldings that help to distribute the weight.

BASEBOARD

Horizontal board, usually trimmed with molding, placed at the bottom of a wall to cover the juncture between wall and floor.

BASILICA

In Roman architecture it was an oblong building used for administrative purposes, with double colonnades inside and a semicircular apse at the end. Many were later converted into Christian churches, which is how the term came to be applied to ecclesiastical architecture.

BASKET GRATE

A freestanding iron basketlike grate first designed to burn logs and, later, coal.

BAS-RELIEF

Universally adopted French term for low-relief sculpture or carving in which the design is raised only very slightly from the background surface.

BASTIDE

An old French house, generally fortified.

BASTION

A projection (much the same as a bartisan) at the angle or corner of a fortification from which the garrison could see and defend the ground in front of the ramparts.

BAT

In masonry terms, a part of a brick; half a bat is half a brick.

BAT'S WING BRASS

An early American hardware design, shaped like outstretched bat's wings, used for handles and escutcheons. Also, a decoratively shaped plate, for backing keyholes, doorknobs, or pulls.

BATTEN

A narrow strip of wood applied to cover the seam between two parallel boards in the same plane.

BATTLEMENT

A parapet with alternating indentations or embrasures.

BAY

A subdivision of an interior space, usually one in a series divided by consecutive supports, such as columns or shafts, or in the ceiling by beams, transverse arches, and so on. Bays can also take the form of external divisions of a building marked by windows or buttresses.

BAY LEAF GARLAND

A Classical decorative motif generally used to enrich large convex moldings.

BAY WINDOW

A window that protrudes from the main wall of a building at ground level, with its own sidewalls and roof.

BEAD MOLDING

Small cylindrical molding resembling a string of beads.

BEAKHEAD

A Norman decorative motif. It involves a row of carved stone bird, animal, or human heads ostensibly biting, or at least holding in their mouths, a continuous decorative molding or projection around a building that is meant either to throw an interesting shadow or to deflect rainwater from the stonework.

BEEHIVE HOUSES

Primitive circular structures built of rough stone set in projecting courses to form a dome. They are still inhabited in Puglia in southeast Italy, where they are known as *trulli*.

BELFRY

Derived from the old French word *berfrei*, meaning tower, it is the upper room or story of a tower in which bells are hung. Also, the timber frame inside a church steeple to which bells are fastened.

BELVEDERE

Italian term for "beautiful view." In architecture it is the uppermost story of a building, open on several sides to allow good views of the surrounding countryside and to let in cooling breezes. Sometimes a lantern-like structure on top of a building, seen particularly in English Renaissance architecture, is also called a belvedere.

BETON BRUT

Adopted French term for "concrete in the raw"; it refers to concrete that is left in its natural state when the formwork, or shuttering, that is the temporary form into which wet concrete is poured, has been removed.

BEVEL

To cut the edge off a piece of wood or stone so that it slants at either more or less than a 45-degree angle. (See also *chamfer*.)

BILLET

A Romanesque or Norman molding made from several bands of raised short cylinders or squared pieces placed at regular intervals. This type of banding was also used for eighteenth-century furniture as inlays around cabinet doors and drawers.

BLIND ARCADE

A nonstructural decorative arcade, with no actual opening, applied to a wall.

BOISERIE

Paneling decorated with carved or molded designs in the French styles of Louis XIV, XV, and XVI.

BOLECTION MOLDING

A molding most often used around wall or door panels, but also around some fireplaces. The molding stands proud of the framing member and is often shaped in a double curve or ogee.

**Edwardian
bolection molding**

**Georgian
bolection moldings**

BOSS

Ornamental knob or projection covering the intersection of ribs in a vault or ceiling, or at the intersection of beams or moldings. Angel or animal heads, foliage, or flowers are common motifs.

BOTTLE GLASS

Pieces of blown glass disks that have been broken off from the blowpipe during manufacture; now often copied in an attempt to make glass windowpanes look old. Also called bull's-eye panes.

BOW WINDOW

A late-eighteenth- or early-nineteenth-century curved window that was mostly used for shops and taverns or inns.

BRACKETS

A support, often S-shaped and either plain or decorated, for projecting features like shelves or cornices.

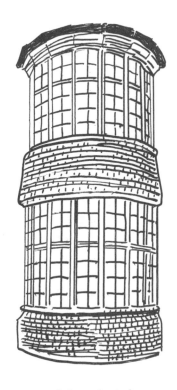

**A two-storied
double bow window**

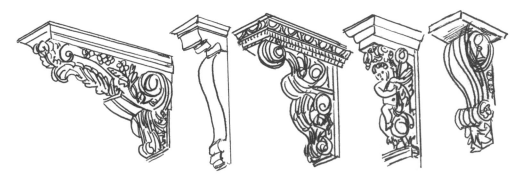

Some decorative brackets

BRATTISHING

An ornamental cresting (edging) or pierced parapet on the top of a cornice, paneling, or screen.

BRESSUMER

A heavy beam used as a massive structural lintel across a wide opening.

BRICK VENEER OR BRICK FACING

A facing of brick laid against a wall but not structurally bonded to the wall. (See also *mathematical tile*.)

BUILDING BOARD

Another term for Sheetrock or plasterboard. Made from repulped paper, gypsum, shredded wood, and other plaster compositions sandwiched between sheets of kraft paper. Building board is usually manufactured in 4 x 8-foot panels and fixed on to lathing strips to create partition walls or ceilings.

BULLNOSE EDGE

Deep, nearly half-round edge on marble or wood tabletops or other pieces of furniture.

BULL'S-EYE WINDOW

A round window. Also, the circular distortion in the center of a disk of crown glass, sometimes known as oeil-de-boeuf. A bull's-eye mirror is another name for a convex or concave mirror set in a circular frame.

BUTT JOINT

The simplest, cheapest type of carpentry joint whereby one piece of wood is butted perpendicular and at right angles to another and then glued, screwed, or nailed together. Such a joint cannot take much strain.

BUTTERFLY WEDGE

Double V-shaped fastener that, since the Vs connect at their points, looks rather like a butterfly. It is used to hold adjoining boards together.

An elaborate Rococo bull's-eye window in Colonial America, c. 1700

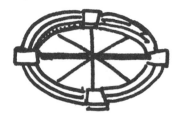

An oval bull's-eye window

CABLE MOLDING

A Romanesque molding that imitates a twisted cord.

CABLED FLUTING

A form of fluting, usually used for pilasters, in which the lower part of each flute is filled with a convex molding.

CAISSONS

Ornamental sunken panels or squares in a ceiling, dome, vault, or arch soffit, found originally in Classical architecture. Also called *coffers* or *coffering*, or *lacunar*. Also, a term for watertight chambers used in construction below water or waterlogged ground.

CAMBER

A surface with a minimal curve, like the soffit or underside of an arch.

CAMBERED COLLAR

A horizontal piece of timber that is slightly curved, like a very shallow arc, and joins two principal rafters.

CAMBERED LINTEL

A shallow, arched timber, stone, or concrete structural component that carries the load over a window or door.

CAME

A soft metal strip used to hold together pieces of glass in stained glass or leaded windows.

CAMEO

A low-relief carving. Cameos were used for decoration on walls and for furniture in the later eighteenth century.

CAMP CEILING

A ceiling that follows the line of the rafters at the sides but is flat across the middle; similar to an attic ceiling. Also, a ceiling with an inward curve suggesting a tent.

CAMPANILE

Italian for "bell tower," a campanile is either round or square and is sometimes freestanding.

CANCELLI

A latticed screen or grille separating the choir from the main body of the church in early ecclesiastical architecture.

CANEPHORA

A sculpted female figure carrying a basket on her head; a device often used as a decorative support for shelves during the Italian and French Renaissance periods.

CANTED

A term usually applied to large elements such as the angles of a half-octagonal bow window, but also something that is angled, sloped, slanted, beveled, or chamfered.

CANTILEVER

A projecting beam or slab supported at one end only. Its stability depends upon the amount of loading applied to the tethered end.

CAP

Shortened term for *capital*, used to describe the moldings at the top of a pilaster, column, or newel-post on a staircase.

CAPITAL

The top part of any column where it spreads to take the load. The capital may consist of carving or molding, depending upon its style or period. Also, the top part of a Classical pilaster.

CARREL OR CAROL

A niche inserted into the wall of a cloister for a monk to sit and read.

CARTON-PIERRE

An easily molded and carved gessolike or plaster of paris–like substance, much used by Robert Adam and other architects and decorators of the eighteenth century, to add high- or low-relief ornament to ceilings, paneling, and furniture. Like gesso, it was first sized and then painted or gilded.

CARTOON

A full-sized, fully detailed drawing used as the plan for a mural, painted panel, or painting. The term derives from the Italian *cartone*.

CARTOUCHE

A convex lozenge shape often edged with elaborate molding to frame some kind of inscription or heraldic figure or figures.

CARYATID

A sculpted female figure used as a column or to support a Classical entablature.

CASSOON

Another name for a sunken panel in a vault or ceiling.

CASINO

A building designed for gambling purposes but originally an ornamental pavilion on the grounds of a large house, and in the eighteenth century, a salon for dancing.

CAST

Generally a plaster-of-paris reproduction of a piece of sculpture.

CAST IRON

Iron containing 3.5 percent carbon, which was first made by the British Darby family in the early eighteenth century, who smelted iron ore with coke instead of the traditional charcoal. Cast-iron columns first appeared as structural elements in 1780, and became a central ingredient of architecture and interiors during the Art Nouveau period.

CATHEDRA

The bishop's chair or throne. It was originally placed behind the high altar in the center of the curved wall of the apse. The word *cathedral*, identifying or designating a church that is the official seat of a diocese's bishop, is derived from this term, as is the term *ex cathedra*, meaning from the bishop's chair or seat of authority.

CATHEDRAL CEILING

High pitched ceiling in a modern home that is somewhat reminiscent of its ecclesiastical counterpart.

CAVETTO

A hollow molding that curves inward, about a quarter of a circle in section.

CELLA

The main body of a classical temple without the portico.

CENTERING

The wooden framework used in the construction of a stone or plaster arch or vault. It is removed, or "struck," when the mortar or plaster has set.

CESSPIT

Large underground waterproof storage tank into which drains are run. Cesspits are mainly used in rural settings where "mains" sewage systems are not an option. It is essential that they be pumped out at regular intervals.

Pair of caryatids

Caryatids used as columns on either side of an elaborate eighteenth-century fireplace

CHAIR RAIL

A molded wood or plaster decoration that runs around the walls of a room about a third of the way up—or at whatever level prevents the backs of chairs from doing damage to the wall finish.

CHAMFER

A symmetrical cut of 45 degrees on beams and lintels that usually dates from the seventeenth century or earlier.

CHANCEL

The part of a church where the main altar is placed, generally reserved for the clergy and choir.

CHEVRON

A zigzag form of ornament much used on Norman arches.

CHIMNEY BREAST

The stone or brick structure projecting into or out of a room and containing the flue.

CHIMNEY SHAFT

A high chimney with only one flue.

CHIMNEY STACK

Masonry or brickwork containing several flues, projecting above the roof, and finishing with chimney pots.

CHIMNEYPIECE

The wood, brick, stone, or marble frame surrounding a fireplace, sometimes with an overmantel or mirror above. Also called a mantelpiece.

CINCTURE

Small, convex molding used around the shaft of a column.

CLADDING

Weatherproofing or decorative surface fixed to the structural element of a wall, such as slates, clapboard, tiles, and so on.

CLAPBOARD

American term (pronounced clabbered) for weatherboarding or cladding on houses. Clapboarding protects outer structural elements from the weather.

CLASSICAL ORDERS

The five styles of ancient architecture—Tuscan, Doric, Ionic, Corinthian, and Composite—based on the proportions and decoration of different types of columns. Sometimes, too, the cycle of all design is based on the sequence: Tuscan and Doric (spare and simple); Ionic (more ornamental); Corinthian (highly ornamental); and Composite (a late Roman composite of elements from both the Ionic and the Corinthian columns). In many ways the flow of design and architectural styles do seem to follow that order over and over again. *Orders* is a term frequently used to refer to column design, but in Classical architecture even the proportions of the different sections of a wall could be based on those of a column.

COMPOSITE   CORINTHIAN   IONIC   DORIC   TUSCAN

The Classical orders of architecture

CLERESTORY WINDOW

Window placed near the ceiling of a high room or hall in order to receive light from above the roofs of neighboring buildings. Also, windows piercing the upper story of the nave of a church.

CLOCHER

French term for *bell tower*.

CLOISTER

A quadrangle or courtyard surrounded by roofed or vaulted passages connecting the domestic parts of a monastery with the monastic church or chapel.

CLOSED-STRING STAIRCASE

Strings are actually the main framing members forming the sides of a staircase. *Closed-string* varieties have their treads housed in the strings, as opposed to an *open-string* staircase, in which the shape of the stairs is cut out with the treads resting on the string. *Wall-string* stairs are fixed to the wall of the stairwell.

COADE STONE

Artificial stone invented by Mrs. Eleanor Coade in the 1770s, and later marketed by Coade and Sealy of London. It was very widely used in the late eighteenth and nineteenth centuries for all types of ornamentation.

COLLAR

A metal cap flashing for a vent pipe that projects above a roof deck, or a raised band that encircles a metal shaft, a wood dowel, or a wood leg. In Europe it is also a horizontal timber spiked to each pair of rafters in a roof to restrain any tendency for the ends of the rafters to pull apart under pressure.

COLLAR BEAM

An English term for a horizontal tension member that runs between the principal rafters of a roof truss. Usually, it has the same thickness as the principal rafters and is morticed-and-tenoned into them.

COLLAR PURLIN

A roof timber that runs below the center of every collar in a series of trusses. It is usually supported in its turn by crown posts.

COLONNADE

A series of regularly-spaced columns that support a lintel or entablature.

COLUMN

Vertical, rounded support for an entablature or arch, varying in shape according to style or Classical order. In fact, the shape of columns is a major factor in determining Classical styles.

COMPOSITE ORDER

Classical Roman order that combines features of the Ionic capital with the Corinthian one.

CONTRACT USE

Term referring to building or furnishing goods of whatever sort supplied to a commercial rather than a domestic building.

CONCRETE

(See *Concrete* in Flooring.)

COPING

A course of quite substantial stones that usually tops a parapet or upstanding gable wall.

CORBEL

A support—usually in stone but sometimes in wood—that projects from a wall to carry the load of a structural member such as a beam.

CORINTHIAN ORDER

Classical order of architecture (along with Tuscan, Doric, Ionic, and Composite). The capitals on Corinthian columns are freely decorated with acanthus leaves and other ornamental devices. It is the most elaborately decorated of the five orders of columns and was a Greek invention of the fifth century B.C. Later adopted and slightly embellished by the Romans, the Corinthian order would, even later, become the prototype for architectural form in the Italian Renaissance.

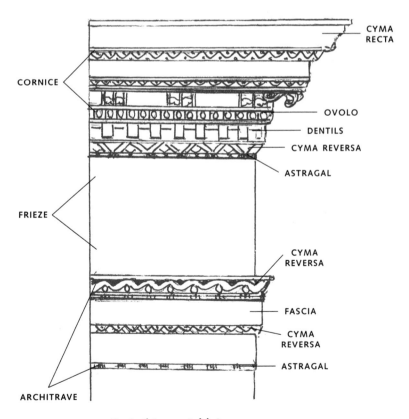

Corinthian entablature

CORNICE

The top of the three parts of a Classical entablature and composed of several different moldings, usually with a fillet and cyma recta (like an asymmetrical flattened-out S-shape with the hollow curve uppermost). Also, the decorative molding that runs around a room at the juncture between ceiling and wall, or any projecting ornamental molding along the top of a building, wall, or arch that finishes or crowns it.

Some decorative cornices

CORRUGATED CONCRETE

Concrete molded with alternate ridges and grooves so that it looks somewhat like corrugated paper.

CORTILE

Italian word for "courtyard"; it is usually internal and surrounded by arcades.

COTTAGE ORNE

An artificial or deliberately rustic building, often with a thatched roof, clapboard, and roughly hewn wooden columns. Such buildings, mostly used for park lodges or pastoral buildings, were products of the Picturesque style of the late eighteenth and early nineteenth centuries in Britain and the United States.

COUNTER BATTEN

Slim fillet of wood nailed to battens running in the opposite direction to provide adequate fixing points for boards, plasterboard, wall boarding, or lathes.

COVE

Large concave molding used like a cornice to join walls to ceilings.

CROWN GLASS

Glass blown into a disk and then cut out to form crown-glass windowpanes or "lights," as they were known up to the nineteenth century. It was the main method of filling in the space between the window mullions until 1830.

CROWN MOLDING

The very top molding above the fascia in a Classical cornice. Also, sometimes the generic term for the cornice between the ceiling and the wall.

CROWN POST

Any vertical timber in a roof truss, especially a king post. The timber is placed in the center of a tie beam, the main horizontal transverse timber in a roof. Longitudinal braces then rise from the crown post to support a collar purlin,

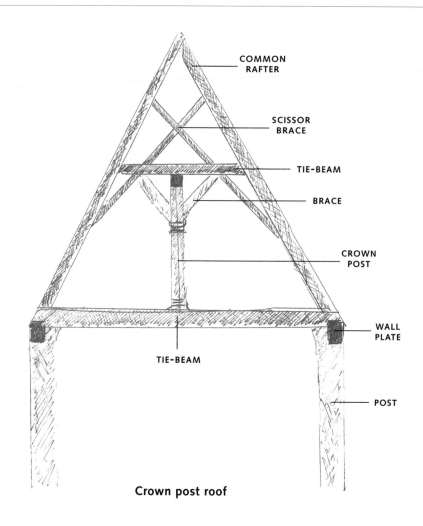

Crown post roof

the single central timber in a roof that carries the collar beams, the transverse timbers that connect pairs of rafters between the apex of a roof and the wall plate. This not only sounds but looks complicated. Examining old roof posts and beams is a fairly fail-safe way of dating a house. (See also *roof construction*.)

CRUTCH OR CRUCK

One of a pair of stout curved timbers that, with a branched effect, rise from the outer walls to support the ridge beam.

They can take the place of both posts for the walls and rafters for the roof. Crutches were used to form the principal framing of old English houses or farm buildings.

CURTAIL STEP

The bottom step of a staircase that is projected sideways and curled around like a dog's tail.

CUSP

Gothic tracery usually took the form of trefoil or quatrefoil ornamentation.

A quatrefoil is composed of four curves, and where they join forms the cusp.

CYMA RECTA

Molding with a double S-shaped curve, concave above and convex below. Also known as an *ogee molding*.

CYMA REVERSA

Molding similar to cyma recta, but instead it is convex above and concave below. It is also known as a *reverse ogee molding*.

DADO

Wood, or simulated-wood, paneling running around the lower part of a room from baseboard to chair or dado rail, or simply to waist height. In Classical terms it is the portion of a plinth or pedestal between the base and the cornice.

DADO RAIL

The piece of molding that divides the dado from the rest of the wall.

DAMP-PROOF COURSE

A layer of impervious material built into the thickness of a wall to prevent moisture rising from the ground into the main structure.

DAMP-PROOF MEMBRANE

Usually a layer of plastic sheeting used in restoration work for damp-proofing.

DEMI-LUNE

Half-moon or elliptically shaped window.

DENTIL

A small, square, tooth-shaped block molding used in series in Ionic, Corinthian, Composite, and, very occasionally, Doric cornices. Also used on its own as a type of molding or cornice in its own right.

DISTRESS

To age a material artificially, whether by scoring, denting, chipping, staining, or by faux painting methods.

DOG GRATE

A freestanding iron or steel basket grate dating from the eighteenth century with a cast-iron fireback and pronounced front legs.

DOG-LEG STAIRCASE

In this case the first flight ends at a half-landing and the stairs then double back in a second flight to the landing itself. The outer string of the second flight is directly, or very nearly directly, above the first.

DOOR CASE

All the joinery work that frames, surrounds, or adorns a door.

DOOR HOOD

A projecting rooflike feature supported on brackets that gives both visual emphasis to a door and shelter for those gaining access.

DORIC ORDER

One of the Classical orders of architecture (the others being Tuscan, Ionic, Corinthian, and Composite). Although the simplest columnar shape is the Tuscan, the Doric is considered to be earlier and exists in both the Greek Doric and the Roman Doric, the former having no base, as on the Parthenon and the temples at Paestum in southern Italy.

DORMER

A window that protrudes from the slope of a roof within its own miniature roofing structure.

DOWN-HEARTH

A fireplace where the fire is laid on the actual hearthstone, sometimes with the help of firedogs.

DROPPED CEILING

A ceiling that is suspended, lowered, or partially lowered from its original height to hide unsightly pipes, ducts, or wiring; to allow space for recessed lights; or simply to change proportions in a room.

DUBBING-OUT

Filling major cavities, depressions, and other scars in a wall with mortar before applying the first coat of plaster.

DUCK'S NEST GRATE

A lower, less elegant hob grate that can rest on firedogs or be self-sufficient, originally used mostly in eighteenth- and early-nineteenth- century kitchens.

DUTCH DOOR

A door divided horizontally so that each section can be independently opened or shut.

EARS

Architectural term for molding that overlaps the uprights of a door or window frame.

EAVE

The edge of a roof sticking out beyond a wall.

Examples of dormers

EGG-AND-DART MOLDING

A continuous string of alternating egg-shaped or ovoid forms and dart or arrowhead shapes, said to represent life and death. It is one of the most classic of moldings used for cornices.

ELEVATION

The facade and general exterior walls of a building.

ELL OR EL

An extension of a building set at a right angle to the principal dimension. More specifically the term is also used to refer to an American single-story lean-to wing containing a kitchen, generally added in the seventeenth century to clapboard, wood-framed New England houses.

EMBRASURE

An opening or recess in a wall, often slightly splayed.

ENCAUSTIC TILES

Patterned earthenware tiles, often glazed, and much favored by Victorian and Edwardian builders.

ENFILADE

The arrangement of doorways connecting a series of rooms running into one another so that if doors are open one can obtain a vista down the whole length of the suite.

ENTABLATURE

The topmost horizontal element of a Classical order or column, consisting of architrave, frieze, and cornice.

ENTASIS

The slight convex curve in the shaft of a column that is built in purposely to correct an optical illusion. Curiously, the slight swell makes the column appear straight.

ENTRESOL

French term in common use for a mezzanine: a low story between two taller levels or the low story over a ground floor. Literally, "between floors."

ESCUTCHEON

A shieldlike tablet containing a heraldic device or coat of arms. Also, the ornamental brass or ormolu

Egg-and-dart molding

protective plate that surrounds the keyhole of a door or a handle.

ETRUSCAN

In decoration, either another name for the Tuscan or Classical Roman Doric order or the intriguing form of decoration mistakenly called "Etruscan" by Robert Adam in the eighteenth century, which was actually based on Greek black- and red-figure vases that were thought at the time to be Etruscan. Excellent examples of Adam's Etruscan-style decorations are to be seen at Osterly Park House, just outside London, and Home House in Portland Square, London.

EXEDRA

A niche or a room opening through a full-width arch into a larger, covered (or sometimes open) space. In Classical architecture, however, it means a semicircular or rectangular extension of a room that forms a recess inside, sometimes with raised seats.

FACADE

The outer face of a building.

FACING

The finish applied to the outer surface of a building.

FANLIGHT

The glazed light (that is, glassed-in section) above a door in eighteenth- and early-nineteenth-century buildings that was often semicircular or fan-shaped with radiating glazing bars or other ornamentation. Sometimes the term is used erroneously for rectangular lights above doors, which are more correctly called *transoms*.

FAN VAULTING

Particular type of vaulting, unique to the Perpendicular phase in Gothic architecture, in which fanlike ribs spring out from a central point. It is also called *palm vaulting*. There is a particularly beautiful example in Westminster Abbey, London.

FASCIA BOARD OR FACIA BOARD

A plain horizontal band in a Classical architrave. Also, a board that runs horizontally under the eaves of a building to which the guttering can be attached.

FENESTRATION

The arrangement and proportions of windows seen from the outside of a building.

FIBERBOARD

Rigid, compressed, wood-pulp panels used for modern-day construction of interior walls, partitions, and ceilings, as well as the interior carcass of cheap furniture. Trademarks include Beaver Board, Homasote, and Masonite.

FIBERGLASS

Strong, pliable, heatproof fiber made from fine filaments of glass saturated with polyester plastics. The result is then poured into appropriately shaped molds to form seating, planters, and so on.

FIELDED PANEL

A wall or door panel with a raised center area that is "fielded" (meaning beveled or slanted) around its sides.

FILLET

A plain narrow band of wood, stone, or plaster that divides more complicated moldings from one another.

FINIAL

A formal turned or carved ornament in the shape of an urn, ball, bun, spike, arrow, fleur-de-lis, or figure at the top of a gable, canopy, pinnacle, or newel-post on a stairway, or at either end of a curtain pole.

FIREBACK

A cast-iron slab with an ornamental design that stands at the back of a fireplace to protect the wall and help reflect heat. Long, low shapes are more typical from the sixteenth century; later ones become increasingly upright.

FIREHOOD

A canopy in metal, plaster, brick, or stone that stands right over the fire on a big open hearth to channel smoke into the flue of a chimney.

FLASHING

A strip of waterproof material used to make watertight the abutments between slates and chimneys, walls and roofs, walls and windows, and so on.

FLIGHT

A continuous series of steps, with no intermediate landings, from one landing or floor to another.

FLITCH

Any part of a tree, or log, that can be thinly sliced to make a veneer.

FLUSH DOOR

A plain, smooth door, with either a solid or hollow core, surfaced with plywood or a laminate.

FLUTING

Shallow concave grooves running vertically on the shaft of a column, pilaster, or other surface. If the lower part of the grooves is filled with a solid cylindrical piece it is called *cabled fluting*.

FRENCH WINDOW

A pair of narrow, glazed doors giving access to the outside, or another room or hallway. French windows generally open inward, as do windows in France, from which their name derives. (Interestingly, such windows in France are called *fenêtres anglaises*.)

FRET OR FRETWORK

Pierced decoration that generally takes the form of a repeated motif on a gallery around a tabletop or on chair legs or stretchers. (See also *Greek key pattern* or *key pattern*.)

FRIEZE

The decorative band along the upper part of an internal wall, or the middle division of an entablature between the architrave and cornice.

GADROON

An ornamental band made up of a series of elongated egg or ovoid forms that project slightly above the surface.

GALVANIZED IRON

Iron coated with zinc to make it rust resistant.

GARGOYLE

A water spout projecting from a roof or parapet carved in the form of human or animal grotesques.

GARRETING

The process of finishing a surface by pressing small stones into soft mortar before it dries.

GAZEBO

Either the turret on the roof of an open ornamental garden summerhouse or the whole structure.

GESSO

Made from gypsum powder or chalk, it is mixed with size or a binding glue to form a dense white absorbent base for the decoration of paneling or for gilded moldings.

GILDING

A process in which gold or other metallic leaf is applied like a transfer to a surface coated with sticky gold size or weak glue.

GIRANDOLE

A seventeenth-century word (derived from the Italian) for "wall light" or "sconce" (in France, however, it meant "a cluster of diamonds" or "chandelier"). By the mid-eighteenth century, however, the term girandole had come to describe the combination of multi-branched, carved, and often gilded wood candle sconces that incorporated a small mirror to add extra sparkle.

An early-sixteenth-century frieze

They were widely used during the Rococo period. During the Neoclassical era they became rather more restrained and were more like mirrors with a sconce or candleholder below, although sometimes they had candle sconces at either side.

GLASS BRICKS

Soda-lime glass molded into hollow blocks that can be sealed together with a vacuum. They can then be mortared together to form glass walls and partitions.

GLAZING BARS

The wooden framing members in a sash window that divide and contain the glass panes. Early bars—that is to say those from the late seventeenth century and Queen Anne period—were wide, flat, and fairly crude. They became progressively finer and more subtly molded in the eighteenth century; early nineteenth-century bars were very slender.

GOLDEN SECTION

An incommensurable ancient Greek proportion that reads like one of those awful intelligence test questions, yet was thought to be fascinating if not divine by Renaissance theorists. It can be defined as a line cut in such a way that the smaller section is to the greater as the greater is to the whole, but it cannot be worked out mathematically as can all other theories of proportion.

GRAND TOUR

An almost obligatory part of education for rich, young eighteenth-century European men, particularly the British, who flocked to Italy and Greece and, to a lesser extent, France, to steep themselves in Classical antiquity. After two or three years they returned laden with sketches of ancient buildings, beautiful pieces of Renaissance furniture, paintings, drawings, vases, sculpture, and so on, as well as new ideas for building splendid homes or improving old ones.

GREEK KEY PATTERN

A horizontal pattern of interwoven horizontal and vertical lines. (See also *fret* and *key pattern*.)

GRIP FLOOR

Mixture of beaten lime and ash, normally used on the ground floor in some early sixteenth-, seventeenth-, and eighteenth-century houses, but occasionally upstairs when it was placed on top of lathes supported by joists.

GRIP HANDRAIL

Heavy Elizabethan or Jacobean handrail with a pronounced roll molding on top.

GROIN

In construction, the curved, rather sharp edge formed at the juncture of two vaulted surfaces.

GROIN RIB

The rib that follows the edge of the groin on a vaulted ceiling.

GROTESQUE

Not ugly, but simply the sort of masks, animal forms, winged creatures, mermaids, and so on created by artists in antiquity and discovered during excavations for new construction or in long-buried ruins known as *grottes*, from which they take their name (as does the Anglicized term *grottoes* and the slang term *grotty*).

GROUT

A cement and sand mixture (mostly cement, with little sand) used for fixing tiles, bricks, and stones in place.

GUILLOCHE

A carved plaitlike band used as decoration on a molding.

HA-HA

A more or less invisible division between a park or garden from the fields beyond. It consists of a sunken retaining wall on the domestic side, deep enough to deter horses, cows, or sheep, with a sloping bank on the other.

HACIENDA

Used in Spanish-speaking countries for the principal long, low house—with verandas or porches and a projecting roof—on a large estate. More recently, it has been adapted for residential structures in the southwestern United States.

HALF-TIMBERING

Walls are built of interlocking vertical and horizontal beams or lengths of timber. To give the impression that the house is more solidly built of bricks, the spaces that are formed are either filled with wattle and daub, lathe and plaster, or brick noggin, or covered by clapboard, plaster, or mathematical tiles. The process is also called *timber-framing*.

HAMMER BRACE

Long, curved bracket made to support a projecting hammer beam in early roof construction.

HAMMER-BEAM ROOF

A particularly medieval system of roof design, but still used through the seventeenth and eighteenth centuries, whereby rafters are supported by short horizontal "hammer beams" that project from wall-plate level on opposite sides of the wall and end in midair. The hammer beams are supported by hammer brackets. The inner ends of the hammer beams support vertical timbers called hammer posts. These in their turn support purlins or horizontal timbers. Anyone interested in such hammer-beam construction would be advised to examine the superb example to be seen at Westminster Hall in London, which was constructed between 1394 and 1406.

HANGINGS

An umbrella term that embraces bed curtains, as well as draperies for windows and tapestries, or decorative fabric hangings for walls.

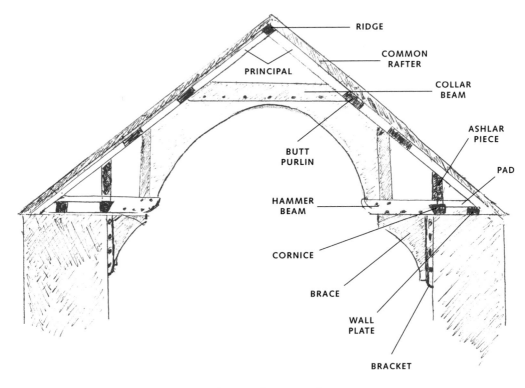

RIDGE

COMMON RAFTER

PRINCIPAL

COLLAR BEAM

ASHLAR PIECE

PAD

BUTT PURLIN

HAMMER BEAM

CORNICE

BRACE

WALL PLATE

BRACKET

Hammer beam roof

HELIX

The inner spiral of the spiral scroll on an Ionic capital at the top of a column, or in a smaller version, on a Corinthian or Composite capital. Also, just a spiral motif.

HERCULANEUM

Ancient Roman city near Naples in southern Italy that was excavated in the mid-eighteenth century. The ruins had a profound influence on the development of Neoclassical English (particularly on Robert Adam), American, French, and European architecture and interiors, and on the Louis XVI period in France.

HERM OR HERMA

Either a Roman boundary marker or an eighteenth-century outdoor sculpture or gatepost in the form of a downward tapering pillar holding a bust of Hermes. Or just a three-quarter length figure on pedestals used decoratively from the Renaissance onward. (See also *term*.)

HERRINGBONE WORK

Stone-, brick-, or tile-work in which the components are laid diagonally instead of horizontally. Alternate courses lie in opposing directions, forming a zigzag design.

HIGH-TECH

An interior design movement from the 1970s that used industrial components for furniture and interiors. (See also *High-Tech* in Styles and Movements.)

HINGES

Basically, these are chrome, brass, nickel, or other metal devices that enable doors to swing and the tops of chests and drop leaves or flaps to flip up and down. Regular hinges consist of two plates joined by a pin and are sometimes quite decorative in their own right. But there are other varieties. In the case of a *butt hinge*, two such plates are fixed inside the door or chest unit so that only the pivot and pin are seen. *Invisible hinges* are *almost* just that. *Double-acting hinges* are so formed to allow doors or panels to swing almost 360 degrees in either direction. *Rustic "HL" hinges* are made from wrought or forged iron and are so called because their structure forms the two letters.

HIP RAFTER

A diagonally placed rafter at the external junction between roof slopes. Internal junctions are called *valleys*.

HIPPED ROOF

A roof with sloped rather than vertical ends.

HIPS

In construction, the external junctions between roof slopes.

HISTORICISM

A nineteenth-century term for respect for the past in architecture. Also, the revival of historical styles in the nineteenth century. Architects took particular care to observe the rules of the past style they were imitating and to reproduce details as accurately as possible.

HOB GRATE

Cast-iron coal-burning grate made from the late eighteenth century onward.

HOOD MOLD

A projecting molding above an arch, doorway, or window to divert rainwater. Used until the eighteenth century. Also called a *drip mold*.

HOPPER WINDOW

A casement window hinged along its bottom edge to enable it to be opened outward. More often than not it is part of a larger window unit.

HORSESHOE ARCH

Moorish or Spanish arch with an exaggerated curve, generally greater than a semicircle or 180 degrees.

HOT TUB

Basically, a round wooden tub made of a close-grained wood, such as redwood, set outside in the open air and filled with steaming hot water for one or more people to enjoy. Hot tubs are available in various sizes and can be fitted with internal seating ledges and whirlpool or jacuzzilike attachments to swirl hot currents of water around. They can also be made from metal with a porcelain finish and installed inside as well as out.

HYPERBOLIC PARABOLOID ROOF

A form of construction in the shape of a double-curved shell. It was used by Felix Candela in his Cosmic Ray Pavilion, University City, Mexico.

ICON

Derived from the Greek word for *image*, in decoration, it is a religious painted panel.

I.M.

The term for the inner measurements of a hollow object, as opposed to the O.M. or outer measurements.

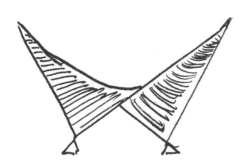

Hyperbolic
paraboloid roof

IMBRICATION

The technique of placing tiles on roofs or walls, or even columns, in overlapping rows like fish scales.

INGLENOOK FIREPLACE

A large open fireplace with a down-hearth and a built-in seat or seats inside the chimney breast. It first appeared in the sixteenth century and was commonly used in the seventeenth century. It continued to be used in rural houses in the early eighteenth century.

INLAID FLOOR

Sometimes described as a marquetry floor—a kind of parquet floor with wood strips laid with and against the grain. The decoration is seldom truly inlaid into the actual carcass timber (that is, framework) of the floor.

INSULATION

A process whereby appropriate insulating materials are installed to ensure that heat is either kept in or out depending on the climate; that sound is kept within proper bounds; and that a structure is generally protected from the outside elements. It should be remembered that electric outlets put back to back on either side of partition walls are sound conductors, and therefore should be staggered.

INTARSIA

A form of mosaic made up of different colored woods that was popular in fifteenth- and sixteenth-century Italy, especially for the floors of libraries, studies, small anterooms in palaces, and the designated choir space in churches.

INTERLOCKING TILES

Tiles designed so that their edges fit mechanically one against another to provide a weather seal.

INTRADOS

The inner curve or underside of an arch. Also called a *soffit*.

IONIC ORDER

One of the Classical orders (along with Tuscan, Doric, Corinthian, and Composite). It originated in Asia Minor in the mid-sixth-century B.C. and has deep volutes or spiral scrolls at the column head but no acanthus leaves.

ISOMETRIC PROJECTION

A three-dimensional schematic view of a figure or object.

JAMBS

The sides of a door opening, or just an opening, whether made of stone, brick, or wood.

JESTING BEAM

A ornamental beam that is rarely structural. In this sense, it is a faux beam.

JIB DOOR

A disguised door fitted within a wall,

paneling, or faux bookshelves, and appearing to be part of the surroundings.

JOINERY

The final finished woodwork in a house, such as doors, trims, stairs, paneling, baseboards, and so on. Also, the fitting and making of such items.

JOINTING

Instead or raking out or "pointing" the mortar joints between bricks or masonry when it is dry, the finishing is achieved while the mortar is still fresh.

JOIST

A parallel timber placed between the walls or s the top of structural beams to support floorboards. In old or traditional houses the undersides are generally exposed to the room below and are then either cleaned up, molded or carved, or have ceiling lathes nailed to them for the attachment of plaster or composition ceilings.

KAKEMONO

An Oriental, and particularly Japanese, style of painting that is mounted on brocaded wall hangings instead of being conventionally framed.

KEEL MOLDING

A molding with a "nib" that in profile looks rather like the keel of a ship.

KEEP

Inner tower of a castle with living quarters large enough to serve the household either permanently or in times of siege.

KEY PATTERN

A geometric ornament of both horizontal and vertical straight lines. (See also *fret* and *Greek key*.)

KEYSTONE

The topmost and central stone—sometimes carved—of an arch or rib vault.

KICKPLATE

A metal or brass plate fixed to the bottom of a door to prevent scuff marks.

KING POST

The middle upright post in a roof truss connecting the tie or collar beam with the roof ridge.

KILN-DRIED LUMBER

Wood that has been artificially dried in a kiln rather than in the open air. This method of drying makes lumber less prone to warping as a result of better control of the evaporation of water.

KNAPPED FLINT

Old method of English construction, particularly in East Anglia or on the

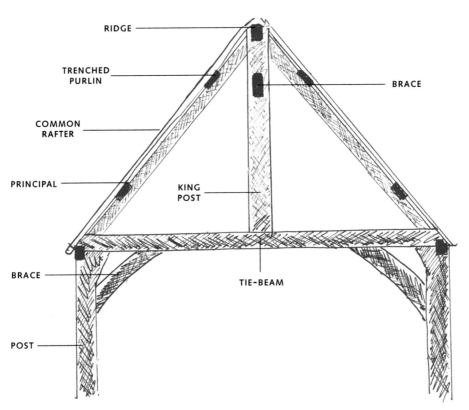

King post roof

East Coast, in which stony flints are split in half and laid so that the smooth black surface of the split side of the flint forms the facing on a wall. (If you split a flint, its inner surface is smooth and black.)

LACUNA OR LACUNAR

The term for a sunken panel in a paneled or coffered ceiling.

LAMBREQUIN

Deeply scalloped piece of fabric or carved wood across a window. Also, a fringelike ornament.

LANCET WINDOW

Slim, arched window used mostly in early-thirteenth-century English architecture or medieval reproductions.

LATH

The narrow strips of wood or metal used to build a supporting structure for plaster, shingles, slates, or tiles.

LATTICE

Open fretwork-type decoration with crisscrosses or squares made of thin strips of wood or metal known as laths.

LIMESTONE

Sandy, sedimented rock that yields lime if burned. It is much used as a building stone and for facades; a crystalline variety is used for floors.

LINENFOLD PANELING

Paneling carved to look like stylized folds of fabric; associated with the sixteenth-century Tudor style.

Gothic lancet
window

Sixteenth-century
linenfold paneling

LINTEL

Structural component usually of wood, stone, or concrete that carries the load over a window, door, or fireplace opening.

LOAD-BEARING CONSTRUCTION OR WALL

Supporting construction or wall to bear the weight of ceilings and upper floors as opposed to frame construction or non-load-bearing walls. If supporting construction has to be removed, or has an arch cut through it into an adjoining wall, it will have to be strengthened with steel supports known as RSJs.

LOGGIA

A gallerylike space that is open on one side and often has pillars. It can also be a quite separate structure near but apart from a main house or building.

LOZENGE PANELING

Diamond-shaped decoration in Jacobean paneling.

MANOR HOUSE

A large house in the country or the largest house in a village. Architecturally, the term is used to denote an unfortified, medium-sized house from the late Middle Ages.

MANSARD OR MANSART ROOF

A type of roof invented by François Mansart in the seventeenth century. (See also *Mansart, François* in Architects, Designers, and Decorators.)

MARTELLO TOWER

A round tower, such as the Mediterranean watch towers used for coastal defense in Europe and in Britain from 1793 onward, and especially during the Napoleonic wars. (Named after the tower first built at Cape Mortello in Corsica.)

MASONITE

Compressed fiber wall or building board. Very rigid but difficult to nail.

MASONRY

Any construction work dealing with the fitting together of bricks, tiles, stone, and so on.

MASTIC

Heavy-duty adhesive for fixing most types of tiles. Also, one of the resins or gums frequently used in the manufacture of varnish.

MATCH BOARDING

Thin softwood boards, used particularly in the United States for lining rooms, sometimes with an edge bead.

MATHEMATICAL TILE

A facing tile, much the size of brick headers (the small ends of bricks), laid across wood-framed exterior walls to give the structure the appearance of being brick-built. Mathematical tiles have been used in England since the early 1700s and were probably first introduced to update and make weatherproof old timber-framed buildings. (See also *brick veneer*.)

MEDALLION

In building, a decorative oval or circle often containing a painting, a plaster head, or a figure in relief.

MITER

To bevel the ends of architraves and moldings so that at corners they butt together at a 45-degree angle.

MODULAR HOUSING

Self-contained living units preassembled in a factory, then transported to the relevant site to be combined, if necessary, with other units as part of a housing complex or a high-rise apartment building.

MOLDING

A shaped length of wood, plaster, or stone used as ornament in a room or on furniture; often used to conceal joints between one building surface and another.

MONTAGE

The overlapping or superimposing of various layers or of various decorative elements.

MORESQUE

A term used to describe decoration based on the Moorish style that was imposed upon Spain and Portugal during the early-thirteenth- and fourteenth-century Moorish occupation. This is exemplified by the exotic Alhambra Palace and Citadel near Granada in southern Spain, with its stunning geometric tiles, plasterwork, fountains, and use of water.

MORTAR

Usually a mixture of cement and sand, and sometimes lime as well, or lime and sand, used to fix bricks or stones together.

MORTISE AND TENON JOINT

An efficient method for joining two pieces of wood, especially for cabinetwork. A mortise is the hole cut in one piece of wood to receive the specially shaped tenon, or projection, of the other.

MUFF GLASS

Early glass used for windowpanes. Muff or cylinder glass was blown in a cylinder form, then slit lengthwise and unrolled into flat pieces from which the panes were cut.

MULLION

A wood or stone, often supportive, upright that divides windows vertically into separate *lights* or windowpanes, as they are now mostly called.

MUNTIN

An intermediate upright framing panel or glass in doors or windows.

MUTULE

Anything projecting from the wall of a building, particularly the ends of beams.

NEWEL

The supportive central post or column around which the steps of a circular staircase wind.

NEWEL-POST

A tall, basically ornamental post at the top or bottom of a stair that supports the handrail. In British construction the term *newel-post* is also used to refer to supportive posts at any change of direction in the staircase.

SCREW STAIR, WINDING STAIR, OR NEWEL STAIR

A circular stair whose steps wind around a central post.

NIB

A small edge on building materials, such as tiles, that enable them to be fixed more securely in place.

NICHE

A recess in a wall—often with an arched top—for a statue, piece of sculpture, or bust.

NOGGING

A short length of wood, not unlike lathe and plaster, that is fixed between the vertical studs of a partition to strengthen construction. In old timber-framed houses, the spaces between posts are filled with bricks, called *brick noggin*.

NOSING

The part of a stair tread that sticks out above the riser. Also, the rounded edge of a wood or marble shelf or tabletop.

OBELISK

A tall, tapering shaft of stone, usually granite or marble, of square or rectangular sections. Its top ends like a pyramid. Much used in ancient Egypt.

OCULUS

A round opening or window. Also, a circular opening at the top of a dome.

OEIL-DE-BOEUF

A small oval or circular window.

OGEE MOLDING

An S-shaped section of molding like *cyma recta* or *reversa*.

OPEN PLAN

A large, open, flexible living space meant to contain various functions such as cooking, dining, sitting, and playing/entertaining.

OPEN-WELL STAIRS

A staircase rising in relatively short flights to quarter-landings, built around an open well. It was first used in the sixteenth century.

ORANGERIE OR ORANGERY

Originally a term for an eighteenth- or nineteenth-century conservatory or hothouse in which orange trees were grown. Now it is often used for any decoratively glassed building that provides seating among exotic plants.

ORDERS

(See *Classical orders*.)

ORIEL WINDOW

A projecting window on an upper floor supported by a corbel or bracket.

ORMOLU

An alloy of copper, zinc, and tin made to resemble gold and used mostly for decorating furniture.

OVERMANTEL

The upper part of a chimneypiece above the mantelpiece shelf. It is usually a panel topped by a cornice or pediment. In the nineteenth century it contained a mirror and shelves as well.

OVOLO

A small quarter-rounded molding.

PAGODA

A Buddhist temple in the form of a polygonal tower with elaborately ornamented roofs projecting from each of its many stories, common in China and India. Pagodas were often incorporated into chinoiserie designs in the West.

PALISADE

A fence of iron or wooden stakes. Palisade construction consists of interlocking vertical wooden boards or planks.

PALLADIAN MOTIF

A rhythmic arcade consisting of twin columns supporting arches; it occurs over and over in Palladian architecture.

Part of an eighteenth-century overmantel

Palladian motif

PALLADIAN WINDOW

Windows consisting of four columns defining three tall windows, the central taller window with a semicircular arched cornice, the two side windows with straight cornices. It was a fashionable component, centered to light the stairwell, in most prosperous mid-eighteenth-century New England houses, often set over Ionic columned porticoes surrounding the front door. It was also much used in Britain, and still remains popular for classically-styled houses.

PALMETTE

A fan-shaped ornament composed of narrow divisions, such as those of a palm leaf. A frequent Neoclassical motif.

PANTILE

Interlocking S-shaped roof tile.

PAPER BOARD

A thick, stiff board, much thicker than regular cardboard, made by compressing together layers of paper or paper pulp. It was used by Buckminster Fuller to make temporary dwellings for the armed forces. (See also *Fuller, Buckminster* in Architects, Designers, and Decorators.)

PARAPET

A low, sometimes battlemented wall, placed to protect any place where there is a sudden drop—for example, at the edge of a flat roof, or on the edge of a bridge or quay.

PARGETING

Ornamental exterior plasterwork in relief or intaglio in vine patterns, other foliage, or figures. It is most often found in eastern England timber-framed buildings.

PARGEWORK

Like pargetry (the bas-relief work on plastered or stuccoed outside walls), pargework emulates old interior Gothic stonework.

PARQUET FLOOR

Wood floor made from thin hardwood blocks (about a quarter-inch thick), often arranged in herringbone or squared patterns on a wood subfloor, then highly polished.

PATERA

Small disklike oval or circular ornament in Classical architecture that was a particular favorite of the Neoclassical architects, such as Robert Adam. It is often decorated with acanthus leaves or rose petals and used on fireplaces or decorative plaster friezes.

PATIO

In Spanish or Spanish-American architecture it is an inner courtyard open to the sky. But it has become a generic English word for an outside paved or bricked area.

PAVILION

A lightly constructed ornamental building often used as a summer or "pleasure" house in a garden. In the United Kingdom the term is also applied to the half-roofed spectator seating attached to cricket, or other sports, grounds.

PEAR DROP ORNAMENT

An eighteenth-century ornamentation in the form of hanging pears, usually used to decorate the top segment of an otherwise plain frieze. It was used on both architectural and furniture friezes.

PEBBLEDASH

Small rounded stones, such as pea gravel, dashed into cement and plaster before it has set to achieve a densely textured wall finish; also a kind of roughcast.

PEDESTAL

The base supporting a column in Classical architecture. Also, the base for a statue, bust, or piece of sculpture.

PEDIMENT

A triangular or segmented feature in wood, stone, or plaster that forms the topmost element of a classical door, window, fireplace, or large piece of furniture, such as a bureau-bookcase or chest on chest. A broken pediment has a gap at the top of the triangle.

PELE-TOWER

Northern English or Scottish term for a small fortified house or tower, formerly ready for sudden defense.

PENTICE

A roof with post, pillar, or pier supports covering an outside staircase. Also, a gallery with its own roof.

PERGOLA

A covered garden walkway or paved area outside a house, formed of upright posts or pillars and horizontal beams. It can be made of wood or stone.

PERPENDICULAR

Name for the last phase of Gothic architecture. It was so named because of its singular use of vertical elements. However, another signature of the style was its exquisite fan or palm vaulting. (See also *Gothic* in Styles and Movements.)

PIER

A solid masonry support as opposed to a column, which can also be decorative. Also, the solid mass between windows or doors in a building.

PILASTER

A flat, rectangular version of a column attached to a wall, more for decoration than structure, often used as the side pieces for a pair of columns supporting a squared arch.

PILLAR

A freestanding upright member that, unlike a column, does not have to be cylindrical or conform to any of the Classical orders.

PLINTH

The base of a column or pedestal, generally chamfered or molded at the top.

PLASTER

Wall or ceiling surface formulated from lime, water, sand, and occasionally, plaster of paris. It needs to be completely dry before applying any sort of wall covering or decorative finish.

PLASTER OF PARIS

A composition made from calcined and ground gypsum, often used as a base for decoration.

PLASTERBOARD

Sheets of plaster composition made from repulped paper, gypsum, and shredded wood, and then covered with sheets of kraft paper and attached to lathing strips to create partition walls and ceilings. Also called building board or Sheetrock.

PLATE GLASS

Very strong glass used for large picture windows. It is made out of a mixture of soda, lime, and silica, which is then rolled into large sheets. The final process is grinding and polishing the surface.

PLEXIGLAS

Trademark name for a moldable, versatile plastic sheet product that is sometimes transparent but also produced in a number of sizes, colors, and thicknesses.

PLYWOOD

Layered wood panels consisting of the same number of thin veneers compressed on either side of a thick, semiporous core. A finished layer is applied to the top.

POCKET DOOR

A standard-sized door (or double doors) that is designed to slide away sideways into an opening fashioned out of the supporting wall.

PODIUM

A continuous base or plinth supporting columns, or the platform enclosing the arena in an ancient amphitheater. Today, the term is also refers to a stand used for making speeches.

POINTING

The mortar filling between bricks or stones in a wall.

PORCH

In the United States, a covered veranda. In Britain, the covered entrance to a building, called a portico if columned and pedimented like a temple front.

PORTCULLIS

An iron gate, or iron-reinforced wooden bars that slide up and down in vertical grooves in the jambs of a doorway. Historically used for the defense of castles and fortified houses.

PORTE-COCHERE

A porch that is big enough for a

car and, formerly, carriages to pass through.

PORTICO

A roofed space, either open or partly enclosed, forming the entrance and centerpiece of the facade of a house, church, or temple. It often has detached or attached columns and a pediment.

PORTLAND CEMENT

Synthetic cement made from a mixture of lime and clay.

PORTLAND STONE

White or creamy white English limestone.

POSTERN

A small gateway that is sometimes deliberately concealed at the back of a castle, monastery, or even a walled town (as in a *postern gate*).

A portico

PREFABRICATED

A term used to describe building units or components that are shaped and finished off-site and then delivered to the construction site, such as windows, doors, frames, and so on.

PREFABRICATED HOUSES

Houses, such as modular houses, constructed from prefinished parts that are assembled on-site.

PROFILE

In architecture, the section of a molding. Also, the contour or outline of a building, or part of it.

PROSTYLE

A term used to describe free-standing columns in a row, often in a portico.

PULLMAN KITCHEN

A small kitchen tucked into a narrow recess or alcove, or a kitchen arranged all down one wall and hidden by a sliding screen wall or by some other device.

PURLIN

A square section of timber that runs lengthwise along a roof and rests on the principal rafters in order to carry the lighter and more numerous "common" rafters. *Collar purlins* are single central timbers that are supported by crown posts in order to carry the collar beams. *Side purlins* are pairs of timbers that appear some way up the roof to carry the common rafters and that are supported, like *clasped purlins*, by queen posts.

PUTTI

Italian cherubs much used in Baroque
and Rococo art and architecture.

QUADRANT MOLD

A quarter-round molding.

QUARRY TILE

An unglazed, nonporous, burned-clay
tile, usually red.

QUARTER ROUND

A convex molding that is one-quarter
of a circle.

QUARTER-SLICED VENEER

Striped or straight-grained veneer that
is achieved by slicing a quarter of a
log in parallel lines at right angles to
the growth rings.

QUATTROCENTO

Italian term for the fifteenth century,
referring to the 1400s and literally
meaning *1400*.

QUEEN POST

A vertical tie post, used in pairs
and placed symmetrically on a tie
beam to support side purlins or
clasped purlins.

QUOIN

A "squared-up" or "dressed" stone
that is square-cut and that forms
the corner of a building.

RABBET OR REBATE

A step-shaped groove cut along the
length of a piece of wood or metal
in order to better fit or receive a
corresponding piece, as in a picture
frame to receive the glass.

RABBET JOINT

An edge joint formed by fitting together
two rabbeted boards or timbers.

RADIANT HEATING

An energy- and cost-efficient way to
heat rooms by building heat coils in
walls, ceilings, or floors, or a mixture of
all three locations. When these surfaces
warm up they retain their heat and
the whole room gets the benefit.

RAFTER

A sloping lateral member that runs
from the top of the walls to the apex
of the roof to support the battens or
lathes from which roof tiles or slates
are slung. *Common rafters* are smaller
members placed along the length of
a roof. *Principal rafters* support com-

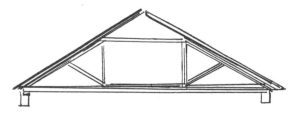

Queen post or double roof truss

mon rafters. (See keys for *crown post* and *king post*.)

RANCH WINDOW

(See *ranch window* in Windows and Window Treatments.)

REEDING

Closely (or sometimes widely) spaced half-round beading often used in nineteenth-century architraves and furniture legs.

REGISTER GRATE

A cast-iron or sheet-metal plate that fills the main fireplace opening with a diminished opening for quite a small fitted grate. It was popular during the second half of the nineteenth century, particularly for bedrooms and smaller rooms.

RENDERING

The first coat of plaster on a solid wall, and sometimes the only coat.

RETURN

In design and decoration, it means a change in direction, like the turn of a cornice or a border at the angle of walls.

REVEAL

The visible exterior parts of a window jamb or door between the frame and the main wall surface.

RIB

A slender, projecting band or member on a ceiling or vault that is usually structural, though it is sometimes merely decorative. Ribs are placed either transversely or at the groins, thereby dividing the surface into sections. Elizabethan and Jacobean plasterwork is usually made up of such "ribbed" designs.

RIDGE

The apex of a pitched roof where one slope meets the other.

RIDGEBOARD, RIDGEPOLE, RIDGEPIECE, OR RIDGEPLATE

The timber running along the apex of a roof and sandwiched between the tops of the rafters and which supports the upper ends of the rafters.

RIDGE TILE

An angled or half-round tile used to weatherproof the junction between the roof slope coverings at the ridge.

RIVEN FLAGSTONE

A flagstone that has been split rather than sawed.

RISER

The vertical face of a step or stair.

ROMANESQUE

A very early style probably current around the tenth century, if not earlier. It predated the Gothic and is characterized by rounded arches as well as simple internal planning, yet each European country seemed to have different Romanesque tower arrangements or no towers at all, as in the south of France. The style had a resurgence in the second half of the nineteenth century and became popular in America in the 1890s.

RONDEL OR ROUNDEL

A rounded medallion or plaque, or a circular disk of stained glass with a stained glass window design, or a design of some sort contained within a round frame.

ROOF CONSTRUCTION

Roofs are as complicated as the skeletal structure of human bodies and consist of almost as many small parts. They are generally named after their principal structural component, which could be a crown post, hammer beam, arched-brace, or king post. (See keys for *crown post* and *king post*.)

ROTUNDA

A building or room that is circular and often domed.

RSJ

A strong support made of rolled steel that is a smaller version of the I-section universal beam. RSJs are generally used to support a ceiling when a supporting wall has to be removed or an opening has to be made. They are then surrounded by plaster or columns to disguise their utilitarian nature.

RUNNING DOG

Classical ornament similar to a wave, often used in a frieze. It is sometimes called a *Vitruvian scroll* after the ancient Roman architect, Vitruvius.

RUSTIC

In the eighteenth century the basement floor was known as "the rustic." In Palladian houses, the lower story was rusticated and acted as a basement podium for one or more smooth-faced upper stories.

RUSTICATION

Masonry cut in massive blocks that are separated from each other by deep joints. It was used to give a bold texture to exterior walls, and particularly to the lower part of the elevation.

SADDLE

In construction, the board or stone slab set below a door.

SANDBLASTING

A cleaning method in which particles of sand are propelled with great force by jets of steam or air to clean old stone or brickwork.

SASH WINDOW

(See *sash window* in Windows and Window Treatments.)

SCRATCH COAT

A preliminary coat of plaster that is applied to a wall and then scratched and scored while still damp. This ensures that the second or finishing coat will adhere well and not flake off.

SCREED

A scrupulously applied level layer of mortar used to provide a smooth surface on which to lay finishes such as tiles.

SCREENS PASSAGE

The passage formed at the lower end of a medieval hall by screening off the main area from the entrance. It often had a minstrel's gallery over the top for the general musical entertainment.

SCRIBING

The technique of fitting moldings, or some sort of wood framework, to an uneven surface. Usually, small pliable strips of wood are used to cover up cracks and irregularities.

SECTION

A vertically sliced view of an architectural structure or molding that shows the silhouette at the same time as the internal construction and dimensions.

SEGMENTAL ARCH

An elliptical arch, which means that it is somewhat less than a semicircle.

SEPTIC TANK

A sealed waterproof tank, usually below ground, in which waste material from a drainage system is biologically decomposed before finally being partly purified and dispersed through a soak away, which is often constructed in conjunction with the tank. Used for country houses not on the "mains" drainage system.

SHINGLES

Thin wooden tiles for covering roofs or the sides of houses, especially popular in the United States. Shingles are generally made from cedar, which weathers into a distinctive silvery gray, although they are now produced in synthetic materials as well.

SHINGLE HOUSE

A late-nineteenth-century American building based on the Queen Anne Revival style of the English architect Norman Shaw. This was sometimes called the "Stick Style" because of the emphasis given to the structural framing sticks, which in itself was a variation on the "half-timber" style of architecture. In the United States, shingles sheathed the wood framework in curved or straight sweeps, and there was a new emphasis on porches.

SHUTTER

In building, an exterior covering for a window to give protection from extremes of weather and to keep out excessive sun. In southern Europe, closed shutters are a ubiquitous sight at midday. In the United States, shutters are mostly decorative.

SILL

The horizontal timber that rests on the foundation, thereby forming the bottom of the frame of a wood structure. Also, the board at the bottom of a window frame.

SKIRTING

English term for baseboard, the molded strip of wood that covers the crack or joint where a wall and the floor meet.

SLATE

A fine-grained stone that is easily split into tiles or slabs. The tiles, laid in overlapping rows, are used to cover roofs. Slate is also an effective flooring material.

SLIPS

Well-finished rectangular slabs—usually of marble or slate, but sometimes of tile or mirror—that surround a fireplace opening.

SOFFIT

The underside of any architectural element (such as an arch, beam, lintel, or cornice). Also, a band of wood or plaster to conceal light fixtures.

SOLAR

The upper living room in a medieval house. The term comes from the Latin *solarium*.

SOLARIUM

A sun terrace, sun roof, or loggia.

SPACKLE

A putty or plasterlike substance used to repair battered or faulty walls, ceilings, or timbers. Spackle is laid over the top of fissures and cracks. The excess is removed and when it is dry it is sanded to create a smooth new surface, ready for painting or sealing.

SPANDREL

The triangular area formed between an arch and the rectangle of moldings in which the arch is placed.

SPECIFICATIONS

The finalized measurements, materials, and details given to a contractor for pricing or bids. Also, the final detailed proposal with relevant prices given to a client.

SPIRAL STAIR, CIRCULAR STAIR, CORKSCREW STAIR, OR SPIRAL STAIRCASE

A flight of stairs (see *flight*) whose treads radiate from a central newel. Also called a *solid newel stair*.

SPIRE

A tall, pyramidical, polygonal, or conical structure rising from a tower, turret, or roof—usually of a church—and terminating in a point.

SPLIT-LEVEL HOUSE

A house built on a series of levels rather than being divided up into actual stories.

SPLAT BALUSTER

A staircase baluster cut from a thin board to suggest the design of a conventional baluster in one of the Classical shapes, such as barley sugar twist, a simple elongated Greek vase, or columns. It was much used in the seventeenth and early eighteenth centuries and is not unlike the splat at the back of a Queen Anne chair.

SPROCKET

In roofing, a small strip of wood that is placed both behind and at the foot of a roof rafter to form projecting eaves.

STANCHION

Usually a vertical rolled steel joist to support a load-bearing wall or beam.

STILES

The outer framing members of a system of paneling. Stiles are used in much the same way to support a paneled door.

STRAP WORK

Form of plaster decoration in the shape of leather straps originating in the Netherlands around 1540 and brought to Britain via pattern books from the Netherlands and Germany. The term is also loosely used to describe Elizabethan and Jacobean ceilings with flat decorated rib work.

STRETCHER

A brick that appears lengthways on the face of a wall. The ones that appear head-on are described as *headers*.

STRUT

Roof component. Either a short vertical or oblique piece of timber positioned between two structural members of a roof truss to hold them apart.

STUCCO

A form of smooth and quite hard rendering that is often painted white or cream and was especially popular for the exteriors of many late-eighteenth- and early-nineteenth-century terrace houses in Britain. The term is used quite loosely for a fine plaster to be used inside, outside as a hard exterior covering, or in the place of stone. More specifically, it is a slow-setting plaster, mainly made from gypsum, sand, and slaked lime with other substances added to make it easier to form or model and to make it durable. The ancient Romans apparently used just such a mixture for ceiling decoration, and the Italians used it for interiors for centuries with marble dust as a strengthener and binder. The Italians first introduced it to Britain in the eighteenth century, but it was later introduced as an outdoor rendering by the British architect John Nash in the Regency period. It does need a good deal of maintenance and careful upkeep but it is undeniably handsome when it is kept in good repair.

STUD

An upright post or support—mostly "two-by-fours" (so-called since the stud is 2 inches deep by 4 inches wide)—that, in a series of other studs, forms the main framework of walls and partitions.

SWAN NECK

A wall coping, pediment, or handrail that adopts an ogee curve.

TENON

The end of a piece of wood, or other material, that is cut away to fit into a mortise. It is an extensively used framing joint.

TERM

A support comprising a carved human head and torso that merges into a downward-tapering pedestal.

TELAMONE

The male version of a caryatid, this decorative sculpted figure is sometimes used instead of columns to support entablatures or ledges and other members.

TERRACE

A paved or graveled area around a house or a building usually edged by a balustrade or low hedge. Also, the British term for a continuous row of houses in a town, or what Americans call row houses.

TERRAZZO

A hard-wearing surface made up of cement and small pieces of crushed marble. It is useful for floors, pavements, and walls, and is particularly popular in warm climates.

TIE BEAM

The most important beam in roof framing, the tie beam is a horizontal timber that connects the lower ends of the two opposite rafters to prevent them from spreading. (See keys for *crown post* and *king post*.)

TOENAILING OR DOVETAIL NAILING

Nails are hammered through one piece of wood to another at opposite angles to make it difficult to pull the pieces of wood apart.

TONGUE-AND-GROOVE BOARDING

When the protruding edge of one board fits into a slot at the edge of the next. It is used for floors and ceilings, though it can also be used for walls.

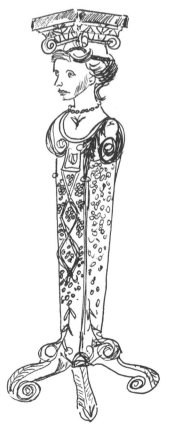

A gilt term made by Benjamin Goodison

TOP RAIL

The uppermost horizontal rail in a system of paneling.

TORUS MOLD

Sometimes called *bull nose*, this is a substantial convex molding used on steps, window sills, and the bases of columns.

TRACERY

The stone mullions on Gothic windows or the decoration sometimes carved on door panels, wall paneling, and chair backs. The intricate form is basically made up of circles; arcs are then formed by intersecting the original circles with other circles so that, in the end, every line is either a circle or the broken arc of a circle.

TRANSEPT

Ecclesiastical architectural term for the part of the church that crosses the nave or central part of the building at right angles near the apse (the semicircular or angular extension in a Christian church).

TRANSITIONAL

When referring to styles, a style that combines established design elements with quite new ones.

TRANSOM

A stone or wood member that divides window openings horizontally into separate panes of glass, or lights. Also, the cross-bar that separates a fanlight from the door below it.

TRAVERTINE

A cream-colored stone or unpolished marble used for floors or tabletops. It is full of small irregular depressions.

TREILLAGE

French term in universal use for ornamental trelliswork in gardens and courtyards.

TRIM

Literally the trimmings of a room: the baseboards, cornices, coves, paneling, wainscoting, dadoes, picture moldings, chair rails, architraves, and window and door surrounds.

TROMPE L'OEIL

French term meaning, literally, "to trick or cheat the eye." A technique in which a painting or mural is so realistically rendered that it looks three-dimensional and therefore real.

TRULLI

The kind of beehive-shaped stone house found particularly in southern Italy.

TRUMEAU

In Romanesque architecture this is the stone mullion in the middle of the carved arch between the lintel of a door and the arch above. In interior decoration it is usually an overmantel filled with a mirror or painting, or the panel over a door. During the reigns of Louis XV and Louis XVI a trumeau was part of the beautiful boiserie those periods produced.

TRUSS

The substantial framework of timbers (also called beams) fitted across a building to support the longtitudinal roof timbers that, in turn, support the common rafters.

TUDOR ROSE

A much-used British royal emblem consisting of a stylized five-petal rose with a smaller rose set in the center. It symbolized the marriage between Henry VII of the Lancasters, whose symbol was a red rose, and Elizabeth of York, whose symbol was the white rose (and it heralded the subsequent end of the Civil "War of the Roses" between the powerful Lancasters and the Yorks).

TUSCAN ORDER

The Roman simplification of the Greek Doric order.

TYMPANUM

The triangular or oblong space in the middle of a pediment above a door or doorway, or the area between the top, load-bearing member of a door and the arch above it. In Romanesque architecture it is usually elaborately carved.

UNIVERSAL JOINT

A joint designed to allow one or both of two connected units to be moved in different directions.

UNIVERSAL BEAM

A rolled-steel support beam bigger than an RSJ.

VALLEY

The junction at the internal angle between roof slopes.

VAULT

An arched ceiling or roof built of stone, brick, or concrete, but sometimes imitated in wood or plaster.

VENETIAN WINDOW

A window with a rounded, arched head closely flanked by two smaller and narrower flat-headed windows. Also known as a Palladian window.

VERANDA

Basically, a European version of an American porch, originally brought back as an idea by soldiers, tea planters, sugar growers, and civil servants who had spent time in India or the East or West Indies. Many houses in the southern United States and in South America sport verandas, too. A veranda is a covered area with open or colonnaded sides that are attached either to one or more sides of a building, or wrapped around it in the manner of a wraparound porch. It was always popular—and somewhat cooler—to relax on a veranda in the heat at whatever time of the day or night. Some have ceiling fans to aid the cooling process.

VERMICULAR

Term for facing stone that has been incised or carved with wavy lines or squiggles to achieve a somewhat distorted texture. It was used a great deal on the facades of Renaissance Italian buildings.

VERNIS MARTIN

An especially hard and brilliant lacquer finish used for both walls and furniture that was developed by the Martin brothers in Paris during the reign of Louis XV. The brothers produced a clear lacquer flecked with gold, as well as some forty other colors, including a particularly beautiful green.

VINETTE

An ornamental molding with a continuous band of entwined leaves and tendrils.

VILLA

A single-family house with various uses and connotations through history: in Roman times it was the landowner's residence; in Renaissance architecture, and particularly Palladian architecture, it was a large country house; in the nineteenth century it denoted a small detached house on the outskirts of a town; and today it can be a detached house anywhere, but is usually a house on a coast, and most often a European coast.

VITREOUS ENAMEL

Porcelain enamel fused to metal.

VITRUVIAN OPENING

A heavy, ancient Egyptian-looking door or window with sides that incline slightly inward toward the top. It gets its name from the ancient Roman architect and architectural theorist Vitruvius, who was a major influence on architecture from the Renaissance through the eighteenth and early nineteenth centuries, and who described it in his writings.

VOLUTE

The distinguishing spiral scroll on an Ionic capital; smaller versions appear on Composite and Corinthian capitals. It was a key feature of Baroque decoration.

WAINSCOT

The paneled wood lining of interior walls in old houses. Also, wainscoting.

WALL PLATE

In roofing, a horizontal member that is fixed longitudinally along the top of the walls to receive the ends of the rafters. In wood-framed construction, the wall plate supports the posts and studs of the wall below that are tenoned into it.

WATTLE AND DAUB

A method of wall construction consisting of branches or thin lathes (wattles) roughly plastered over with mud or clay (daub). It was often used as a filling between the vertical members of old timber-framed houses.

WEATHERBOARDING

Overlapping horizontal boards covering an exterior wood-framed wall. Known in the United States as *clapboard*.

WEATHERING

Making horizontal surfaces, such as windowsills, on a slight slope to throw off rainwater.

WEATHER SLATING OR SLATE HANGING

An exterior wall covering of overlapping vertical rows of slate on a timber substructure; provides protection against moisture.

WIDOW'S WALK

A railed rooftop walkway, usually on early coastal houses, particularly on the East Coast of the United States. Widow's walks were built to make it easier to look out to sea for approaching boats, with the connotation that they did not always return safely home.

WINDER

A tread of a stair that is wider at one end than at the other and is used on staircases with quarter turns.

WHITEWOOD

Trademark name for the otherwise characterless wood used for the interior parts of furniture or for furniture that is intended to be painted or veneered.

WROUGHT IRON

Literally, iron that has been wrought, bent, twisted, formed, and re-formed. Iron that has been drawn out and extended by heating.

XYSTUS

In Greek architecture, a long portico used for athletic contests. In Roman architecture, a long covered walkway or open walk bordered by trees or a colonnade. In ecclesiastical architecture, an ambulatory or a semicircular aisle used for processional purposes.

ZIGGURAT

An ancient Mesopotamian temple tower that looked like a truncated pyramid and was built in smaller and smaller layers, each reached by ramps. A good example is the famous tower of Babylon; the best-preserved is at Choga Zanbil (1250 B.C.) in Iran.

ZOOPHORUS

A carved relief of animals decorating a frieze.

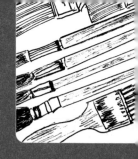

COLORS, PAINTS, VARNISHES, AND DECORATIVE FINISHES

I believe in Michelangelo, Velázquez, and Rembrandt; in the might of design, the mystery of color, the redemption of all things by beauty everlasting.

George Bernard Shaw (1856–1950), from *The Doctor's Dilemma*, Act IV

In general, color and its various gradations and subtleties are the most immediately noticeable and the least-expensive elements in decorating. I say *in general* because the *way* color is introduced and its cost vary considerably. Specialty decorative paint finishes and varnishing are a great deal more expensive than regular paintwork, and of course color can also be introduced with fabrics, trims, carpets, rugs, paintings, prints, posters, objects, books, plants, and flowers—all of which can be much more expensive than a can of paint.

This section covers the whole array of color and paint terms and the vocabulary of the possible decorative paint techniques as well as the brushes and equipment needed for accomplishing them. Color and paint can seem simple enough subjects, but the verbiage surrounding them can be complicated and often quite bewildering. The list of possible paints to use is longer than one might imagine. In fact, for the average home owner the task of dreaming up appropriate color schemes for walls, ceilings, and woodwork or trim is quite difficult enough, without having to battle with color breakdowns, accents, complementary colors, tones, and shades, let alone the right mediums.

All the same, the ability to learn to really *look* at and analyze colors, paint techniques, and appealing color schemes is what will give confidence. Analyze why something is particularly attractive to you. Break down the tones and shades and juxtapositions, and bear them in mind for the future. Suit tones to their visual counterparts and try to familiarize yourself with them, and you will be well on the way to using the many facets of color to their best advantage.

ACCENT COLOR

Contrasting colors or different tones used in small amounts in a room's color scheme to provide variety. Accent colors are often chosen from the opposite side of the spectrum from the main color of a room, and are generally used for pillows, cushions, throws, flowers, rugs, and so on.

ACRYLIC COLOR

Quick-drying artists' colors that are excellent for stenciling. The pigments are mixed in a water-soluble polyacrylic base, resulting in clear, matte colors. They can be used undiluted for an opaque effect or can be diluted with water for a transparent effect.

ADVANCING COLORS

Warm colors, such as reds, yellows, apricots, and oranges, appear to bring surfaces closer and to make objects look bigger. They are useful in large rooms to "bring-in" walls or to "lower" ceilings. Dark shades of cool colors have similar effects.

ALKYD

A synthetic resin used in paint in the United States that now mostly replaces oil-based paint used for interior or exterior painting.

ANTIQUING

A method of artificially aging the look of paint, usually by rubbing over a newly painted surface with a "dirtying" glaze or with a color wash of raw umber, burnt umber, or burnt sienna (although an excellent "antiquing" product is commercially available through Jocasta Innes Paint Finishes). On furniture, the surface may then be wiped over with a cloth, leaving the darker colors in the crevices. Also, rubbing off new paint with steel wool produces a patchy, worn look.

BADGER BLENDER

The finest badger-hair brush for blending and softening a color wash or glaze that has been applied with a different brush, a sponge, or a rag and is not yet dry. A *dusting brush* is a less-expensive substitute.

BAGGING

Creating a textured finish by wrapping a rolled-up cloth in a plastic bag and then working it over a newly applied oil-glazed surface, either in a particular pattern or at random. If areas more than 2 square yards (2 square meters) are worked at a time, the glaze will dry before it has been textured.

BASE COAT

A coat of paint applied before topcoats of paint or glaze to give good coverage and to prepare the surface. When painting a lighter color over a darker one, it's best to apply two base coats and one topcoat, thinning the first coat with a little water. When painting a dark topcoat over a lighter base coat, the base coat should be tinted with a little of the topcoat, or an appropriately tinted commercial base coat may be used. On a new surface, such as plaster or wood, it is best to apply a primer before applying a base coat.

BROKEN COLOR

Two or more coats of different colored paints, in which the top layer is partially removed to reveal the color beneath.

BRUSHES

Many different specialized brushes are used in painting, depending on the method used. These include, among others, a *badger blender, dragger, dusting brush, fitch, flogging brush, mottler, over-grainer, stenciling brush, stippling brush*, and *sword striper*.

BUTTERMILK PAINT

(See *milk paint*.)

BUTTON POLISH

A quick-drying orange-colored shellac that can be used on furniture but also over metal leaf to simulate gold. (See also *shellac*.)

CASEIN PAINT

A paint made from pigments in a casein (milk-curd) medium. It is opaque and powdery (though less powdery than distemper). For a color wash, it is thinned down with two parts water; for cream and pastel shades, it is thinned with white casein. It is tough, water-resistant, and inexpensive, but not, unfortunately, widely available except through specialty paint stores.

CHALKBOARD PAINT

Used for creating a chalkboard on a surface such as a portion of wall in a child's room or on a large piece of primed and undercoated board fixed to a wall or used on an easel.

CISSING

The reverse of spattering, this is achieved by applying a coat of glaze or color wash to a dry base coat and then, while the glaze is still wet, spattering on mineral spirit or turpentine (for oil-based paint) or water (for water-based paint).

COLOR WASH

A delicate, transparent wash of color for walls. It was achieved traditionally with a watered-down, tinted distemper, but today is generally done using a latex, gouache, or acrylic paint diluted with water.

COLOR WHEEL

The seventeenth-century British physicist Sir Isaac Newton developed the original color wheel when he was studying the effects of a beam of light shining through a glass prism. A prism splits light into the colors of a rainbow, and the color wheel is the prismatic spectrum displayed in a circular form. It consists of twelve colors, from which all of the other identifiable hues or gradations of colors are derived. It is based on the three *primary colors* (red, yellow, and blue), which are spaced equally around the circle. Between these are the

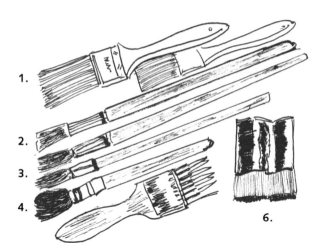

1.

2.

3.

4.

5.

6.

7.

8.

9.

10.

1. Draggers, dragging, or flat varnish brushes

2. Fitch

3. Fitches

4. Mop or softer fitch

5. Over-grainer

6. Mottler

7. Dusting brush or jamb duster

8. Oval varnish brush

9. Badger blender or softener

10. Another dusting brush or hog's hair softener

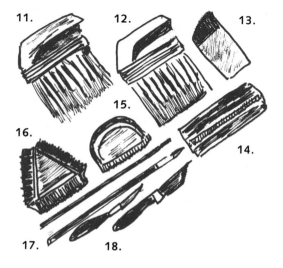

11.

12.

13.

15.

16.

14.

17.

18.

11. Large stipple brush

12. Small stipple brush

13. Heartgrainer (curved rubber or plastic stamp incised with a pattern resembling the heartgrain in pine or oak)

14. Heartgrainer

15. Rubber comb for "graining"

16. Combination rubber comb

17. Artists' brushes for very fine work

18. Sword liner

Brushes

secondary colors (violet, blue, and orange). The remaining six colors are *tertiary colors*. All other colors are variations of these basic colors mixed either with each other, or, for a tint, with black or white.

COMBING

A broken finish with a pattern that resembles a basket weave, achieved by dragging a coarse comb or a specially cut piece of stiff cardboard, plastic, wood, or steel through a wet glaze.

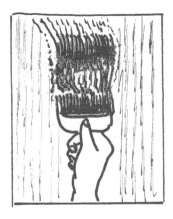

A wide-toothed comb is pulled through the glaze.

COMPLEMENTARY COLOR

A complementary color is a color achieved by mixing two primary colors together in equal parts. The complement of one primary color is made by mixing the two other primary colors. So, the complement of red is green, which is a mixture of yellow and blue (the other two primaries); the complement of blue is orange (red and

yellow); and the complement of yellow is violet (red and blue). Complementary colors fall opposite one another on the color wheel. When equal amounts of two complementary colors are mixed, they form gray. In decorating terms, however, the phrase "complementary colors" often means colors that go well together.

CONTRASTING COLORS

Technically, when talking about color, a contrast is what you get when you put a secondary color next to a primary one. But in normal parlance, the term means colors that are not near one another on the color wheel. Contrasting color schemes include complementary schemes (using complementary colors) and triadic schemes (using colors that are equidistant from one another on the wheel). Such schemes generally work best if one color (usually the major receding or cool color) predominates. Small amounts of contrasting color are useful as accent colors in a room scheme.

COOL COLORS

(See *receding colors*.)

CRACKLE GLAZE

A substance obtainable from specialty paint stores that imitates the effect of old, peeling paint. Crackle glaze is applied between two different colored coats of water-based paint, after which it then produces a series of cracks in the top layer of paint through which the layer underneath is just visible.

CRAQUELURE EFFECT

A method in which two varnishes known to dry at different rates are applied to a painted surface to imitate the delicate cracking (called crazing) that develops in layers of old varnish. It produces a finer crazing than crackle glaze, but it is more time-consuming and expensive.

DECORATOR'S BRUSH

A term for any nonspecialist brush used for painting walls and any other large surface.

DISTEMPER

A powdery paint that can be mixed to make extremely pretty pastel colors and color washes. Also known as *whitewash*, it is made from animal glue, whiting, pigments, and water.

DISTRESSING

To make surfaces look older and more time-worn through techniques such as *antiquing* and *broken color*.

DRAGGER

A long-bristled brush used for dragging paint.

DRAGGING

The process of dragging a dry brush—such as a *dragger* or a *flogging brush*—through a wet glaze or color wash to produce an irregular, fine-lined effect.

A dry brush is dragged through wet glaze.

DUSTING BRUSH

Used for small-scale stippling work, such as on baseboards, doors, and window surrounds. It can also be used for softening and blending (instead of a *badger blender*), or for dragging (instead of a *dragger*). The soft, medium-length bristles should be very carefully cleaned and must never be immersed in solvent or they will drop out.

EGGSHELL FINISH

A finish, usually painted, with a low, subtle sheen.

ENAMEL

An oil-based paint so dense that only one coat is needed. It is most often used for small areas, woodwork, or metal.

EPOXY ENAMEL

A tough, oil-based enamel paint with a hard finish that resists dirt, grease, and scratches. It is ideal for painting over ceramic tiles, porcelain, fiberglass, masonry, and metal.

EQUAL TONES

Many successful room schemes are formed from a mixture of colors of *equal tone*—in other words, colors having approximately the same brightness, depth, and lightness or darkness. Therefore, pastel pinks, roses, yellows, and peaches used together will look harmonious and well balanced, as will, in a much more dramatic way, a combination of strong reds, blues, and yellows. In nature, the quality of light often has the effect of reducing colors to equal tones—the pale colors of early dawn, the soft colors of dusk, the more brilliant colors of sunset—while in decorating, white, gray, or black is often added to colors to produce a similar effect.

FITCH

A small, rather stiff bristled brush used for small-scale work such as detailed stippling or spattering. It is available in fan, angled, oval, and flat shapes.

FLOGGING BRUSH

A long-bristled brush used for dragging and graining. It picks up the glaze easily when pulled across the surface. The brush is used with a slapping technique, hence its name.

FRESCO

A wall painting made by applying water-based paints to damp plaster. This originally Italian technique,

named after the Italian for "fresh," originated in the fourteenth century.

GILDING

Adding a gold finish to a surface. Traditional gilding uses gold leaf or some other metal leaf, which is then fixed to a surface with gold size. A gilt effect can be reproduced using bronze, silver, or aluminum powders; commercial products are also available. However, these methods do not produce the subtlety of traditional gilding.

GLAZE

Traditionally, a transparent oil-based finish (also known as *scumble*). However, a water-based acrylic glaze can now be bought commercially that dries much faster. A tinted glaze has to be applied before any sort of broken finish can be attempted.

GLUE SIZE

(See *size.*)

GOLD LEAF

(See *gold leaf* in Furniture and Upholstery.)

GOLD SIZE

A quick-drying oil varnish usually used as an adhesive in traditional gilding and as a medium for some quick-drying paints.

GOUACHE

Concentrated colors in a water base that give an especially clear, fresh matte finish. Use it "neat" (decorator's terms for undiluted) to decorate paneling or furniture, or use it to tint water-based colors or color washes.

GRAINING

A highly specialized art of painting and staining softwoods to make them look like various hardwoods that have discernible patterns in the graining. It is mostly achieved with special graining brushes—such as over-grainers and heartgrainers—although some decorative painters improvise their own tools for certain specific wood grains or nodules. It was was often practiced in the late seventeenth century as well as in the Victorian and Edwardian eras, and is currently favored again.

GRISAILLE

A painting or design carried out in variations of neutral grays and beiges so that it gives the impression of a basrelief panel. Such a technique was popular for panels over mantels and doors in the French Louis XVI period and during the Neoclassical era all over Europe. Many of the great eighteenth-century British furniture designers used the technique for medallions and plaques.

HARMONIOUS COLORS

These colors are close to one another on the color wheel and as a result are close either in warmth or coolness. For example, a harmonious monochromatic scheme might be composed of a light tone like pearl gray, moving through middle tones such as flannel gray, and ending with a deep tone like charcoal. Or, it could be buttermilk moving from a deep putty to a dark greige. Either way, the effect can be intensified by dashes of noncolors like black or white, and the occasional accent color.

HUE

A pure color to which neither black nor white has been added.

IMPASTO

Thin layers of opaque pigment mixed with an oil glaze that are placed one upon another to create a particular feeling of depth. This was a technique developed by the Venetian painter Titian.

INCARNADINE

A seventeenth-century term for a fleshy pink color verging into light crimson.

INCISED LACQUER

An Asian design process in which many coats of lacquer are applied to a cabinet, tabletop, tray, or screen. Each coat is allowed to dry thoroughly until a particular thickness is achieved, at which point a design is cut into the raised surface.

JAPANNING

An old term for lacquering in the Asian style. It dates back to seventeenth- and eighteenth-century imitations of imported lacquerwork from the Far East. (See also *japanning* in Furniture and Upholstery.)

LAC

The sixteenth- and early-seventeenth-century name for *lacquer*. Lac was the principal ingredient of shellac (and various other varnishes) made from the resinous deposit, usually found on trees, that is created by an insect known as *Coccas lacca*.

LACQUER

Western lacquer is made from shellac dissolved in alcohol and usually mixed with pigment to form a waterproof opaque or colored varnish. *Oriental lacquer* is made from the sap or gum of the lacquer tree.

LACQUERING

A technique involving the patient application of many coats of varnish, one upon another over paint, wood, or metal. Each coat is sanded down when dry before another coat is applied, to create a smooth, lustrous finish. The original technique, developed in the Far East, involved applying many coats of a lacquer made from the sap of the lac tree. Lacquering is used for walls, furniture, screens, boxes, and so on. Walls can be given the effect of lacquer by applying a semi- or high gloss varnish over a painted and sanded surface (with a roller, to avoid brushstrokes), or by using a tinted glaze over paint. (See also *japanning* in Furniture and Upholstery.)

LATEX PAINT

Water-based paint consisting of pigment bound in a synthetic resin called *latex*. It is available in matte or flat, satin or semigloss, and gloss finishes. Latex is soluble in water, is quick-drying, and covers so well that it does not necessarily need an undercoat, though the effect is always that much more professional if one is applied.

LIMING

The process of "whitening" wood, particularly oak, very popular in the 1930s. Good for new paneling and for elderly, as opposed to "good" old furniture. Liming paste for producing this effect is available from specialty paint stores.

LINING BRUSH

A thin brush used to make narrow decorative lines. Artists' sable brushes work well for this, or you can use a sword liner.

MARBLING

The technique of producing faux marble. Sometimes a particular type of marble is copied as closely as possible or sometimes just the general effect of marble is reproduced. The latter approach is sometimes known as marbleizing.

MEDIUM

The term for the liquid in which pigments are mixed to form either paints or some sort of lacquer or glaze. It can vary from water to oil, egg, resin, buttermilk or skimmed milk, and others.

To create a marbled effect, randomly lay on two colors of glaze (left). Stipple selectively with another brush (right).

Then blur the color by lightly brushing with softener (left). Use crumpled paper or cloth to rag glazed surface (right).

Final marbling touches: vein the surface with a darker or contrasting color by twirling and dragging a goose feather over the mixed glazes.

MILK PAINT

A simple casein paint in which powdered colors are mixed with buttermilk or skimmed milk. It was widely used in Colonial America and produces lovely clear colors and a smooth clean-looking finish, although it smells for a bit. Protect with a matte varnish.

MINERAL SPIRITS

A solvent used to dilute oil-based glaze or paint and to soften old latex finishes.

MONOCHROMATIC SCHEME

A type of color scheme that utilizes one basic color in a variety of tones. This type of scheme is benefited by using as many different textures as possible, as well as the occasional accent color. (See also *harmonious colors*.)

MOTTLER

A brush used to mottle, highlight, or distress glazes.

NEUTRAL COLORS

These include the noncolors black, white, and grays—ranging from the palest of silvers to charcoal—and also off-whites, for example, creams through putties, camels, caramel, and nutmeg to browns.

OIL PAINT

This is the equivalent of alkyd paint and comes in four finishes: matte, eggshell, semigloss, and gloss. It is soluble in turpentine or mineral spirits and takes much longer to dry than water-based paints, but it can be washed down easily, provides a good surface, and lasts longer.

OMBRÉ

Literally translated as "shaded" or "shadowed," this is a French term in common use for a painting effect that uses one color graduated into different shades.

OVERGRAINER

A very small brush with clumps of small hairs—like several long, pointed, artists' brushes bound to one handle. It is used to add fine details or a darker grain to a grained surface—in other words, it is used to delicately build up color and details. (Most decorative paint finish brushes tend to take off color, rather than add it.)

PALETTE

This refers to the assortment of colors that are used by an artist or designer for a particular painting or room scheme, as well as the actual board on which artists' paints can be mixed.

PASTEL COLORS

Pastels are the soft and gentle colors produced by adding a good deal of white to other colors; for example, with the addition of white, pink is derived from red, lilac from purple, apricot from orange, and a pale celadon green from green. Pastels are always pale.

PIGMENT

The coloring element in paint. It is available in many forms, including powder, compressed cakes or artists' blocks, artists' oil, gouache, acrylic colors, and tinting colors. In general, like should be mixed with like: solvent-thinned pigment with solvent-thinned paint, and water-thinned pigment with water-thinned paint. Tinting colors, however, can be mixed with either oil or water-based paints.

POLYURETHANE VARNISH

(See *varnish*.)

PRIMARY COLOR

Each of the three primary colors—red, yellow, and blue—is a pure color and cannot be produced by mixing other colors. All other colors are derived from the primary colors.

PRIMER

A primer is generally used on a hitherto untreated surface, such as wood or plaster, in order to seal it before applying an undercoat and the final finish coats.

QUADRATURA

The Italian term for a type of trompe l'oeil painting consisting of architectural elements like columns, colonnades, entablatures, and cupolas painted on walls and ceilings to create deliberately foreshortened perspectives.

RAGGING

Using rags to achieve a particular painted finish. The final effect depends upon the type of fabric used. Burlap, for example, will produce a coarser effect than bunched-up cotton.

When ragging, pat cloth over glaze with one hand.

RAG-ROLLING

Using a rolled rag to get the desired effect when ragging.

Use both hands when rag-rolling.

RECEDING COLORS

Blue, violet, and green, or colors to which these three have been added, are known as receding colors. They are also referred to as cool colors. They can make rooms seem larger because they make surfaces appear to move away from the eye.

ROTTENSTONE

A fine, gray, abrasive powder bought from specialty paint stores. It is mixed with lemon oil, baby oil, or sunflower oil to make a paste that is used to give the final polish to a wall that has been lacquered or varnished.

SATURATION

The intensity, brightness, or purity of a color. The opposite of a saturated color is a muted color—often referred to as "dirty" or "knocked back." Sometimes, in an otherwise muted scheme, it is a good idea to add the occasional dash of a saturated color, which will then seem to sing out. However, it is not necessarily a good idea to add knocked-back color to a saturated room scheme since a "dirty" color against a lot of bright and clear colors tends to simply look dirtier.

SGRAFFITO

Italian "scratched" technique dating from the sixteenth century, but still used today. Tinted or colored plaster is covered by a layer of white plaster—or the other way round—and when dry, scratched to reveal the bottom layer. The scratching could be haphazard or disciplined to produce recognizable motifs such as arabesques.

SECONDARY COLOR

An equal mixture of two primary colors produces a secondary color: red and yellow make orange, blue and red make violet, and yellow and blue make green. Each secondary color is a complementary color of the primary color not used in its making.

SHADE

This is the tone produced by adding black to a hue. In decorating terms, a shade can also mean the color produced by adding gray or white or small amounts of other hues to a color.

SHELLAC

A quick-drying, spirit-based varnish available in "transparent" form (actually a yellowish-brown), orange (also known as *button polish*), white (which is almost clear), and brown.

SIZE

Also known as *glue size*, this serves as a medium to bind paint. In addition, it can be used as a sealant instead of a primer to prevent fresh plaster and unpainted wood from absorbing too much paint when being painted, or too much paste when being wallpapered. Plastic-based sizes, such as PVA (polyvinyl acrylic), are used with synthetic paints, such as latex, and natural paints, such as casein and distemper. The best quality size is made from rabbit skin.

SOLVENT

A substance used to dilute paint, glaze, or varnish and to clean brushes. Mineral spirits and turpentine are both solvents for oil-based products; water is the solvent for water-based products.

SPATTERING

A simple broken-color technique that consists of spattering a dry surface with dots of color. It is known as an *additive technique*.

SPECTRUM

A beam of light that when shone through a glass prism is broken up into its constituent wavelengths, represented by bands of red, orange, yellow, green, blue, and violet, just like a rainbow. Studying this phenomenon led the physicist Sir Isaac Newton to develop the color wheel. As odd as it may seem at first, white is produced by a balanced mix of all the colors of the spectrum, while black is a total absence of color.

SPONGING

This technique can either be *additive* (by sponging color—or tinted glaze—onto a previously painted surface) or *subtractive* (by gently dabbing glaze off for a more subtly painted distressed effect). Either way, it is one of the easiest paint effects to achieve.

STENCILING

An application, which is usually repeated, by dabbing paint through

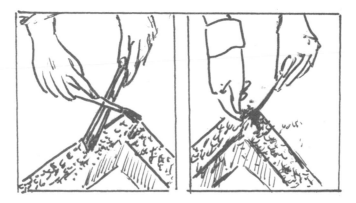

When spattering, tap the brush hard to produce a bold effect (left).
Flick the bristles for a fine speckle of color (right).

An ambitious stencil scheme.

cut-out shapes using a stenciling brush or small sponge. So that it will be long-lasting, a stencil that will be used for walls should be cut from oiled Manila paper, oiled stencil board, or acetate. Oiled Manila paper and acetate are thin, light, easy to wipe clean, and easy to move around but still tough. Also, it is useful that acetate is transparent. In contrast, paper tears easily and gets messy with paint that can be transferred to the clean surface, and it often curls up and won't hold firm. Wood is not as maneuverable and does not wipe off as well, either.)

STENCILING BRUSH

A short plump brush with shorn-off hog's hair bristles, which looks a little like a shaving brush. It gives a crisper edge than that achieved with an ordinary brush.

STIPPLING

An effect produced by gently dabbing a stippling brush against a coat of wet glaze or paint. This is a good soft finish for a large area.

STIPPLING BRUSH

A rectangular brush with long and short detachable handles. The long one is used for stippling walls and large surfaces like doors; the shorter for close work. It lifts off fine flecks of paint to produce the typical stippled or freckled effect. Cheaper alternatives are an old hairbrush or an old clothes brush.

SWORD STRIPER

A type of lining brush used for making fine thin lines, particularly for marbling. Its bristles taper to a point.

TEMPERA

A very early painting medium that produces a tough, permanent finish. Powdered color or pigment is mixed with fresh egg yolks, thinned down with water, and then applied to a panel or surface prepared with gesso. As it dries, the color pales, as is the case with most paint media.

TINTING COLOR

A synthetic dye that is attainable in good art supply or specialty paint stores. Tinting colors can be used for tinting paints and glazes, and can be used for either oil-based or water-based paints.

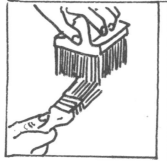 

**Prime stippling brush with a little glaze (left).
Wipe off excess glaze with a rag (right).**

TERTIARY COLOR

A tertiary color is made up of equal quantities of *primary colors* and *secondary colors*—for example, lime green is composed of yellow (primary) and green (secondary).

TINT

The tone of a color that is produced by the addition of a very small amount of white or a slightly darker shade. Tints can be only *marginally* different from the principal colors in a scheme.

TONE

This term refers to the gradation of a color from its weakest intensity to its greatest—for example, the range from palest pink to a dark rose red.

TOSSAWAY BRUSH

An inexpensive brush that can be thrown away after use, often used for varnishing.

TROMPE L'OEIL

An illusionistic painting effect often applied to walls and created, in particular, by the use of shading, highlights, and clever perspective. Literally, to "trick, cheat," or "deceive the eye."

TURPENTINE

A solvent used for cleaning brushes, as well as for thinning artists' oil paints.

An early example of trompe l'oeil. The Ixion Room, House of the Vetti, Pompeii, first century A.D. Above the simulated marble dado, pictures are set in simulated three-dimensional frames.

A twentieth-century example of trompe l'oeil. The entire room is painted to a design by the Italian architectural painter Renzo Mangiardino.

UNDERCOAT

A standard paint applied as a thin coat (or coats) and left to dry before the main coat of paint is applied.

VARNISH

A final transparent layer of varnish is used to harden and protect a decorative finish. Varnishes come in matte, flat, eggshell, semigloss, and gloss finishes. Quick-drying acrylic water-based varnishes are superseding the older polyurethane and oil-based finishes.

WARM COLORS

(See *advancing colors*.)

FABRIC AND WALLPAPER

Whatever you have in your rooms, think first of the walls, for they are what make your house and home, and if you do not make some sacrifices in their favour you will find your chambers have a makeshift, lodging house look about them.

William Morris (1834–1896)

The history of fabric and wallpaper is a fascinating one to follow as much for what it reveals about the tastes of the day—which were influenced, beginning in the seventeenth century, by the importation of textiles from the Far East and India—as for developments over the centuries in weaving, dyeing, and printing. Interestingly, an appreciation for the usefulness and beauty of fabric and wallpaper is a common thread throughout human history. In the eighth century B.C., Homer was always going on about rich embroidered fabrics in both the *Iliad* and the *Odyssey*, and China and Japan produced stunning woven and painted silks from the earliest times. Medieval European bed and wall hangings known as "stuffs" were often the most prized of household possessions. They were packed up and transported from property to property in those peripatetic centuries to transform bare cold rooms as they were hung and rehung. Early American settlers set out to produce simple homespun cloths to adorn their homes almost as quickly as they had built them, just as fabric and wallpaper today form the fundamental "dressing" of a home. Many of the extant letters and journals of the eighteenth and nineteenth centuries mention the choices and purchases of fabrics and papers as preeminent factors in people's lives.

Contemporary manufacturers of fabrics and papers rely a very great deal on being able to reproduce and re-color old patterns—"documents" as they are known in the trade—while developing new patterns, synthetic materials, and technologies. Yet some of the oldest ethnic tribes around the world are still producing surprisingly sophisticated traditions of patterns, color juxtapositions, and weaves that have hardly changed over the centuries and are increasingly valued. This section, then, encompasses a vocabulary that is both ancient and traditional, but which has been added to over the decades with each innovation.

ACETATE

Cellulose acetate fiber, or any thread, yarn, or fabric made from it. It is not as strong as cotton, but it dyes and drapes well.

ACRYLIC

A type of synthetic fiber or fabric. It is stronger than natural fibers and will not shrink or crease, but it does attract dirt.

ALPACA

Fine silken cloth that is soft to the touch, light in weight, and made from the hair of Peruvian alpacas, which are a kind of cross between a sheep and a llama. The cloth may be woven entirely from alpaca hair or from alpaca blended with additions of silk, cotton, and regular sheep's wool.

ANAGLYPTA

A particularly tough, embossed wall covering made of wood or cotton-fiber pulp. It was introduced in England in the 1880s as an alternative to the more expensive, heavier Lincrusta, made from the same materials as linoleum, and meant to emulate late-seventeenth- and early-eighteenth-century embossed leather wall coverings. Anaglypta papers usually look better painted and are useful for hard-wearing areas and for covering old and battered, or irregular—but not damp—walls. They were often used to cover ceilings in the nineteenth century as much for their lightness as for

An Anaglypta peacock paper in the Art Nouveau style, ca. 1900

their decorative surfaces. Now they are more often used to cover dadoes or wainscoting, the area between dado or chair rails and baseboards. (See also *Lincrusta paper*.)

ANGORA

Soft, long, hairlike wool from the Angora goat, a native of Anatolia (the old name for Turkey), but now also raised in Texas. It is often used in combination with wool, mohair, and other fabric blends.

ANILINE

A term applied to dyes used to color fabrics; aniline dye is derived from coal tar.

ARABESQUE WALLPAPER

This dates from the eighteenth century and was generally supplied and hung as separate panels with either printed borders or set in paper frames depicting architectural motifs. These papers had light, airy designs inspired by sixteenth-century engraved ornament, Raphael's famous series of pilaster designs for the Vatican Logge that he executed in 1519, and also by motifs taken from Pompeiian wall decorations. They were particularly popular in France among the aristocracy.

ARCHITECTURAL WALLPAPER

Like Arabesque paper, architectural paper dates mainly from the eighteenth century, although some black-and-white papers imitating elaborate low-relief plasterwork (mostly meant for ceilings) were introduced in the late seventeenth century. Good eighteenth- and nineteenth-century architectural paper, particularly recommended for halls and staircases, imitated sculpture and various architectural features, either in the Gothic or Classical style, with trompe l'oeil depictions of masonry or stonework, arches, Classical pillars, marble, wainscot paneling, and, later, brickwork, tiling, and wood grain. As J. C. Loudon explained in his *Encyclopaedia*, first

Portion of a chiaroscuro "pillar and arch" architectural paper (ca. 1769) left over from the eighteenth-century decoration of the Old Manor Bourton-on-the-Water, Gloucestershire, England

published in 1833, "For entrance lobbies and staircases one of the best designs was a paper simply marked with lines in imitation of hewn stone because if it was damaged a piece the size of one of the stones could be removed without the repair being obvious." Apparently, the Classical styles were particularly popular in America, and the Gothic in England and Europe. Horace Walpole used many Gothic papers in his famous house, Strawberry Hill, entirely carried out in the Gothic taste. "Pillar and Arch" papers often used both Classical *and* Gothic features in one design and often represented arcading or a facade punctuated by sculptures in shallow arched niches. Gradually, more figurative elements crept in, sometimes in the shape of memorials and monuments. A late-eighteenth-century American paper depicts the defeat of the British and the declaration of American independence; another a memorial to George Washington complete with figures of Liberty and Justice. In 1795, a Parisian paper manufacturer called Durolin advertised an extensive range of "architectural ornaments in grisaille (papers printed all in tones of gray or beige) and highlighted with gold; papers imitating Brazil wood and book spines of all sizes; grille-work imitating that of bookcases, open as well as closed; trellising, brickwork, stonework, ashlar, marbles, granites, columns, pilasters, margents, banisters, cornices, architraves, stayes, swags, parterres, corners, borders, paneling and overdoors of all kinds...." In the 1840s and '50s, wallpaper panels were printed in grisaille to represent sculpture collections. Toward the end of the nineteenth century, however, tastemakers vociferously objected to the sham of imitating one material in another, although such papers were just part of a decorating tradition that has woven in and out of the centuries in a somewhat tongue-in-cheek manner.

ART LINEN

Plain weave, cylindrical yarn with a very soft finish used as a needlework base.

AWNING STRIPE

Heavy, firm-woven cotton duck or canvas with either yarn-dyed or printed or painted stripes. Typically used for awnings and beach umbrellas.

BAIZE

A coarsely woven, reversible fabric with a feltlike surface. It was often used to cover connecting doors between servants' and living quarters, in the days when many people had live-in help—hence the expression "beyond the green-baize door." In fact, it is actually made in a range of colors besides green and looks good edged or studded with brass- or copper-headed nails. It can also be used for covering walls as well as for curtains and shades.

BARATHEA

A tightly woven fabric with a characteristic pebbly weave either of silk or rayon or a blend of the two.

BARK CLOTH

A woven fabric with a rough texture, used primarily for curtains.

BATIK

Generally, fabric dyed using the batik method originating from Indonesia, in which portions of a piece of fabric are coated with wax so that only the unwaxed area will take on the dye. The operation can be repeated several times with several colors for a more idiosyncratic effect. The effect is now often machine imitated.

BATISTE

A soft, sheer fabric named after Jean-Batiste, an early French weaver. It usually comes in white with wide streaks. It can be woven from cotton, silk, linen, wool, or synthetic fibers.

BEDFORD CORD

A vertically corded material of cotton, worsted, or silk, or a blend. It was first made in Bedford, Massachusetts.

BENGALINE

A finely woven fabric with a raised horizontal rib.

BOBBINET

Curtain material made with a round-hole mesh. The closeness of the mesh and the fineness of the thread determine the quality.

BOMBAZINE

Crepelike black fabric used for mourning clothes in the nineteenth century, hence the expression "mourning crepes."

BORDERS

Borders, both for wallpapers and textile hangings, were originally developed in the late seventeenth century to hide the tacks with which papers and hangings were fixed to the walls (in those pre-paste days). In the eighteenth century, borders were generally made to match the papers and were considered indispensable. John Walsh, a paper importer in Boston, wrote to his agent in France complaining, "Do let the borders match better—the (back) grounds ought to be alike." And a Rhode Island importer wrote crossly to his English suppliers that "the paper hangings came without borders and are now lying useless." In the late eighteenth century George Washington wrote, when ordering a wallpaper border, "I do not know whether it is usual to fasten it with Brads (tacks) or Glew (glue)." (It is hard to imagine present incumbents of the White House paying so much attention to domestic details.) Contrast borders, for decoration as much as for neatness of finish, were developed in the nineteenth century once pasted papers became the norm. Borders are still manufactured and sold for both purposes and are sometimes used alone over painted walls as a substitute for decorative cornices, chair rails, and baseboards or to form the appearance of paneling.

BOUCLÉ

A general term, from the French for "buckled" or "ringed," for a fabric with a buckled or looped appearance caused by the drawn-out looped yarn with which it is woven.

Some late-eighteenth- and nineteenth-century wallpaper borders

BROCADE

Jacquard-weave upholstery and drapery fabric (also, in lighter form, used for evening clothes) with interwoven raised patterns emphasized by contrasting surfaces or colors, sometimes outlined by gold or silver thread. The name derives from the French "to ornament."

BROCATELLE

A variation of brocade with a higher relief or repoussé effect, meant, originally, to be an imitation of the old Italian tooled leather. Warp and filling yarns are unequally twisted with an extra set of yarn for backing.

BUCKRAM

Once this was the term for a rich, heavy cloth, but it now refers to a stiffened material, usually cotton mixed with

Brocade

glue sizing, to stiffen drapery headings, valances, and curtain tie-backs.

BUMP

Thick, loosely woven, blanketlike cotton or polyester interlining for curtains, or used as a lining for "walling," or fabric-covered walls.

BURLAP

A coarse cloth woven from jute, hemp, or cotton and used to cover springs in upholstery and quite often for textured wall coverings. It is available in its natural color or, for walls or even curtains, in a variety of colors. For walls it can be paper-backed for easier application. In Britain it is called hessian.

BUTCHER'S LINEN

A coarse, homespun linen-weave cloth originally used for butchers' smocks.

CALICO

A plain-weave, inexpensive, printed cotton fabric originally from Calcutta, India. The British term for unbleached muslin.

CAMBRIC

A fine, tightly woven white or solid-colored cotton fabric with a glazed appearance on the right side. It can be used for curtains, but also shirts and nightwear.

CAMEL HAIR

Hair from camels that is lustrous, soft, and wool-like in texture with natural colors ranging from sand to a deeper brown. It can be used for luxurious upholstery and wall coverings, blankets, throws, pillows, rugs, and coats.

CANVAS

A tightly woven cloth, usually of linen, hemp, or cotton, used for upholstery or tapestry work, or stretched on a frame as a surface for a painting.

CASEMENT CLOTH

A broad term that covers many curtain fabrics, usually of a light, plain, and neutral color. The weave structure is plain twill.

CASHMERE

Silken, soft, wool-like hair from goats of Kashmir, India, Iran, Iraq, and the southwest of China. True cashmere is originally brownish in shade. It is used for expensive throws and pillows, as well as sweaters and clothing.

CAVALRY TWILL

Strong, tough material with a pronounced raised cord. It can be used for upholstery but is most often used for trousers.

CHALLIS

Soft fabric of silk, worsted (mainly blends of smooth, well-twisted nylon or polyester yarns), or rayon. It is available in solid colors or printed and is is often used for curtains.

CHAMBRAY

A fine quality plain-weave fabric with a linenlike finish that is woven in solid colors, checks, or stripes. It can be used for light curtains, pillows, and so on and is especially breezy and fresh looking for summer rooms.

CHEESECLOTH

Plain-woven, soft, low-count cotton also known as *gauze*. Coarse grades are used for cheese wrappings, dust cloths, and fine sieving, and finer grades for lightweight bed and window draperies.

CHENILLE

Fabric made by weaving a thick, soft weft with a small, hard warp, which binds the weft threads together. Split into stripes, this forms the chenille yarn used for weaving the fabric. The cut edges of the yarn form a plush surface.

CHEVIOT

Lightweight tweed made from the cheviot sheep bred in the Cheviot Hills in Scotland. It is mainly used for sports coats but can also be adapted for upholstery.

CHIAROSCURO

From the Italian words for "light" and "dark," chiaroscuro refers to a pictorial representation done in shades of gray, without color. Many chiaroscuro wallpapers were produced at the beginning of the nineteenth century.

CHIFFON

A thin, gauze fabric of plain-weave construction made of silk. Used mainly for clothing, but also for airy curtains.

CHINESE WALLPAPERS

These were first introduced to Europe and subsequently to America in the late seventeenth century in panels, when they were called, somewhat hazily, either *India* or *Japan papers*. By the mid-eighteenth century, with the popularity of chinoiserie and Chinese motifs (such as butterflies, flowering trees, and Occidental figures walking through Oriental landscapes), they became increasingly fashionable and were copied by English and French printers.

CHINO

A hard-wearing cotton fabric woven of combed yarn in a twill weave. Used mainly for armed services summer trousers, but also for upholstery.

CHINTZ

Originally any printed cotton fabric, named after the Hindu word for "spotted," but now available both patterned (mainly with flora) and solid. The only really durable chintz that will withstand washing or dry cleaning is one that has a protective glaze made of resin—thus its name *glazed chintz*. *Unglazed chintz* is also known as *cretonne*. Chintz is used for curtains, shades, and slip- and bedcovers.

CORDUROY

Mostly all-cotton cloth with narrow-to-wide wales backed by a plain twill weave for extra durability. It can be obtained in washable, stretchable, and durably pressed varieties. It is useful for upholstery.

COTTON

The term refers both to the cotton fiber itself and the fabric that is made from it, which devolves from the seed-case of a cotton plant. It is an incredibly versatile fabric and comes in a wide range of weights and textures. Cotton fiber is grown in America, Central America, China, Egypt, India, Israel, Mexico, and Peru. Very fine qualities come from Egypt; the finest of all is the Sea Island variety originally grown—before the Civil War—on the islands off the Carolinas and Georgia, but now in Central America and Mexico.

CRASH

A coarse fabric with a slightly lumpy texture obtained by weaving together thick uneven yarns. It can be made of jute, rayon, linen, cotton, or a blend, and is mainly used for curtains.

CREPE

A general term for lightweight fabric of silk, rayon, cotton, wool synthetic, or a mixture of any of the synthetic fabrics with the natural ones. It is characterized by a crinkly surface. (See also *bombazine*).

CRETONNE

Drapery and slipcover material first made by a Monsieur Cretonne in France. It is similar to unglazed chintz but usually has somewhat larger designs.

CREWELWORK

Embroidery worked in colored worsted yarns with a variety of stitches, but mostly chain stitch, on cream-colored cotton, linen, or wool.

DAMASK

Firm, rather glossy jacquard-weave fabric first introduced to the West by Marco Polo in the thirteenth century. He had discovered it in Damascus, at that time the center of the fabric trade between East and West. It is similar to brocade but flatter and reversible, though the pattern changes color on the wrong side. (Incidentally, looking at—and often choosing—the "wrong" side of a fabric is a good decorator's trick to remember. That wrong side might achieve just the right subtle shade.) Damask is now available in linen, cotton, rayon, or silk and used for draperies, bed dressing, and upholstery, as well as for table linen.

DECAL

Decal designs are printed in reverse on thin paper attached to a backing and then transferred to the chosen surface. They are particularly useful for children's room decoration since they can be easily removed and replaced as tastes change. The English term for decal is *transfer*.

DENIM

Heavy twill made of coarse cotton yarn, though some for dress goods may be finer. The name, originally *serge de Nîmes*, comes from France. Available in others colors, as well as shades of blue, it is used for upholstery and general furnishing fabric as well as for jeans.

DIAPER MOTIF

An allover square, diamond, or rectangular trellis design sometimes enclosing leaf or floral designs or dots. It is mainly used for borders on wallpapers and fabrics.

DIMITY

Lightweight, sheer cotton fabric, often woven with an integral stripe or check that launders well and is good for bedspreads and curtain sheers as well as clothes.

DOESKIN

This is really a soft, malleable leather made from the skin of a doe and used for luxurious upholstery, but the word is also used to describe a napped finish on one side of a wool or heavy satin-weave cotton, hence "doeskin finish."

DOTTED SWISS

Sheer plain-weave cotton fabric woven with dots that originated at Saint Gallen in Switzerland around 1750. It is often used for sheer curtains.

DOUPPIONI OR DOUPION

Originally a slubbed silk made from the thread of two silkworm cocoons that have nested together. The double thread is not separated during spinning. The same effect is now achieved with synthetics.

DUCK

Tightly woven, heavy, generally cotton fabric considered to be the most

Dotted Swiss curtains

durable on the market. Excellent for upholstery.

EMBOSSED PAPER

The generic title for papers like Anaglypta and Lincrusta, Vynaglypta and Supaglypta, as well as flocks. They are all exceptionally hard wearing and usually have some insulating qualities as well.

FAILLE

Soft, ribbed fabric of silk, rayon, or cotton belonging to the grosgrain family. It drapes well for curtains.

FAKE FUR

Cotton or man-made fibers used for woven or knitted simulations of various furs that are flameproof and dry cleanable. Good for throws as well as outdoor coats and jackets.

FELT

Thickish wool fabric made by pressing rather than weaving. It is sometimes paper-backed and sold in a generous range of colors for wall coverings; non-paper-backed felts can be stuck straight onto the wall or stretched on battens. Since it is very wide it can be quite cost-effective. A thicker version is made for inexpensive carpeting, and is practical for short-term rentals that need to be brightened up.

FIGURING

The slub or tiny raised areas caused by the weaving method on some fabrics, or somewhat abstract designs on papers.

FILLING

In weaving, a term for the individual warp yarn that interlaces at right angles with a weft yarn (hence the expression "the warp and weft" of a fabric). It is also known as *pick* or *filling pick*, and in the United Kingdom as *weft*.

FLANNEL

A cotton, rayon, wool, or worsted fabric napped on both sides. It is used for blankets, warm sheets, wall coverings, and draperies, as well as clothes.

FLOCK OR FLOCK PAPER

A process invented in the seventeenth century whereby finely chopped wool was sprinkled all over sheets of paper with designs filled in with glue. The wool stuck only to the sticky surfaces and the rest was blown off, producing

Fragment of an architectural, flocked block print paper in the neo-Gothic manner, originally printed by Cowtan & Son in 1840. Reproduced by Cole & Son

a raised cut-velvet effect. The original paper was so well received that, in the 1750s, Madame de Pompadour is said to have replaced precious tapestries in her sumptuous dressing room/ bathroom at her Chateau de Chimys with the new "English paper," as flock was then called. Today it is machine implemented, and is also adapted to produce an allover solid suede or velvet effect.

FOAMBACK

Fabric that has been laminated to a backing of polyurethane foam.

FOIL PAPER

Like Mylar paper, and equally steam-resistant, foil paper is useful for bathrooms, or anyplace where a bit of sparkle and reflection helps to enhance available light. It is fairly fragile though, so must be used with lining paper. It should not be used on uneven walls, since it will merely make any unevenness more apparent, or in sunny rooms where it might cause glare.

GABARDINE

Firm, tightly woven fabric with a close diagonal twill-weave surface and a flat back. It can be made from most major fibers either alone or in blends. It can be used for hard-wearing upholstery.

GAUZE

Thin, sheer-woven cotton similar to cheesecloth and named after fabric first made in Gaza. Used for sheer curtains.

GENOA VELVET

Figured velvet with a satin ground and multicolored pile. It can be used for upholstery, pillows, or curtains.

GINGHAM

Checked plain-weave cotton fabric used for curtains, pillows, slipcovers, and upholstery, as well as clothes.

GLAZE

In fabrics, a finish that provides a sheen, luster, or polish to the fabric surface (such as with glazed chintz). Glazed fabrics can be used for curtains, upholstery, and lamp shades.

GRASS CLOTH

Cloth made from rough-textured vegetable fibers that are woven together. When backed with paper it can be used as a wallpaper. It is also used for draperies.

GRAY GOODS

Cotton and cotton-mixture fabrics straight from the loom before they are finished or dyed. Similarly, silks and rayons fresh from the loom are known in the trade as *greige goods* (as the name implies, they are a gray-beige color).

GRENADINE

Loosely woven, fine fabric made from silk, rayon, or wool that is usually plain, or woven with dots. Used for draperies.

HAND

In fabric, the feel of a piece of material.

HAND-BLOCKING

A printing method that involves cutting or carving a design onto some sort of block made of wood, linoleum, and so on. Paint or dye is applied to that surface, which is then pressed onto the fabric or host material. Since the cut or incised lines will not print onto the fabric or host material, the paint or dye adhering to the flat surface will form the design.

HANGING

An umbrella term that embraces bed curtains, as well as draperies for windows and tapestries, or decorative fabric hangings for walls.

HARRIS TWEED

Tweed made of virgin wool that is spun, died, and handwoven by islanders from Harris and other Hebrides Islands off Scotland.

HERRINGBONE

A pattern made up of rows of parallel lines that in any two adjacent rows slope in opposite directions.

HOLLAND

Plain-woven cotton or linen that is heavily sized or starched and sometimes given an oil treatment for opacity. It was traditionally used for shades (called Holland blinds), and is sometimes known as *shade cloth*.

HOMESPUN

Loosely woven fabric formerly spun by home weavers but now sometimes imitated by manufacturers to resemble handwoven Colonial material.

HONEYCOMB WAFFLE

A raised effect that looks like the cellular combs of a beehive. The raised areas on one side of the material are the recessed areas on the other side. The high point on one side of the material is the low point on the reverse. It belongs to the piqué family of fabrics, and is used for curtains, bedspreads, and table linen.

HOPSACK

Rough-surfaced basket-weave patterned cotton, linen, or rayon.

HOUND'S-TOOTH CHECK

A broken-check effect available in a variety of sizes.

INDIENNES

A French term, generally used to describe the Indian print cottons made during the seventeenth and eighteenth centuries and imported by the Dutch East India Company.

JACQUARD

An intricate method of raised weaving invented by Joseph Jacquard between 1801 and 1804 and used for damasks, brocades, and machine-made tapestries.

JARDINIÈRE VELVET

A silk velvet originally produced in Genoa, Italy. It makes use of multicolor designs that look like flower arrangements—hence the name. Several levels of uncut loops are set against a silk or satin background.

JASPÉ

A French term for upholstery or other fabric incorporating a series of faint stripes formed by light, medium, and dark yarn of the same color.

JERSEY

Plain-stitch knitted cloth, mostly made of wool.

JUTE

A coarse brown fiber from the stalk of the Indian Bast plant. It is mainly used in the weaving of burlap (hessian) and as a backing for carpets.

LACE

Fine, open-work fabric with patterns of knotted, twisted, or looped threads on a ground of net or mesh. The name is derived from the old French word *las*, itself derived from the Latin *laquens*, which means a "noose" or to "ensnare."

LAMÉ

Brocade, brocatelle, or damask in which metallic threads or yarns are integrated into the weave. Copper, silver, or gold are the most popular threads.

LAWN

Light, thin, combed-cotton fabric first made in Laon, France. It is mostly sold in plain white, although it comes in prints, or with a faint, and sometimes satin, stripe. It is crisper than voile but not as crisp as organdy and has a crease-resistant finish. Good summer fabric.

LINCRUSTA PAPER

Very similar to Anaglypta paper, but made from linseed oil welded to a backing paper and then embossed with a burlap, hessian, or tilelike texture. Like Anaglypta, Lincrusta can be over-painted.

LINEN

Fabric made from the bark of the flax plant. It is favored in summer because of its rapid moisture absorption and its tendency not to soil easily, as well as for its smoothness and luster. But it does crease easily. Used for curtains or tightly stretched upholstery, as well as clothes and bed and table linen.

MADRAS COTTON

Strong cotton fabric from India woven with a brightly colored plaid or check.

MADRAS MUSLIN

Gauze fabric, usually white, with thick weft threads. It is used for light curtains and sheer draperies.

MAN-MADE FIBERS

As the name implies, fibers that are not found naturally. Formerly called synthetic fibers.

MARQUISETTE

Lightweight, open-mesh cloth made of cotton, silk, or man-made fibers such as glass fiber, polyester, acrylic, or nylon and very popular for easily laundered sheers.

MATELASSÉ

A French word meaning "cushioned" or "padded," and here describing a quilted surface produced on a loom, or a figured or brocaded cloth with a raised pattern. Used for luxuriously thick curtains, bedcovers, pillows, or upholstery.

MERCERIZED

A treatment for thread or actual fabric to give added luster.

MERINO

The finest quality wool available.

METALLIC CLOTH

Any fabric, but usually silk, woven with integrated metal threads. Metallic yarns made with Mylar polyester film withstand higher temperatures than acetate-type yarns. Silver or gold lamé is a metallic cloth.

MOHAIR

Extremely strong hair culled from the Angora goat, one of the oldest-known animals. Mohair is cultivated in South Africa, western Asia, Turkey, and now in the United States—in California, Oregon, and Texas—and is two-and-a-half times stronger than wool, which it easily outwears. Used for blankets and throws, as well as clothes.

MOIRÉ

A watermark or wavy finish given to cotton, silk, rayon, acetate, nylon, and so on, that gives both light and dim effects.

MOLESKIN

A type of cotton fabric that is fleece-lined with a thick, soft, suede-effect nap.

MONK'S CLOTH

Coarse, canvaslike material made of heavy cotton yarns, sometimes containing flax, jute, or hemp. Originally woven for monks' habits, it wears extremely well and can be used for curtains, upholstery, and wall hangings and coverings. Also known as *friar's cloth*, it is not particularly easy to sew or manipulate.

MUSLIN

Generic term for a variety of plain-weave cotton fabrics varying in fineness.

MYLAR PAPER

Much like foil paper. When used—and strengthened—with lining paper it is useful in any room that gets much steam, such as a bathroom or laundry room. Avoid using it over uneven walls because it has a tendency to highlight any imperfections, or in very sunny situations where it will cause problems with glare.

NAP

Not to be confused with pile, it is, rather, the fuzzy or downy surface of a cloth with its fibers raised to the surface, as in flannel.

NATURAL FIBERS

Fibers produced from natural materials or sources (as in silk from silkworms), cotton (from cottonseeds), and wool (from sheep), as opposed to synthetic or man-made fibers.

NET

Open-mesh work and also the British generic term for sheer fabrics used as curtains.

NINON

Smooth, transparent but highly textured voile. If used for curtains it is woven with glass fibers.

NOTTINGHAM LACE

Flat lace used for tablecloths and sheers, originally handmade in Nottingham, England, but now machine made.

NOVELTY WEAVE

Any small weave made from a combination of two or more basic weaves (such as twill, satin, basket, and rib).

NYLON

A man-made fiber adapted into filaments of extreme toughness and elasticity that are then knitted into fabrics.

OILCLOTH

Fabric treated with a linseed oil varnish to resemble patent-leather and used for table covers or for lining shelves, as well as for waterproof coats, various containers, bags, and luggage.

OILED SILK

Thin silk fabric that has been soaked in boiled linseed oil and left to dry, thereby making it waterproof. It is often used for shower curtains.

OLEFIN

A soil-resistant, insulating man-made fiber used as a component in sturdy upholstery fabrics and in the manufacture of outdoor carpeting.

ORGANDY OR ORGANDIE

Fine, transparent cotton cloth or lawn chemically treated to maintain its crispness. Used for curtains, baby's crib dressings, and numerous other purposes.

ORGANZA

Very thin but stiff woven silk or man-made fiber.

ORGANZINE

Expensive two-ply silk.

OTTOMAN

A heavy silk or man-made fiber fabric with a ribbed effect. It is used for both clothes and furnishings.

PAISLEY

Multicolored amoeba-shaped designs of Persian and Indian descent, woven or printed on normally natural fabrics. Shawls using these designs were also woven in the town of Paisley in Scotland. (See example on the next page.)

PALAMPORE

An Indian cotton printed with tree-of-life designs intermingled with peacocks and other exotic birds among the

Paisley

foliage. It was first introduced to Europe in the late seventeenth and early eighteenth centuries.

PANNÉ

Satin-faced velvet or silk with a high luster made possible by powerful roller-pressure treatment.

PASHMINA

A luxuriously soft and light mixture of silk and wool from domestic Himalayan goats.

PASSEMENTERIE

A French term—from *passement*, meaning a strip of lace—in common use for fabric trimmings for upholstery and curtains. They can be made of ribbon, grosgrain, braid, cord, beads, or gimp.

PAYSAGES OR PAYSAGES-DECORS

(See *scenic paper*.)

PEAU DE SOIE

A soft, tightly woven satin with a low-luster finish. It is usually made of silk.

PERSPECTIVES

The English equivalent to nineteenth-century French *paysages*.

PICK

Another term for the *weft* in weaving.

PILE

A fabric surface made of upright ends, as in fur, and distinct from nap. Corduroy and velveteen are examples of cut pile, while Turkish toweling or terry cloth are examples of uncut pile.

PILLS OR PILLING

Little balls of fiber that form on the surface of a cloth, caused by abrasion or wear and tear.

PIQUÉ

The French term for medium to heavyweight, generally cotton fabric with raised cords that run in the warp direction.

PLAID

A pattern formed from colored bars and stripes that cross one another at right angles, as in a Scottish tartan.

PLAIN WEAVE

A weave structure in which the weft goes over one and under one warp.

Examples include gingham, voile, muslin, taffeta, and pongee.

PLISSÉ

The French term for cotton, acetate, or rayon fabric that has been chemically treated to give a crinkled or pleated effect.

PLUSH

Warp-pile fabric with a surface of cut-pile yarns. Derived from the French word *peluche*.

POINT D'ESPRIT

A fabric with small dots or woolen figuring, somewhat similar to dotted swiss.

POLYESTER

A man-made fiber that is strong and durable but pills and soils easily. It blends easily with natural fibers like cotton and linen to give them greater versatility.

PONGEE

Thin, natural tan-colored fabric that was originally made from wild or raw Chinese silk with a slightly nubby rough weave. Hence its name, which comes from the Chinese *pun-ki*, meaning "woven at home" or "from one's own loom." Nowadays, it is also made from a combed-cotton fabric or simulated in man-made fibers.

POODLE CLOTH

Looped bouclé or knotted yarn that somewhat resembles the coat of a French poodle. Originally made of wool and mohair, it is now made from other fiber mixtures as well.

POPLIN

Fine, cotton, ribbed fabric, usually mercerized, which wears well.

PRATHER

Originally a stray three-dimensional body of indeterminate size and shape. In fabric it is characterized by the small raised irregular nubs found in raw or wild silks, shantungs, some linens, and homespun weaves.

PRINT ROOM

A mid-eighteenth-century term for a room decorated by a method whereby unframed prints and etchings were stuck straight to walls in an arrangement. Cut-out borders, festoons, ribbons, and friezes were then arranged to accent the prints and to "frame" them. (See example on the next page.)

RAMIE

A natural fiber made from the stalk of a plant native to China.

RATINÉ OR RATINE

From the French word meaning "frizzy" or "fuzzy," rather loose tapestry-woven fabric with a nubby surface mostly used for coats, but which can also be used for some upholstery.

RAW SILK

Sometimes called *wild silk*, it is made from the cocoon of the silkworm

Fragment of an eighteenth-century print room

before the natural gum has been removed. It has a slightly nubby, rough finish.

RAYON

A lustrous synthetic fiber made by converting cellulose (wood pulp or cotton linters) into a filament by means of a chemical and mechanical process. It is more lustrous but less expensive than silk, but also not as strong.

REP

A fabric that looks a little like poplin with a heavier, wider cord. Very popular curtain and upholstery material.

REPEAT

One complete repetition of a pattern in fabric, wallpaper, and carpets or rugs.

SAILCLOTH

Sturdy close-weave cotton canvas or other close-weave man-made fiber material normally used for sails, but sometimes for upholstery or shades.

SANFORIZED

A patented preshrinking process.

SATEEN

Mercerized cotton fabric with a satin weave. More expensive grades resemble silk-satin. Most often used for lining curtains.

SATIN

A lustrous-surfaced fabric with a broken twill weave, and usually woven with silk threads, but it can also be made of rayon. It has an interesting texture when used back to front. The name originated from Zaytun (tzu-t'ing Zaitun) in China, where it was first woven.

SAXONY

Originally a high-grade fabric used for topcoats or overcoats, it is made from Saxony merino wool from sheep raised in Germany. The term now describes a highly-twisted worsted yarn that is used to make luxurious upholstery and curtain fabric.

SCENIC PAPER

Panoramic, landscape, or *paysage* wallpaper mainly of French origin and among the most ambitious, and expensive, of all decorative papers. One theory is that scenic papers were the French answer to the then ubiquitous English flock papers. In any case, they were supposed to have been somewhat instrumental after the French Revolution in restoring confidence in French design panache. They were printed from woodblocks on anything up to thirty individual (to suit particular spaces) lengths of paper and meant to be hung as a continuous mural. Although they were so highly detailed that from a distance they could be mistaken for a proper painted mural, they also had their roots in the large-scale French tapestries woven in the Gobelins and Beauvais workshops, as well as in the popular painted panoramas, such as those painted by the great German architect Karl-Friedrich Schinkel (see also *Schinkel, Karl-Friedrich* in Architects, Designers, and Decorators). Occasionally, they were printed in grisaille, which made them less expensive than the full-color designs. Subjects varied from city scenes, mythological subjects, and Classical and historical scenes to parks and pastoral delights. They were hung in reception rooms as much as in

A scenic paper or *paysage* depicting Boston Harbor, from Vue d'Amerique du Nord, designed by Jean-Julian Deltil for Zuber, issued in 1834

hallways, dining rooms, and salons. And since manufacturers could foresee the varying difficulties of hanging them, they were mostly divided into scenes with natural divisions like rocks, walls, or trees that could be trimmed or even sacrificed altogether. Sometimes they were hung just above the chair rail all around a room. Sometimes they came right to the baseboards, or had balustrades that formed their own dado or wainscoting. Others, however, were meant to be hung as single panels with printed paper borders or paper pilasters to act as framing devices. Naturally, with these papers, paintings, mirrors, tall pieces of furniture, and lamp brackets all had to be avoided or kept to a minimum. Leading manufacturers were Dufour of Paris and Zuber et Cie of Alsace-Lorraine. The latter is still producing them.

SCOTCHGARD

Highly advisable fluorochemical water, dirt, and oil-repelling finish for fabrics and leather made by the Minnesota Mining and Manufacturing Company. It is odorless, colorless, safe for to washing and dry cleaning, and does not affect the "hand" of the fabric or leather so treated.

SEERSUCKER

Cotton, nylon, silk, or rayon fabric with a crinkled surface and usually a faintly striped pattern.

SELVAGE

The tightly woven fabric edges that prevent fabrics from unraveling.

SERGE

One of the oldest of textile terms that now implies any smooth-faced cloth made with a twill weave. Worsted serge holds a crease very well but turns shiny with age. French serge has a fine, lofty, springy feel and is one of the best cloths available.

SCRIM

A coarse type of lightweight voile made in different constructions and weights. It can be used for sheer curtains or buckram. Cheesecloth, when bleached and firmly sized, is also known as scrim.

SHANTUNG

Nubby fabric that is very similar to pongee, but somewhat heavier. It too, as the name implies, was originally woven from Chinese silk, but is now often made with man-made fibers or blends of man-made fiber and silk.

SHARKSKIN

A very durable worsted fabric that resembles the skin of a shark and comes in a number of patterns including stripes, plaids, windowpanes, and bird's eyes.

SHETLAND WOOL

Tough, rugged wool from the Shetland Isles in Scotland, used for tweeds, homespuns, cheviots, and throws or car rugs.

SILK

The only natural fiber that comes in filament form. It is obtained by unraveling the cocoons of Japanese silkworms, which vary anywhere from 300 to 1,600 yards in length. The term also applies to fabric woven from silk threads.

SIZING

Any chemical substance applied to a fabric to provide greater stiffness, a smoother surface, or increased strength.

STRIÉ

Cloth that has irregular stripes or streaks that are practically the same color as the background.

SUEDE FABRIC

Woven or knitted cloth made from major textile fibers to resemble suede leather. Excellent for upholstery and sometimes shades.

SUPAGLYPTA PAPER

Supaglypta is a very heavyweight cotton fiber paper with a deeply embossed pattern, and, like the other "glypta" papers, looks best painted, especially with a gloss paint. Like the Anaglyptas, Vynaglyptas, and Lincrustas, Supaglypta is extremely hard wearing and differs from the others only in texture and effect.

SYNTHETIC FIBER

Fiber made through chemical and machine processes as opposed to natural fibers. Also called *man-made fiber*.

TAFFETA

The name applies to several different types of fine, crisp plain-weave fabrics having a sheen and being smooth on both sides. The name comes from the Persian (Iranian) fabric known as taftah, which comes from the Persian verb *taftan*, "to shine" or "to twist, to spin." It is usually solid colored, though it can be printed or woven in such a way that its colors seem to change depending on the angle that one looks at it. It was originally made of silk but is now often made from man-made or synthetic fibers.

TAMBOUR

Machine-made embroidery in chain stitch to resemble work done on a tambour frame. It is also a variety of Limerick lace made in Ireland.

TAPESTRY

Originally a handwoven pictorial subject, then a handwoven fabric made with a bobbin worked from the wrong side on a warp stretched vertically or horizontally. Now it can be machine made.

TARLATAN

A thin, gauzy cotton fabric glazed for stiffness that can be used for curtains or headings.

TERRY CLOTH

An absorbent fabric used for toweling that is woven or knitted with a looped pile.

TICKING

A striped cotton fabric originally used to cover mattresses but now frequently used for upholstery, wall coverings, and, in a finer grade, curtains.

TOILE

Finely woven cotton or linen with translucent qualities; also often a shortened term for toile de Jouy.

TOILE DE JOUY

Originally an eighteenth-century copperplate-printed cotton fabric from France, printed with pictorial scenes in a single color on a white or cream background. Modern versions and excellent reproductions are widely available.

TWEED

Rough-surfaced wool fabric of mixed, flecked colors, good for upholstery as well as clothes.

TWILL

Heavy cotton fabric.

TWILL WEAVE

Weave structure in which the weft moves one step to the right or one step to the left with each line, producing a diagonal texture.

UNBLEACHED MUSLIN

Plain-weave inexpensive cream-colored cotton fabric.

An original George Washington toile de Jouy

UNION

Plain-weave fabric in which the warp and the weft are of different fibers. In particular the term is used for a sturdy linen and cotton upholstery fabric known as *linen union*.

VAT DYE

A dye process used to obtain permanent color.

VELOURS

Fabric with a short pile surface resembling velvet.

VELVET

All warp-pile fabrics except plush and terry cloth.

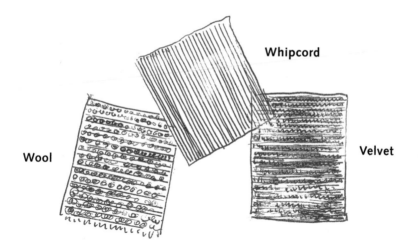

VELVETEEN

A fabric with a short cotton pile meant to be an approximate imitation of silk velvet.

VINYL

Nonwoven plastic capable of being embossed or printed to produce any desired finish.

VINYL PAPERS

Vinyl paper is made from backed polyvinylchloride with a plastic coating and stands up well to grease, finger-prints, cooking splashes, and so on. It is tougher and more waterproof than ordinary washable papers, and a very great deal tougher than expensive non-washable handprinted papers. It must, however, be stuck on with a fungicidal adhesive or mold will collect under-neath. If you use a wallpaper border,

make sure that it is vinyl, too, or that you use a special vinyl paste to ensure that the wallpaper adheres properly to the vinyl paper.

VOILE

Translucent plain-weave fabric, often of cotton, but sometimes made of silk. Used for sheer curtains and shades.

VYNAGLYPTA

Similar to Supaglypta, but made of vinyl.

WARP

The set of yarns running lengthwise on cloth, across the *weft*.

WEAVE

The characteristic structure of a fabric produced from interlocking strands of yarn.

WEFT

The set of yarns running crosswise to and interlaced with the *warp* to produce a woven fabric. Also rather confusingly called *woof, filling, pick,* or *shoot.*

WHIPCORD

A ribbed material formed by floating the warp threads over several large weft threads. Very sturdy.

WILD SILK

An alternative name for *raw silk.*

WOOL

A natural fiber produced from sheep. Also, fabric woven from yarn made of wool fiber. All wool types—depending on the breed of sheep—share the qualities of warmth and elasticity, and are adaptable to blending with other fibers, whether natural or man-made, for added strength, beauty, and smoothness.

WORSTED

Originally a smooth, tightly woven fabric made of uniform and well-twisted wool yarns, but now also made with nylon or polyester yarns.

YARN-DYED

A term used to describe fabrics woven of yarn that has been dyed before it is put into the loom.

FLOORING

A good floor says that the entire foundation of a room is sound.... In recent years,
however, the battle for rich design in
flooring has gained considerable ground;
Modernists and Traditionalists alike
have rediscovered the infinite possibilities
that lie underfoot.

Mark Hampton (1940–1998),
from *Mark Hampton on Decorating*

I t is not an exaggeration to say that there have never before been so many flooring options. Once you make the decision of whether to go hard or soft—although you can combine hard and soft surfaces or textures by, for example, choosing some sort of tile or wood with the softening factor of rugs—you then have to decide on precisely what sort of hard floor or what sort of carpet best suits your lifestyle, location and, not least, pocketbook.

Aside from your decision on texture, you must decide what role flooring will play in your overall decorating scheme. Generally speaking there are two schools of thought on this matter. One school maintains that the floor should be chosen before any other elements of a room are set in place and that that choice should provide the starting-off point, for the final scheme. The other maintains that the best sort of floor, whether hard or soft, is a totally anonymous one, serving as a neutral background against which the other ingredients of a room can be set. Whichever school you follow, you would be hard put in the twenty-first century not to find exactly what you want within the boundaries of practicality, suitability, good design, and cost.

Again, however, there are confusing terms to master. What is the difference, for example, between Wilton and Axminster? Are they the names of long-established manufacturers or are they types of weaves of carpet? What is the difference between the textures of Brussels weave, say, and Velvet? Which natural floor coverings are both handsome and practical—marble, travertine, granite, or limestone? And what about slate, bricks, quarry tiles, or encaustic or ceramic tiles? What about the different kinds of parquet or strip wood floors and how should they be treated? Answers to these questions and others can be found in this section.

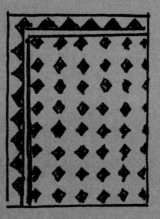

ACRYLIC

In carpets, a man-made fiber that looks a lot like wool and is nonallergenic and cheaper, but slightly less stain-resistant and resilient.

AXMINSTER CARPET

Woven carpet named after the loom on which it is woven, which positions the pile tufts at the same time as it weaves the backing. Because the threads are not carried along the back of the carpet, it is possible to weave Axminsters in a great variety of colors. Although Axminsters always have a cut pile, they can be woven long and shaggy, stubby or sculpted, as well as short or smooth. The strongest weaving quality is generally 80 percent wool, 20 percent nylon, but it can also be woven in an acrylic or a blend.

Axminster cut pile; tufts are inserted one by one into the backing before being cut.

BERBER CARPET

A carpet traditionally made of natural undyed sheep's wool with a dense, looped pile, and named after the original handwoven squares made by North African Berber tribes. Berber carpets are now made by machine (sometimes in olefin, a light, dirt-resistant, highly insulating synthetic fiber) in white, cream, beige, fawn, gray, and dark brown. The term is often used loosely to refer to similar multilevel, looped, neutral-colored carpets.

BOUCLÉ

The pile formed by uncut loops of yarn in, for example, a Brussels-weave carpet.

BRICK

A good, tough, easy to clean flooring material for ground floor spaces in country houses. Once bricks have been warmed up, they maintain a comfortable temperature in winter and are cool in summer. They can be laid in herringbone and basket-weave patterns, as well as the more common parallels. Contemporary bricks made especially for floors are thinner

New brick floor

and lighter than traditional bricks and are preglazed to combat stain-ing, although you may prefer to use more mellow old bricks, which are quite often a bargain, although they will need to be sealed. Architectural salvage companies and local contrac-tors interested in old houses are good sources. Along with the thin brick tiles known as "pavers," contem-porary bricks are comparable in price to good wood or ceramic tiles.

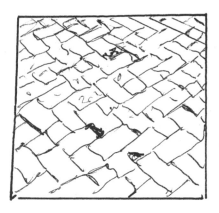

Old brick floor

BROADLOOM

A term describing the standard widths of carpet (12 feet and 15 feet) as opposed to narrower widths for Wiltons and runners.

BRUSSELS WEAVE

A type of weave that results in a tightly looped carpet with a neat, crisp appearance that lends itself to geometric and other graphic designs. Brussels weave carpets look handsome in living rooms that do not get a lot of traffic, as well as in master and guest bedrooms.

They do, however, snag easily, so any loose ends that appear need to be quickly and carefully snipped.

Brussels weave; it is woven like cut pile but the loops are not cut.

Brussels carpet weave

CARPET CONSTRUCTION

Carpets are made in a variety of methods, the main being *weaving* and *tufting*. Woven carpets are the most durable because the weaving process links the backing and the surface pile. They are, however, more expensive than tufted carpets. There are several types of carpet weaves and looms; among the most common types are velvet, Wilton, Axminster, and tapestry or flat weave. A *velvet weave*, which should not be confused with a velvet *texture*, is the simplest kind of weave, producing both looped and cut textures. Patterns are limited to tweeds and stripes. *Wilton* is similar to a velvet loom but capable of producing multi-colored designs; however, the larger size of the *Axminster* loom, along with its more complex construction, allows a greater variety of patterns than the Wilton, in which the number of colors in any design is limited to five. Thus Axminsters are generally patterned, while the majority of Wiltons are solid colored. However, Wiltons are woven in one continuous length, permitting the surface pile and backing to be woven together for a special strength. In patterned Wiltons, the colors not appearing in the surface pile are carried along the back to form an extra pad of fiber that cushions against wear—hence the patterned Wilton's reputation for hidden value. *Tapestry* or *flat* weave is used mainly for kilims and dhurrie rugs. Sisal carpets—and those made of other grasslike fibers, such as seagrass and coir—are available in many different kinds of weave, including herringbone, bouclé, and twill. Tufted carpets are constructed by a method similar to sewing: that is to say, a machine fitted with hundreds of needles stitches the pile through a backing material, which is then coated with latex to secure the tufts. Additional backing is then added to strengthen the carpet. Tufted carpets can have a looped or a cut pile and are generally an excellent value for domestic use.

CARPET DENSITY

The density of a carpet or rug is measured by the number of stitches per inch or centimeter and is the most important aspect of carpet construction to understand. A very closely woven or tufted carpet will assure years of wear whatever the height of the pile. A good test is the so-called "grin test": when choosing a carpet, fold a bit back on itself. If a lot of backing shows, it is not going to be very durable. Many people make the mistake of thinking that a deep pile carpet looks more expensive. In fact, high pile on a carpet often means that it is rather loosely woven and that the pile will flatten easily when walked on.

CARPET TEXTURE

This refers to the surface finish of a carpet and it depends on which type of pile the carpet has. Some of the most common types are:

CUT-AND-LOOP PILE: This is a combination of the two basic types of pile—cut pile and loop pile. If the two different types of pile are different heights, a sculpted effect is produced; if they are of the same height, the effect is a more subtle contrast of textures. Carpets with this type of texture are produced in both solid and multicolor forms. Also known as *high-and-low pile*.

FRIEZE PILE: Another hard-wearing cut-pile texture, but in this case the pile yarns are twisted so tightly that they appear almost curly and therefore somewhat textured. This low, thick pile surface is good for halls, stairs, and corridors, and any rooms that get a lot of traffic.

FUSION-BONDED PILE: Fusion-bonding (fusing a carpet to its backing) produces a very hard wearing carpet with very dense cut pile. It is available in mostly solid colors.

LONG OR SHAG PILE: An informal type of carpet with 1–2 inch-high cut pile that was thought the height of luxury in the mid-twentieth-century, though it is not now much favored. It is made like a velvet pile, that is to say, tufted in high loops. But the loops are then cut through with a shearing knife, as with a sheep's coat, to give it a distinctive shaggy look. It comes in many densities, but the cheaper varieties—those in which yarn is less tightly packed—tend to flatten easily. It gets dirtier than short pile and is not easy to clean. If you want a similarly textured but more practical rug or carpet, it would be best to buy the Greek Flokarti type, which is always woven in white but is easily cleanable and springier.

LOOP PILE: This pile is formed by loops of yarn. It looks good but can snag so is best employed in rooms that do not get too much traffic. If it does snag, snip off the offending thread or tag carefully, or, if the carpet is loose-laid, turn it back and pull the snag through the backing.

SAXONY PILE: A particularly soft, mid-length cut pile of high quality. Here the pile, though cut, consists of pile yarns that are slightly more twisted than those of velvet or plush varieties. This produces an exceptionally smooth and durable carpet for formal rooms.

VELVET OR PLUSH PILE: Sometimes also called *velvet weave*, this is a short, dense, smooth finish with all loops formed in the manufacturing process sheared to the same height. It looks elegant, feels luxurious, and is recommended for rooms intended more for looks than heavy use, such as formal living rooms and other rooms in which there is not too much through traffic since footprints show. It is also less resistant to dirt than a more tightly woven looped carpet. Velvet pile carpets are available in a huge range of colors and designs. Velvet is also the name of a carpet loom, as is Wilton or Axminster.

Velvet weave tufted carpet

CARPET TILE

A square of carpet in woven, tufted, or bonded form and in various combinations of wool and man-made fibers. Carpet tiles are available in various sizes ranging from 28-inch-square to 36-inch-square. They do not require padding or underlay and are flat, thin, and comparatively hard wearing, although they lack the softness underfoot of fitted carpet. They can be laid by amateurs quite easily, all in one color, or in checkerboard fashion, or made into random designs. Their advantages are that they are fairly inexpensive and that if one or two get stained or worn they can be removed and replaced. New tiles will soon tone down to the general effect.

CERAMIC TILE

Ceramic tile looks decorative in the right setting and climate and is pleasantly smooth and cool to walk on (though clearly cold in colder climates). Tiles come in a wide variety of colors and styles. Either handmade or machine made from clay, they are fired at high temperatures. For outside use you must choose the frost-proof or vitrified variety. It is important that the tiles be both nonslip and floor weight.

COIR MATTING

Increasingly a favorite for many rooms because it is a good background for rugs, coir matting is made from coconut-husk fibers and is comparatively inexpensive and hard wearing. It comes in area-rug sizes (that are bound to prevent fraying and to add a finishing touch), mats, tiles, and broadloom forms, and is available mostly in natural colors, though it is sometimes made from dyed fibers. Latex backing prevents dirt falling through. It can be adhered directly to a floor, but lasts longer and is more comfortable if an underlay is put down first.

CONCRETE

A strong building material made by mixing mortar, gravel or sand, and water.

Invented by the ancient Romans, concrete is still considered to be one of the most current and malleable of materials, since it can be molded into any shape or used in any thickness. It is extremely practical since it is both heat and cold resistant, as well as scratchproof and reasonably priced. It makes good-looking floors (in large tile form), which can either be stained and waxed or painted and sealed, but since concrete floors take a month to cure properly they are best installed in houses while they are being built or undergoing major renovations.

CORD CARPETING

A low-loop, woven carpet that looks a little like corduroy (see also *corduroy* in Fabric and Wallpaper). It is woven in much the same way as a solid Wilton, but is much cheaper and not particularly soft underfoot, though nicely textural.

CORK

Cork is made from the compressed and baked pieces of the bark from cork oak trees and is long lasting, especially when mixed with vinyl, which also makes it easier to clean. It comes in a range of natural colors, as well as some dyed ones, and is warm, soft, and quiet underfoot. It is therefore efficient in offices, hallways, family bathrooms, and kitchens, but is especially good in children's rooms. It does come in sheets, but is much more usually available in presealed tiled form. If it is not sealed and mixed with vinyl, it should be varnished after laying. As with wood, cork should be left in the room to which it is to be laid for at least three days prior to the installation in order to give it a chance to adjust to the atmosphere of the house. Also, always sweep cork floors very carefully to avoid any grit or sand scoring the surface.

CUT PILE

As the name implies, strands of yarn are cut rather than left in loops. All Axminster carpets and some Wilton carpets have cut pile.

DHURRIE

A tapestry-weave cotton or wool rug that generally comes in all kinds of designs and colors. Dhurries are inexpensive and the Indian equivalent of kilims.

ENCAUSTIC TILE

Widely used soft, matte-look Victorian and turn-of-the-twentieth-century tile inlaid with a pattern, used for halls, ground-floor corridors, and conservatories. Now, they look particularly good

in conjunction with plain terra-cotta tiles and are popular for restoration work. They are generally smaller than other floor tiles—about 3–4 inches square.

FELT

A woven wool and sometimes cotton cloth heavily napped and shrunk. Carpet-thickness felt comes in a good range of colors and is not at all expensive. It is therefore a good choice for cheering up rentals or a rented vacation house.

FLAT WEAVE

An alternative term for tapestry weave, the traditional weave for kilims and dhurries. As the name suggests, flat

Four examples of encaustic tile

weave rugs have no pile. Flat weaves are made out of cotton, linen, wool, and occasionally silk, and are generally cheaper than pile carpets.

FLAGSTONE

The term derives from the word flag, which is a hard stone that splits into flat pieces for paving. Flagstones are cut mostly from bluestone or slate, but sandstone or limestone (both should be sealed for durability and for easier cleaning) can also be used as slabs as opposed to the smaller tiles. They are as attractive inside (mainly country) houses as they are outside on terraces. Old flagstones in old houses are used mainly in hallways and sometimes in other ground floor rooms; yet they can be new as well. Flagstones can be bought in irregular slabs or can be custom-cut and laid on top of concrete screed (the term for

concrete that is slightly ridged) or a plywood subfloor. They are somewhat expensive to install, though they are generally cheaper to buy than terracotta or ceramic tiles.

FRIEZE PILE

(See *carpet texture*.)

FUSION-BONDING

(See *carpet texture*.)

GRANITE

Less expensive than marble, granite is the hardest stone used for floors. It has an attractive grain and is less likely to scratch or stain than marble, and it is less slippery. Like marble it comes in slabs but is also available in very thin tiles, which means it can be installed in upstairs rooms set on plywood as long as the floor

Flagstone floor

is level and firm. Interestingly, it comes in some fifty colors and in either a matte or polished finish; the former is less slippery, but the latter is more splendid.

INDIAN CARPET

A wool, looped-pile carpet, knotted at the back for greater wear. It is always off-white, comparatively inexpensive, and can be bought in rug sizes as well as in broadloom widths.

JUTE MATTING

Matting made from the fiber of an Asian herbaceous plant. It feels relatively soft compared with sisal, having a near-silky feel, but it is not particularly hard wearing.

KILIM

A traditional flat-weave rug from Turkey or Afghanistan. The fiber is usually wool and the pattern geometric. Vegetable dyes are used to produce warm, rich colors that mellow with age.

LINEN CARPET

A comparatively new addition to the carpet scene, linen carpet has an interesting texture and looks very handsome with natural slub (term for those little bits of stuff that give texture to some linens and natural silks) and has the feel of coir or sisal carpets. It provides a good background for designs, and could, perhaps, be designated as the contemporary version of the old painted floorcloth. In any case, it is very handsome, but

expensive and not hard wearing, so it is best for extremely elegant decoration rather than practicality.

LIMESTONE

For centuries this has been a building component for facades but it has become a favorite choice for contemporary floors. It is formed from a sandy, sedimentary rock that contains calcium carbonate, which exudes lime when burned, hence its name. It should be laid on a cement bed on a concrete subfloor, like marble or granite, and is as happy indoors as out. It is usually a pale, creamy beige but can veer toward gray.

LINOLEUM

This is made from a compound of linseed oil, pine resins, wood, ground cork, and pigment pressed into a jute backing. As usual, with such unlikely mixtures, one wonders how on earth the formula came to be created. But it did, in the nineteenth century, when it reigned supreme in almost every institution and the "below stairs" area of countless homes for decades. Now, since it is nonslip, burn resistant, easy to lay—and is available in many colors—it is becoming popular once again as a flexible entity. One of its biggest pluses is that the material can be inlaid and spliced to make handsome and distinctive customized designs that are a far cry from the sticky old brown "lino" that covered so many institutional floors in the greater part of the twentieth century. Whether you are using the sheet form or linoleum tiles, you should glue the material to a spotlessly clean and level, preferably plywood, underlay.

MARBLE

Marble, which is actually highly polished crystalline limestone, has been used for cladding since ancient Roman times and comes in a range of colors from pure white and gray (much of it quarried, perhaps surprisingly, in New England and the southern United States, as well as in Carrara, Italy) to rust and rosy reds, greens, a tawny or rosy yellow, and various shades of black. Most of the colored varieties are imported from Italy. It normally comes in 6 x 6-inch or 12 x 12-inch tiles, although it is available in slabs. The most decorative grades with the more interesting veining and coloration are often the most fragile and expensive. The more solid grades are usually classified A and B, while the more delicate grades are C and D. The disadvantages of marble are that it scratches and stains easily, but to many people the aesthetic advantages easily outweigh the impracticality. It should be laid on a cement bed on a concrete subfloor, or, if using the very thin tiles, on a very flat plywood or chipboard base.

MOSAIC

There are three types of mosaic tiles—clay, marble, and glass silica—and they are normally supplied on small sheets of plastic mesh (usually 12 x 12 inches), although other sizes are available. It is also sold in numerous shapes for flooring apart

from the usual 12 x 12-inch squares, and in a flooring weight as well as a lighter weight for walls. During installation the plastic mesh is stuck into an underlying adhesive, leaving only the tiles visible so that you do not have to grout between each one. Mosaic floors are easier to clean if you continue the floor about 6 inches up the wall all around at more or less normal baseboard level.

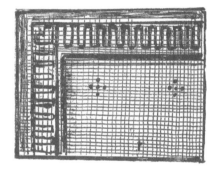

Ceramic mosaic tile

NYLON FIBER

In its various forms this is the most popular man-made fiber used for carpeting. It is nonallergenic, resistant to water-soluble stains, easy to clean, and easy to dye, taking color more evenly than wool. Newer varieties are more expensive than the old since they now have built-in static control (a former problem) and are more resistant to soiling.

PARQUET FLOORING

Strips of wood—sometimes of different colors—that are inlaid to form different floor designs.

Sometimes they are used for floors of immense complication and beauty, as at the Palace of Versailles and in many grand Beaux Arts houses of the late nineteenth century.

number of strands twisted together to form one whole strand), and the density of the tufts. A deep, high pile is not necessarily as expensive or as good quality as it may look. In fact, a high pile is often a sign that it will flatten easily.

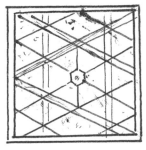

Two patterns for parquet flooring

Densely woven wool pile

PLUSH PILE

An alternative term for *velvet pile*.

POLYESTER FIBER

Like nylon, polyester is nonallergenic and is moisture and abrasion resistant. It makes for thick-cut pile carpets that have a luxurious feel, but it does have a tendency to pill like a sweater.

POLYPROPYLENE FIBER

Also known as olefin, this man-made fiber is strong, resists moisture and mildew, and is reasonably priced. Carpets containing it are a good choice for bathrooms, family rooms, powder rooms, children's rooms, and basement rooms, or anywhere where there is a likelihood of dampness, water spills, or splashes.

PERFORMANCE RATING

This is a widely used grading system to indicate a carpet's suitability for whatever use it is intended. Most systems have a five-point scale: the higher numbers signify an ability to withstand heavy wear.

PILE

The tufts or loops of fiber above the backing of either a woven or tufted carpet or rug. The quality of the pile is affected by several factors: the fiber size and weight, the ply of the yarn (the

QUARRY TILE

Rustic ceramic tile made from unrefined high-silica clay. It comes in a range of terra-cotta tones, but also a series of grays. The unglazed type is dense and nonslip, but somewhat absorbent. The glazed variety is a little more slippery, but tougher.

RUBBER TILE

Rubber flooring is hard wearing, softer, warmer, and quieter underfoot than linoleum or vinyl. It is also resistant to burns and dents, and because in some cases it contains self-releasing wax, it can often cure itself of minor scratches. All this makes it ideal for contract work, although it comes in domestic as well as industrial qualities. It is available in sheets and tiles in a large range of colors. Studded patterns of various sizes are the most common, and they are much used in High-Tech settings. It and another ribbed variety are nonslip. There is also a slatelike tile form.

RUSH MATTING

This is a centuries'-old form of flooring. Rushes can be woven into thickly textured and braided lengths or sold in squares. It is heavy and therefore can be laid loose over concrete or other hard floors without need for an underlay but is not particularly kind to high heels. It needs the occasional sprinkling of water to keep it in good shape, and to stop it from drying up and disintegrating, but looks wonderfully rustic in a country or rural setting.

SANDSTONE

This has been a favored building component for facades and is formed from sedimentary rock made up of particles of grit and sand bound in a natural cement. But it can be bought in slabs cut like flagstones, or in straight-cut slabs and tiles, and can be polished. It can be rather soft, but the hardest varieties come from Italy, near Florence (*pietra bigia* and *pietra serena*); India; or Yorkshire, England. (Various suppliers now sell beautiful old sandstone and limestone floors retrieved from demolished European houses. These suppliers advertise in decorating magazines and at the more expensive hard-flooring showrooms.)

SAVONNERIE

This terms refers to carpets, rugs, and tapestries produced by the Savonnerie factory founded in France in 1604. (The factory produced soap before carpets. *Savon* is French for "soap," hence the name.) The handwoven high pile is usually produced with distinctive but delicate pastel floral and scroll designs. Unusually, the factory made use of some Eastern techniques, such as the Ghiordes knot (see also *Ghiordes knot* in Oriental and Other Rugs). Savonnerie was merged with the Gobelins factory by Louis XIV in the late seventeenth century to better provide a unified French style, but it still produces beautiful carpets and rugs under its own name.

SEAGRASS

A plant fiber grown in a paddy field and used for matting. It has an interesting texture, is comparatively inexpensive, is water and stain resistant, and is reasonably hard wearing. Like sisal and coir matting, it provides a good unifying element for an eclectic mix of furniture and a good background for rugs.

Seagrass

SHAG PILE

(See *carpet texture*.)

SLATE

Slate is derived from metamorphic rock that splits easily into slabs, but it is also available in tiles, in colors that range from pale gray, green, and blue-gray to a darker green, bluish purple, and near-black. The slabs should be laid on a layer of mortar or concrete or a plywood subfloor on ground level floors. But the thinner tiles are light enough to use over a plywood subfloor upstairs. Slate is more stain resistant than marble and often used as an alternative since it is solid, handsome, and fairly easy to maintain, though expensive. It can be left untreated, but it is equally effective if sealed and waxed.

SILK

Silk fibers can be made into beautiful, extremely expensive rugs. It is one of the best of all fibers and is usually hand-loomed.

SISAL

Tough, durable white fiber that can be dyed easily and always looks crisp and neat. It is woven into many interesting textures that look handsome with or without rugs. It is softer than coir but not as soft as jute.

SISAL-LOOK

A term used to describe carpets that are made of wool, man-made fibers, or a mixture of the two, and are woven to look like sisal. These carpets have the advantage of being softer underfoot than sisal, but are usually more expensive.

TAPESTRY WEAVE

Like *flat weave*, a term applied to both carpets and rugs that are woven but have no pile. They are usually made of cotton, linen, or wool, though occasionally of silk. Traditional types of tapestry and flat weave are Middle Eastern, Turkish, North African, and South American kilims, Indian dhurries, and Native American Navajo rugs, as well as the elegant and expensive French Aubussons and their excellent Chinese, Portugese, and Romanian copies.

TATAMI MAT

A straw mat, about 3 x 6 feet in size, used singly or together in groups of more than one. Tatami mats have been available in Japan since the tenth century and are still going strong.

TERRA-COTTA TILE

Unglazed clay tile. The most attractive are handmade out of natural clay, kiln-fired, and produced in Mexico, Italy, Portugal, and Spain, although a more regularly shaped machine-made variety is available. Like bricks, terra-cotta tiles retain heat in winter and stay cool in summer. The disadvantages are that they scratch easily from grit retained on the bottom of shoes; but on the other hand, they develop a very attractive natural patina with age.

TERRAZZO

This flooring material is made from marble chips set into a cement or resin base and polished to a high sheen. It is reasonably nonslip, durable, and handsome. Like marble itself, it is available in tiles or slabs and is normally laid in panels. Cement-based terrazzo needs to be laid on a concrete substrate, but the resin-based variety can be laid on a flat plywood base.

TRAVERTINE

This is a handsome creamy-colored limestone from Italy that is pitted with small irregular depressions. It comes from the Tiber valley and was used for buildings by the Romans from the earliest times, as it is still, especially for cladding and for floors. It should be installed as for marble or granite.

TUFTED CARPET

This is the most common and least expensive type of carpet, but generally a good value. Each fiber is punched into a base material rather than woven on a loom. The fibers are then secured with adhesive and usually sealed with a waterproof backing. Tufted carpet can have a loop or cut pile.

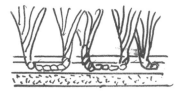

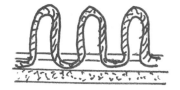

Tufted cut pile; a newer weave that is less expensive than Wilton or Axminster.

VELVET PILE

(See *carpet texture*.)

VINYL TILE

This is made from polyvinyl chloride and basically comes in two qualities: the more expensive, long-lasting solid variety and the cheaper composition vinyl that is a mixture of fillers and pigments with a thermoplastic binder, which can be either cushioned or flat. The former provides good sound insulation, and is quite bouncy and more resilient underfoot. The latter is flexible and molds itself easily to a floor. Vinyl tiles come in solid colors, but also in fairly realistic copies of marble, granite, terrazzo, limestone, brick, terra-cotta tiles, and various woods. It is usually best to buy the inlaid composition variety in which the design runs through all layers, as opposed to the rotogravure type in which the design is merely printed on the surface. All vinyl is available in sheet or tile form, can be formed into various inlays and designs like linoleum, and is reasonably priced and easy to clean. It can be laid on existing wood, tiled, or linoleum floors (if still smooth), or on a concrete subfloor.

WILTON

Woven carpet that gets its name from the loom on which it is woven, as does Axminster. But unlike Axminster, Wilton is woven in one continuous length, usually 27 inches wide, so that the surface pile and backing are woven together for more strength. It comes in a very large range of solid colors

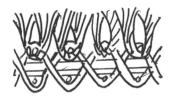

Wilton cut pile. Woven on a loom in loop form, the loops are then cut to form the pile.

in varying piles and various mixtures of fibers, as well as pure wool and a mixture of wool and man-made fibers. Patterned Wiltons are comparatively rare since the number of colors in one design is limited to five.

WOOD

Wood flooring is available in every price bracket, tone, and finish, and can be used in any room in the home. As well as using new wood, consider reclaimed beams and boards from old houses and industrial and farm buildings. Softwoods (including hemlock, spruce, fir, and pine) and hardwoods (including cherry, walnut, beech, oak, the extra hard maple, teak, ebony, iroko, mahogany, Australian ironwood, hackwood, and rosewood) are all used for floors; some are easier to obtain than others. There are even more exotic woods to choose from. Floorboards are available in solid or laminated woods, and strips differ in width from about $3\frac{1}{2}$ inches to 8 inches or even wider, if older. Parquet blocks usually come in interlocking pieces, typically about 12 inches square. Always remember to take delivery of the wood and store it in the room into which it is to be laid several days before installation so that it can become acclimatized; otherwise it may shrink or buckle. If the wood is to be laid over concrete on a ground floor, a vapor retardant, or some moisture-retardant material like roofing felt, should be laid in between to deter mold.

FURNITURE AND UPHOLSTERY

Furniture is, in origin, of two species: furniture that supports and furniture that contains. The former suggests animal forms; the second architecture. The chair is inspired by the horse. The linen chest, like a coffin for that matter, is inspired by the house.

Mario Praz (1896–1982), from
*An Illustrated History of Interior Decoration,
from Pompeii to Art Nouveau*

Furniture-making is one of the world's oldest trades—providing basic and necessary goods—and yet when crafted by the best hands and designed by the best minds, it is also an art. It is not surprising that it has produced a startlingly large vocabulary of terms, paralleling an equally large range of shapes, styles, and construction methods. From the most primitive carpenter-made benches and trestle tables we progressed via increasingly handsome chests and beds to the most exquisitely carved, gilded, and inlaid cabinetry (now rather more prosaically called *case goods*), chairs, and tables of every sort. Each successive period supplied new pieces made in different woods as they became available, in different styles, and with differing elaboration. Ornamentation went in and out of fashion. But with all the improvements—including methods of construction, the introduction of machines to ease the hardest jobs, and the revolutionary Modernist choices of materials other than woods—there has been little, at least in chair, design that has surpassed the exquisitely proportioned chairs made in ancient Greece.

Leaving aside mechanized furniture-making, there have also been surprisingly few changes in the furniture maker's tools since the eighteenth century. The extant tool chest belonging to the great American furniture maker Duncan Phyfe (1768–1854) contains what all furniture makers needed: saws (mounted in the lid), a fret saw, clamps, chisels, gouges, planes, awls, and measuring devices—though most of the chisels had ivory handles, fitted with blades of the usual eighteenth-century shape, tapering from the cutting edge of the shaft, rather than the parallel blade produced in the mid-nineteenth century. According to *The Book of Trades or Library of the Useful Arts* (London, 1804), the cabinetmaker's chief tools were "Saws, axes, planes, chisels, files, gimlets, turn-screws, hammers and other tools which are used in common by the carpenter and the cabinet-maker; but those adapted to the latter are much finer than the tools required by the house-carpenter."

Upholstery has been a different story. Its professionals once had a more pivotal role in furniture-making and furnishings in general. In the early eighteenth century, upholsterers—then identified as the "stuffers and coverers of a chair or settee-bed"—were regarded as "being in charge" of furniture-making establishments, with the cabinetmakers as their right hands, so to speak, and in fact they often segued into the role of interior designer. Happily, however, for the current users of furniture, modern upholstery is far superior in comfort to that which came before.

An exuberant, seventeenth-century
variation on the acanthus leaf

ABATTANT

French term (derived from *secrétaire à abattant*) for a fall-front or drop-leaf secretary.

ACANTHUS LEAF

The thick scalloped leaf of *Acanthus spinosus* used since Classical times (and revived during the Renaissance) in stylized forms on the tops of columns (notably the capital of Corinthian and Composite columns); for architectural moldings; and, on a smaller scale, as carved decoration on furniture, particularly mahogany furniture made between 1725 and 1760.

ACORN

A turned wood acorn used for a furniture foot, knob, drawer-pull, or finial on seventeenth-century furniture.

ACORN CHAIR

A seventeenth-century Jacobean chair with acorn-shaped pendants used as decoration along the cross rail of the chair.

ACT OF PARLIAMENT CLOCK

A hanging clock with a large (non-glass covered) wooden dial usually painted black with gold numerals and a short trunk that could be any number of shapes, from oblong and paneled to bulbous and fiddle-shaped. This type of clock was in vogue during the eighteenth and early nineteenth centuries.

ADIRONDACK FURNITURE

Rustic furniture made from roughly hewn and bent branches and logs and produced in upper New York State since the middle of the nineteenth century. Adirondack chairs are made from wood slats with a slant back and wide arms (excellent for setting drinks on) and are much reproduced today for garden furniture.

AJOURÉ

A pattern of pierced holes in ceramics, wood, metal, and parchment lamp shades. The latter creates attractive spatters of light.

ALCOVE CUPBOARD

A seventeenth- and eighteenth-century cupboard often integrated into the paneling of a room or used in corners.

ALMONRY

A room set aside in a monastery to store food, and possibly money, to be given to the penurious or the elderly as alms.

AMERICAN CHIPPENDALE

The term given to furniture made by mid- to late-eighteenth-century cabinetmakers working in the Chippendale tradition, who adapted designs from Chippendale's *Gentleman and Cabinet-Maker's Director* (1754).

The best known were William Savery, Jonathan Gostelowe, Thomas Tufts, and Benjamin Randolph from Philadelphia; John Goddard and his Townsend kinsmen Job, Christopher, and John from Newport; Benjamin Frothingham of Charleston, Massachusetts; Marinus Willett and Andrew Gautier of New York; Aaron Chapin of Hartford, Connecticut; and Webb and Scott of Providence, Rhode Island. Pieces signed by any of these craftsmen are highly prized and correspondingly priced.

AMERICAN EMPIRE

This followed the French Empire period in France and covers American furniture and decoration from approximately 1820 to 1840. Heavy and self-important, this style

One of a pair of alcove cupboards flanking a fireplace in the dining room of a Philadelphia house, ca. 1761–62

Eighteenth-century American Chippendale lowboy by William Savery of Philadelphia

of furniture was veneered mostly with mahogany, cherry, maple, and curly maple and embellished with various Empire motifs, for example, pineapples, cornucopias, Egyptian sphinxes, and lions' paws. (See also *Empire* in Styles and Movements.)

ANCILLARY FURNITURE

Backup or incidental furniture to the "anchor," or main, pieces in a room, which are pimarily used to make a room more comfortable. Some ex-amples are screens, side tables, consoles, lamp tables, side chairs, stools, benches, and coffee, cocktail, display, and end tables.

ANGEL BED

A wooden bed with a cantilevered integral canopy that, like a fabric half-tester, is about a third of the length of the mattress.

ANDIRONS

A pair of upright metal or iron supports with a transverse rod to hold back burning logs in a fireplace. A form of firedog.

ANTHEMION

Classical Greek motif that resembles honeysuckle leaves. It is as much used in furniture decoration as it is in buildings, particularly those that incorporate the Classical orders.

APRON

The often-ornamental strip of wood at the bottom edge of the seat of a chair or settee, below the frieze of a cabinet, or between the base of a tabletop and its legs.

ARABESQUE

Decorative scrollwork or other intricate ornamentation using interlacing branches, foliage, animal forms, curvilinear shapes, and so on, derived from Muslim ornament. Also found on ancient Roman tombs.

ARCADING

A series of arches with supporting columns or piers used to decorate panels on chairs and cabinetwork from the sixteenth century onward.

ARCHITECTURAL FURNITURE

Furniture incorporating architectural motifs and the Classical orders. Much of it was produced in the eighteenth century in Britain and America when architects such as Christopher Wren, James Gibbs, William Kent, Isaac Ware, and the Adam Brothers either designed furniture themselves or published books of patterns and designs that were then copied internationally by other architects, cabinetmakers, and craftsmen.

ARCHITECT'S TABLE

An eighteenth-century invention combining a drawing table with a desk. Its hinged lid can be adjusted to the best angle for drawing. (See also *drawing table*.)

ARMOIRE

French term for a large two-door cupboard used either as a wardrobe or freestanding closet, or a storage cupboard fitted with shelves. More recently, it has been used as a receptacle for a stereo or television or as a bar.

ARROW-BACK CHAIR

An American form of the Windsor chair in which the back spindles flare outward. Popular from around 1830.

ARTE POVERA

Literally "poor man's art," this is much the same technique as decoupage. Prints and engravings were cut out from publications, hand-colored, stuck to furniture, and then varnished or lacquered over.

ASTRAGAL

Small convex beaded molding used on the edge of glazing bars or doors of cabinets. Popular from around 1750.

ATHENIENNE

A slender French late-eighteenth- and early-nineteenth-century tripod table made in the Louis XVI/early Empire period and often used as a basin stand.

AUMBRY

Derived from the Latin for "chest" or "cupboard," originally an ecclesiastic cupboard to hold communion vessels, books, or altar linen. Also, a cupboard kept especially for provisions for the poor. Later the term applied to any closed cupboard.

BACHELOR CHEST

A small, plain chest of drawers normally no more than 2–3 feet wide by 2 feet 6 inches by 3 feet tall, often used in pairs as end or bedside tables.

BACK STOOL

A term used in the seventeenth and eighteenth centuries for an upholstered single chair (a chair that looked like a stool with a back)—not to be confused with the kind of angled stool-like chair so useful for back sufferers.

BAG TABLE

Worktable with a cloth bag or pouch of some kind under one or two drawers. It was first made in the eighteenth century and was popular on both sides of the Atlantic.

BAGUETTE

Small convex bead molding used in furniture decoration.

BAIGNEUSE

French term (from the verb *se baigner*, meaning to bathe) for an early-nineteenth-century upholstered daybed with a back that swooped down into sloping sides, making it look not unlike an old-fashioned tub.

BAIL HANDLE

In the past, the term referred to the type of brass drop handle hanging from

Early-eighteenth-century bail-type handles

a half-moon shaped back plate found on many William and Mary–period drawers. Now it refers to any similarly shaped drawer-pulls.

BALDACHINO BED
OR BALDEQUIN BED

Originally an Italian Renaissance–period wood canopy supported on columns over an altar or pulpit; or a cloth canopy held over the Blessed Sacrament or a statue in a procession. The term is now used mostly to describe a tester or half-tester—that is, a wood or fabric canopy fixed to the wall and extending fully or just slightly over a bed.

BALL FOOT

The rounded end of a turned leg resting on a shallow coinlike pad. This form of leg was much used for cabinets and tables in the seventeenth century.

BALL AND CLAW FOOT

An old Chinese motif suggesting power in the form of a ball or rounded jewel grasped by a bird's or dragon's claw. It was much used for the feet of furniture—particularly seating and cabinets

in Dutch furniture of the early eighteenth century, as well as furniture of the Queen Anne period, when furniture, silks, and porcelain were first being imported from China.

BALL AND RING LEG

A style of furniture leg that displays spherical turns separated by flattened rings or disk shapes.

BALL AND STEEPLE FINIAL

A popular decoration on American eighteenth-century furniture, including cabinets, highboys, secretaries, and so on. It took the form of a turned sphere topped with a number of graduated wood rings tapering to a peak, not unlike a church steeple.

BALLOON BACK

Late-eighteenth-century hoop-shaped chair back. George Hepplewhite used them for some of his designs, as did the equally famous French cabinetmaker Georges Jacob in the Louis XVI period, although Jacob called his chair the Montgolfier, to honor the Montgolfier balloon ascent. (See examples on the next page.)

**English balloon-back chair,
late eighteenth century**

**Montgolfier chair (the French equivalent
of the English balloon-back chair)**

BALUSTER

In furniture, a turned stretcher between chair legs or part of a chair back.

BALUSTRADE

In furniture, a small series of balusters topped by a rail used as decoration in some eighteenth-century furniture.

BAMBOO

Easily maneuverable, inexpensive furniture with distinctive nodules, made from the bamboo plant. It first became popular in the late seventeenth and eighteenth centuries with the introduction of Oriental furniture and furnishings. This was followed by *faux bamboo*—simulated, stylized bamboo—furniture and accessories made from painted and sometimes gilded wood, which became fashionable, particularly in the early nineteenth century and again in the Victorian era.

BANDEROLE

A painted or carved ribbon-based decoration that originated during the Italian Renaissance.

BANDING

Ornamental, inlaid border, or a border of contrasting wood used as an edging to tabletops, chests of drawers, drawers, and panels. In the late eighteenth century, satinwood or other exotic woods, cut in different ways, often edged mahogany. *Crossbanding*, for example, meant that the grain of the wood ran at right angles to the edge. *Straight banding* meant that the wood had been cut along the length of the grain. *Feather banding* and *herringbone banding* were cut at an angle between crossbanding and straight banding. Herringbone inlays and straight crossbanding were often used in walnut furniture as well.

BANDY-LEGGED

Early American colloquialism for the outward-curving cabriole-legged furniture introduced in the late seventeenth and particularly eighteenth centuries. (See also *cabriole leg*.)

BANISTER-BACKED CHAIR

Early American chair with a back formed from vertical split balusters, spindles, or flat bars. These chairs were often made of ebonized maple.

BANJO CLOCK

An early-nineteenth-century American clock that resembled an inverted banjo.

BANK OF ENGLAND CHAIR

An English Regency serpentine-seated variation of a tub chair, often with cabriole legs. It was first made, presumably, for the Bank of England.

BANQUETTE

An upholstered bench without a back; from the French term.

BARCELONA CHAIR

A twentieth-century classic in polished stainless steel, leather, and leather strap suspension designed by Ludwig Mies van der Rohe in 1929 and first exhibited at the German Pavilion at the International Barcelona Fair that year. Today it is made by Knoll Associates, New York. It is also the name of a late-seventeenth-century ladder-back Spanish chair with a deeply carved cross-slat.

BARLEY-SUGAR TWIST

As the name implies, a barley-sugar or twisted-rope turning. It was used for legs and stretchers on some mid- and late-seventeenth-century and Victorian chairs.

BARREL CHAIR

Originally a rustic chair based on a wine barrel that had been cut in half. Since the nineteenth century it has been an upholstered barrel-shaped chair with its back often upholstered in vertical ribs.

BASALT

A deep green or reddish-brown stone used in ancient Egypt for statues, and revived for the tops of chests and side tables in the French Empire period because of its Egyptian associations.

BAT'S WING BRASSES

Brass backings or escutcheons for keyholes, handles, and so on, in the shape of outstretched bats' wings.

BEAD MOLDING

Small convex molding resembling a string of beads, or a narrow, semi-circular section of a small plain molding that runs around a panel called a bead flush. Used on drawers, cabinet door panels, and other cabinetry. (See also *astragal*.)

BEAR'S PAW FOOT

A naturalistic, carved furry bear's paw occasionally combined with a ball; used for chair and other furniture feet in the late seventeenth and early eighteenth centuries, though it was very often used right through to the nineteenth century on Eastern European and Russian furniture. Thomas Chippendale occasionally used the device.

BEAU BRUMMEL

A dressing table aptly named after an arbiter of English Regency fashion that was—with its adjustable mirrors, differently shaped drawers, and a candle-stand—all that a dandy could require.

BED CHAIR

The Dutch bed chair can be counted as one of the numerous, ingenious, space-saving, and multipurpose furniture inventions of the eighteenth and nineteenth centuries that was made possible by strong hinges. The armed, cabriole-legged bed chair was designed so that the back could be let down to join the seat, which could then be pulled out to form a much longer surface. A concealed extra leg could then be released to support it, and the arms lowered to be joined together with the regular legs for added stability.

BED STEPS

Another eighteenth-century design, this time to make it easier to clamber into the high beds ubiquitous during that period. Like the bed chair, however, bed steps were also multipurpose, some-times resembling an antique version of modern-day folding-ladder kitchen stools, or incorporating a chamber pot.

BENTWOOD FURNITURE

Furniture made by a process invented in the mid-nineteenth century whereby wood could be steamed to soften it enough to allow it to be bent and then molded into the requisite shape. Michael Thonet, an Austrian, became a master of the process, and his original scrolled rocking chairs and other furniture pieces are still eagerly sought.

BERGÈRE

An eighteenth-century French armchair with a wide seat, exposed frame, and upholstered back and sides. It was first introduced during the *Régence* period as a welcome alternative to the grandly uncomfortable chairs of the Louis XIV period. It was so appreciated that its production continued during the subsequent reigns of Louis XV and Louis XVI.

BEVEL

This usually refers to an applied molding with sloping sides often used to edge a mirror or painting frame.

BIBELOTS

A French term in common usage for small art objects—collections of various boxes, for example—and small ornaments. (See also *objets d'art*.)

BIBLE BOX

As its name implies, a box in which to keep the family bible. These boxes were generally carved, and later, often had a sloping lid to serve as a reading stand.

Bed steps

A bergère armchair, introduced in
the mid-eighteenth century

A staple in many homes from the seventeenth century to the nineteenth century.

BIBLIOTHÈQUE

Internationally used French term for a usually handsomely detailed bookcase with doors inset with either glass panes or grilles. A *bibliothèque-basse* is a low version of the same.

BIEDERMEIER

Simpler, lighter, less-expensive German version of early-nineteenth-century French Empire furniture. (See *Biedermeier* in Styles and Movements.)

BIRDCAGE SUPPORT

Early Anglo-American term for the cage-shaped construction that enables a tilt-top table to be tilted or rotated.

Sometimes such English "cages" were designed with miniature columns.

BIRD'S-EYE MAPLE

Term for the look of the small marks made—particularly on maple-wood furniture—when the indentations that appear on the annual rings of a tree trunk are cut on a tangent.

BLACKAMOOR

Plant, vase, or sculpture plinth in the form of an exotically dressed, or mostly half-dressed black man, popular in the nineteenth century as a decorative accessory.

BLANKET CHEST

Originally an American or European chest with usually one or two drawers inside and a separate lidded section on top. It was used both for storing clothes or blankets and as a seat.

BLOCK FOOT

A square or cubed foot at the bottom of a straight furniture leg.

BLOCK FRONT

This term is most often used in relation to the type of eighteenth-century fall-front desks, secretaries, and highboys made by John Goddard and the Newport, Rhode Island, school of cabinetmakers. It refers to the fronts of such pieces, which are divided into alternating convex and concave panels, usually with a recessed (concave) center panel with a projecting (convex) panel at either side.

BOBBIN TWIST

This form of turning, used for chair and table legs and stretchers in the seventeenth century, was based on a series of bobbins or spool shapes, or reels of cotton or wool.

BOISERIE

The French but now universal term for carved paneling used for both walls and pieces of furniture from the seventeenth and eighteenth centuries. During the Rococo period this paneling was most often painted in pale pastel colors and gilded.

BOLECTION MOLDING

Molding that is rounded or ogee-shaped and that projects from the paneling of walls or doors. Although used mostly for interiors and doors, it is also sometimes used for furniture paneling as well.

BOMBÉ

French term, universally adopted, for a convex front to a chest of drawers, a commode, or a bureau. The literal meaning of the word is "blow out."

BONHEUR DU JOUR

Another French term (literally means "happiness" or "good luck" of the day) for a small, rather frail-looking desk with tall, slim legs, raised drawers or a small cabinet at the back, and, sometimes, space for women's toilet necessities.

BONNET TOP

The curved or rounded top of a late-seventeenth- or early-eighteenth-century highboy, secretary, bureau-bookcase, or other tall piece of furniture.

BORNE

A large round, or sometimes shamrock-shaped, upholstered sitting piece with an upholstered central core. It was mainly used in the nineteenth century, although there are earlier examples. It was typically placed in the middle of a large room or public foyer.

BOSTON ROCKER

Essentially American, early-nineteenth-century rocking chair in which the wooden seat usually curves up in the back and down in the front. The design is often attributed to the illustrious Benjamin Franklin. The rockers sometimes have a stenciled design of some sort on the deep top rail above the spindled back. Many of them were made in Lambert Hitchcock's factory along with the Hitchcock "fancy" chair.

BOUILLOTTE TABLE

A slender round gaming table invented in France in the eighteenth century for a card game of the same name. These tables had a low brass or bronze gallery around the circumference of the marble top, and generally had two drawers for the cards as well as a pair of candle slides that could be pulled out from recesses in the apron.

BOULLE OR BOULLE WORK

Andre-Charles Boulle and his four sons were master French cabinetmakers to Louis XIV, and later, the *Regence*, in the late seventeenth and early eighteenth centuries. Today, the name conjures up grandly ornate cabinet furniture, sometimes made of ebony and more often than not veneered or inlaid with the opulent marquetry process Boulle invented, now known as Boulle work. This involved fusing sheets of tortoiseshell and brass or silver, cutting out a design through both pieces, and then setting either the metal into the tortoiseshell or vice versa.

BOW BACK

A curved or hooped chair back most often seen on eighteenth-century Windsor chairs.

BOW FRONT

The convex, or outwardly curving, front of a chest of drawers or bureau.

BOX BED

As the name suggests, a bed enclosed on three sides, as in an alcove, often with curtains or draperies, or even shutters, on the open side for privacy and to resist drafts. The term also describes a bed that folds up against a wall behind a panel—a sort of early form of today's Murphy bed.

BRACED BACK
OR FIDDLE-BRACED BACK

A chair back, usually of a Windsor chair, strengthened by two extra spindles that are fixed to a small extension behind the seat at the bottom and to the chair rail at the top, making a V-form.

BRACKET FOOT

Straight corner–edged and curved inner–edged design frequently used for the legs in both American and English eighteenth-century cabinetry or case or carcase furniture. The legs usually project slightly from each corner.

BREAKFAST TABLE

Term promoted by Chippendale for a small table, sometimes with a long drawer, and usually with drop leaves. Similar to a Pembroke table.

BREAKFRONT

A large, originally eighteenth-century cabinet piece—such as a bookcase, a display cabinet, or a secretary—with a center section that was either recessed or advanced from the two end sections. The term also describes an upper bookcase or series of shelves set back from cabinets or shelves beneath.

BREWSTER CHAIR

A solid-looking chair with large, turned posts, a double row of spindles on the back, and a rush seat. It was made in New England in the seventeenth century and was named after Elder Brewster, an early governor of the Massachusetts Bay colony.

BROKEN PEDIMENT

A triangular architectural element that is interrupted in its middle. It was often used to crown the top of eighteenth-century bookcases, cabinets, highboys, corner cupboards, and so on. The central open area is usually filled with a carved urn, shell, or finial of some sort, though sometimes it is just left empty.

BRONZE-DORÉ

A French term in common usage for the gilded bronze used for candlesticks, candelabra, and ornaments in the seventeenth, eighteenth, and nineteenth centuries; it was also used for brackets, mounts, and moldings for furniture. (See also *ormolu.*)

BUFFET

A French term used for a cupboard or sideboard for storing dishes and serving food.

The original carved oak
Brewster chair, ca. 1650

BULLION

A heavy fringe made from lengths of cord wrapped in silver or gold thread; sometimes used to trim upholstery.

BULLNOSE EDGE

An almost-180-degree rounded edge on a table, desktop, or slab of marble.

BULL'S-EYE MIRROR

A convex mirror with a round frame, used particularly in the Regency and Empire periods in the early nineteenth century.

BUN FOOT

A slightly flattened ball foot used on furniture; introduced in the second half of the seventeenth century.

BUREAU

A French term with several meanings. Thomas Sheraton called it a "common desk with drawers." Most experts say it is a hinged slant-top desk that opens down to form a writing surface, with pigeonhole compartments and drawers underneath. Since the nineteenth century in the United States it has also meant a bedroom chest of drawers.

BUREAU-BOOKCASE

A desk as above with a bookcase or cabinet with shelves over the top.

BUREAU À CYLINDRE

A French term for a rolltop desk.

BUREAU-PLAT

A French term for a flat writing table.

BUREAU-TABLE

The name given to a kneehole writing table designed by John Goddard of Newport, Rhode Island, in the late eighteenth century.

BUREAU-TOILETTE

A French term for a combined writing and dressing or toilet table.

BURR WALNUT

The figured or circular whorls distinguishable in transverse slices of walnut wood caused by growths on the trunk of the tree. It was much used as a furniture veneer in the eighteenth century.

BUTLER'S TRAY TABLE

A wood, japanned metal, or silver tray mounted on a folding stand or on legs. If wooden, it usually has hinged flap sides and cut-out handles so that it can be lifted and carried around if necessary. It was much used in the eighteenth century and has remained popular.

CABINET

A general term derived from French for "closet," but now meaning a unit of case furniture with shelves or cupboard doors, or a wooden or metal housing to enclose an object like a television or stereo.

CABINETWORK

Case goods made with skilled design and execution by a cabinetmaker, as opposed to less-skilled carpentry or joinery, or to tables and seating.

CABRIOLE CHAIR
OR CABRIOLET CHAIR

French term for an anglicized version of a small Louis XVI chair with curved or cabriole legs and an upholstered back set in a framelike surround topped with a carved ribbon tied in a bow. Thomas Chippendale and George Hepplewhite both designed similar versions.

CABRIOLE LEG

A leg that curves outward at the knee or top and tapers in an elongated S-shape toward the foot. It was presumably so called because cabriole in French is to "leap" or "caper." It was the most popular furniture leg in the Rococo period in France and came into general use in Europe and then America. It can finish in a club, hoof, bun, scroll, or ball and claw foot. The latter was very popular in the Queen Anne period in England and America.

CACHEPOT

Decorative container for a plant or flowerpot. It can be made from china or pottery, wood, or metal.

CACQUETEUSE OR CAQUETEUSE

Originally a French "conversational" chair, meant, as the translation of the name implies, to be used by gossiping women. It was adapted by the Scots in the late sixteenth century and had a tall narrow back, spreading arms, and a triangular seat. Occasionally, such chairs can be found with a swivel base, all the better for chatter back and forth.

CAMEL BACK

A sofa or chair back with a dipping or serpentine shape like a camel's hump, much promoted by both Chippendale and Hepplewhite in the eighteenth century and still popular.

CAMPAGNOLA

A term used to describe simple Italian provincial or rural furniture.

CAMPAIGN CHEST

A tall, narrow nineteenth-century army officer's traveling chest of drawers. For protection from wear and tear, its corners usually had brass or metal edges.

CANAPÉ

A French term for a small two-seater sofa or love seat. Originally, the term applied to a seventeenth-century sofa with a canopy.

CANDELABRA OR CANDELABRUM

A candlestick or chandelier made up of many branched candlesticks, or today, candlesticks with flame-shaped electric bulbs. They can be made of silver, brass, crystal, or wood.

CANDLE SLIDES

An eighteenth-century device consisting of thin, small, pull-out boards tucked away at the sides of desks and tables to pull out when necessary to support a candle.

CANE

The stems of different plants or grasses, including bamboo and rattan, that can be woven into a pliable mesh used for comfortable and, though light, supportive seating. Cane (the term derives from *canna*, the Latin word for "reed") has been popular for furniture, on its own, or mixed with

French *Régence canapé*, upholstered in brocade

wood for, say, chair backs, since the seventeenth century.

CANTERBURY

A small, ancillary piece of furniture with deep open partitions and a drawer between the legs, ostensibly for holding sheet music. Nowadays it is used as a decorative magazine and newspaper rack, but it originally was called a Canterbury, according to the cabinetmaker Thomas Sheraton, because "A bishop of the See first gave orders for those pieces."

CAPTAIN'S CHAIR

A nineteenth-century chair made for sea voyages and specifically for the captain's cabin. Both the back and the arms are curved and supported by small spindles, the seat is rounded, and the simply turned legs are joined by turned stretchers.

CARCASE OR CARCASS

Both the framework and structure of furniture before the finish, veneer, or any carving is applied. Also, a term for any furniture used for storage purposes, as opposed to chairs and tables. (See also *case goods*.)

CARD CUT

Low- or bas-relief carving in a Chinese fretwork design. Chippendale used it for his chinoiserie-style furniture, known as Chinese Chippendale.

CARD TABLE

Today, a utilitarian, collapsible, square, green baize-topped table. In the Queen Anne period, there were handsome walnut versions with cabriole legs and

Late-seventeenth-century card table with "seaweed" marquetry

candlestick corners. Card tables first appeared in the seventeenth century.

CARLTON HOUSE TABLE

A D-shaped side table, mostly designed in satinwood during the late eighteenth and early nineteenth centuries. Thomas Sheraton illustrated them in *The Cabinet-Maker and Upholsterer's Drawing Book* (1791–94), and they were named after tables originally made for the Prince of Wales's London residence, Carlton House, designed by Henry Holland (but now destroyed).

CARTONNIER

Eighteenth-century equivalent of an ornamental cardboard box or box file made to hold papers, but a great deal more decorative than those available today and is thus highly collectible.

CARTOUCHE

A central motif—such as an escutcheon—on a cornice, the back of a chair, or the center of cabinet pediments or fire surrounds. It usually takes the form of a scroll, but it can also be an oval, a rondel, or a shield shape; it most often provides a field for a monogram, an inscription of some kind, some sort of bas-relief portrait, or a coat of arms. It is also frequently referred to by the Italian term *cartoccio*.

CARVER CHAIR

Plain, square-shaped, early-American turned chair, usually made of ash or maple, with a rush seat. It was named after John Carver, the seventeenth-century governor of Plymouth, New Hampshire, and is very similar to the Brewster chair named for Elder Brewster, governor of Massachusetts Bay. Also, a general term for a dining chair with arms.

CASE GOODS
OR CASE FURNITURE

Furniture essentially made for storage purposes, such as wardrobes, armoires, bookcases, highboys, chests, chests of drawers, secretaries, and so on.

CASSONE

Early Italian, richly-carved, and sometimes painted chest made between the late fourteenth and early fifteenth and seventeenth centuries.

CASTOR *OR* CASTER

A small swiveling wheel made of metal, wood, leather, and sometimes even ivory, attached to the legs of furniture for easier maneuverability.

CAUSEUSE

A small French late-seventeenth- or eighteenth-century sofa or love seat, or even a particularly wide armchair, with a carved frame and open sides. It was often covered in tapestry.

CEDAR CHEST

Cedar chests are generally carved and have been made for centuries. Since cedar wood is anathema to moths and other scavenging insects, it is used to either line or to make linen or blanket chests.

CELLARETTE

A cabinet, sometimes lined with lead, made especially for storing bottles. It can be portable or part of a sideboard. Thomas Sheraton included designs for a cellarette in *The Cabinet-Maker and Upholsterer's Drawing Book*.

CHAISE-BRISEE

A daybed or chaise longue conveniently constructed in two parts for easier handling.

CHAISE LONGUE

French for "long bed," in general usage it's a day bed.

CHAMFERED EDGE

A beveled, faceted, or smoothed-off edge on some pieces of furniture. Or, an edge that has been symmetrically cut off from a square at an angle of 45 degrees.

CHANNELS

Parallel grooving found on many columns, and often on seventeenth-century oak furniture.

CHEST ON CHEST

As the name implies, one chest placed upon another. The lower chest usually has a series of wider drawers; the upper drawers are often divided into two sets.

CHESTERFIELD

A nineteenth-century deep, usually button-backed sofa named after English peer Lord Chesterfield.

CHEVAL GLASS

A French term (from the French for "horse"), universally used for a full-length dressing mirror suspended between two uprights forming a frame that allows the mirror to be tilted. A little confusingly, *horse* was the old name for a frame with legs on which something is hung or supported, as in "clothes horse." Horse is also another term for one of two or more trestles supporting a table.

Cheval glass

CHEVAL SCREEN

A fire screen suspended between two "horses" (as used in a cheval glass), often with bracketed feet.

CHIFFONIER

An anglicized French term (originally meaning a "rag-and-bone man") for a small cupboard or sideboard with double doors concealing drawers used for collections of this and that. It sometimes has stepped-back drawers on top and is occasionally topped with a mirror as well.

CHIMERA

A composite, half-beast/half-human or other monsterlike creature, used as legs or supports for Renaissance and late-nineteenth-century post-Renaissance furniture.

CHINESE CHIPPENDALE

Furniture designed by Thomas Chippendale in the second half of the eighteenth century based on Chinese motifs, mainly inspired by Sir William Chambers's book *Designs for Chinese Buildings* (1757).

CHINESE EXPORT

Eighteenth- and early-nineteenth-century designs with occidental figures and motifs produced by the Chinese on furniture and ceramics for export only.

CHIPPENDALE FURNITURE

A graceful style of furniture named after the first and most eclectic of English eighteenth-century cabinet-makers who had worldwide influence on furniture design through their pattern books. (Thomas Chippendale published his pattern book *Gentlemen and Cabinet-Maker's Director* in 1754.) Chippendale's variety of styles included chinoiserie, French Rococo, Gothic, and Queen Anne, and he created a range of extraordinarily exotic beds as well as chairs, beautifully carved mirrors, side tables, girandoles, and cabinets. (See also *Chippendale, Thomas* in Architects, Designers, and Decorators.)

CLUB CHAIR

A comfortable, upholstered, easy armchair that may or may not be skirted and that has different-shaped and -sized arms and backs depending upon the style.

CLUB FENDER

A version of a brass or iron fender that extends across, and is then angled around, the front of a fireplace. Either the side parts of the fender take the form of two raised upholstered seats, or the fender has a continuous narrow upholstered top. Either way, the seat parts are usually covered in leather or some other tough upholstery fabric. Such club fenders are an excellent way to provide extra seating without taking up "visual" space.

Chippendale chair, ca. 1760

CHINOISERIE

European and American versions of Chinese designs imported from the Far East since the late seventeenth century. (See also *chinoiserie* in Styles and Movements.)

CLOCHE

French term, universally used in decoration (meaning "bell glass" or "dome") to describe the nineteenth-century habit of placing a protective glass dome over various *objets*, such as a statue, plaster cast, vase of artificial flowers, stuffed bird or animal, or even a clock.

CLOSE STOOL

An early pot cupboard, sometimes called a "necessary stool," with a hinged top concealing a pan.

CLUB FOOT

A rounded pad, in the form of a club, used to terminate cabriole legs; from the early eighteenth century.

COCK BEADING

A small astragal or convex molding applied to the edges of drawer fronts from around 1730 to 1800.

COLONNETTE

A favorite Classical and Renaissance motif consisting of miniature columns—often Corinthian—used for the backs of chairs or as supports for tables. Also, in the late eighteenth century, fluted or reeded quarter- or half-round pilasters applied to the front corners of chests of drawers or bureaus.

COMMODE

An originally French, and now universal, term for a low chest of drawers, or two-drawered or two-doored chest, possibly derived from the early-eighteenth-century *bureaux commodes*, which were tables with drawers. By the later eighteenth and early nineteenth centuries, they were often serpentine in shape. Interestingly, in the latter part of the nineteenth century the term came to be used for a chair with a hinged seat that concealed a chamber pot or pan, similar to a close stool. In the twentieth century it became quite a furnishing conceit to possess a thronelike chair concealing a proper flushing toilet.

CONFIDANTE

A French-derived term for an elegant, upholstered two- or three-seater, or a sofa with two angled end seats separated by arms from the main structure. Hepplewhite included one in his book *The Cabinet-Maker and Upholsterer's Guide*, and it was popular—as were the similar companion chairs, tête-à-têtes, or *siamoises*, and bornes—in the mid to late nineteenth century.

CONNECTICUT CHEST

An early American chest, usually painted black, with oak fronts and side and pine backs, tops, and bottoms. It had two rows of double drawers and was supported by short legs.

CONSOLE TABLE

Console was originally a French term for a bracket, but from the early eighteenth century the name was given to a form of side table that had hitherto been called less gracefully a *clap table*. Such tables often had marble tops and were fixed to a wall by two curving brackets. Similar side tables followed, with legs or supports at the front only and occasionally with gilded eagles with outstretched wings. Consoles were almost always, as they still are today, surmounted by a long mirror.

COQUILLAGE

Carved Rococolike ornamentation in the form of shells or shells and flowers or tendrils. It was often used in the center of a chair rail or a settee in the Chippendale period.

A confidante or borne, from the third edition of *The Cabinet-Maker and Upholsterer's Guide* by George Hepplewhite

CORNUCOPIA

A design motif based on a stylized horn of plenty. It was used particularly in the Empire and mid-Victorian periods for the scrolled arms or legs of sofas or chairs, the latter ending in lions' paws.

COROMANDEL SCREEN

A Chinese lacquered screen, introduced in the middle of the seventeenth century and often made in Peking. It was usually fashioned from hard, dark coromandel wood, also known as Macassar ebony, which had intense brownish-black stripes on a reddish background. However, the look of the wood was often reproduced with clever lacquering. Coromandel screens, or *faux coromandel* screens, were mostly decorated with allover bas-relief patterns or allover landscape scenes.

COUCH

Originally an early term for a chaise longue or a daybed with one end in the shape of a chair back. Now it also denotes a sofa.

COURT CUPBOARD

A French-derived term—meaning "short"—for a low, late-sixteenth- and early-seventeenth-century carved display cupboard. It stood on legs with an open base.

CREDENZA

The Italian term for a buffet or serving table.

CRESTING

Carved wood decoration, often consisting of a crown and cherubs, surmounting or forming the top rail of a chair, settee, mirror, or cabinet. It was introduced around 1730.

CRICKET TABLE

A round three-legged table supported on a triangular frame and first made in the English Jacobean period.

CROSSBANDING

A contrasting narrow band of wood veneer, cut across the grain and used as an inset border or frame for doors, tabletops, panels, and so on.

CROSS RAIL

The horizontal slat or rail that forms part of the back of a chair.

CROSS-STRETCHER

An X-shaped stretcher used on some early chairs.

CUIVRE

The French term for "copper." Cuivre d'oré is gilded copper.

CURULE CHAIR

A seventeenth-century chair based on an ancient Roman prototype with the frame shaped like a backward S in profile, or like two Cs on top of each other when full frontal. Normally, strips of leather provided the backrest and the seat. The shape became popular again in the early nineteenth century. Sheraton included a version in *The Cabinet-Maker and Upholsterer's Drawing Book*.

CURULE LEG

A Classical Greek and Roman inward-curving X-shaped leg for stools, resurrected during the Renaissance and still used.

CYLINDER FRONT

A quarter-round front of a desk or secretary that can be pivoted.

CYLINDER TOP

A rolltop front for a desk or secretary that, unlike a tambour top, does not roll up on itself.

DAVENPORT

A confusing term in that it refers both to a small nineteenth-century kneehole desk with a shallow sloping top and side drawers, as well as an exposed-framed overstuffed American sofa originally made to a Sheraton design by a Mr. Davenport of Boston, Massachusetts.

DAYBED

A long chair, usually with one chair back–like end (although it can have two ends or, in some modern versions, no end at all). It was first introduced in the seventeenth century. (See also *Chaise Longue*.)

DEAL

Fir or pine softwood used to make the carcase of veneered furniture or cut into planks to make simple unadorned furniture.

DECALCOMANIA

A cheap way to decorate furniture and accessories. It is not unlike a transfer technique. Designs are printed in reverse on thin paper, attached to a backing, and then transferred to the surface to be decorated.

DECOUPAGE

An inexpensive decorating technique for furniture, accessories, screens, trays, boxes, dadoes, and so on. It dates back to the eighteenth century and consists of assembling assorted clippings, transfers, magazine illustrations, and so on, and reassembling them on the chosen surface in a variety of patterns that are then varnished over with a clear lacquer.

DEMI-LUNE

A French term in common parlance, literally meaning "half-moon" and

Seventeenth-century black lacquered and cane daybed

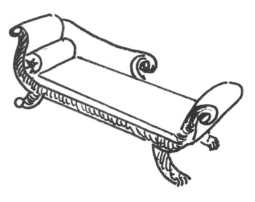

Nineteenth-century Regency daybed

applied to semicircular side tables, consoles, commodes, or sideboards.

DENTIL or DENTELLE

Rows of small toothlike rectangular blocks with regular spaces in between them, used as a molding on a cornice or on eighteenth-century furniture.

DESK BOX

An early form of desk, a little like a bible box, consisting of a wood box to contain writing materials with a sloping hinged lid to form a writing surface.

DIP SEAT

A curved ergonomically designed chair seat, lower in the center than at the sides. This was a form sometimes used by Chippendale.

DISK FOOT

A flattened ball or disk-shaped pad for the foot of a cabriole leg.

DISK TURNING

Flat wooden disks used as ornamentation on furniture.

DISTRESSED FINISH

This term refers to aged wood furniture with small scratches, signs of wear, and indentations. The effect of distressed furniture can be simulated on new pieces.

DOCUMENT DRAWERS or DOCUMENT BOXES

Small deep drawers or cavities with doors at either side of the central interior section of secretaries and fall-front desks. In old desks, they are often decorated with colonnettes.

DOMED BED

A dome-shaped tester or canopy above a bed. An eighteenth-century treatment that was much swagged and draped. Also called *un lit à la Polonaise*, or a Polish bed.

DOVETAIL

In cabinetry, wedge-shaped projections in the side of a drawer that interlock with alternating grooves in the front to form secure right-angled joints. In high-quality furniture, from the eighteenth century on, such joints were concealed by an overlapping piece of wood.

DOWEL PIN

A round, headless wooden peg to hold two pieces of lumber together in cabinetry.

DOWER CHEST

A chest meant for storing a trousseau, such as a Connecticut chest or the painted Pennsylvania Dutch or German chests. (See also *hope chest*.)

DRAFT CHAIR

An eighteenth- or nineteenth-century wing chair with enclosed side wings to diminish drafts.

DRAW TABLE

A refectory table with three leaves. When the two end leaves are drawn out, the third slips down into the gap created in the middle.

DRAWING TABLE

An artist's worktable with an adjustable height so that it can be used while sitting or standing. In a much-emulated Sheraton design, a small flap can be drawn from the top to form a base to support a still life or whatever inanimate object is being drawn or painted. There are sliders at either end to hold lights or drawing equipment.

DRESSER

An old term for a sideboard or buffet with a cupboard and shelves for plate and dish storage and display. In the United Kingdom, this term still applies to a hutch or a two-doored cupboard with shelves, or a smaller cupboard with shelves above. In the United States, the term applies to a long chest of drawers usually placed in a bedroom.

DRESSING TABLE

Usually a kneehole table with compartments or drawers for makeup or toilet necessities, and with either a fixed or separate mirror.

DROP LID

The hinged top or front of a desk that, when closed, conceals the interior, and when dropped and supported, forms a flat surface for writing. (See also *fall front*.)

DRUM TABLE

A round table with drawers inset into a deep apron. It is usually set onto a tripod base. It is similar to a *rent table*.

DUCHESSE

A French term for a chaise longue with two ends, the head end higher than the foot and a flat piece in the middle. Or, as Sheraton described it: "two bergères with a stool in the middle."

DUCHESSE-BRISÉ

Another French term for a two-piece chaise longue. (See also chaise-brisee.)

DUMBWAITER

A mid-eighteenth-century invention to help with self-service in dining rooms. It consisted of a wooden column with a tripod foot supporting trays or shelves of diminishing circumference. It was set by dining tables to hold food, plates, and utensils and was often made to revolve. In some nineteenth-century town houses, the term applied to a small food elevator installed between a basement kitchen and first-floor dining room to obviate unnecessary stair-climbing.

DUST BOARD

A thin wooden partition fixed between drawers in commodes, dressers, and chests of drawers to ward off dust.

DUST RUFFLE

Hemmed fabric that extends from under the mattress of a bed to the floor, both hiding the bed frame and supposedly resisting dust. It can be tailored, kick-pleated, generally pleated, or shirred.

DUTCH DRESSER

A hutch or dresser with open shelves above and drawers or a two-doored cupboard below.

DUTCH FOOT

A pad foot at the end of cabriole legs on late-seventeenth- and early-eighteenth-century furniture.

DUTCH LEG

A late-seventeenth-century wood-turned leg made up of rounded forms interspersed with small flat oval disks that end with a squared section resting on a small oval foot.

DUTCH SETTLE

A wooden settle or armed bench with a hinged back that could be flipped down to rest on the arms and form a table.

EAGLE MOTIFS

The eagle and the eagle's head have been used as military symbols as well as motifs for furniture and decoration all through history. *Spread eagles, double-headed eagles,* and *eagles rampant* weave in and out of furnishings from the ancient world of the Middle East and Egypt through Greece and Rome, Byzantium, the Italian Renaissance, the eighteenth-century revival of Classicism, the Napoleonic Empire, and finally, as the bald-headed eagle for the American Revolution. Yet Georgian England used eagle heads for the termination of chair and sofa arms, as well as spread eagles for the tops of round convex mirrors, fully as much as post-Revolutionary America.

EAMES CHAIRS

The Eames produced radical new concepts for chairs—such as separating chair backs and seats within their supporting frames, wire-frame chairs with snap-on upholstery, and, for more resiliency, using molded laminated plywood and steel models with rubber disks. All of these—as well as the famous Eames Lounge Chair (designed 1956), with its plywood shell, star-shaped metal pedestal base, patent snap-off soft leather upholstery, and matching ottoman—are twentieth-century classics, still sold by Knoll. (See also *Eames, Charles and Kaiser, Ray* in Architects, Designers, and Decorators).

EASY CHAIR

Any comfortable upholstered armchair, although the term used to refer to a high-backed wing chair or the French bergère.

ÉBÉNISTE

The French term for cabinetmaker dating back to the sixteenth century, when a good deal of furniture was made from fine-grained ebony glued onto stained black pearwood. Ebony, imported from Ceylon (now Sri Lanka) and India, was particularly popular during the reign of Louis XIV and the king's cabinetmaker was known as the *Maître ébéniste*.

EBONIZED WOOD

Wood stained black to simulate ebony, used as the trim for Beidermeier furniture and for nineteenth-century oriental-type cabinets. It was called *bois noir* in France.

ÉGLOMISÉ

As in *verre églomisé*, a painting process that was done on the reverse side of glass and often gilded, then protected by varnish or another piece of glass. It was named after a Monsieur Glomy, an eighteenth-century French framer and gilder, and was particularly used for the borders of mirror frames.

ÉGOUTTOIR

A French country piece with wooden open-rack shelves for drying and storing plates or dishes.

EGYPTIAN DETAILS

Although the ancient Egyptian civilization preceded those of Greece and Rome, very little was known about its art and architecture until the time of the Napoleonic campaigns in Egypt. From 1800 or so, sphinxes, lions' heads and paws, lotus-headed capitals, palmetto leaves, soaring stone Cleopatra's needles (as in Paris and London), and X-shaped legs all became part of the design language. There was a resurgence in Egyptian-inspired design after the discovery of the Rosetta stone at the end of the eighteenth century and yet another after the archeological discoveries and the excavation of the pyramids in the 1920s.

ELBOW CHAIR

A chair first developed in France during the mid-eighteenth century with an upholstered seat and back, a carved frame, and cabriole legs. Later, it was simply a chair with arms placed at the head of a table, often known as a carver chair—a chair from which carving can be done or on which elbows can be rested—as opposed to the early-American *Carver chair*, named after Colonial Governor Carver.

EMPIRE, FRENCH EMPIRE, *OR* AMERICAN EMPIRE

Early-nineteenth-century furniture and architectural style. (See also *Empire* in Styles and Movements.)

EMPIRE BED

Low nineteenth-century French bed with curved or sweeping foot and head, usually set sideways against a wall or in an alcove. It is similar to a boat, gondola, or sleigh bed.

ENCOIGNURE

A French term in general parlance for a built-in corner cabinet or cupboard, often part of the architecture.

Empire bed

END TABLE

A convenient, small table specially made to be placed at the end of a sofa or couch or at the side of a chair to hold lamps, books, drinks, and so on.

ENTABLATURE

In Classical architecture, the top part of the Classical order consisting of architrave, frieze, and cornice that rests upon a column. The term also applies to the top part of some cabinets or cupboards designed in the Classical manner.

ENTRELAC

A decorative, interlaced carved motif much used in the French Louis XVI period. (See also *guilloche*.)

ENVELOPE TABLE

Originally a late-eighteenth-century design from the French Directoire period (see *Directoire* in Styles and Movements) in which a square table has four close-fitting hinged flaps that can be folded outward to increase the size of the surface.

ÉPERGNE

A French term in common use for a table centerpiece. It usually consists of a decorative stand with a dish on top. Sometimes there is a slim container rising above the dish for a flower arrangement or there are candelabra branches extending below the dish for candles; sometimes, both occur.

ERGONOMICS

A design principle based firmly on the needs of the human body. The term is often overused to describe what is hoped to be a comfortable chair design. One of the first steps toward the application of ergonomics was made in 1947 by Denis Young, when he used a "seating box" of modeling clay to record the body shapes and postures of sixty-seven people; the resulting data formed the basis for the design of his "shell" chair.

ESCABEAU

A French term in common use for an early, often painted, carved stool or bench supported on decorative trestles.

ESCRITOIRE

A French term in common use for an early-eighteenth-century straight-fronted (as opposed to slanted) writing cabinet, with drawers, pigeonholes, and sometimes a secret compartment.

ESCUTCHEON

A shield-shaped plaque containing a heraldic device. Also, in hardware, a shield-shaped or otherwise decorated brass or ormolu plate for the surround of a keyhole, door or drawer knob, or pull.

ÉTAGÈRE

A French term in common use for a set of hanging or standing open shelves for the display of collections of objects or ornaments. It is also sometimes referred to as a "whatnot."

FACADE

The main front or face of a building or of a piece of architectural furniture.

FALL FRONT

Usually a slanting, but sometimes vertical, hinged top to a desk that conceals the contents, but which can also be let down to form a writing surface supported by concealed slides. (See also *drop lid*.)

FAN DESIGN

A much-used semicircular motif in eighteenth- and early-nineteenth-century furniture carvings as well as for decorating fanlights, the semicircular windows set above the doors of so many houses of the time.

FANCY CHAIR

A very popular late-eighteenth- and nineteenth-century occasional side chair; it was small-scale and easy to move around.

FARTHINGALE CHAIR

A special chair with a wide seat and no arms made to accommodate the voluminous skirts or farthingales of the Elizabethan period. Similar chairs were made to accommodate the hooped crinolines of the nineteenth century.

FAUTEUIL

French term often used for an armchair with a wood frame and open sides. Arms normally have upholstered tops or elbow pads. Early versions had the arms placed in line with the legs. Later *Regence* and Rococo versions had slightly shorter legs with the arms stepped further back.

FESTOON

In furniture or decoration (as opposed to curtains or draperies), a sculptured, molded, painted, or carved garland of leaves, flowers, or fruit—or all three—curving between two points.

FIDDLEBACK CHAIR

Early rush-seated eighteenth-century chair with a fiddle- or vase-shaped back splat and cabriole or bandy legs.

FIELD BED

Originally a small collapsible four-poster campaign bed, often only about 5 feet high, for soldiers to take to the battlefield. It was also known as a *tent bed*. However, because field beds were usefully small they came into general use and were sometimes taken on long travels to obviate the then common risk of bed bugs. Chippendale designed such a bed with simple bedposts and a small tester that he thought to be suitable also "for single persons and for smaller rooms in villas and superior cottages."

FIELDED PANEL

A flat central panel surrounded by beveled edges.

FIGURING

The marks and striations on various woods used for furniture, whether solid or veneered.

A cast-iron fireback

Some different late-eighteenth-century firedogs

FIN DE SIÈCLE

A French term in common usage for the end of a century, but also used specifically to describe the end of the nineteenth century and its particular opulence.

FINIAL

The ornamental device, such as a carved pineapple, arrow, spear, knob, urn, flame, or cluster of acanthus or other leaves at the end of a pole or post.

FIREBACK

A decorative cast-iron or metal screen placed behind a fire in a fireplace to both conserve and reflect the heat, and to protect the brickwork.

FIREDOG

Either of a pair of upright iron, brass, or nickel supports—usually with a decorative upstand at the front end—used to keep logs in place while they burn. (See also *andiron*.)

Chimneypiece and firedogs in a parlor, Newport, Rhode Island (1758)

FIRESCREEN

Originally an ornamental screen or guard to set in front of a fire to protect against flying sparks or falling logs and coals, or to conceal an empty fireplace when no fire was lit. Smaller, more graceful versions with tripod legs were used to protect the face from too much heat. The term also now applies to glass screens that can be pulled down or up.

FIRESIDE FIGURE

A not quite life-size and generally exotically dressed figure made of plywood, canvas, or papier-mâché meant to act as a heat protector. Fireside figures were particularly popular in the late seventeenth and early eighteenth centuries. They were also known as picture board dummies.

FLAMBEAU

A French term, often used for a flame or flaming-torch decorative motif.

FLANEUSE

A term taken from the French verb *flaner*, meaning "to lounge or wander around with no fixed purpose." It generally describes a garden or conservatory-type chair with a matching footrest and a cane seat and back, a kind of early deck chair.

FLAP TABLE

A seventeenth-century variation of a gateleg table, with a fixed center and two side flaps that can be pulled up and out, and supported also by pulling out the appropriate legs.

FLEMISH

The old term describing things and people from Flanders, the area that is now much of northern France, Belgium, and Holland, and used to describe furniture from that area.

FLEMISH CHAIR

A typical late-seventeenth-century high-backed, elaborately crested chair with a central back panel and seat of woven cane (though occasionally the back panels of such chairs were upholstered with tapestry or velvet). Back legs were straight; front legs were turned and curved outward. These chairs were also known as *Carolean* or *Restoration chairs*.

FLEUR-DE-LIS OR FLEUR-DE-LYS

Stylized lily or iris motif on furniture, representing France and the long line of French kings.

FLUTING

Vertical or horizontal parallel grooves on a column, frieze, pilaster, chair, or table leg. The opposite of reeding, which consists of rows of convex molding.

FLY RAIL OR FLY BRACKET

A term for the folding brackets that support drop- or fall-front desks, drop leaf or Pembroke tables, or other hinged flaps.

FOOTRAIL

The bottom supporting stretcher between two chair legs.

FORNASETTI

Idiosyncratic and highly prized lacquered black-and-white architecturally themed chairs, cabinets, plates, and so on designed by the late-twentieth-century Italian designer Enrico Fornasetti. In some ways they are a kind of updated version of the seventeenth-century Anglo-German Non-such furniture that incorporated marquetry designs based on stylized versions of one of Henry VIII's palaces. (See also *Fornasetti, Enrico* in Architects, Designers, and Decorators.)

FRANKLIN STOVE

The combined stove and fireplace invented by Benjamin Franklin in the mid-eighteenth century in an effort to keep more heat in a room and less going up the chimney.

FRENCH POLISH

This was introduced around 1820, when dark resinous shellac (a natural resin) was melted, strained, dissolved in spirit, applied to furniture in several brushstrokes, and then left to harden to a high shine. Much the same formula is still used today, but it is not recommended for dining tables, serving tables, or sideboards since it does not react well to heat.

FRENCH PROVINCIAL

Generally a simplified interpretation of the Louis XV or Rococo style. Like all provincial or rural furniture, it is much less decorated than more sophisticated city furniture and rarely, if ever, makes much use of veneer, carving, or complicated decoration.

FRET TABLE

Generally a tea table with a gallery formed from cut-out, geometric ornament such as pierced trelliswork or a Greek key pattern.

FRINGE

In upholstery, the decorative edging or trim with twisted threads or loops and tassels used to "finish off" a chair or sofa. (See also *bullion*.)

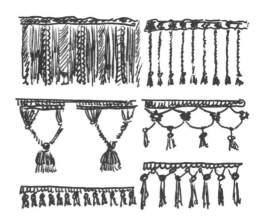

Early-eighteenth-century fringes used to trim upholstery

GALLERY

In furniture, the small decorative railing set along the edge of some tables or trays, or the brass, or other metal, rod running along the back of late-eighteenth- and early-nineteenth-century sideboards. In grand country houses, the wide corridorlike space used to show off family collections of paintings. In apartment buildings, the wide corridor or hallway connecting rooms.

GALLOON OR GALON

A narrow silk braid, often woven with gold or silver thread, used as an edging or trim for upholstery or curtains. It was (and probably still is) frequently used as a cover-up for poorly finished work. A galloon can also be a continuous embroidered or lace band with scalloped edges.

GAME TABLE OR GAMING TABLE

A table specially designed for different card games, chess, and gambling.

GARNITURE

This usually applies to the arrangement of objects on a mantelshelf, but it can also mean the enrichment of any tabletop or surface.

GATELEG TABLE

A circular or oval table, dating back to the seventeenth century, with rounded, hinged flaps supported, when flipped up, by gatelike legs that can be swung out from underneath the central section.

GILDING

Gilding is an ancient art known to be used by the Egyptians and used in Europe from the fifteenth century on with either a water or oil base. Water

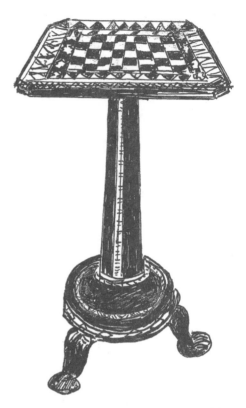

Mid-nineteenth-century game table in Tunbridge ware marquetry

gilding achieves a higher luster, but oil is cheaper and more durable. Gilders were much in demand in the seventeenth and eighteenth centuries for gilding friezes, cornices, and leather hangings, as much as for gilding furniture. Frequently, judging from contemporary accounts, the cost of the gilding exceeded the cost of the actual furniture it decorated.

GIRANDOLE

Originally, a wall sconce for a candle that was usually mirrored to reflect the flicker of the flame and thus the sparkle. Girandoles were much used in the late seventeenth and eighteenth centuries. In the nineteenth century the term was also used for round convex mirrors topped with gilded eagles and candlesticks attached either side of the frame.

GOLD LEAF

Thin sheets of an amalgam of tin and copper, also known as *Dutch gold*, are laid over the relevant furniture or mirror frame surface that has been previously dampened and prepared with gold size, shellac, or some sort of tacky adhesive. "Lay on your gold," advocated John Stalker and George Parker in *A treatise of japaning and varnishing: being a compleat discovery of those arts, with the best way of making all sorts of varnish...together with above an hundred distinct patterns for japan-work...*(1688), "pressing it gently and close...if your work be sufficiently moist, you'll perceive how lovingly the gold will embrace it, hugging and clinging to it like those inseparable friends, Iron and the Loadstone" (loadstone or lodestone being magnetic iron ore). Their advice still holds ture.

GONDOLA BED

A French nineteenth-century Empire bed with a scrolled headboard and footboard that looked like a Venetian gondola.

GOOSENECK

A pediment with double curves frequently used on American and English furniture of the eighteenth century. (See also *swan neck pediment*.)

GOUT CHAIR

A chair specially designed in the eighteenth century for gout sufferers. A trundlelike footrest could be pulled out from under the chair seat so that the bad leg could rest at the required angle. The stool could be pushed back when not needed.

GOUT STOOL OR GOUTY STOOL

Another eighteenth-century design for gout sufferers. The stool had an adjustable top.

GRAIN

The figuring caused by annual growth rings indigenous to all types of wood used for furniture.

GRAINING

(See *graining* in Colors, Paints, Varnishes, and Decorative Finishes.)

GRANDFATHER CHAIR

An oversized wing chair that was popular during the Queen Anne period.

GRANDFATHER CLOCK OR LONGCASE CLOCK

A clock 6 feet tall or higher with a waisted and hooded case protecting the pendulum and weights. It made its first appearance in the seventeenth century and has remained popular.

GRANDMOTHER CLOCK

A smaller, fined-down version of a grandfather clock.

GRECIAN SOFA

A graceful early-nineteenth-century Empire and Regency period couch or recamier (after the literary Madame Récamier) with a higher head than foot, though both ends roll or curve over.

GRIFFIN

A mythical animal used as a decorative motif on friezes and in both Gothic period carving as well as in early-Georgian decoration. The chimerical creature has the body of a lion and the head and wings of an eagle, and is also much used in heraldry.

GRIS TRIANON

The term for the aged gray-white color (based on white lead) of much late-eighteenth-century furniture that was originally painted white. The color is named after the white-painted furniture originally ordered for the Petit Trianon near Versailles.

GROS POINT

Wool cross-stitched tapestry on a coarse linen or canvas backing. This work is often used for covering stools and chair seats.

GROTESQUES

Not ugly, but simply the sort of masks, animal forms, winged creatures, mermaids, and so on created by artists in antiquity and discovered during excavations for new construction or in long-buried ruins known as *grottoes*, from which they take their name (as does the slang term *grotty*).

GUÉRIDON

A French term for a small round table, stand, or pedestal, sometimes used as a candlestand. It was a popular piece of ancillary furniture borrowed from a French design during the early-eighteenth-century Queen Anne period. A *guéridon à crémaillière* was much the same sort of piece but adjustable in height and usually topped with a piece of marble surrounded by a small brass gallery.

GUILLOCHE

An ornamental Renaissance-designed band of continuous interlacing circles or figure eights. It has been a popular decoration for furniture from the sixteenth century onward.

HADLEY CHEST

An early-eighteenth-century New England dower chest on four legs with one or more drawers, made in Hadley, Massachusetts. It was usually incised—rather than deeply carved—with patterns. In addition, it sometimes bore its owner's initials and was stained scarlet, a deep mulberry, or black. The height was determined by how many drawers the chest had.

HALF-TESTER

(See *tester*.)

An early-eighteenth-century
Hadley Chest or dower chest,
made in Hadley, Massachusetts

HALL CHAIR

A formal, sometimes armless, but usually decoratively backed eighteenth-century chair designed specifically for halls.

HALLMARK

A stamp of approval from the Goldsmith's Company in London, with the maker's initials, coded date, and so on, imprinted on silverware and gold utensils.

HANDKERCHIEF TABLE

A space-saving, triangular-shaped table made to fit into a corner. A second similarly shaped hinged top is attached to the first so that when the table is pulled out, the second top can be flipped back to form a larger rectangular surface.

HANDLES

In furniture, the knobs or pulls in various shapes, sizes, and materials

A hall chair with arms designed by
Thomas Chippendale, ca. 1755

that are used to pull open drawers or doors. In the sixteenth and seventeenth centuries these were made from turned wood or wrought iron. Brass was introduced to hardware during the reign of William and Mary in England and then found its way to America. A ring hanging from a lion's mouth was popular, but the French, and much of mainland Europe, favored decorated ormolu, a kind of gilded bronze, for their own mounts and handles.

HANGING SHELVES

In the seventeenth and eighteenth centuries, such shelves in a variety of shapes and styles, some of them highly decorated, were popular for the display of objects, collections of this and that, and books. Today, they are valued for their space-saving qualities; contemporary versions tend to be simply designed.

HARDWARE

Umbrella term for general door and drawer "furniture," including metal hinges, handles, pulls, knobs, knockers, escutcheons, finger plates, bell pulls, and bells.

HARLEQUIN TABLE OR DESK

An eighteenth-century form of the Pembroke table designed with all kinds of pigeonholes, secret compartments, and small drawers. The central nest of drawers is raised and lowered by a weight or spring system called harlequin. When the drawers are lowered the surface becomes flat again, allowing it be used alternately as either a dressing table or desk.

HARVARD CHAIR

A seventeenth-century American turned three-cornered chair.

Harlequin table, ca. 1790, shown with the central drawers in the raised position

HARVARD FRAME

Trademark for a steel bed frame, generally bolted to a headboard (and a footboard if there is one) to support the bedsprings and mattress.

HARVEST TABLE

A long and narrow table of eighteenth-century design with drop leaves with either square or gently rounded ends and either straight or turned legs. It was probably a good size for harvesting feasts.

HASSOCK

A small thick cushion or mat used as a kneeler in churches or as a small ottoman or footstool in a domestic setting.

HEPPLEWHITE FURNITURE

George Hepplewhite was the second of the triumvirate of eighteenth-century English furniture designers who had a worldwide influence through their published pattern books. His book *The Cabinet-maker and Upholsterer's Guide*, published posthumously in 1788, promulgated a certain lightness of construction with many charming heart, hoop, and shield-shaped chair backs; wheat sheaf, floral or honey-suckle swag, and fern decorations; and Prince of Wales feathers. He almost always favored a spade foot and fluted chair legs, and also designed many satinwood and inlaid pieces as well as some interesting japanned pieces. (See also *Hepplewhite, George* in Architects, Designers, and Decorators.)

HIERACOSPHINX

An ancient Egyptian motif on furniture consisting of a lion's body with a hawk's head.

HIGHBOY

Called a *tallboy* in England, this eighteenth-century chest on legs, originally introduced in Holland during the reign of William and Mary, became very popular in America. It usually had cabriole legs, four or five drawers, and was capped by either a flat top with a carved cornice or a pediment or broken pediment.

Early-eighteenth-century highboy in curly maple

HIGH DADDY

As opposed to a highboy or tallboy, an American eighteenth-century tall chest of drawers with at least six drawers.

HIGH RELIEF

On furniture, figuring or ornamental designs so deeply carved that they appear almost three-dimensional, as opposed to bas-relief.

HIGH-RISER

Another space-saver piece in the form of a well-upholstered couch, with no back or arms, that hides a slightly smaller mattress and a collapsed frame underneath it. The mattress can be pulled out and raised to the couch seat level so that the whole becomes a double bed.

HITCHCOCK CHAIR

A popular nineteenth-century American "fancy" chair made between the early 1820s and the 1850s, and named after its manufacturer Lambert Hitchcock. It had an oval turned top rail and either wooden, rush, or cane seats, and was generally painted black. It was principally distinguished by its stenciled top rail and its splat, which was decorated with colored or gilded fruits or flowers.

HOOF FOOT

A chair foot in the form of a small goatlike hoof.

HOOPBACK CHAIR

A Queen Anne chair, also a Hepplewhite design, on which the uprights and the top rail of the back of the chair were combined in a continuous hoop.

HOPE CHEST

A chest used to store items for a hopeful wedding trousseau.

HORSE

In furniture, a simple squared or V-shaped support for a trestle table. Also, vertical supports for a swing (cheval) mirror or fire screen.

HORSESHOE TABLE

A late-eighteenth-century design that was sometimes also called a *hunt table*. It had a somewhat narrow horseshoe-shaped top.

HUNT CHAIR

Originally a Sheraton design for a chair with a built-in wooden strip to act as a foot rest.

HUNT TABLE

(See *horseshoe table*.)

HUTCH

An American term for an English *dresser*, it is usually a scrubbed pine cabinet or cupboard. Or, more specifically, it is a set of open shelves within a frame—sometimes flanked by a pair of narrow cupboards—set over a buffet or second set of shelves or cupboards closed off by double doors. The name drives from the old French *huche* for a chest.

INLAY

Like Boulle work, or marquetry in furniture, this is a technique whereby a design is carefully cut out of the surface to be decorated, thus allowing space for the resulting gaps to be filled with exact-fitting contrast material or color. These insets may be of ivory, horn, shell, stone, mother of pearl, various metals, or wood veneer.

INTAGLIO

A process in furniture-making whereby designs are cut out of a surface in order to create a relief design in reverse. The result is a design sunk below the surface material.

INTARSIA

An Italian incising process for mosaic or furniture-making that was particularly popular during the fifteenth and sixteenth centuries. Similar to later inlay work, different colored woods or stone were inlaid with contrasting materials such as shell, bone, ivory, and so on.

INTERLACED CHAIR BACKS

A late-eighteenth-century French design, as well as designs by Hepplewhite and Sheraton, for carved straps or ribbons that interlace with one another as intricately as geometric fretwork.

IRISH CHIPPENDALE

Like American Chippendale, this term refers to furniture made in Ireland using Chippendale designs fashioned from mahogany. That the Irish of the time must have had a fascination for lions is proved by the preponderance of leonine masks and paw feet used in the designs.

JALOUSIE

A well-used French term for louvered shades, based on the premise that people are annoyed or *jealous* when deprived of a neighboring interior view, especially at night.

JAPANNING

In furniture, the various imitations of oriental lacquer achieved in the late seventeenth century by using different resins or gums dissolved in strong spirit or wine. The resulting varnish was then mixed with metals like German brass dust to simulate gold, the duller English silver dust, or powdered tin in a "green-gold" or "dirty gold," as well as different coppers. These mixtures were then used to paint flowers, houses, views, and so on. However, there were long hours of preparation before the final coats could be applied. According to the instructions issued by John Stalker in 1688, great attention had first to be given to achieving a really smooth surface with several coats of whiting and size to seal the original wood grain. The ground was then "black varnished" by applying three coats of varnish mixed with lampblack. This was followed by six further coats that were also mixed with lampblack but thinned down somewhat with "Venice" turpentine. Each coat, of course, was allowed to dry thoroughly before it was rubbed down again to prepare the surface for the next coat. And these nine coats were just the preliminary. After that, twelve further similar coats were applied with the same drying and smoothing processes. After the twelfth coat, the furniture was allowed to stand untouched for five or six days to allow the surface to harden. It was then given a final polish and finished with a mixture of lampblack and oil before any ornamentation was painted or incised. If all these steps were conscientiously followed, John Stalker promised that the results "would be as good, as glossy, as beautiful a black as ever was wrought by an English hand and to all appearances it was no way inferior to the Indian" (geography, as usual, being still a somewhat hazy science). (See also *gold leaf*.)

JARDINIÈRE

A stand or container for plants made from painted metal, wood, or porcelain in varying degrees of elaboration.

JIGSAW DETAIL

Mid- to late-nineteenth-century fretwork or cut-out designs achieved with a jigsaw, which was one of the first "power tools." The technique was used for furniture, but it was particularly used to decorate the outside of buildings, including the fanciful "gingerbread" and "steamboat Gothic" designs.

Detail of a jigsaw of a fretsaw back of a garden bench.
Taken from William Halfpenny's *New designs for Chinese temples,
triumphal arches, garden seats, palings, etc.* (1750–52)

JIGSAW MIRROR

A detailed mirror framed with all sorts of fanciful scrolls that were first hand-cut, then achieved by the new jigsaw.

JOINERY

A technique in which joiners are used to assemble furniture with the help of dovetail joints, mortise and tenons, and dowels. This carpentry method is used more for tables and chairs than for case or cabinet pieces.

JUDGE'S CHAIR

Upholstered high-backed chair especially shaped to cradle the head and shoulders. Box stretchers connect the four generally square-cut legs.

KAS

The Dutch version of the French armoire brought over to America by early Dutch settlers. It usually had a simple but heavy cornice, double doors, and ball feet.

KETTLE BAS

Another term for a bombé-shaped chest or commode, so-called because of the fanciful parallel with the shape of a kettle.

KEYSTONE

The central wedged-shape pieced at the apex of an arched form on a piece of furniture.

KIDNEY DESK OR DRESSING TABLE

A slightly curved concave-fronted kneehole desk or dressing table popular in the eighteenth century.

KLINE

A curious multifunctional ancient Greek couch that was used for sleeping, lounging, and eating. It had a sweepingly curved back at one end while the front legs curved forward and the back legs curved backward.

KLISMOS

The Classic Greek chair, much emulated in the French Directoire, English Regency, Duncan Phyfe, and American Empire periods. The chair had a concave curved back rail and splayed-out legs.

KNEEHOLE DESK

A desk that, as the name implies, provides a central leg space flanked by rows of drawers.

KNIFE BOX

A decorative receptacle for knives that tested the design prowess of several great cabinetmakers in the eighteenth century. Pairs of knife boxes—sometimes shaped like urns, sometimes square with a sloping top—were often perched symmetrically on sideboards.

KNIFE URN

An urn-shaped predecessor of the knife box that, being metal-lined, could also hold water.

KNOLE SOFA

A 1920s design based on a seventeenth-century sofa among the furnishings of Knole Park, a stately home in Kent, England. It had a high back and hinged arms secured in an upright position by loops of rope or twisted heavy braid.

KNUCKLE CARVING

A design element, often used by Chippendale, in which the outer edges of a chair's arms were shaped to resemble the knuckles on hands.

LADDER-BACK

A chair back with ladderlike horizontal cross rails flanked by two vertical stiles; it is a provincial alternative to the splat back.

LAMINATE

Many layers of wood glued together like plywood, often with some sort of veneer on top to form a unit.

LAMPADAIRE

Usually a rather grandly decorated pedestal to hold a lamp or candlestick.

LANCASHIRE SPINDLE-BACK CHAIR

A pleasant eighteenth-century country chair from northern England with a rush seat and a front stretcher with a knoblike centerpiece, as well as a shell-like motif in the middle of the top rail. Generally, two rows of spindles are

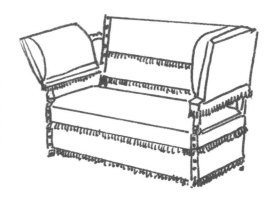

A knole sofa with adjustable drop ends, ca. 1600

framed by one or two horizontal rails in addition to the top rail.

LANTERN CLOCK

A brass, lantern-shaped clock for a mantel or regular shelf first made in the seventeenth century. It was sometimes also known as a *birdcage clock*.

LATTICEWORK

The name is applied to the open tracery sometimes used to screen the doors of cabinets or bookshelves, as well as to form radiator covers. It is also a well-known chair-back design promulgated by Sheraton.

LAZY SUSAN

A revolving circular tray, or series of trays on a stand that is an American variation of the old English dumbwaiter. It is set in the middle of a large tabletop to enable guests to help themselves, or to provide a choice of condiments.

LEAFWORK

A decorative carved motif in the form of foliage used in the eighteenth century for chair legs and seat slats and as borders on cabinets.

LECTERN

A support for a bible or large book set on a carved or turned pedestal.

LIBRARY CHAIR

Although Thomas Chippendale designed some large comfortable chairs especially for libraries, whose patterns remained standard, several ingenious eighteenth- and nineteenth-century multipurpose space-saver versions were also invented. One of them was a padded leather armchair with a saddle-shaped seat, an adjustable hinge flap on which to put a book, and compartments in the arms for holding pens and inks and a candlestick. Another was a chair and library steps in one (not unlike modern kitchen stool-stepladders) in which the were steps concealed under the seat. Tipping the seat over converted the chair into steps for reaching high shelves.

LIBRARY STEPS

Libraries clearly exercised the ingenuity of furniture designers. Since shelves were often very high in high-ceilinged old rooms, several library-step devices, including long black tubes with a slit down the middle, could be snappily pulled apart

A library chair designed by
Thomas Chippendale, 1768

to form slim triangular-shapedladders. (A version of this was reproduced by the British designer David Hicks in the 1970s.) Sheraton proposed a unit that could be a library table one moment or open out to a ladder with a conveniently tall grip handle the next.

LIBRARY TABLE

A large writing table with drawers, although many people use circular drum or rent tables.

LINENFOLD PANELING

Carved paneling, derived from Flemish design work, imitating vertical folds of linen, and ogee-shaped at top and bottom. Later, it was over-carved with bunches of grapes, tassels, and other similar emblems. It was very popular from the late fifteenth through the sixteenth centuries for chests and cupboards, as well as for paneling. (Also called *parchment paneling*.)

LIT EN BATEAU

A French term in common usage for a boat-shaped bed with curving ends, very popular in the nineteenth-century Empire period.

LIT À LA FRANÇAISE

A French canopied bed meant to be placed against a wall or in an alcove. Thomas Jefferson had just such a bed at his Virginia home, Monticello.

LIT À LA POLONAISE

A late-eighteenth-century "Polish" bed with an elaborate raised canopy.

LIVERY CUPBOARD

An all-purpose cupboard mentioned many times in sixteenth- and seventeenth-century inventories of household goods. It consisted of shelves as well as a cupboard and was used for storing the *livre*, the name at that time for provisions or food and drink kept for the night, as well as the relevant eating and drinking vessels and candles.

LONGCASE CLOCK

The more formal term for a *grandfather clock*.

A bed with an elaborate raised canopy believed to have been developed in Poland during the eighteenth century and thus called a *lit à la Polonaise.*

LOO TABLE

A large nineteenth-century oval or round card table with a tip-up top and a pedestal base. It was meant originally for playing the card game called "Loo" that was popular at the time.

LOOSE SEAT

A separate seat that can be slipped out of the frame of a chair or stool for easy recovering or upholstery.

LOTUS

An ancient Egyptian motif based on the water lily of the Nile that was popular, along with all things Egyptian, around 1810. It was also an Indian and Eastern motif.

LOUNGE

An alternative name for a living room, much used in the early part of the twentieth century. It also applies to a deep, comfortable armchair in which one can literally lounge.

LOVE SEAT

An upholstered two-seater sofa or settee.

LOWBOY

An eighteenth-century American low chest of drawers often made to accompany a highboy. Also, a late-seventeenth-century English table with one long drawer flanked by two smaller, but often deeper, drawers.

LOZENGE

A diamond-shaped motif used on panels and for general carving, from medieval times.

LUNETTE

In furniture, a demi-lune or semi-circular shape often filled with ornamental carving especially in the case of oak furniture. In the late eighteenth century the lunette was filled with marquetry or other inlaid or painted designs.

LYRE BACK

A carved lyre-shaped splat much used by Adam, Sheraton, and Hepplewhite in Britain in the eighteenth century and by Duncan Phyfe, in America, in the early part of the next.

MARLBOROUGH LEG

A late-eighteenth-century, rather heavy-looking grooved leg with a block foot. Chippendale often used it.

MARQUETRY

Usually, the term describing the designs made by inserting contrasting and interestingly colored woods into a wood veneered surface so that both surfaces remain flush. It was much used for both floors and furniture in the Renaissance period as well as the seventeenth and eighteenth centuries. The same process could also be repeated with bits of metal, mother of pearl, horn, and tortoiseshell.

MARQUISE CHAIR

An early-eighteenth-century French wide chair or love seat variation in the bergère tradition. It was designed to make it easier for women to sit wearing the wide skirts of the period.

MARRIAGE CHEST

A chest usually used for a marriage trousseau or for storing household linens. It took many forms over the centuries, from the magnificently carved and decorated Italian *cassones* of the Italian Renaissance period to the simple painted *hope* or *dower chests* of the nineteenth century.

MARTHA WASHINGTON CHAIR

Martha Washington gave her name to pieces of furniture much as British monarchs bestowed their royal coat of arms to their various purveyors of goods. The eponymous chair, sometimes called a *lolling* chair, had a low upholstered seat and high upholstered back, with slender tapered and often reeded legs and open arms.

MARTHA WASHINGTON SEWING TABLE

A useful oval table with sensibly deep storage pockets flanking the generally reeded legs. The bags were accessed through lift-up hinged flaps at the two curved ends, a system that also accessed the fitted central tray.

MILK SAFE OR PIE SAFE

A nineteenth-century substitute for a refrigerator with a pierced tin panel or grille to allow air to circulate. They were often made of painted pine.

MIRROR

A polished or smooth surface that reflects images. The earliest mirrors date from Greco-Roman antiquity and were actually made of highly polished silver or metal, but silvered-glass mirrors were made in Venice as early as the fourteenth century. Mirrors are often used decoratively and, since they reflect light, to brighten a space.

MODERNE

A term for 1920s furniture and accessories.

MODULAR FURNITURE

Related pieces of case furniture or seating that are made to a module, or a given set of dimensions, and to fractions of that module. They can then be assembled to choice with connecting devices within a given space.

MODULAR SEATING OR SECTIONAL SEATING

Pieces such as upholstered corner seats, seats with right arms, seats with left arms, backless seats, seats with backs, foot stools, convenient dumping surfaces, and so on that can all be put together in whatever way best suits the user and his or her given space.

MULE CHEST

A hefty, double-sized chest with drawers and a centered supporting foot as well as the normal side-kicks and two handles to help move it. The precursor of the modern double chest of drawers.

MURPHY BED

The trade name for a modern space-saving "hideaway" bed that can be hidden away behind apparent closet doors, an alcove, a bookcase, or a series of shelves.

NACRÉ OR MOTHER OF PEARL

This describes the pearly, opalescent lining to some sea shells that is much used as an inlay for furniture and accessories, particularly nineteenth-century papier-mâché pieces.

NEEDLEPOINT

Tapestrylike cross-stitch on canvas, net, or coarse linen that incorporates different methods like the coarser *gros point*, with twelve stitches per inch, and the finer *petit point*, with twenty per inch. It has been used as an upholstery covering and for pillows and cushions since medieval days. Other examples can be found in eighteenth- and nineteenth-century samplers usually featuring the alphabet and a quotation carried out in different stitches and colors.

NEW COLONIAL

A mass-produced early-twentieth-century revival of the earlier Colonial period in both architecture and furniture. It amalgamated—in a simplified way—all the salient features of the first Colonial eras using later Federal, Greek Revival, and American Empire motifs.

NONSUCH DESK

Germans in Germany as well as Germans who settled in London in the sixteenth century made these desks decorated with marquetry designs of arches and architectural fantasies. The designs were reminiscent of Henry VIII's now nonexistent Palace of Nonsuch (meaning unequaled or nonsuch), but not literally based on it. In a way, the late Italian designer Piero Fornasetti's twentieth-century black-and-white lacquered architectural-motif furniture and objects are somewhat reminiscent of this work.

OBELISK

An Egyptian-inspired column that narrows to a pyramid-shaped top. The form is used in miniature for decorative objects.

Nonsuch writing desk inlaid with various woods, second half of the sixteenth century

OBJET D'ART

A French term in general use, literally translated as "art object," although it is usually small and could include collections or individual items of fine porcelain, snuff boxes, decorative boxes of all shapes and materials, miniatures, ivories, and so on. (See also *bibelots*.)

OCCASIONAL CHAIR

A small maneuverable chair that can be pulled up to a conversational group in a living room, family room, or drawing room.

OCCASIONAL TABLE

An umbrella term for any convenient small table used as a side table, end table, coffee table, cocktail table, or sofa table.

OEIL-DE-BOEUF

Literally, "bull's eye." A French term in common use for a round or oval window or mirror.

OPEN BACK CHAIR

Any unupholstered chair back that has a decorative open frame like a *shield back* or a back with a central splat.

ORMOLU

Gilt or gilded bronze used either for sculpture and ornaments or objets d'art, or for mounts, moldings, and decoration on furniture. The name derives from a corruption of the French *bronze dore* into *d'or mulu* (bronze gilded with ground gold).

OTTOMAN

A backless upholstered bench or a large, upholstered footrest often designed to partner a club chair or armchair.

OVERSTUFFED

An American term for well-upholstered, comfortable seating generally with concealed frames.

OXBOW FRONT

A front on cabinets and case furniture characterized by a concave center flanked by convex sides. Used in the eighteenth century.

PAD FOOT

The disklike foot very often found attached to a cabriole leg.

PAGODA

In furniture and decoration, a motif or decorative element often found in eighteenth- and nineteenth-century chinoiserie. It follows the shape of Buddhist Chinese multistoried temples in which each level has its own upswept roof, each smaller than the preceding one.

PAKTONG

An Eastern, eighteenth-century, silvery-colored alloy imported from China and made from copper, nickel, and zinc. In the West it was called white copper and used for fireplace furniture such as grates, fire irons, and so on.

PANEL-BACK CHAIR

A seventeenth-century oak chair with a high panel-back, usually a carved crest, and heavy legs and stretchers. It is also sometimes known as a wainscot chair because of its paneled appearance.

PAPER SCROLL

A carved scroll resembling unfurling rolled-up paper that is sometimes placed at the end of a top chair rail. Chippendale showed some similar designs in his *Gentleman and Cabinet-Maker's Director*. Such scrolls are also known as spiral scrolls and spiral volutes.

PAPIER-MÂCHÉ

French term in general use for a popular nineteenth-century material used for making light chairs, occasional tables, trays, and other decorative items. It was made from pulped paper mixed with whiting and glue that was then molded into appropriate shapes. The finished items were then japanned or painted black and inlaid with mother of pearl and other inlays. A similar material called *paper stucco* was used in the late eighteenth century as a substitute for plaster moldings and ceiling designs.

PAPYRUS

Papyrus plants were primarily used to make paper in ancient Egypt and China but they were also much used as the inspiration for a decorative motif for furniture in those countries and, after the Napoleonic Egyptian campaigns, in the West during the Neoclassical era.

PARQUETRY

Inlay for furniture worked in geometric designs in different color woods.

Parquetry of oyster shell veneer on a late-seventeenth-century cabinet on stand

PARSONS TABLE

Simple, unobtrusive, allover square occasional tables named after the Parsons School of Design in New York City. They could and can be made in many colors and finishes, and were a great favorite of the late interior designer Billy Baldwin, who passed on the liking to many of his peers and their followers.

PARTNERS' DESK

A large pedestal kneehole desk that has drawers on either side and is wide enough for two people to work opposite each other. It was introduced in the nineteenth century and was a variation of large eighteenth-century writing or library tables.

PATINA

The sheen or glow that settles on well-cared-for furniture over the years. Also the greenish coat that settles on bronze and copper through a chemical reaction.

PAW FOOT

The carved animal paw often used to finish off a furniture leg in the late seventeenth to the eighteenth centuries.

PEACOCK CHAIR

An overscale rattan or wicker chair with a high back made in the Orient in the late nineteenth century. Much the same design is still used today.

PEAR DROP ORNAMENT

(See *pear drop ornament* in Architectural, Building, and Decorating Terms.)

PEDESTAL

In furniture, the support for a bust, statue, vase, or piece of sculpture that can be plain or carved. It is also called a *plinth*.

PEDESTAL CHAIR

This chair first appeared in the mid-twentieth century and was set on a single slim support with a larger rounded or flared base made of metal, fiberglass, plastic, or wood. A particularly good example is the Eero Saarinen tulip chair on which the seat is molded with the base.

PEDESTAL DESK

(See *kneehole desk*.)

PEDESTAL TABLE

A round or oval table attached to a single base. Sometimes the base is a substantial column that either goes straight to the floor or ends in a heavy base with sturdy spreading feet. A smaller occasional pedestal table is supported by slimmer columns that often branch off into a tripod base halfway down the column or stem. Such tables in various guises have been popular since the eighteenth century, and many modern variations exist, including the Saarinen companion piece to the tulip chair.

PEDIMENT

In furniture, a triangular feature carved in wood, very similar to an architectural pediment, that is used to crown a mirror or a case piece like a bookcase, highboy, tallboy, bureau-bookcase, or secretary. The pediment can be plain, broken to support a bust or vase, segmented, scrolled, or swan-necked.

PEMBROKE TABLE

A drop-leaf table on four legs with a drawer set in the frieze, or apron (the part immediately below the table surface). The leaves, which are supported by hinged wooden brackets when flipped up, are generally slightly rounded and narrower than the fixed central portion.

PENDANT

A suspended or hanging ornament on furniture, chandeliers, sconces, and so on.

PENNSYLVANIA DUTCH FURNITURE or GERMAN FURNITURE

Furniture with simple lines made originally by the German and Swiss Mennonites who settled in Pennsylvania between the late seventeenth/early eighteenth and the nineteenth centuries. In this case "Dutch" is a corruption of *Deutsch* (German). It was usually painted with various superimposed motifs like the hex sign to ward off evil (usually a circle with a six-pointed star), hearts, peacocks, roosters, leaves, and so on.

Inlaid satinwood Pembroke table, ca. 1790. The set of pigeonholes and drawers rises on springs and is the feature that gives it the alternative name of *harlequin table*.

PETIT POINT

A fine version of gros point embroidery often used for upholstery and worked in tent stitch (a series of parallel stitches worked diagonally across the intersection of the threads of the canvas backing), rather than cross-stitch. Where gros point or needlepoint use about fifteen stitches per linear inch, petit point makes use of twenty.

PIECRUST TABLE

A small table with a shallow scalloped raised edge like a piecrust.

PIER GLASS

This was originally a long mirror propped against a pier, or solid masonry wall, between windows or supporting a high arch. Also, applies to a tall mirror set above a side table, console, or pier table (also set between windows).

Piecrust table, ca. 1750

Pier glass designed by
George Hepplewhite

PIER TABLE

A narrow table set between windows or against a pier, generally topped by a *pier glass*.

PHILADELPHIA CHAIR

A version of the ubiquitous *Windsor chair* made in Philadelphia in the eighteenth century.

PIERCED SPLAT

Cut-out (like fretwork) or openwork design on the central splat of a chair.

PIERCED WORK

Openwork woodwork used for screens or window shutters (as in Moorish architecture) or for the backs of chairs.

A pier table from the third edition
of *The Cabinet-Maker and
Upholsterer's Guide*
by George Hepplewhite

PIETRA DURE

Early Italian Renaissance technique for inlaying stone with chips of marble and semiprecious stones. The technique is still practiced for tabletops, the tops of low cabinets, and so on.

PIGEONHOLES

The small storage compartments in a bureau, fall-front desk, or secretary.

PILASTER

In furniture, it is a vertical carved ornamental representation of a flattened rectangular column, often reeded.

PILLOW-BACKED CHAIR

Not as it sounds, but a kind of "fancy" or Hitchcock chair with a block in the middle of the top rail flanked by turned decoration.

PINEAPPLE FINIAL

A stylized carved version of the fruit used for topping off bedposts, newel-posts on stairs, and occasionally pediments. It was then and is today a symbol of wealth and of prosperity.

PLAQUE

A small panel or tablet inset into wood or plaster, usually made of porcelain or metal and ornamented in some way.

PLATFORM BED

A bed made up of a mattress set on a platform, sometimes recessed into a frame with a shelf, and sometimes appearing to float over a recessed base.

PLINTH

As with a pedestal, a support for a bust, piece of sculpture, large vase, or urn. Also, the square base of a column or a cabinet.

POLE SCREEN

A small, decorated fire screen to deflect heat from faces. It is made from an adjustable panel mounted on a slim pole.

POUDREUSE

A French term for a small dressing table with a lift-up lid, lined with a mirror, which shuts off a space for cosmetics.

POUF *OR* POUFFE

A French term in universal use for a large round upholstered stool.

A corded pouf, or what the French call *pouf à cordages*

PRÉ-DIEU

A French term for a kneeling chair that is designed for prayer. It is normally in the shape of a very low seated armless upholstered chair with a broad upholstered shelf, or wood shelf, in place of a top rail.

PRESS *OR* LINEN PRESS

An early name for a cupboard or armoire used to store linens or clothes. In the seventeenth century the term was sometimes used for a closet or cupboard to store books before bookshelves became necessities.

QUATREFOIL

A symbol or design element with four foils, lobes, or leaves—such as a stylized four-leaf clover—much used in Gothic furniture and decoration.

RAIL

In furniture, the horizontal tie-bar of a chair, such as the top of the back, or a stretcher running from leg to leg. Also the horizontal strip of a panel or a frame.

RAM'S HEAD

A popular motif in the eighteenth century, often used by Robert Adam.

RAM'S-HORN STUMP

A motif of double-curved arms on some eighteenth-century chairs that shows a similarity to skinny ram's horns.

RATCHET CHAIR

A high-backed eighteenth-century chair with stout, reeded Marlborough legs and upholstered arms that had a reclining mechanism. The back was attached to the armrest via a ratchet device that facilitated several different degrees of incline.

RECAMIER

A graceful nineteenth-century French chaise longue in the spare but elegantly curved Grecian style. It was named after Jacques-Louis David's portrait of Madame Recamier, the great literary hostess, reclining on just such a couch.

RECLINING CHAIR

A chair, not unlike some dentists' or airplane seats, in which the mechanism allows the back to fall backward and a footrest to come up simultaneously. Such chairs were being designed as early as the nineteenth century.

RED FILLER

An American finish for country pieces made from a reddish-brown pigment mixed with linseed oil. It stopped being used in the first half of the nineteenth century.

REEDING

Parallel convex curves, as opposed to fluting, which is concave. The decoration is used vertically on chair and table legs, horizontally on borders and edgings.

REFECTORY TABLE

The term applies to most long, narrow dining tables whatever the legs and whether the top is formed from planks or a solid piece of wood.

RENT TABLE

Originally a landlord's table for both collecting and filing rents. They are round or octagonal with seven drawers—numbered for every day of the week—set into the apron under the tabletop.

REPOUSSÉ

Design on metal. The effect is produced by hammering or otherwise forcibly pressing the metal from the reverse side to create a raised design.

RESTORATION CHAIR

A high-backed cane-paneled chair from the reign of Charles II, otherwise called a Carolean chair. The legs and uprights were usually spiral-turned, and there was generally some decorative carved cresting on the top rail. Sometimes this carving took the form of a crown held by cherubs, decorated all around with roses and the peripatetic acanthus leaves, which had become such a popular form of decoration during the Renaissance period. (See also *Carolean* period in Styles and Movements.)

RETICULATED

Allover lattice- or netlike design on furniture.

RIBBAND BACK

Carving resembling interlacing ribbons, sometimes used by Chippendale.

RIBBON BACK

A carved central splat, such as puckered or creased ribbon bows, often used in the Louis XVI period in France and adopted and adapted by Chippendale and his peer group.

ROLLTOP DESK

A nineteenth-century variation on the normal pull-down or fall-front desk in which the rolltop consisted of a curved slatted panel that folded up on itself.

ROPE BED

A mattress set on a base of rope laced back and forth, as when lacing a shoe. This takes the place of an open or closed spring base.

ROYCROFT COMMUNITY FURNITURE

A style of American Arts and Crafts furniture characterized by simple designs with tapering legs from ash, oak, and mahogany, often with copper fittings or hardware and obvious mortise and tenon joints. The Roycroft Community, which produced the furniture, was founded by Elbert Hubbard in 1896.

RUSH SEAT

A seat made of woven rushes. Before cane became available for furniture and rugs, as well as for other flooring such as sisal and coir, rushes were widely used for both chair seats and flooring.

SAARINEN PEDESTAL TABLE AND CHAIRS

A graceful, now classic set consisting of a round white table and chairs. The distinctive pedestal design that supports the table and chairs is like an elongated trumpet that flares out at the base and just below the table or chair seat.

SABER LEGS

A chair leg that, in the Greek manner, splays forward in front and outward behind, following the lines of the Greek *Klismos*.

SALEM ROCKER

A New England rocking chair with a straight spindle back, rather lower than the Boston rocker, and heavy scrolled top rail, arms, and seat. It was first built in the early nineteenth century.

SAWBUCK TABLE

Unadorned tabletop supported on X-shaped trestles. It is also known as a *plain trestle table*.

SCAGLIOLA

A seventeenth-century Italian finish made of gypsum or plaster of paris inset with marble chips, then colored and polished to look like marble or another ornamental stone. It was much in demand in eighteenth-century England and was often used as a material for chimneypieces as well as for tabletops.

SCALE

This is important to take into account when buying furniture or moving furniture around. It means equating the dimensions of a piece of furniture in relation not just to the height and width of the room in which it is to be placed but also to other pieces in the area (and also making quite sure that any given piece will comfortably fit through the appropriate doorways, into elevators, or up stair turns). When drawn to scale, a drawing is reduced or enlarged in relation to a particular ratio, such as one-quarter of an inch equals one foot.

SCREEN TABLE

One of Sheraton's bright design ideas for a lady working at her writing desk near a fire. A small proportional screen was slotted into an opening at the back of the desk and could be slid up and down as needed to protect the face or body from too much heat.

SCROLL

A much-used motif in furniture design based on a spiraling line like a rolled piece of paper.

SCROLL FOOT

An early-eighteenth-century flattened scroll finishing off a cabriole leg.

SEAWEED MARQUETRY

An inlay of different woods forming arabesque and seaweed patterns often used on William and Mary– and Queen Anne–period furniture.

SECRETARY OR SECRETAIRE

A writing desk with a fall-front with drawers underneath and a cabinet or bookcase on top. *Secretaire*, the French term, is also much used.

SECTIONAL FURNITURE

As in "modular" furniture, upholstered pieces made to be put together in different variations. Sectional upholstery, for example, usually consists of two or more seats with an angled or curved corner piece, but pieces can just as well stand on their own.

SEDAN CHAIR

An enclosed chair with sidebars enabling it to be carried by four men. It was the taxi of the seventeenth and eighteenth centuries and named after the town of Sedan in France where it was first made. In France, however, it was known as *chaise à porteur*.

SEMAINIER

The French term for a seven-drawer chest—one for each day of the week (which is *semaine* in French).

SETTEE

With a name derived from the early wooden *settle*, the early-eighteenth-century settee was like two joined-up upholstered chairs with an extra front leg placed before the seam, or join, or the two chairs, so to speak. The term is still often used to describe a regular sofa.

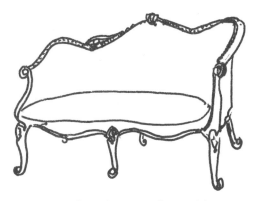

French-style settee favored by Thomas Chippendale

SETTLE

A medieval wooden bench with a high back and arms. Superior versions were paneled and carved. If they had hinged seats with storage capacity underneath they were known as *box settles*.

SEWING TABLE

A small, practical table, first designed in the eighteenth century, that was equipped with a shirred cloth bag for necessary materials, as well as drawers, spool racks, and trays. It was also called a pouch table.

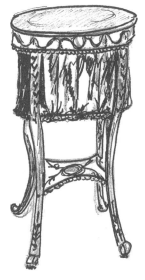

Sewing table, ca. 1790

SGABELLO

A distinctive Italian Renaissance chair, heavily carved, usually painted, with an octagonal seat, carved trestle supports instead of legs, and a carved back splat. It is still reproduced.

SHAGREEN

Green-dyed sharkskin (or untanned horse or mule skin) much used for objets d'art and for covering small pieces of accessory furniture in the eighteenth century. Such pieces were considered to be highly collectible in the 1920s, as indeed, they are still.

SHAKER

A term describing furniture, metalwork, and textiles produced by the Shaker community in North America from the late eighteenth century onward. Shaker furniture is characterized by its simple, functional appearance, tapering legs, swallowtail joints, use of local woods, and meticulous attention to detail. Chairs were made so that they could hang from the wall to save space.

SHEAF BACK

An eighteenth-century design for chair backs based on a bunch of stylized wheat fanning out to the top rail.

SHELLWORK

A form of collectible nineteenth-century decoration that uses shells of various shapes, sizes, and colors mounted in metal as ornaments or vases, or applied to plaster on boxes or for mirror frames.

SHERATON FURNITURE

Designed by Thomas Sheraton, Sheraton furniture was light and graceful and was characterized by a preponderance of straight lines, satinwood veneers, and much inlay. Sheraton was the last member of the triumvirate of British eighteenth-century cabinetmakers (Chippendale, Hepplewhite, and Sheraton) and was

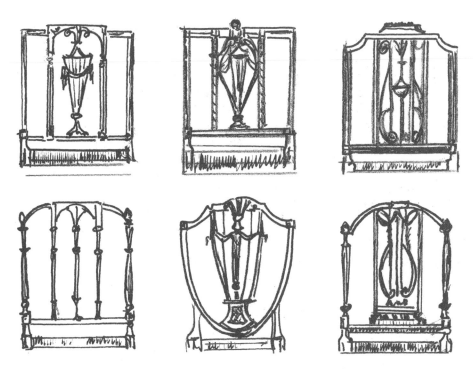

**Some chair backs designed by Thomas Sheraton
and shown in *The Cabinet-Maker and
Upholsterer's Drawing Book* (1791–94)**

generally influential through the many ideas and models in his *The Cabinet-Maker and Upholsterer's Drawing Book* (1791–94), although Sheraton was in turn much influenced by Hepplewhite and Chippendale. (See also *Sheraton, Thomas* in Architects, Designers, and Decorators.)

SHIELD BACK

A late-eighteenth-century chair back, much used by Hepplewhite, in which the chair rail and stile (the upright section) form the shape of a shield. Sometimes the shield shape would contain a carved splat with the Prince of Wales's feathers, always a popular motif, or sometimes a sheaf of wheat

.

SHOJI SCREEN

A Japanese screen formed of rectangular black-framed and sectioned panels filled with some sort of translucent material, from rice paper to sheer fabric. These screens are variously used as room dividers, screens, and sliding doors operated by ceiling and wall tracks.

SIDEBOARD

A comparative latecomer to the range of case furniture (but then so was the dining room, which it was meant to furnish), the sideboard was designed to provide serving and carving as well as drawer and cupboard space. Robert Adam is credited with creating the first such piece. Another eighteenth-century English cabinetmaker, Thomas Shearer, somewhat influenced by Hepplewhite, is credited with transforming the piece to its present shape, and both Hepplewhite and Sheraton for perfecting it.

SIDE CHAIR

A generic title for an armless chair.

SIDE TABLE

Any table designed to be placed against a wall. In a dining room, it is a serving or secondary serving table.

SLIPPER CHAIR

A small, useful upholstered chair with a low seat most often used beside fires and in bedrooms.

SOFA

In its present form it is an upholstered couch with two solid arms and a back in a variety of shapes and lengths.

SOFA BED

A space-saver sofa that converts to a bed.

SOFA TABLE

Originally it was a table, similar or the same as a Pembroke table, which stood in front of the sofa or couch. Now it is almost always placed behind.

A sideboard with a serpentine front, from the third edition of
The Cabinet-maker and Upholsterer's Guide **by George Hepplewhite**

SPANISH COLONIAL FURNITURE

Generally rather heavy, somber, recti-linear furniture with usually massive legs and a dark brown-to-black color. It shows to best advantage in spare white rooms. American Southwest furniture shares much the same characteristics.

SPINDLE

A slender rod used for chair backs.

SPINDLED SHUTTER

One of a pair of interior shutters formed from slim spindles, used mostly in Spain.

SPLAT

The central member or panel in the middle of a wood chair back. It can be plain, carved, or pierced; decorat-ed with tracery, fretwork, marquetry, or a plaque; or be fiddle- or vase-shaped.

SPLAY LEG

A furniture leg that flares, turns, or angles out from a chair, table, or case piece.

SPOOL FURNITURE

Turned furniture in the form of strings of spools or cotton reels, often made of stained pine, mass-produced in America in the eighteenth century.

SPOON-BACK CHAIR

A chair with a high, curved back and low-set arms that rise from the seat, then make a neat sweep up to the top of the back and down and around again, forming the top rail in the process. The center splat is usually either plain or vase- or urn-shaped. The shape was often used during the Regency, Biedermeier, and American Empire periods.

SQUAB

A removable cushion for a chair seat, often tied to the back with tabs.

STACKING CHAIR

A twentieth-century space-saving chair designed to fit one on top of another.

STILE

In chairs, the outer upright member of a chair back.

STOOL

A seat without a supporting back or arms. Stools and also benches without supporting backs or arms used to be the main form of seating for everyone except the lords of the manor. In the seventeenth century, first backs and then arms were added to form side chairs, at which time stools became relegated to incidental seating or footrests.

STORAGE WALL

A space-saving mid-twentieth-century introduction whereby modular units of all shapes, styles, colors, and sizes were hung or stood against a wall (or used as a space divider) to include TV, DVD, and stereo storage, as well as storage for books, files, cassettes, tableware, drinks, glasses, desktops, computer hardware and games, and so on.

STRAP WORK

A stylized representation of woven, interlaced, or plaited leather straps or strips. The motifs were often used in Elizabethan times, and Chippendale resurrected and flattened them for some chair splats.

STRETCHER

The crosspiece that connects and strengthens chair and table legs.

STRINGING

In furniture, a narrow band of inlaid wood, or, in the early nineteenth century, brass. In decoration it can be the "strings" of molded plaster, wood, or fiberglass that are part of a cornice or a crown molding.

STUDIO COUCH

A space-saver couch with an internal mechanism to convert it into a bed.

SUPER LEGGERE

A classic twentieth-century chair designed by Gio Ponti, the *super leggere* combines very light, crisp-lined black-stained ash with a woven cane seat and a back that slopes back above the middle rail. It is made by Cassina, Milan.

SWAG

In furniture decoration, a carved or painted garland of fruit, flowers, and leaves.

SWAN NECK

The generic term for moldings with an ogee curve, as, say, at the end of a curved handrail.

SWAN NECK PEDIMENT

A broken pediment made up of two opposite-facing S-shaped curves. There is often a miniature central pediment in between, topped by a stylized vase, ball, pineapple, or some other motif. (See also *gooseneck*.)

SWING-LEG TABLE

A table with an extra leg to swing out at right angles and support a hinged flap.

TABLE CHAIR

An early space-saver, an oak chair with turned legs and a drawer under the seat.

TABORET OR TABOURET

A French term still used by antique dealers for a type of low upholstered stool.

TESTER

The canopy over a bed or the top part of a four poster. A half-tester is a canopy that extends only just past the pillow section of a bed.

TIER TABLE

A table with several tiers lessening in size as the tiers ascend.

TILT-TOP TABLE

Space-saving pedestal table. A hinge on a block at the top of the pedestal allows the top to be hung vertically when the table is not needed.

TIRETTE

French term for a small pullout extension unique to many French country or provincial refectory tables. They were—and still are—invariably used for children or extra guests at traditional family Sunday lunches and other family occasions.

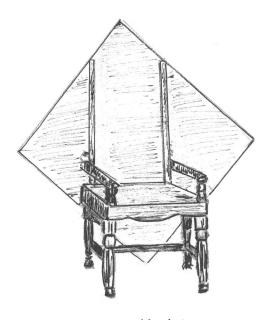

**Puritan table chair,
seventeenth century**

TOP RAIL

The rail that connects the uprights of a chair and upon which any cresting is superimposed.

TORCHÈRE

French term in general use for a pedestal or decorative stand supporting a candelabrum or large candlestick. Now a tall uplight, and receptacles for the glamorous gas-fired flames that are sometimes used outside restaurants, hotels, or house entrances.

TRAY-TOP TABLE

An occasional table with a small brass or wood gallery around three, or sometimes all four, sides.

TREFOIL

Popular Gothic motif in the shape of a cloverleaf.

TRELLISWORK

Pierced, fretted, crossbarred, or lattice effect used not just used for treillage but also often as grilles for bookcases, radiator covers, and so on.

TRIPOD STAND

A small tabletop to support a round planter or an urn or similar container, and supported in its turn by a columnlike shaft ending in a triple-legged spreading support.

TRIPOD TABLE

A generally round table with a pedestal support ending in three outward curving feet.

TRIPTYCH

A three-panel mirror, screen, or painting, especially an altarpiece.

TRIVET

Small, generally iron or metal stand to keep a hot container off the surface of a dining or side table.

TROMPE L'OEIL

French term in general use that means "tricking, cheating, or fooling the eye." The term refers to the technique of painting scenes on walls, screens, canvas, or wallpaper, complete with perspective, foreshortening, and shadows that are realistic enough to seem three-dimensional. The same effect can be achieved with inlay.

TRUE-LOVE CHAIR OR COURTING CHAIR

A forerunner of the *love seat*, the true-love chair was a double upholstered chair that looked like two chairs with their backs joined together but with a single seat. It was popular during the reign of Louis XIV in France and again in the Queen Anne period in England and America.

TRUMEAU MIRROR

A late-eighteenth- and nineteenth-century mirror set into an overmantel.

Often a painted scene or carved panel was set above it.

TRUNDLE BED OR TRUCKLE BED

An early space-saver, it is a small bed on rollers or castors that can be rolled under a larger bed. The trundle bed is a forerunner to the hideaway bed.

TUB CHAIR

Comfortable occasional chair with a rounded back like an upholstered version of the old barrel chair.

TUB SOFA

Love seat or two-seater sofa with ends that sweep round in embracing curves so that the people sitting on it have no choice bit to turn slightly toward each other.

True-love chair or courting chair, ca. 1715

TUNBRIDGE WARE

Miniature mosaiclike wood veneer that originated in Tunbridge Wells, Kent, in southern England. It was made by arranging dozens of differently colored drinking straw–sized dowels of wood into a design and gluing them together. These clusters of dowels were then cut horizontally into wafer-thin slices so that the veneer appeared on each slice. The veneers were then used for decorative surfaces on boxes, mirrors, and other accessories.

TUXEDO SOFA

Slim-armed, crisply lined sofa. The sides and back of the sofa are the same height.

UNDERFRAME

The part between the legs and the superstructure of a piece of furniture.

UPHOLSTERED WALLS

Walls lined with a filler fabric, like Bump or Dacron, then carefully covered with trimmed and stapled panels of the chosen fabric. Staple marks are generally hidden by braid or thin fillets of brass.

VALANCE

A decorative board or finish to curtains, shades, bed hangings, and sometimes undraped or uncurtained windows and occasionally doors. It can be made of carved or painted or gilded wood, wood covered with fabric, fabric alone, or fabric stiffened with buckram. Other names are *pelmet* or *lambrequin*, but the term should not be confused with the English term *valance*, which also means a bed skirt. (See also *valance* in Windows and Window Treatments.)

VENEER

Ultra thin slices of the more handsomely grained woods sliced either laterally or vertically across the relevant log (or flitch, the old English word for a side of something). These piles of slices more or less share the same grain and can be quite easily matched. They are then applied to the surfaces of furniture made from less beguiling or sturdier trees so that the

Example of veneered panels on an eighteenth-century cabinet, probably designed by Robert Adam (Victoria & Albert Museum, London)

effect is of one solid piece. For example, it was fashionable in the William and Mary period at the end of the seventeenth century to veneer oak furniture with burr walnut veneers. Strips of veneers were also used as inlays to contrasting woods. Great cabinetmakers often switched around, using satinwood and the then much rarer mahogany for veneers as well as for solid construction.

VERMEIL

French term in general use for silver gilt, silver objects given a wash of gilt. But it is also the term for a kind of vermilion or orange-red lacquer.

VERNIS MARTIN

A clear lacquer containing flecks of gold that was a French Rococo approximation of oriental lacquer. It was invented by the five Martin brothers, hence the name, but the brothers developed some forty other colored lacquers for walls as much as furniture and bibelots. The most popular was a beautiful deep green.

WAINSCOT CHAIR

Also known as a *panel-back chair*. Both names were applied to these early-seventeenth-century high-seated and somewhat thronelike chairs because they bore a distinct resemblance to wainscot paneling.

WASHSTAND

Before the advent of modern plumbing, washbasins were set on special stands. Some eighteenth-century designs had hinged covers to hide the small basins and drawers, or corner units with drawers and a conveniently sized hole for a basin. In the nineteenth century, such stands were more likely to be more tablelike, with practical marble tops and drawers for wash things.

WASSILY CHAIR

Another twentieth-century Bauhaus classic designed by Marcel Breuer in 1925. It was made from chrome-finished tubular steel with seat, back, and armrests made from bands and tubes of leather wrapped around the frames. It was named after the painter Wassily Kandinsky, also a member of the Bauhaus, who used it in his house.

WELSH DRESSER

A hutch or combination of cupboards and drawers with a pot board below and shelves above.

WHATNOT

A decorative shelf unit that is usually designed to stand or hang in a corner (hence its French name of *encoignure*) and used for odds and ends or collections of this and that.

WHEELBACK CHAIR

As the name implies, a chair with a back shaped like a wheel or an oval with spokes radiating from a central boss or plaque. Robert Adam used this type of back, as did George Hepplewhite.

WINDOW SEAT

In the eighteenth century, small seats were made to fit into deep window recesses. Now, a window seat is more likely to be a built-in bench, sometimes with a lift-up lid for storage, with a seat cushion and pillows.

WINDSOR CHAIR

An eighteenth-century design popular on both sides of the Atlantic, the basic Windsor had a long back filled with vertical rods or spindles and a double-vase-shaped central splat. The arms and lower rail were sometimes connected in a hoop-rail effect. The spindles and bowed shapes were originally made in Windsor, near Windsor Castle, hence its name. In the

Windsor armchair

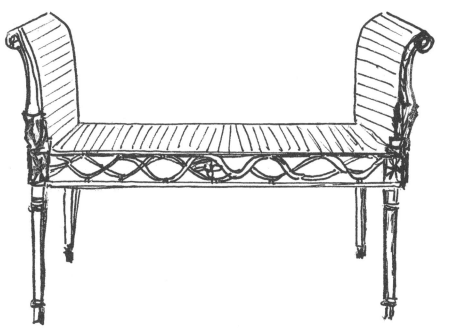

A window seat designed by George Hepplewhite

beginning the chair had cabriole legs, which were changed in time to the turned variety. Through the years there have been all kinds of variations on the theme. Early New England Windsors were lighter and eschewed the wide back splat. Pennsylvania versions had ball feet. Some had a specially wide writing arm, or a wheel back, fan back, low back, or some other kind of version, and some nineteenth-century Windsors had bamboo turnings.

WINE TABLE

Rather like a club fender, horseshoe-shaped wine tables were designed to fit around the front of a fireplace with the wine tasters sitting facing toward the fire.

WING CHAIR

A mid-seventeenth-century uphol-stered design with a high back and side wings that were meant to keep out drafts. There have been many variations on the original, with cabriole legs, turned legs, and straight legs, and lower backs, medium backs, deeper seats, and shallower seats.

X-SHAPED CHAIRS

A very ancient design that uses X-shaped legs at either side of a chair (or, in some cases, X-shaped stretchers at the base of a chair). X-shaped chairs were used in antiquity, the medieval ages, the seventeenth century, and in the current incarnation of folding camp chairs or director's chairs.

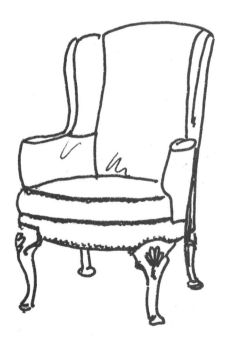

Wing chair, ca. 1720

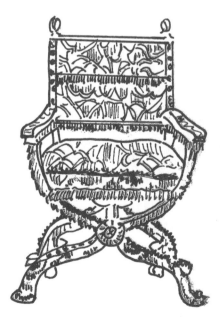

Early-seventeenth-century
X-shaped armchair (the framework
is covered with fabric)

GLASS AND CERAMICS

> *The interior represents the universe for the private individual. He collects there whatever is distant, whatever is of the past. His living room is a box in the theater of the world.*
>
> Walter Benjamin (1882–1940),
> from *Schriften*, Vol. I

Luckily for museums and amateur collectors all over the world, if the history of fine furniture is long, the history of glass and ceramics is as long, or even longer. Grecian vases, Roman glass, Far Eastern ceramics (including china, stoneware, celadon ware, and pottery), and the great European porcelain and glass factories and producers of tin glaze earthenware like faience, not to mention delftware and majolica, all provide coveted collectibles of varying rarity and prices.

The list of venerable producers in these fields is just as long as production life spans, which often last hundreds of years. Not surprisingly, there is often much confusion among neophyte collectors about the various types of ceramics and the terms used to describe them: hard paste and soft paste, stoneware and earthenware, porcelain and artificial porcelain, and bone china and regular china. But quite apart from learning the different types of ceramics, there remains the awesome task of recognizing differences in production wares between august names like Meissen and Coalport, Sèvres and Chelsea, Bohemian glass, Waterford and Lalique, as well as the identification marks they use.

Best of all, though, in my opinion, is the entertaining story of the shenanigans that went on in the china trade from the earliest days in the Far East and from the seventeenth century onward in Europe. In their way, ceramics producers were just as openly desperate as gold prospectors, but usually a good deal more subtle. Moreover, the often highly questionable maneuvers peppered throughout the history of ceramics —whether they were internecine fights between emperors and war lords in China and Japan, or rivalries between the monarchs of old Europe—regularly involved the crowned heads of a region.

Although the glass trade seems altogether more gentle, there is no doubt that acts of piracy, kidnapping, and the often quite desperate cloak-and-dagger searches among hopeful ceramic producers for secret recipes, the right firing temperatures, and successful formulas are the stuff in which crime fiction revels.

ACID GILDING

A process to embellish porcelain with low-relief gold patterns whereby designs are etched with hydrofluoric acid and then gilded and burnished. It was invented by the British porcelain factory Minton in 1873.

AIR TWIST

The delicately spiraled stems of many early English seventeenth- and eighteenth-century glasses.

AMPHORA

An ancient Greek storage jar with an ovoid body and two handles reaching from the mouth or neck of the jar to the shoulder.

ANHUA

A Chinese term meaning "secret decoration." It describes very faintly incised or painted decoration in white diluted or liquid clay, called *slip*, on a white body. It was developed during the Ming Dynasty.

ANNAMESE PORCELAIN

Porcelain actually from Hanoi in Vietnam, but which takes its name from Annam (translated as "the pacified south"), the ancient name for the area that is a hangover from the Chinese occupation of the country from 1407 to 1428 (north Vietnam, lying just south of China). The ground color of this porcelain is often a very pale gray or buff but there are green and brown monochromatic shades as well and almost all pieces are neatly

Armorial plate, famille rose in Meissen style, Qianlong period (1753–95)

supported on much shorter, square-cut foot rims than the higher variety of feet favored by the Chinese.

ARITA

One of the earliest and largest porcelain-producing areas in Japan. Relatively inexpensive and mainly blue-and-white Japanese porcelain came from Arita along with celadon wares to sate the demand from the West. Arita kilns also produced Imari ware (named after the port from which it was shipped) and the polychrome or variegated enameled porcelain first made by the legendary Kakiemon family in the late seventeenth century. Kakiemon was much admired and emulated in Europe from the time it was first exported there in the eighteenth century.

ARMORIAL PORCELAIN

Porcelain decorated with the coats of arms of the European commissioning owners, which are either painted or transferred onto the pieces in question. It was first developed during the Ming Dynasty.

BACCARAT

Very fine French crystal, produced since the nineteenth century, much of it skillfully cut with geometric designs, but some of it enameled. The *cristallerie* (glass works) produced heavy ornamental decanters, dishes, vases, enameled drinking ware and table services, and many splendid chandeliers and sconces.

BASALT WARE

Unglazed black stoneware, originally called "basalts," and first produced by Josiah Wedgwood in England in the late 1760s. Other subsequent producers included Spode, Elijah Mayer, and Neale.

BATAVIAN WARE

Broadly painted blue-and-white bowls, teacups, and saucers with the outsides coated in a coffee-colored wash. It came from Batavia (now known as Jacarta), in Java, which was the Dutch staging post for the exportation of Chinese porcelain in the eighteenth century.

BELLEEK

An Irish porcelain manufacturer established in 1863 and still producing glazed *parian ware* (statuary porcelain meant to resemble marble). So-called "First Period" Belleek ware *without* the words "Co. Fermagh Ireland" printed on them are now considered to be highly collectible.

BERLIN PORCELAIN

A German porcelain manufacturer (founded in 1751 in what was then Prussia) that has had a long, if checkered, career. For a short time the factory produced delicately painted (although it tended to flake) and extremely fine white porcelain with a slight yellowish-gray tinge, which was identified by a blue "W." But the founder, W. K. Wegely, sneakily tried to seduce workmen and trade manufacturing secrets away from the Meissen factory during the Seven Years War (1756–63) between Prussia and Saxony. When the Prussians won the war and were able to buy the superior Meissen wares anyway, Wegely gave the business up. Johann Ernst Gotzkowsky tried to restart the factory in 1761, calling it the Berlin Konighliche Porzellan Manufaktur (KPM), which it has been called ever since. When Gotzkowsky went bankrupt, Frederick the Great purchased it himself and commissioned many dinner services and decorative pieces for his various castles. Like the Viennese ceramicists, the Berlin craftsmen used their porcelain pieces like a canvas for some delectably fine paintings. When Friedrich Wilhelm II took over the throne in 1744, the company switched over from the Rococo decoration enjoyed by its late owner to some handsome Neoclassical motifs. The new king, though a great afficionado of architecture and furniture, and committed to developing a definite German Style, was not particularly interested in his inherited porcelain factory. Nevertheless, it came into its own again in the late eighteenth and nineteenth centuries with the much stronger patronage of Friedrich Wilhelm III and the expansion of the bourgeoisie. The factory then started employing distinguished artists, including the versatile architect and painter Karl Friedrich Schinkel, and began to produce its highly collectable, often gold-rimmed, pictorial and portrait plaques.

BISCUIT WARE

Unglazed earthenware that has been fired only once.

BISQUE

Often wrongly thought of as another term for biscuit ware. In fact it is a formula normally used for the manufacture of unglazed doll heads and bodies.

BLANC DE CHINE

Chinese cream-colored (not white as the name implies) porcelain made in the province of Fujian from the fourteenth century Ming Dynasty onward. As soon as it was imported into Europe it was much imitated.

BLANK

The name for any undecorated piece of porcelain.

BLUE-AND-WHITE WARE

Generic term for any blue-and-white ceramics that includes decorative vases and tableware imported from the Far East (China, Korea, and Japan) in the late seventeenth and early eighteenth centuries. The term also includes the many copies of Eastern patterns as well as new designs that started to be made first in Holland in the seventeenth century and then throughout Europe in general from the eighteenth century. Now blue-and-white ware is made all over the world.

BOHEMIAN GLASS

This refers to a great deal of reasonably priced glassware—as well as much more rare and expensive decoratively colored, cut, and engraved commemorative work—that has been produced in Bohemia (now a region in the Czech Republic) since the nineteenth century. More distinguished enameled or gilded pieces were decorated with designs by leading Austrian artists. The glass works are still going strong, and the pieces are still called Bohemian glass.

BONE CHINA

A mixture of clay and kaolin (a fine white china clay) with a little added animal bone ash, which produces a modified true porcelain. The formula was introduced in England at the very end of the eighteenth century and is credited to Spode, one of the Staffordshire factories, which at the very least so perfected the process that it has been used for English porcelain

A bohemian vase and pedestal (ca. 1878) thought to have been designed by Josef Ritter von Storck for J & J Lobmeeyr at Meyr's Neff's Bohemian Glassworks. Made of amber-colored glass with enameled decoration.

more or less ever since. Apart from the fact that it needs a lower firing temperature than hard paste or true porcelain, and thus saves fuel, it has a clean white finish, good translucency, and allows all kinds of decoration. The new formula meant that Staffordshire became as unquestionably the center for porcelain in England as Limoges in France. The term is often just shortened to *china* (without the *bone*).

BOW PORCELAIN

One of the two first, along with Chelsea, English porcelain factories of the eighteenth century, and like the latter, hugely collectible. Bow was started in 1744 by Thomas Frye and Edward Heylyn, but unlike Chelsea, which always aimed for exclusivity, Bow looked for a much wider market and their designs ranged from the early quite inexpensive "sprigged" (small low-relief ornaments attached to the body of a piece by a thin slip of diluted clay) and blue-and-white porcelain to much finer quality figures and vases. Bow also quite aggressively sought an export market and to this end imitated both Japanese and Chinese designs right down to producing famille rose and underglaze blue designs. Bow even designed its factory after an East India warehouse in Canton, calling it "New Canton." The factory also used a bone ash formula for its body rather than the lighter, glassier Chelsea recipe, which turned out to be a particularly successful mix for its well-known Bow figures. Although the factory continued with its familiar famille rose designs during the 1750s, it also added popular white ware sprigged with raised prunus blossoms, Japanese Imarilike patterns in underglaze blue and overglaze iron-red and gilt, and much the same Japanese Kakiemon-inspired designs as Chelsea, as well as its well-known Partridge and Quail patterns and a vast amount of blue-and-white. Dinner services were a specialty. In the 1760s Bow's standards slipped and the factory slowly declined till it was sold in 1776 to William Duesbury of Derby (who had also bought the Chelsea factory in 1769–70). It did not really have a consistent distinguishing factory mark, although during the 1760s it often employed an incised anchor-and-dagger mark, and some of its pieces were dated.

BRISTOL

Much-collected glassware produced in Bristol, in southwest England, since the eighteenth century and known for its deep colors, particularly its deep blue, green, and cranberry.

CACHEPOT

A porcelain or pottery pot made to hide a more ordinary flowerpot.

CANTON PORCELAIN

The European name for a Chinese export design of flowered or figured panels on a gilt and green scrolled ground called Rose Medallion. Rather confusingly, in the United States, Canton was the name for a late-

eighteenth- and early-nineteenth-century style of decoration consisting of blue landscapes within a stylized border that was applied to biscuit earthenware, then glazed, and fired.

CAPO DI MONTE

The most famous Italian factory, set up in 1743 by Charles III of Bourbon (when he became King of Naples and Sicily) to make Rococo figures, plaques, and wall brackets in a soft-paste, or "artificial," porcelain made from white clay and brightly colored ground glass. The eighteenth-century Capo di Monte mark was a blue fleur-de-lis impressed within a roundel at the base of the figures and other pieces. There is a very splendid chinoiserie room in the Capo di Monte Palace in Naples made entirely from the porcelain—including the wall tiles—modeled by Giuseppe Gricci, the then chief modeler at the factory. In 1759, Charles III took over the throne of Spain on the death of his father and moved the Capo di Monte factory, together with the workmen, to Madrid. There Gricci modeled his other extraordinary completely porcelain room, the Salon di Porcellana in the Palace of Aranjuez. Some of the late-eighteenth-century Capo di Monte took the form of creamware rather like the British Wedgwood Queen's Ware. A hard paste was introduced in 1803 but the factory was destroyed by the British in 1812. In the meantime, Charles III's son, now King Ferdinand IV of Naples and Sicily, had revived the Italian factory, this time making the newly fashionable Neoclassical pieces with a new mark, a crown over an "N" in blue, and adding tea, coffee, and dinner services to the range. Contemporary, rather garish plaques, boxes, and lamp bases are still named after the original factory.

CAUGHLY PORCELAIN

Founded in 1772, Caughly was a big eighteenth-century British producer of blue-and-white Nanking-like porcelain, complete with complicated chinoiserie designs, from a factory near Worcester on the River Severn, in Shropshire. Caughly's Chinese imitations (on a body that used soapstone, a form of steatite, as a hardener rather than kaolin, a fine white clay that was in more general use) fairly tumbled out of the factory during the 1780s and '90s, but then, as now, the British manufacturer simply could not match the Chinese prices. Caughly also produced some handsome bright blue-and-white floral designs in the manner of the French Chantilly factory, including some finely painted commemorative pieces and some equally finely painted dessert services with landscape and architectural scenes, as well as a great many toy tea services. The Caughly mark, when they bothered to imprint it, was either a "C" or an "S" (the "S" was for Salopian, the name given to people from Shropshire, just as Salop, with the usual British illogicality, was short for Shropshire); flat ware, however, was impressed with the word Salopian once the factory had changed its name in the 1790s to the Royal Salopian Porcelain Manufactory. In 1799 it was taken over and merged with the nearby Coalport Factory.

CAVETTO

The term for the slight depression or well in the middle of many plates.

CELADON

Mainly, Chinese stoneware, an opaque ceramic midway between earthenware and porcelain, with a distinctive gray-green glaze, made in China from the Warring era between 480 and 221 B.C. The northern Chinese celadon ware had a rich olive green glaze over granular gray clay. Exposed bits of the latter sometimes turned a rusty brown when fired, hence the odd brownish bits you often see among the green. The southern variety was a somewhat colder blue-green. The blue-green bowls described by Marco Polo on his travels through the China of Jenghiz (Genghis) Khan were perhaps *quinbai*, sometimes known as *yingquen* (translated as "cloudy, misty, or shadow blue"), which was first produced during the Song period (960–1279) and ranged from pale green or blue to a rich sky blue. The celadon of the later Yuan (1280–1368) and early Ming (1368–1644) Dynasties was much more complex and sophisticated. Apparently very little celadon "of any note" was produced after the fifteenth century in China. Southeast Asian countries also produced celadon ware: the Koreans from the tenth century followed by Annam (now Vietnam) and Thailand. In Japan, in the seventeenth century, the Nabeshima celadon glaze was considered particularly fine. Nowadays the term *celadon* is also applied to any glaze of this color.

Celadon bowl from Korea, twelfth century

Chantilly cachepot, ca. 1735–40

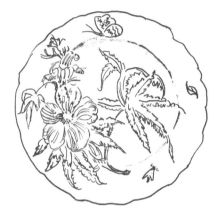

Chelsea porcelain botanical plate

CHANTILLY PORCELAIN

French eighteenth-century porcelain produced by a factory set up in 1725 by the Duc de Condi. The factory was best known for its pieces painted in the popular Japanese Kakiemon style based on the duc's large collection of Kakiemon porcelain. It also produced versions of the Chinese famille verte, and sometimes pieces that showed a mixture of both Japanese- and Chinese-style figures. Up until 1750, Chantilly wares could be distinguished from other French porcelain by the use of an opaque tin glaze. From then on, a normal, slightly creamy lead glaze was used. Another distinctive Chantilly production was its tableware, which was known for its decorative blue or pink flowers either in underglaze decoration or enamel and particularly its design of flowers on a blue and gold trellis background. After 1755, the factory stopped making its finest pieces in order to comply with a royal edict forbidding any competition with the Royal Factory at Vincennes, near Paris.

CHELSEA PORCELAIN

Much-coveted English eighteenth-century porcelain. The Chelsea factory was unusual in the eighteenth century for several reasons: it concentrated its entire output on the luxury market; the ingredients of both the body and glaze were changed more often than by any other factory; and the history of the company falls into four distinct periods, each with its own mark. The Chelsea factory was started by a Huguenot silversmith from Liège in France named Nicholas Sprimont. His early designs—with white moldings on a white ground, Rococo shell motifs, and asymmetrical curves, or with restrained Oriental influence "tea plant" or strawberry-leaf moldings— were very like his earlier original silver pieces with repoussé designs. Occasionally, the molded designs were finished in enamel colors. The mark for this first period, which lasted from 1744 to 1749, was an incised triangle. Then the factory moved premises and was relaunched in 1750 with an advertisement offering "a great Variety of Pieces for ornament in a Taste entirely new." And indeed a new, more utilitarian recipe was used for the porcelain, producing a beautiful soft white body (whitened by the addition of tin oxide) with a waxy glaze, and the former Rococo shapes gave way to a whole new range of ideas and figures, somewhat influenced by the German Meissen factory. Decoration either followed the popular Japanese Kakiemon style of the late seventeenth century (depicting oriental birds, banded hedges, trees, flowers, and bamboo in the distinctive Kakiemon coloring of dark green, yellow, turquoise, blue, and iron-red, sometimes subtly gilded), or used more conventional florals, figures, and landscapes. The mark for this phase of the factory's output (1750–56) was a raised anchor surrounded by an oval medallion. Chelsea figures from this period are often considered to be the finest of all the English factories. Yet another mark, this time a red anchor, was introduced in 1753, shortly followed by a new formula that made the porcelain more transparent, more apt to craze, and rather lighter. The famous Chelsea fruit and vegetable designs belong to this period, along with the naturalistic animal and bird tureens and refined botanicals inspired by the proximity of the Chelsea Physick Garden. Another Chelsea specialty of the 1750s was its extremely collectible "toys": miniature scent bottles, etuis, seals, and bonbonnières or sweet dishes. In the latter part of the 1750s, the business was interrupted again, this time by Sprimont's poor health. When he recovered he decided to add a proportion of bone ash to his porcelain recipe, a great deal more gilding (following the influence of the French Sèvres factory rather than Meissen), and yet another mark, this time a gold anchor. Different ground colors were introduced, including the famous Chelsea dark mazarine-blue, as were different grouping of figures and some opulent vases. Chelsea came more or less to the end of its glory days in 1769 when Sprimont sold the factory to William Duesbury of Derby (who, the sort of "Murdoch" of the china industry, also bought and then closed the Bow factory), although it went on producing wares until 1784, when it was finally closed.

CHINA

Originally a shorter term for the chinaware imported from China in the eighteenth century, although it is also a shortened term for English *bone china*, and is often loosely applied to any porcelain.

CHINA CLAY

Another term for *kaolin*, a fine white clay and a form of aluminum silicate that, together with ground petunse, a Chinese feldspathic rock, forms a hard-paste, or true, porcelain.

CHINAWARE

The original name for imported Chinese porcelain.

CHINESE EXPORT

Broadly speaking, the name given to all Chinese exports to America and Europe. But the term has also come to mean chinaware decorated with occidental-looking figures and designs produced by the Chinese, as opposed to wares with their original Chinese designs. These included some three thousand complete dinner services decorated with the coats of arms or crests of European and American families as well as many commemorative pieces. The Chinese were gifted copyists and were adept at fitting any occidental print, engraving, drawing, bookplate, and armorial bearings sent out for special commissions onto whatever porcelain blanks had been chosen. (It seems that the Chinese sent representatives on arduous journeys to the West to take special orders and to show the various shapes, borders, and styles available—much as leading London tailors and shirtmakers still send representatives to the United States and the Antipodes to measure and take orders.) These naturally non-Western-language speaking artists could be relied upon to copy everything with the utmost care and to the letter, literally. In fact, sometimes everything was copied so painstakingly and faithfully that customers frequently found their hopefully helpful instructions reproduced onto their wares. For example, where one owner had written coloring instructions for his coat of arms, the Chinese had copied them diligently onto every piece of the set as a part of the design.

CLARICE CLIFF (1899–1972)

British Art Deco ceramic designer for Wedgwood whose jazzy work is much collected.

CLOISONNÉ

An extremely attractive Oriental enamel technique where various colors are separated by ultra thin wires. It was much used for larger items like trays and urns. In the last part of the nineteenth century the Japanese started to use the same technique for porcelain.

Cloisonné teapot, ca. 1867

COALPORT

Another Staffordshire porcelain factory (now part of the Wedgwood Group in Stoke-on-Trent). By the 1820s, having taken over the Caughley factory in the last year of the eighteenth century, Coalport had become a prosperous manufacturer of mainly tea- and table-wares marked by pattern numbers that ran rather like some motor vehicle licenses up to 1–999 and then started all over again at 2–999, and so on. The bulk of Coalport's prosperity at that period came from white wares that they sold to other people to decorate, although they also produced some very fine dinner services, such as their Imarilike design in pink, blue, and gold, now displayed in King George IV's Brighton Pavilion. It also employed the eminently talented ceramicist and painter William Billingsley, late of the elegant Swansea and Nantgarw porcelain factories, and his son-in-law, the equally talented potter Samuel Walker. Later the firm became famous for its Rococolike flower-encrusted pieces, marked "Coalbrookdale," "CD," or "C.Dale." These were more successful as single pieces or as garnitures for mantelpieces than for tea sets since their elaborate encrustation made them almost unusable. Also in the 1820s, Coalport began to make elaborate vases, desk sets, and dessertware based on the French Sèvres designs and using their special ground colors—the *bleu celeste* (heavenly blue) and *rose Pompadour* or *rose du Barry* (tactfully, or ingratiatingly, named after the royal mistresses, the French being more forgiving in these matters). In the 1830s, Coalport employed two special painters, Cook and Randall—Cook's specialty being flowers and Randall's birds—which segued into realistic tropical varieties in the 1860s and '70s. Any Cook or Randall pieces are very collectible. One word of warning: curiously, since 1875, the Coalport mark included the date "AD1750," the inaccurate date of the factory's founding (it was actually founded in the 1790s, which is still pretty venerable), causing many people to believe that 1750 is the date of the piece.

COPENHAGEN PORCELAIN

A Danish factory started in the 1730s and taken over as the Royal factory in the 1770s when its name was changed to Royal Copenhagen. It was formed into a company in 1774 with the Queen of Denmark as principal shareholder and taken over in 1779 by the King. It is probably most famous—apart from the talented designers it has employed over the centuries—for its Flora Danica service, which was started as a commission for Catherine II of Russia in 1789 but not finished until 1802. Its designs were based on a book by Oeder (1761), and the paintings were executed by J. C. Bayer from Nuremburg, Germany. Still, the long execution time paid off—the service is still being produced.

CRACKLE

A ceramic glaze with an intentionally cracked surface, as opposed to "craze," which is unintentional, although both are caused by the glaze shrinking more than the body after an item has been fired. It was originally a Chinese technique developed during the Song Dynasty (1128–1279).

CREAMWARE

Creamy, as the name implies, lead-glazed earthenware developed in the mid-eighteenth century by Wedgwood, among others. It is much collected.

CRYSTAL

A clear, colorless, and very fine glass that is of superior quality to ordinary glass.

DAUM BROTHERS

Decorative glassmakers, members of the late-nineteenth-century School of Nancy in France, and followers of Emile Gallé, the leading glassmaker of the Nancy group and, indeed, the time. They produced some outstanding opaline glass vases in blues and creams, and sometimes rose, as well as some oriental-like celadon and jade greens in *pâte verre* (glass paste).

DAVENPORT

Founded in 1794 and closed 1887. Davenport was best known for its earthenware but also produced, up until about 1812, both the hard-paste (or true) porcelain bulb pots that were very popular in that period, and, from about 1800, some high-standard bone china tea and dessert services and rare vases. The factory made a specialty of ornamenting its tableware with landscapes painted in the Picturesque style in both monochrome and poly-chrome. Indeed, the Prince Regent (later George IV) who visited the factory in 1806 was heard to remark that they "deserved equal with old Seve," meaning the desirable French Sèvres. The first Davenport bone china pieces were unmarked, but in the early 1800s the factory used the name "Longport" in red script until 1812 or so, when the name Davenport became standard with or without an anchor. Again, highly collectable.

DEGUÉ

Extravagantly decorative glass that was made in the Degué glassworks (also known as the Cristalleries de Compiègne) between 1926 and 1939 in Compiègne, France, northeast of Paris. The factory was started by David Gueron, as colorful in character as his glass. Born in Turkey of Spanish parents he joined the French Foreign Legion, fought in World War I, visited the 1925 Exposition des Arts Décoratifs in Paris (from which the term *Art Deco* was taken), and was so impressed that he set up his own manufactory for glass objets d'art. The Cristalleries, trading under the name of Degué, was commissioned to design six thousand individual glass panels for the first-class public rooms and suites on the *Normandie*, the French ocean liner that was used as a showcase for French taste, style, cuisine, and sense of luxury. Together with René Lalique, Gueron also produced many of the stunning light fixtures in the ship. Degué's extraordinary jardinières and vases graced some of the best of

American and French collections from the 1930s, and today any Degué piece is highly coveted.

DELFTWARE

Mainly blue-and-white earthenware that was glazed with a glassy white tin oxide (known as tin glazing) to resemble, as near as possible, Chinese porcelain. The tin glazing method was actually first developed in Italy in the sixteenth century, where it became known as *faience* after the town of Faenza. After the formula spread to France, Spain, and Antwerp, where it was also known as *majolica* or *maiolica*, it was taken up with enthusiasm in Holland. From the beginning of the seventeenth century and the confiscation of two Portugese shiploads of Chinese porcelain, later auctioned in Amsterdam, the Dutch potters did their best to imitate the Chinese blue-and-white late-Ming dishes, first in Haarlem and Rotterdam, and then in Delft, which during its golden age (from roughly 1650 to 1750) gave its name to an increasingly profitable industry known preeminently for its blue-and-white wares and tiles. Delftware started to be made in England in the seventeenth century, where it continues to be known by that name.

DELLA ROBBIA

Generally round majolica plaques or medallions containing mostly white bas-relief ceramic figures on blue backgrounds garlanded with multi-colored fruit and foliage. The process

Extra large delft tile (ca. 1694) commissioned by William III for Queen Mary's dairy at Hampton Court, "in which her majesty took great delight."

was started by a family of fifteenth- and sixteenth-century Italian sculptors called Della Robbia—notably by Luca Della Robbia (1399–1482), who turned from sculpting in marble and bronze to ceramics—and was continued by Andrea (1435–1525) and Giovanni (1469–1529). Della Robbia work had a different character from the work of traditional majolica workshops in that its glaze was generally dry and not very vitreous, its colors were opaque and applied thickly, and its decoration was distinguished.

DERBY PORCELAIN

Known since 1890 as Royal Crown Derby, the factory was started in 1750 and for its first six years produced only vases, its core figures, and other

Derby Imari-pattern cup and saucer, ca. 1890

ornamental pieces. In 1756, it was taken over by the ubiquitous William Duesbury (who was later to acquire both the Chelsea and Bow factories) and for the next decade so faithfully followed everything produced by Meissen that it was actually described in contemporary advertisements as "...The Derby or second Dresden..."— Dresden being the then home of the Meissen factory. Certainly, Derby figures had a great deal in common with the Dresden figures. However, one quite distinctive Derby characteristic of the early period was the miniature figures in landscape that adorned items like inkwells, potpourri containers, and saltcellars. Another was its flatware that, when held up to the light, showed tiny bubbles trapped in the paste (as did some of the Chelsea pieces). The tea wares that Derby produced from 1760 were

dogged by bad luck, because the porcelain had a most unfortunate tendency to crack on contact with boiling water. This was a very real marketing setback because the newly introduced tea-drinking habit was enormously popular. The problem was not really solved until 1780. After the takeover of Chelsea, known as the Chelsea–Derby period (1770–84), Derby produced its first factory mark, which was a "D" conjoined with an anchor, and came more under the influence of the French Sèvres than the German Meissen. The factory also started to make the first of its well-known Derby "Japan" Imari patterns, beautifully detailed unglazed animal figures, as well as a whole cache of national heroes and theatrical and allegorical subjects. Derby prospered well until the years between 1811 and 1828, known as the Bloor–Derby period, so called because the factory was taken over from the last remaining member of the Duesbury family by Robert Bloor, formerly the firm's clerk. Under the new management, the quality of the porcelain deteriorated and had a tendency to stain, though the standard of decoration remained high. Marks used were a printed crown and a "D" or "Bloor-Derby."

DING YAO

Chinese porcelain dishes and bowls made from the tenth century onward. Ding Yao porcelain has an ivory-white body with a distinctive creamy glaze.

DOULTON

A well-known British earthenware, tile, and stoneware producer from 1858. Although Doulton did not start producing porcelain until 1882, what it did produce was of fine quality, whether it was its distinguished tableware or its handsome decorative pieces. In the early twentieth century, Doulton seemed to specialize in figures, one of the best-known being its Art Deco–style Bathing Girl (1930).

DRESDEN

Dresden is the name of the location of the first Meissen factory (opened in 1710) that made, among other things, particularly delicate ornamental figures of people and animals. The well-known phrase "a complexion like a Dresden shepherdess" is based on the exquisitely luminescent and milky white quality of these early porcelain figures.

By the nineteenth century, Dresden had become a generic term used to describe the numerous copies of Meissen figures and vases that were being produced with similar bodies and glaze by small Dresden factories.

EARTHENWARE

Generic term for all low-fired ceramics, as opposed to stoneware, which is high fired.

ENAMEL

In ceramics, to decorate or overglaze the body with colors made from glass paste pigmented with metallic oxides.

ENCRE DE CHINE

Eighteenth-century Chinese porcelain that is decorated almost entirely in gray and black. It is also known as *grisaille* (after the decorating style), because of its tones, and Jesuit ware, because much of the experimental work for the decorative techniques was achieved with the help of Jesuit fathers at the court of the Qing Dynasty.

FAHUA

The Chinese stoneware (an opaque ceramic somewhere between earthenware and porcelain) produced during the Ming Dynasty between 1368 and 1644.

FAIENCE

Tin-glazed earthenware named after the Italian town of Faenza, where the formula was perfected.

Faience "helmet" jug, ca. 1710

FAMILLE NOIRE

Eighteenth-century Chinese decoration from the "black family," consisting of black enamel overlaid with a translucent green glaze.

FAMILLE ROSE

Eighteenth-century Chinese decoration from the "pink family," using opaque pink and carmine enamels made from colloidal gold introduced from Europe. The earliest group of famille rose wares was known as Kangxi yuzhi after the four character marks enameled on the bases meaning "imperially made in the years of the Kangxi period."

FAMILLE VERTE

Eighteenth-century Chinese decoration from the "green family," recognized by its vivid green enamel decoration—although the famille verte also includes the underlay of black from the "black family," as well as some iron-red, blue, yellow, and eggplant.

FAVRILE

The trademark for the iridescent art glass introduced by Louis Comfort Tiffany in the 1890s as blown glass vases, flower holders, and other decorative glass objects. It is also known as *Tiffany glass*.

FELDSPAR

Another name for the Chinese petunse or the ground Chinese rock that is an essential ingredient of hard-paste, or true, porcelain. It is also an ingredient of Parian ware. Equally, it can be used to form a glaze. (See also *Parian ware* and *glaze*).

FIRING

The process of baking pottery or porcelain in a kiln. The temperature should vary from 1472 degrees Fahrenheit (or 800 degrees Celsius) for pottery to 2642 degrees Fahrenheit (or 1450 degrees Celsius) for hard-paste, or true, porcelain.

FLATWARE

The term for plates, saucers, and dishes as opposed to hollowed-out items like cups, tureens, soup bowls, and so on.

FLOW-BLUE

Flow-blue ceramics (known simply as flow-blue), also emulating Chinese designs, were first produced from the 1830s in early Victorian England, America, and Europe and are popular collector items. They were decorated with underglaze transfer-printed patterns applied to hard white-bodied earthenware. But the ink forming these patterns was made to "bleed" or "flow" into the undecorated portions of the piece during the firing of the glaze. This flow of the blue ink (not, as one might suppose, the least bit messy) was achieved by adding lime or chloride of ammonia into the sagger (the refractory clay box in which more delicate ceramic pieces are fired).

FRIT

Term for the powdered glass (fused, then ground) that is added to clay to make soft-paste porcelain.

GALLÉ, EMILE

The central figure of the French Art Nouveau "School of Nancy," started in 1881, although not officially founded until 1901. Like Louis Comfort Tiffany in America, Gallé made very fine, highly collectible glass vases and ornaments, although in Gallé's case, his glass was sometimes inscribed with verses by members of the Symboliste literary movement, whose work he much admired, such as Poe, Baudelaire, Mallarmé, and Maeterlinck, as well as with cyclamen flowers, butterflies, and dragonflies. He also created some beautiful sinuous polychrome and opaline glass jugs and vases, some of them handsomely mounted in bronze.

GARDNER PORCELAIN

A porcelain factory established in Russia at Verbilki, Moscow, in 1765 by Englishman Francis Gardner. Gardner used the help of technical experts from Meissen and was reputed to have produced such high quality pieces that they were considered almost as good as those of the Imperial factory. His mark was a "G" in blue underglaze.

GARNITURE DE CHEMINÉE

A French term in general use, but generally shortened to *garniture* to describe the three, five, or seven cylindrical or baluster-shaped jars or vases with which it was almost de rigeur to decorate the drawing room mantelpiece during the eighteenth, nineteenth, and early twentieth centuries.

GLAZE

In ceramics, it is a form of glass that is either sprayed, dusted, or coated over an item so that after firing the surface becomes impermeable. It can be colored with a range of different pigments and made to produce varying effects. Glaze can also be formed from feldspar, also known as petunse, the ground rock ingredient of true porcelain or hard paste.

HARD PASTE

Also known as *true porcelain*, it is a mixture of kaolin or china clay and ground petunse or Chinese rock. The formula was discovered in China as early as the Tang Dynasty (618–906) and in Europe, by Johann Friedrich Bottger, an alchemist, working for Frederick I of Prussia, for Meissen, at least nine hundred years later, in 1708. The European search for the secret, as it were, of true porcelain, is almost worthy of a Stephen King novel and is worth recounting here. In 1675, Count Ehrenfried Walter Von Tschirnhausen (1651–1708) of the first Meissen factory, bedazzled by the marketing possibilities inherent in the newly imported Chinese porcelain, was conducting experiments with radiant heat and a mirror in an effort to find out the melting point of difficult-to-melt, refractory substances such as kaolin or china clay. (Kaolin, deposits of which had been found in Saxony, near Meissen, was actually the vital ingredient of true porcelain, though it must, as it later turned out, reach 2640 degrees Fahrenheit, or 1450 degrees Celsius, in the kiln). Although Tschirnhausen had been able to manufacture a form of soft-paste, or artificial, porcelain, he was unable to discover the real secret until he inveigled a young Johann Friedrich Bottger, still in his teens, into the search. Mr. Bottger, however, feared he was unequal to the task and fled from Berlin and the count in 1700. Unfortunately, or fortunately, for Meissen and the porcelain trade, he was seized by Augustus of Saxony (often known as Augustus the Strong) and hauled off to the Castle of Albrectsburg, where Augustus somehow forced him to go on assisting Count Tschirnhausen in

the search for the great secret formula. This time he was successful. The first experimental pieces were produced in 1708 (ominously perhaps, the year of the count's death) and Meissen went into production with them in 1710, with Bottger as manager of the factory until his death in 1719 at the age of thirty-seven.

IMARI

The Japanese port through which the Kakiemon-style beautifully enameled wares from Arita were shipped. It also gave its name to the wares, which were greatly prized in Europe and in America. Characteristic Imari underglaze decoration was in blue, iron-red, and gilt.

An imari bottle with enameled flowers in high relief, ca. 1690

JACOBITE GLASS

Not so much glass from the Jacobite period in England as somewhat subversive, politically motivated glass—engraved with various Jacobite motifs (like the Stuart Rose) and often with slender air-twist stems—made by and for supporters of the exiled future king, Charles II, whose cause they espoused. Subversive or not, the glasses were mainly beautiful, certainly interesting, and are obsessively collected.

JAPANESE PORCELAIN

Although the Japanese have been making stoneware for some three thousand years, they did not actually start making porcelain until the early seventeenth century, and then mostly because of the Koreans. Many Korean potters infiltrated Japan at the end of the sixteenth century, either as prisoners after the Japanese invasion of Korea or as immigrants; but whatever the reason, they combined to introduce new and more sophisticated kilns into, for better or worse, their new country. At first these kilns were located near the port of Karatsu, which was also near to the jumping-off point for the Korean invasion; the new potteries flourished, but after some twenty years, the area around Arita started to make porcelain along with the stoneware, possibly because mounds of the clay used for porcelain, which derives from decayed granite, were found in the area. Perhaps the Japanese began to make porcelain as a result of their trade rivalry with China, or maybe it was because the ultra-powerful Dutch East India Company had tentatively begun to test-buy small quantities of the new porcelain; but whatever the reason, the Japanese anticipated the growing demand from the West for reasonably inexpensive blue-and-white along with the more popular celadon ware, which they were accustomed to shipping to southeast Asia. The Arita factories rose to this anticipated demand and manufactured at first simple designs, and then increasingly added more complex forms to their range, which, by the end of the seventeenth century, resulted in sophisticated and colorful enameled pieces called Imari after the port from which they were shipped. These were inspired by the stunning Kakiemon family enameled ware that the Arita area also produced. Meanwhile, the Dutch, who knew exactly what they could sell and in what quantities, and who were apparently having some difficulty in always getting the precise shapes they wanted from the Chinese, noted how flexible the Japanese were with the Southeast Asia market. They therefore made the decision to turn more toward Japan, most particularly because at that time they would be the only Europeans with direct access to the country and could more easily control the colors and shapes, getting what they preferred. In a curious turn of events, the Chinese then started to buy large quantities of Japanese imitations of their own porcelain designs to sell to European nations other than Holland, as well as to America. In an even more bizarre twist, the Dutch mostly showed

Japanese potters not the beautifully executed Chinese originals, but painted wooden models of what they wanted, sent from Holland and painted by Dutch painters. In short, the Dutch home market then ended up "with Japanese versions of European pastiches of Chinese originals that had already made concessions to European taste" (*Sotheby's Concise Encyclopaedia of Porcelain*, Conran Octopus, 1990.) None of these commercial shenanigans, of course, should detract from the fact that a very great deal of Japanese porcelain from the eighteenth and nineteenth centuries was both very beautiful and very influential to the burgeoning European porcelain producers.

JASPERWARE

The red stoneware produced as an alternative to porcelain by Johann Friedrich Bottger when he managed the Meissen factory (at that time in Dresden, Germany) between 1710 and 1719. Like the porcelain, the red stoneware was based on Chinese pieces (mostly teapots) imported from Yixing, which had already been copied by the delftware potter Arij de Milde. Bottger's versions were called jasperware because the pottery he produced was harder than both the Chinese and Dutch varieties, enabling it to be polished to as high a shine as jasper, an opaque quartz that could be yellow or brown as well as red. It could also be engraved and cut in a number of different designs.

JESUIT WARE

(See *encre de chine*.)

KAKIEMON

Highly prized Japanese enameled porcelain named after the legendary potter Sakaida Kakiemon, who is supposed to have invented the enameling process. The name now denotes both a particularly delicate style of enameled decoration as well as the use of a distinctive palette of green, blue, and red translucent enamels on a milky white body, produced from the 1680s. The Kakiemon factory also produced some gentle underglaze blue-and-white porcelain that is altogether more subtly decorated than the more sumptuous Imari ware. The Kakimon style of porcelain had a profound influence on the major European porcelain manufacturers.

KANGXI WARE

Chinese porcelain produced during the sixty-year reign of the Emperor Kangxi (1662–1722), the second ruler of the Qing Empire, although half of his

Kangxi stem cup

reign, ceramically speaking, took place during the so-called Transitional period between late Ming and early Qing. Court patronage and—perhaps more importantly—control resumed in 1683. But although the finest pieces went to the emperor, the blue-and-white export pieces apparently reached a quality and technical excellence that had not been seen before—nor, as it happens, since—in the West. Other remarkable products were pieces decorated in a gilded powder blue known as *bleu soufflé*; in the famille verte, famille noire, and famille rose modes; in "egg and spinach" (mottled yellow, green, and eggplant pieces); and in the stunning peach-bloom. Kangxi dragon decoration is quite distinctive, with the dragon being very lean and long, with its belly up somewhere near its shoulders, outlined in an underglaze blue, and its forelegs executing a peculiar kind of backflip.

KAOLIN

The fine white clay derived from decayed granite that is an essential ingredient of true porcelain.

KOREAN CERAMICS

Koreans were the first of the Southeast Asian countries to produce celadon-glazed stoneware. Their tenth-century wares were somewhat similar to the wares being produced simultaneously in China, but they rapidly achieved a distinctive look of their own with glassy, translucent glazes ranging from a beautiful grayish-green to a sea green and a yellowish-green.

Many of their surviving incised or carved twelfth-century pots are based on vegetal and flower forms, not at all unlike the natural motifs used in the late-nineteenth-century Art Nouveau style, which thought itself quite unique. And there is some inlaid decoration unique to Korea. Moreover, most Korean pieces have a most pleasing informality about them. Korean porcelain manufacture dates back to the twelfth century, and it was the unwilling Korean potters who had been taken prisoner, as well as Koreans forced to flee to the enemy country, who "helped" to get the porcelain industry started in Japan after the Japanese had overrun Korea in the 1590s. Korea did not really begin to recover the stability of its own porcelain and stoneware industry until the eighteenth century, when it, too, started to create blue-and-white porcelain to feed the ever-expanding world demand.

KUTANI

"Old Japanese Kutani" enameled porcelain dates back to the middle of the seventeenth century and consists mainly of dishes, large plates, and some jars. They are more connected by their distinctive and various shades of eggplant, dark greens and yellows, and underglaze blues than their geographical locations of manufacture. Many of the extant designs, particularly the geometrics—with their spare aesthetics—look as though they could have been executed today; others leave no millimeter of a plate unenameled.

Longton Hall rustic
cabbage sauce boat,
ca. 1755–58

Longton Hall "Snowman figures," ca. 1753–56

LALIQUE, RENÉ (1860–1945)

One of the great French decorative glass producers as well as Art Nouveau jeweler. Lalique glass was also particularly prominent during the Art Deco period.

LIMOGES

The major porcelain-producing area of France since the 1830s. Inspite of France's well-known chauvinism, one of the best-known Limoges firms is Havilland & Co., first started in 1842 by an American, David Havilland, to export products of French factories like Gibus et Cie and Pouyat to the United States. After setting up his own workshop to provide a decorating service, Havilland started producing his own porcelain, too. Most Limoges factories concentrate on producing tableware, although they are quite capable of producing luxury wares as well.

LONGTON HALL

Founded in 1750, and closing ten years later, Longton Hall is thought to be the first Staffordshire factory to succeed in the manufacture of porcelain. Nonetheless, its beginnings, though enthusiastic, were also clumsy; in fact, so much so that its first white figures came to be called The Snowman Family. Throughout its short life, it produced blue-and-white pieces in the convoluted "Chinese taste," as interpreted by English delftware producers, that were pleasing and are collectible today, as are the charming rustic "cabbagey" leaf-molded plates, dishes, sauceboats, and baskets with their well-defined deep-red veins and quite distinctively fresh shades of green. Other collectibles are the flatware pieces with delectable bird and flower paintings, as well as charming rural scenes of castles and ruined arches and the various somewhat energetic–looking figures. There is rarely a mark, but some of the figures do display a "K."

LOWESTOFT

A small eighteenth-century English factory founded by four partners in 1757 and situated all on its own on the East Anglican coast, quite remote from the main ceramic-producing areas. Nevertheless it produced unpretentious but inventive dark inky blue-and-white designs in the ubiquitous Chinese manner, as well as made a feature of some fetchingly naïve and eminently collectible commemorative china (it used a bone ash formula thought to have been obtained from a worker at the Bow factory)—with inscriptions and dates of births, marriages, and deaths—and pieces depicting local East coast villages and towns. These last are particularly collectible. In the 1770s, the factory hired an anonymous "tulip" painter who was responsible for some distinguished florals that nearly always included particularly full-blown tulips. (See also *Bow porcelain*.)

MAJOLICA OR MAIOLICA

This is another European version of tin-glazed earthenware produced in Italy and Spain. It is brightly decorated and glazed with a glassy white tin-oxide glaze that bears a passable resemblance to the surface of Chinese porcelain. The other European tin-glazed earthenware products are delftware (in Holland and Britain) and faience (in France and Germany, though the name faience derives from the Italian town of Faenza). A good deal of Persian (Iranian) earthenware is finished with a similar glaze.

MASON

Popular collectible, mostly in the patent ironstone china. The factory was started by Miles Mason, a Chinese man with an unlikely anglicized name, who decided to go into production himself in England after the cessation, in 1791, of the trade in Chinese export porcelain through the Dutch East India Company. Mason worked first in Liverpool in partnership with Thomas Wolfe and then by himself in Staffordshire from 1802. His early porcelain was a hybrid hard paste, but he changed to bone china in 1806. He produced some well-decorated and gilded pieces and many tea services with mandarin patterns, flowers, and landscapes, some of which were left unmarked others had an imprinted mock Chinese seal mark—some with and some without the name "M. Mason." He retired in 1813 and the business was taken over by his two sons, Charles James and George, who then patented a particular ironstone that had—and still has—great success.

MEISSEN

The oldest and one of the most famous porcelain factories in Europe, Meissen was started in 1710 on the strength of its discovery of the "secret" formula for hard-paste or true porcelain. (This formula was much helped by the fact that deposits of kaolin, an essential ingredient, had been found near the

Meissen black-glazed Bottger stoneware overpainted in gold, ca. 1715

factory.) Johann Friedrich Bottger, its young inventor—or perhaps, in this case, rediscoverer (China had perfected the formula at least nine centuries before, during the Tang Dynasty in 618–906)—managed the factory starting in 1710, when the first experimental porcelain wares went into production. Two of his interesting early introductions were his jasperware—shiny, polished-looking red stoneware based on the dark red stoneware, particularly teapots, imported from Yixing in China—and a special pink luster, called variously mother of pearl pink or Bottger luster. But by the time he died an untimely death at the age of thirty-seven in 1719, Meissen was in near financial ruin. The new manager, Johann Gregor Herold, quickly hired some very fine painters and generally enhanced the Meissen color palette with, for example, a beautiful clear turquoise, a soft sagey green, a subtle iron red, russets, and gilt. To capitalize on the fashion for tea and coffee drinking, he produced tea and coffee services, most of the early ones unmarked. As was normal at the time, Meissen produced a lot of adapted chinoiserie, but in the 1720s, Herold produced it with a twist, setting delicately Orientalized, peopled scenes in charming terraces within lacework cartouches, most often in red and gold, and even in the odd European scene as well. In 1724, he introduced the first mark—"KPM" (Konigliche Porzellan Manufactur)—and a year later started using the cross swords in underglaze blue that are still used today. In the next decade, Meissen started producing its copies of the Japanese Kakiemon wares, taken from the originals in the prescient collection of Augustus of Saxony (who had strong-armed Bottger, Meissen's first manager, back to Berlin to unlock the secret of true porcelain; see also *hard paste*), which proved to be extremely popular and were copied all over Europe. The factory also developed an interesting mixture of the Kakiemon style and the Chinese famille verte, which eventually developed into the famous Meissen flowers, known as *Indianische Blumen* (a reference to the East India Company rather than India), painted between 1720 and 1740. Other beautiful but European flower paintings produced in the 1730s by the painter J. G. Klinger are great collector pieces. By the 1750s, rather more naturalistic flowers and birds frequently decorated Meissen dinner services. The factory was also, of course, particularly known for its figures, many of them in the often strange (at least to contemporary minds) eighteenth-century taste, such as Meissen's monkey band, dwarves, saints and religious figures, Italian comedy figures, miners, and street vendors as well as shepherds and shepherdesses. The figures have proved enduringly popular, and have been enduringly copied. In the nineteenth century, Meissen had to give up its preeminence to the factories of Berlin, Vienna, and the French Sèvres, all of which were producing Neoclassical designs of high quality, although Meissen did produce the stunning dessert service commissioned in 1819 to commemorate the Duke of Wellington's victory over Napoleon at the Battle of Waterloo. The factory,

sadly, never regained its glory days although it still lives on successfully enough with the various technical innovations it has made over the decades and the revivals of so many of its former triumphs.

MING

To most ceramics neophytes the word *Ming* conjures up Chinese ceramics in general—a kind of "Chinese Ceramics 'r' Us" syndrome. Certainly the porcelain and stoneware production during the long Ming Dynasty (from 1368 to 1644) has a distinguished history; it was also mostly responsible for the West's passion for blue-and-white since the seventeenth century. To the expert, the Ming ceramics produced during the fifteenth century are quite simply the best—the most beautifully patterned, the most beautifully balanced between pattern and form, and the most beautifully glazed, with miniscule bubbles that make the underglaze decoration look appealing and soft. Sixteenth-century Ming—though not considered quite as fine in quality (many of the pieces were also a little slipshod and mechanical by comparison)—exhibits a greater variety of more free-flowing designs, including some different colored enamel decoration. However, it was the sixteenth-century Ming—the much more common and garden variety *kraak-porselein*, as the Dutch called it—that caused all the excitement. Those not acquainted with Dutch might suppose that the term *kraak-porselein* referred to less than perfect china,

Ming "Transitional"
blue-and-white jar, 1630–40

but in fact it derives from the Portugese boats called *carracks* (which the Dutch called *kraaks*) that originally started to bring cargoes of porcelain and other Eastern silks and lacquers to Europe. (The Portugese, being the first around the Cape of Good Hope in 1497, had therefore been the first to open up the trade routes to India, Southeast Asia, China, and Japan.) As it happened, the Dutch captured two of these carracks in the very early 1600s and confiscated 150,000 pieces of porcelain, which they proceeded to auction. This caused intense excitement in Europe in general, especially among the rich cognoscenti, including various crowned heads. Henry IV of France bought some, as did James I of England to add to the already fine collection of Queen Elizabeth I (her collection was unusual at the time since hardly anyone in Europe knew about Chinese porcelain until the seventeenth century). In fact, it was this very public excitement that caused the wily trading Dutch, who had just started their Dutch East India

Company in 1602, to include porcelain among the spices, peppers, teas, and so on that were their original target merchandise. From that time on there was scarcely a painting done by the various notable Dutch still-life artists that did not include a piece of late Ming export ware, mostly in the form of dishes piled with fruit or oysters. There is no way of knowing whether the stimulus of new markets and challenges stimulated the designers, but the fact is that the decoration of porcelain seemed to have had a new impetus during what is known as the Transitional period, the period that covers the last years of the Ming Dynasty and the beginning of the Qing. There were many more naturalistic motifs, including flowers, mythical beasts, scroll paintings, and cloudy landscapes or mountain gardens, as well as much more natural–looking figures, as opposed to the stiff and wooden figures of the sixteenth-century designs

MINTON

Much-loved English Staffordshire factory established in 1793 that produced at least nine hundred patterns in its first sixteen-year period, mostly to grace tea and some dessert services as well as punch bowls and a few purely ornamental items. Many Minton pieces showed a delicate chinoiserie influence and are still selling to this day, as are its original copies of Imari and other Japanese patterns. The earliest pieces were not marked, but from about 1805 Minton

Minton pâte-sur-pâte
vase, 1903

Open Minton pattern book with a
corresponding cup and saucer, ca.1830

used a device of crossed "L"s, which could have been confused with the somewhat similar Sèvres mark except that they were set above the letter "M." In the Victorian era, Minton leaped forward to become the leading porcelain factory in Europe, with some interesting interpretations of historic styles and various new techniques. In the 1830s, the factory produced an enormous number of ornaments, from clock and thermometer cases to the more usual potpourri bowls and vases, some of which were not only painted with flowers but also were flower-encrusted and occasionally adorned

with porcelain "lace" as well. In 1849, the firm was joined by a master potter from Toulouse in France named Leon Arnoux. He was given the post of "Ceramic Technical Director with freedom of initiative" and was responsible for many technical improvements, including a new translucency, a new lustrous glaze, and an improved color palette. For the last task, he perfected Minton's version of *bleu-celeste*, or heavenly blue, and *rose-du Barry* (actually the same as *rose Pompadour*), the ground colors for Minton's Sèvres-style collections produced over the rest of the nineteenth century. The factory was also well known for its many Parian figures (see also *Parian ware*), and its *pâte-sur-pâte* designs, built up with layer upon layer of slip. In the 1840s, Herbert Minton, the son of the factory's founder, Thomas Minton, worked very closely with the High Gothic architect A. W. N. Pugin on the interiors of the new Houses of Parliament. Many of the resulting Gothic-style designs were meant for tiles and for earthenware manufacturers, but Pugin's designs also graced two well-known bone china tea sets produced by Minton in the 1860s: his Fleur de Lis and his Blue Gothic Border. In the last part of the century, Minton also hired one of the leading Aesthetic Movement designers, Christopher Dresser, who had been much influenced by Japan and its artifacts, especially Japanese cloisonné, as well as by his own training as a botanist. Dresser produced some very fine designs, as did various Art Nouveau and Art Deco designers. Because of its habit of commissioning distinguished architects, designers, and painters in various periods, who did not nec-essarily have anything to do with porcelain, Minton could be said to have been the forerunners of Swid Powell—the American tableware company who in 1984, a century or so later, unveiled a collection it had commissioned from architects like Charles Gwathmey and Rober Siegel, Richard Meier, Robert A. M. Stern, Arata Isozaki, Laurinda Spear, and Stanley Tigerman and Margaret McCurry.

NABESHIMA

Very beautifully shaped and decorated porcelain first made in Okawachi, a little north of Arita, Japan, at the end of the seventeenth century. These early pieces were commissioned by the Nabeshima Lords of Hizen (now Sag-ken), who wanted to present them to the shogun and to officials of the court. However, the best Nabeshima period is the first half of the eighteenth century,

and the most typical pieces of the time were stunning curved dishes in three sizes: 6 inches, 8 inches, and 12 inches. They were characterized by a skillful use of glaze and a method of using underglaze blue to outline areas that were then enameled. Nabeshima also produced a particularly fine celadon glaze, sometimes used in conjunction with blue-and-white glazes as well. The Nabeshima potters also produced blue-and-white porcelain with or without the addition of overglaze enamel, although the undersides are invariably in under-glaze blue. The porcelain bears no mark.

NANKIN OR NANKING

Chinese blue-and-white export porce-lain produced in the late eighteenth and early nineteenth centuries. The deco-ration consisted mainly of landscapes surrounded by rather complex borders.

NANTGARW

Welsh porecelain. (See also *Swansea porcelain*.)

NEW HALL

Another English Staffordshire factory of late-eighteenth-century origin, starting in 1781. It first manufactured its wares in hard-paste, or true, porcelain, but switched over to bone china in 1814. In the beginning, it specialized in tea services aimed at the middle-class market, but its most collectible wares were those painted in a fairly distinctive style by the French painter Fidelle Duvivier. Until well into the nineteenth century, New Hall, displayed no factory mark. In the early nineteenth century, the factory produced some handsome dinner services showing specific country houses that were bat-printed, that is to say, decorated with a rather short-lived variation of transfer printing. The same technique was used to transfer prints in the style of the well-known nineteenth-century English painter George Morland, and for some winsome studies of women and children, as well as more regular fruit and flower groups. Flatteringly—or, more likely, annoyingly—several other English factories copied various New Hall designs. The factory closed in 1835.

NYMPHENBURG

Bavarian factory, famous to this day for its figures although it also produced some rather grand tableware, including a well-known pattern decorated with trompe l'oeil prints on fine wood-grained grounds. The factory was founded in 1747 as a kind of wedding present for Maria-Anna Sophia, the granddaughter of the same Augustus the Strong of Saxony who forced the fleeing young alchemist Johann Fredereich Blottger to return to Berlin to work on discovering the secret formula for Chinese true porcelain. Apparently, Maria-Anna Sophia's new husband, Prince Max II Joseph of Bavaria, thought to encourage her intense interest in porcelain by opening a new porcelain factory in an old hunting lodge at Neuduck. The factory flourished and in 1754 it was joined by F. A. Bustelli, considered to be one of the greatest modelers of European figures, who was deeply influenced by the wood sculptor F. I. Gunther. Bustelli is well known for his set of sixteen Italian comedy figures sporting particularly dramatic poses and for some charming groups of figures set among ruins. In 1761, the factory was moved to Nymphenburg, to the Palace of the Elector of Bavaria, but Bustelli, like so many of the principal figures in the eighteenth-century ceramics business, died young, only two years later. Many of his figures are still being produced. The Palatinate took over the factory in 1770. Early Nymphenburg figures can be recognized from new models by their rather creamy white color, which became grayer around 1775 to the end of the century. The nineteenth- to twenty-first-century copies are much whiter and also bear the shape of the impressed Bavarian shield. However, as in the case of so many porcelain factories, it is not quite so easy to judge the exact decade of the earlier models because there is an ongoing argument about how many figures were left white pending painting, which could often be some years later.

PARIAN WARE

Unglazed porcelain or earthenware simulating marble and made from a mixture of china clay and feldspar or petunse, ground Chinese rock. It was introduced in 1845 and was mostly used in the production of figures, copies of classical sculptures, and busts, many of them in miniature.

PÂTE-SUR-PÂTE

A French word literally meaning "paste-upon-paste," it is the technique of building a design by using successive layers of liquid slip or diluted clay.

PEACH-BLOOM

A Chinese glaze for which copper was the primary coloring agent and that was first used on Kangxi wares. When it was fired it took on a number of hues from a beautiful peach color, hence its name, to a most un-peachlike sage green.

PHILADELPHIA

A location of porcelain production between 1770 and 1773 under the management of Gousse Bonnin and George Anthony Morris, with kaolin found in South Carolina, clays from Delaware, and a little bone ash. Therefore, the paste produced was very similar to that made by Bow in London a little earlier in the century. Interestingly, some American porcelain did look and feel very like hard-paste, or true, porcelain, even though it was more like the English bone china. In 1827, America's first commercially successful porcelain factory was also started in Philadelphia by William Ellis Tucker. It operated for twelve years and during that time turned out a great variety of wares with a couple of different glazes—one making the goods take on a greenish translucency, the other a straw color that occasionally veered toward orange.

Pickle stand, Philadelphia, 1770–72

PILLEMENT, JEAN

A French painter (1728–1808) who designed chinoiseries that became very popular in England during the eighteenth century.

PORCELAIN

The umbrella term covering true porcelain (hard paste), artificial porcelain (soft paste), and bone china. Interestingly, all American porcelain is soft-paste or artificial porcelain, although some has the appearance of true porcelain even though analysis proves it to be otherwise. The reason for this is that the kind of clays and feldspar available in the United States do not seem to react to the proven formula in the same way as their European and Oriental counterparts. An exception was the fine bed of kaolin discovered in the eighteenth century in South Carolina, which was used to produce Philadelphia wares, but even then, a small amount of bone ash was added.

QING

The dynasty, starting in 1644, that immediately followed the end of the Ming Dynasty in China. Qing wares can be identified by several distinct periods: the innovative and beautiful wares of the Kangxi period (ending in 1722); the spare and elegant minimilism of the Yongzheng period (ending in 1735); the controlled decoration of the Qianlong period (ending in 1795); the overdecorated Jiaqing period (ending in 1820), and the Daoguang period (ending 1850). It bowed out with the sad decline of aesthetic standards at the beginning of the twentieth century.

ROCKINGHAM

An eighteenth-century Yorkshire pottery that was manufactured on the estate of Earl Fitzwilliam, who later became the Marquess of Rockingham. When the pottery factory hit hard times, the Earl helped it financially and by 1826 it had started to produce porcelain. During the English Regency period the factory released some handsome vases, figures and animals, as well as covetable tea and dessert services (the saucers are marked with a griffin and various different permutations of letters printed in red under the base; in 1830, this changed to puce lettering). Yet, the factory was never really well managed financially and had to close in 1842. However, any collectors of Rockingham should beware of its many imitations in hard paste stamped with the griffin mark that were manufactured in Paris and of the fact that Rockingham never made

Qing Dragon and Phoenix bowl, Kangxi mark and period, 1662–1722

the sheep and poodles with simulated wool coats that for some reason are ascribed to it.

SAINT-GOBAIN

A French glass manufacturer particularly well known in the 1920s Art Deco period for its many interestingly decorated goblets and carafes.

SAINT-LOUIS

A French crystal manufacturer and contemporary of Baccarat that produced much fine-quality decorative glass- and tableware in the early twentieth century.

ST. PETERSBURG (THE IMPERIAL PORCELAIN MANUFACTORY)

This was Russia's leading porcelain producer, thought to have been founded in 1744. By 1800 it moved to the forefront of the market, helped by several artists hired from the French company Sèvres and the German company Berlin Porcelain, with the production of a whole series of elegant Neoclassical wares, as well as by the useful addition of new kilns and various other technical improvements. Fortunately, the factory had no need to be worried by tiresome financial situations. After the death of Tsar Alexander I, Tsar Nicholas I took control. Its copies of Greek, Roman, Etruscan, and Egyptian forms were much sought after, as were its portraits of the Russian generals who won the battle against Napoleon in 1812. One of its triumphs was the sumptuous one-thousand-piece dinner service it made for a Count Guryev, which it began in 1809. Painted views of Saint Petersburg on a dark-red ground—complete with its city dwellers, various craftsmen, and peasants all going about their daily business—were surrounded with gilded borders of acanthus leaves, laurel leaves, and other kinds of foliage. In the 1830s the manufactory specialized in figurative groups in biscuit dressed in Russian costume, as well as a number of ornamental pieces like candlesticks, baskets, and clocks based either on Russian antiquities or ideas from Sèvres, Meissen, and the Orient. Although St. Petersburg went on to win various prizes for its work under Tsar Alexander II in the 1860s and '70s, these awards were more for technical proficiency than for any marked originality.

SALT-GLAZE STONEWARE

Stoneware that has a clear, impermeable glaze caused by throwing salt into the kiln that then fuses with the clay and vitrifies at a very high temperature.

SANG DE BOEUF

Dark brownish-red or, literally, *oxblood*-colored glaze developed during the Qing dynasty in China.

SÈVRES

Along with Meissen and later Minton, Sèvres was—and still is—one of the most famous European porcelain manufacturers. It was first known as Vincennes—since it had been started in 1740 as a workshop at the royal

A combined work-writing-reading table veneered on oak with tulipwood and gilt bronze mounts and fitted with Sèvres porcelain plaques (1783, Wallace Collection, London)

Chateau de Vincennes near Paris—and began by experimenting with soft-paste, or artificial, porcelain, made with a form of opaque glass that was very easy to scratch, hence the epithet "soft." The Vincennes workshop was quite successful in producing a nice white body with a good transparent glaze and, by 1746, had also perfected a satisfactory way of firing the pottery both in its unglazed and glazed states; and, two years later, developed a kiln that could fire decoration at a low temperature. This was just as well because in 1745 the workshop had been given a royal warrant to virtually copy the work of Meissen (see also *Meissen*), the first factory in Europe to produce genuine hard-paste, or true, porcelain. Vincennes, however, did not have the benefit, as Meissen did, of nearby deposits of the kaolin needed to make such hard paste. Eleven years later, in 1756, the workshop was promoted to a purpose-built factory for porcelain production in Sèvres, a village midway between Paris and Versailles, and changed its name to that of the new location. In the meantime, however, the eleven-year lead-in to the change of venue and name had been very productive for the old Vincennes workshop. After many experiments with pigments to produce clear pure colors and with gold for better gilding, Vincennes had started a thriving production line. Its first items were a whole range of porcelain flowers to decorate lamps, wall sconces, and chandeliers, as well as a series of enameled figures. It soon diversified into tableware and porcelain items for the dressing table, and did a good deal of research into current tastes in decoration and shapes. Moreover, in 1751, a new director, Monsieur J. Hellot of the Académie des Sciences, had been hired to improve all the various aspects of this production, and had perfected the most beautiful blue called, unsurprisingly, *bleu beau*. Because it ran a little at the edges, the decorators traced over those edges with gold. In the next few years the company produced some other virtuoso colors: its famous *bleu celeste* and its green, called *verte*, and finally, from the new factory in Sèvres, its *rose Pompadour*, named after its patroness, Madame de Pompadour, Louis XV's mistress of renowned taste and discernment. (As an aside, when the English copied the pink, as they inevitably did, they called the color *rose du Barry* after the French king's next mistress). Sèvres proceeded to go from strength to strength adding more and more products, such as dinner services, coffee and tea services, decorative clocks, barometers, inkwells, vases, and even sculptures. In 1768, when deposits of kaolin were discovered in France, Sèvres was able, finally, to produce hard-paste, or true, porcelain like its rival Meissen. In fact, it went on producing both true and artificial porcelain products until 1804, when it finally gave up the soft paste altogether. Both Louis XV and Louis XVI helped the factory by commissioning lavish dinner services to give as presents to royalty and foreign governments around the world, as well as for their own residences.

Sèvres's soaring success was somewhat curtailed by the French Revolution, but it picked up again with the ascent of Napoleon, and Sèvres finally overtook Meissen as the most copied factory in Europe. It has hardly looked back.

SOFT PASTE

Artificial porcelain as opposed to true porcelain. (See also *Sèvres* and *hard paste*.)

SPODE

A well-known English porcelain factory started in 1770 by Josiah Spode I. Like the rest of the European porcelain producers, Spode I conducted many experiments with his paste, adding this component and that in a search for the best body material. But it was Josiah Spode II who, by adding a particularly large percentage of calcined animal bones to the mix, perfected the bone china formula that revolutionized the British China industry. (See also *bone china*.) And it certainly *was* perfected. It did not craze or go creamy instead of white, its enamel decoration did not flake, its gilding stayed rich and glowing, and its shapes were impeccable. It also produced a very good range of blue-and-white earthenware, and some patterns are still produced to this day. Spode's polychrome painted and gilded pieces produced between 1805 and 1822 are highly collectible, as indeed are all its Regency patterns.

STONEWARE

An opaque ceramic, halfway between earthenware and porcelain, that has been produced since earliest times in the Far East and in Southeast Asia and that was introduced to Britain in the late seventeenth century from Germany. It is fired at a very high temperature—higher than earthenware—which vitrifies the formula and makes it watertight without the necessity of glazing.

SWANSEA PORCELAIN

A fine example of Welsh early-nineteenth-century porcelain with a particularly high standard of painting and design. The factory had first been set up in 1813 in Nantgarw, near Cardiff, by William Billingsley, originally from Derby and one of the most talented and creative painters and ceramicists of the period, who dreamed of creating a porcelain to equal that produced by the French. After much somewhat abortive experimenting at various English midland factories, Billingsley eventually arrived in Wales with his two daughters and his son-in-law, the potter Samuel Walker. With the financial aid of a Quaker entrepreneur, William Weston Young, he finally did manage to produce a beautifully translucent Sèvreslike porcelain, but difficulties in production led to unacceptable losses in the kilns. Billingsley then transferred to Swansea in 1814 and entered into an arrangement with Lewis Weston Dillwyn who, between 1814 and 1817, went on experimenting with the formula while

Billingsley resumed his role as master painter, and his son-in-law, Samuel Walker, that of master potter. The resulting Swansea porcelains fell into three main categories: the "glassy" variety, which was beautiful and translucent and did indeed look like the French hard-paste, or true, porcelain of the period; the "duck egg" variety, with a slightly green–tinged translucency; and what Dillwyn described as "a good, sound, tolerable body," although it had an olive-brownish tinge and a grubby-looking pitted glaze that the London porcelain dealers immediately rejected. The two finer-quality varieties, however, were made into some of the best and most interesting shapes of the period by the modeler Isaac Wood under the direction of Billingsley, and decorated by the latter, to make some of the most charming ornamental pieces, as well as dinner, dessert, and tea services made in the British Isles. Not all Swansea pieces, however, were decorated by Billinglsey, who also hired some of the most talented painters and gilders of the time. Marks included an impressed "Dillwyn & Co"; "Swansea," impressed, transfer-printed, or painted in red; "Swansea" in italics in red, gold, and occasionally other colors; and crossed tridents. In 1817, Billingsley left Swansea, followed by Walker, and went back to Nantgarw, where for three years he managed to produce a stunning, translucent, soft-paste porcelain with a pure white glaze that he sent to London both for decoration and sale. Nantgarw's main output was then dinner, dessert, and tea services, pen trays, inkwells, and

tazza vases with the impressed mark of "NANTGARW" over a "CW." In 1820, however, depressed by the factory's financial losses, the talented Billingsley and Walker left Wales and went to Coalport, where Billingsley remained until his death in 1828. (See also *Coalport*.)

TIFFANY GLASS

World-renowned, highly decorative, colored Art Nouveau glass vases, decorative objects, and lamp shades designed by the painter Louis Comfort Tiffany (1848–1933) from the late nineteenth century. Tiffany also invented a particular type of iridescent glass that he trademarked as "Favrile," though it is often also referred to as Tiffany glass.

UNDERGLAZE

The colored decoration, or in some cases, just coating, that is applied to the biscuit—or as yet unglazed porcelain—before it is glazed and then fired.

UNION PORCELAIN WORKS

Nationalistic American porcelain factory founded in 1863 in Greenpoint, New York, known for its ewers and pitchers (mostly made for hotels) with molded eagles placed under the spouts, as well as for its eagle paperweights and plaques with relief portraits of well-known Americans. Its products were widely copied. It stopped production in the 1920s.

Tiffany coffeepot, creamer, and sugar bowl, ca. 1877

WATERFORD GLASS

Consistently high-standard Irish cut glass that has been in production since the nineteenth century. It is now owned by Wedgwood.

WEDGWOOD

Interestingly, although the name Wedgwood is world renowned and the pottery started in 1759, it was known above all for its fine and original earthenware, not its porcelain, which its founder, Josiah Wedgwood, considered nothing but "a gulf" in which to venture. It did not actually start producing bone china until 1812 under Josiah Wedgwood II, but that exercise faltered commercially and began to decline after 1820, stopping altogether in 1829, and was not resumed again until 1878, though it's been in production since then to the present day. Those early porcelain wares that were produced are, however, highly collectible and are marked with the name "Wedgwood," usually in red. Wedgwood also made a parian body (see also *Parian ware*) that was called Carara after the Italian marble, as well as its matte black Basalt Ware. And in the first part of the twentieth century, it produced its well-known "Fairyland" lusterwares that were bowls, vases, and plaques painted and printed with gold and decorated with elves and fairies designed by Daisy Makeig-Jones in 1914, at the beginning of World War I.

WORCESTER

One of the great English porcelain factories and the only eighteenth-century factory to have remained in continuous production until the present day. It was first started in 1751 by Dr. Thomas Wall and fourteen other partners on the banks of the Severn River and united with Benjamin Lund's ex-Bristol factory the following year. Lund had concentrated on mainly blue-and-white wares and a soapstone formula, but his various prior experiments with porcelain helped Worcester to obtain its early sophistication in the field. Its first decorations were mainly inspired by the Chinese famille verte and some Japanese designs, resulting in many ethereal and fanciful chinoiserie scenes with figures in flowing robes, scattered blossoms, floating islands, and long-necked cranes, all adorning shapes that were mostly based on silver originals. Worcester had one particular advantage over its early rivals and that was the ability of its porcelain tea wares to withstand boiling water—an essential element for the making of tea. The factory also introduced transfer printing over the glaze between 1753 and 1754 and was soon unequaled in this technique. By the late 1760s it had developed a more opulent style of decoration as well as its now typical rich underglaze-blue grounds embellished with overglaze designs within circular, oval, and mirror-shaped panels, which were decorated with exotic birds, flowers, or oriental patterns, and landscapes enriched with gilding.

Worcester openwork basket in blue and white, ca. 1770–72

LIGHTING

More light.

Johann Wolfgang von Goethe
(1749–1832), his last words

If color is the most immediate transformer of a home, good lighting is the most subtle. Even though good lighting shops and lighting designers abound, and there are some excellent books on lighting, there still seems to be a curious unawareness of its full potential, its flexibility, and its ability to transform any space at all with the right mixture of light fixtures and dimmer switches. Indeed, good lighting is to spatial decoration what herbs and spices are to cooking. It can provide as wonderful a variety of effects as herbs and spices provide flavors, with light and shade, coolness and warmth, and brilliance and calm.

How can you begin to make the best use of lighting? The first step is to build some basic awareness of its qualities. Simply by noting, for example, that the sun neither stands still nor blazes continuously down from overhead—like those ubiquitous central light fittings—is a great start to improving your lighting awareness. Study lighting effects you like and how they were achieved, taking note of the type of bulb and fixture used as well as the placement of the light within the given room.

However, being aware of lighting and its many possibilities is not enough. Lighting should be planned for and any rewiring or extra outlets installed long before any decoration is undertaken so that both the installation and the necessary wires can be neatly concealed. (The same planning applies to extra wiring for stereos, computers, printers, televisions, telephones, burglar alarms, and so on.) But if you are restricted or prohibited from rewiring projects, whether because you're in a rental or you have a depleted pocketbook, there are ways to vary lighting cosmetically with uplights, downlights, and three-way switches.

One of the reasons, I always think, for the comparative underuse of imaginative lighting in such a sophisticated electronic age—for example, artificial light can now emulate the many, many degrees of sunlight—is the complication of its vocabulary, which, being sprinkled throughout with scientific terms, can be off-putting to the novice or amateur home decorator. In this section tried to present the lighting terms as clearly as possible.

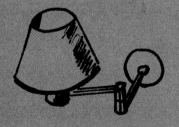

ACCENT LIGHT

Light used to highlight particular paintings, objects, and textures, and an important aspect of any good lighting scheme.

AKARI LAMPS

Japanese rice-paper lanterns with separate lamp shades; especially those designed by Isamu Noguchi in the 1950s.

AMBIENT LIGHTING

The hopefully unobtrusive, overall lighting of a room.

AMP

The short term for *ampere*. This is the base unit of electrical current that measures the speed at which current flows.

BAFFLE

A device meant to lessen or to prevent glare from lighting fixtures, such as downlights, for example, where a cowl is usually lined with concentric black grooves. Similarly, strip lights above a work surface are shielded by a *pelmet*, just as cove lighting is recessed behind a *cornice*.

BALLAST

A stabilizing unit used to control the flow of current and thus prevent overheating in fluorescent, mercury-vapor, metal halide, and high- and low-pressure sodium bulbs (which are grouped together in the trade as discharge lamps).

BARN DOORS

In lighting, adjustable hinged flaps attached to the front of some spotlights to control the shape of the beam.

Barn doors

BAYONET BULB

A European incandescent bulb that has two lugs (small metal bits), as opposed to a screw base, to enable it to be firmly attached to the holder.

BEAM

The spread of light from a bulb. The beam width is labeled "narrow," as from a PAR spot bulb; "medium," as from a PAR flood bulb; or "wide," as from an R40 flood bulb.

BULB

A bulb is the glass or quartz enclosure that protects the filament or other light-producing part, but most people use the term for the whole structure.

CABLE

The sheathed bunch of insulated wires used to transmit electrical current.

CABLE SYSTEM

Tensioned cables that support miniature low-voltage track lights that can be moved along the length of the cables and adjusted to various angles.

CANDELA

This term can be confusing because it can be used to describe either the unit of intensity of light from a given source (also called *candlepower*), or the unit of brightness of a source when used in terms of area, such as "so many candelas per square inch or yard."

CANDLE

In light-measurement terms, a standard candle produces 12.57 lumens of light. It is still the gentlest and most flattering form of lighting for any number of situations.

CANDLEPOWER

Though it seems anachronistic in this high-tech world, the term is still a measure of light intensity. For example, a 150-watt PAR spot bulb has the intensity at the center of its beam of 11,500 candlepower, or *candelas*, whereas a 150-watt PAR flood bulb has an intensity of 4,000 candlepower, or candelas.

CIRCUIT

The path of an electrical current as it passes along supply cables to electrical outlets and light sources.

CIRCUIT BREAKER

The special switch attached to an electrical consumer unit that carries out the same function as a fuse, but without the fuss. In abnormal or potentially dangerous circumstances, it will cut off the electrical flow to circuits, and simply needs to be switched back to restart the flow.

COLOR RENDERING

Things appear to be different colors under different sources of light. Bulbs are rated, among other factors, by their color-rendering index, normally judged against how close an object looks to its appearance in daylight. This takes the form of a number between one and one hundred—the higher the number, the truer the color rendering. However, the numbers are meaningless out of their technical context, so it is still safer to experiment with different bulbs.

CONTRAST

In lighting, this means the contrast between the brightness of an object or surface and the brightness of the background against which that object is set.

COOL BEAM BULB

These are useful wherever it is desirable to reduce heat from lighting on people and objects, such as in stores, food shops, galleries, and museums. The beam of light from these bulbs contains only one-third of the heat (infrared) energy of a conventional PAR bulb of comparable wattage.

DIFFUSED LIGHT

Light that is softened by some sort of translucent fabric shade.

DIFFUSER

A device that filters light from a given source. An example is the Plexiglas or Perspex diffuser that is often used over a fluorescent bulb.

DIMMER SWITCH

An invaluable control switch that allows the lighting level of bulbs to be subtly lowered or raised. Most lighting systems, and most areas for that matter, benefit from this kind of control.

DIRECT LIGHTING

The kind of light that is provided directly from a light source without bouncing off walls or ceilings, or being diffused.

DIRECTIONAL LIGHTING

Lighting that is designed to illuminate an object from a given direction. This is usually provided by adjustable spots or desk or work lights.

DISCHARGE BULB

A bulb whose light is produced by an electrical discharge through a gas, a metal vapor, or a mixture of both. It is generally cheaper to run than incandescent light and lasts longer, though it is correspondingly more expensive and usually gives a less attractive light. Fluorescent, mercury vapor, metal halide, and sodium are all discharge bulbs.

DOWNLIGHT

Light provided by a tungsten or halogen bulb in a fitting that is usually ceiling-recessed, ceiling mounted, or wall mounted to throw light vertically or steeply downward. The fittings themselves are generally called downlights.

EYEBALL SPOT

An adjustable recessed spotlight that resembles an eyeball.

FILAMENT

The thin wire, usually made of tungsten, in an incandescent bulb that emits light when it is heated to incandescence by an electrical current. In the

Three examples of directional lighting: a classic tungsten work lamp (left) and two tungsten desk lamps (right).

United Kingdom, incandescent bulbs are often called tungsten bulbs after the filament substance.

FLOODLIGHT

Any spotlight containing an incandescent reflector bulb that produces a relatively wide beam of light.

FLUORESCENT BULB

A variety of discharge bulb that is more energy efficient than an incandescent or halogen bulb, it is cheaper to run, and lasts longer. Although it had, in the past, a reputation for a less attractive light than the regular household or halogen bulbs, it now provides a much wider variation of color renditions. (See also *discharge bulb*.)

FRAMING PROJECTOR

This is the Rolls Royce of directional spotlights designed to *exactly* illuminate a painting or object without any light spillage. Its attachments allow precise control over the focus of the beam. It is expensive but worth the price for the accuracy it provides. Other terms are *profile spots* or *pinhole projections*.

GLARE

Undesirable brightness that causes annoyance, discomfort, or a loss of visual performance since some parts of the visual field become brighter than their surroundings.

GOOSENECK LAMP

A table lamp with a flexible stem so that the direction of the beam of light can easily be adjusted.

GROUND

A most necessary connection between an electrical circuit and the earth that can conduct electrical current out of harm's way if a fault occurs in the wiring, such as a break in a circuit cable or its insulation. Without such a connection a light fixture or an appliance could become lethally "live."

HALOGEN BULB

A bulb containing a normal tungsten filament that is surrounded by halogen gas, which extends the bulb's life and gives a brighter, whiter punch of light than a regular incandescent bulb of the same wattage. It is also known as *quartz halogen* or a *tungsten halogen* bulb.

HID BULB

A high-intensity discharge bulb used for outdoor lighting.

HURRICANE LAMP

A decorative glass cylinder or cover to set over a candlestick and candle to keep the flame from blowing out. It is, therefore, useful for alfresco dining.

INCANDESCENT BULB

The regular domestic lightbulb with a tungsten filament, and the original type of lightbulb invented by Thomas Edison. Technically, a halogen bulb is also incandescent since it contains a regular filament as well as halogen gas.

INDIRECT LIGHTING

Lighting that is bounced off ceilings and walls and any other large surfaces.

ISL BULB

Internally silvered bulb more generally known as a reflector bulb.

An ISL bulb

KICK SWITCH

Highly sensitive switch that is installed at the base of some modern light fixtures so that they can be controlled by the touch of a foot and so obviate a lot of tedious bending down.

LAMP

Confusingly, the trade name for a bulb.

LENS

An accessory that can be used over the top of a fixture to achieve different lighting effects. For example, a frosted lens can produce an apparently more even wash of light.

LOW-VOLTAGE BULB

A good choice for lighting art and for accenting objects, it has to be used in conjunction with a transformer. As a result, a recessed low-voltage spot needs a reasonable amount of ceiling cavity space. It is available in both incandescent and halogen varieties.

LUMEN

The SI unit of luminous flux that in lay talk means the amount of light that is given off by a light source, or the amount of light received by a given surface. SI is short for *Système Internationale d'Unités*, the internationally agreed upon system of scientific light-measuring units.

LUMINAIRE

The trade term for a light fitting. That is to say, a housing unit designed as a bulb and bulb holder to protect the light source, and also to provide a means of safe connection to the electricity supply as well as to direct and control the light.

LUX

The term for lumens measured by the square yard or meter. Also, the SI unit, which is the measure of light leaving a surface in whatever direction.

NEON BULB

A bulb containing neon, an inert gas at low pressure. It throws off a reddish or pinkish light when voltage is applied.

OPAL FINISH BULB

An opalescent bulb that has an internal coating of silica to give a milky or opal appearance to the resulting light.

OVERSPILL

In lighting, light that spills over from the main profile of a beam, as in the overspill of light around a painting lit by a regular spotlight or wallwasher. This sort of spill is obviated by a framing projector.

PAR BULB

Shortened term for a *parabolic aluminized reflector*, whick is a sealed beamed bulb with a front of tough, heat-resistant glass. The rear of the bulb is parabolic in cross section and the bulb is internally aluminized to reflect or throw off a more powerful beam of light. This type of bulb is weather resistant, so it is especially useful outside.

A Par 38 bulb

PENDANT

A light fixture suspended or projected from the ceiling.

PHARMACIST LAMP

A floor-standing brass, nickel, or chrome light fixture with a semicircular shield to shade the bulb. The light can be twisted around to direct the light source.

PHOSPHOR

A substance used for the inner coating of fluorescent bulbs that emits visible light when bombarded with electromagnetic radiation.

REFLECTOR BULB

Spot or flood bulb with an internally silvered surface for better reflection.

A typical reflector or R bulb

SCONCE

A wall bracket to hold candles or electric bulbs. There are a very great number of stylish interpretations.

SIDELIGHTING

A technique for lighting something from the side in order to emphasize either its texture or its three-dimensionality.

SON BULB

The trade term for a high-pressure sodium bulb used for street or outside lighting.

SPOTLIGHT

An internally silvered reflector bulb with a directional beam that is used for

Swing-arm wall lamp

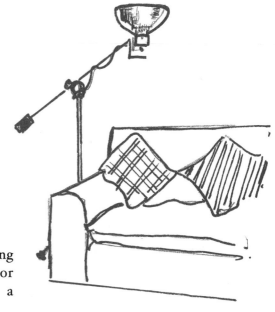

**Swing-arm floor lamp designed
by Mariano Fortuny**

highlighting an object or providing accent light. It can be recessed or surface- or track-mounted from a ceiling, wall, or floor.

SWING-ARM LAMP

A wall or floor lamp, usually made of brass, nickel, or stainless steel, which can be swung at different angles for maximum ease of reading or work.

TASK LIGHTING

This is lighting specifically meant to facilitate a task, whether it is cooking, writing, painting, drawing, sewing, or pleasurable reading.

THREE-WAY BULB

This mostly American bulb (I cannot imagine why it is not sold everywhere) has two filaments. Each filament can be operated separately or in combination with the other. It is a good energy saver and can be turned high for various tasks, such as reading, or lower for TV viewing, conversation, or a gentler ambience. The lowest setting

can be used as a night-light. In other words, it individually performs the services of a dimmer switch. Three-way bulbs are generally available from a 30/70/100-watt range to a 100/200/300 one. You need a special three-way socket and switch to take advantage of the three-way effect. Since there are two filaments in the bulb there are two contacts in the base. Making sure that the bulb is tight enough in its socket will also ensure that both these contacts are properly connected.

TRACK LIGHTING

Tracks of different lengths, available straight or curved, that can be mounted on ceilings or walls to support adjustable spotlights or wallwashers.

They can either work from the main supply or take low voltage.

TRANSFORMERS

These transfer electricity from one circuit to another with a decrease or increase in voltage. They are essential to the installation of any low-voltage bulbs but are often small enough to be concealed within the fixture.

UL

Short for *Underwriter's Laboratory* and the seal of approval for electrical appliances. This independent laboratory tests to make sure that all appliances and fixtures meet specialized safety requirements; you should not buy a fixture or appliance unless it has a UL stamp. This stamp should also indicate whether or not the fixture is suitable for wet or damp locations.

UPLIGHT

Any light fixture that throws light upward so that it is reflected back from the ceiling or walls. Inconspicuous floor-standing uplights are extremely useful for backlighting both objects and plants, highlighting corners, and for providing indirect light when you are unable to install recessed lighting (if, for example, you're in either a rental or a building with concrete ceilings).

VISUAL ACUITY

The ability to be able to distinguish fine detail. This ability is enhanced by well-thought-out task lighting

VOLTAGE

The term for the pressure of electricity as it flows through an electrical circuit. The greater the pressure the higher the number of volts. Main supply voltage varies from country to country: it is 120 volts in the United States, 240 volts in the United Kingdom, and 220 volts everywhere else. A transformer reduces low-voltage lighting to 12 volts.

WALLWASHER

A downlight or spot that literally washes or bathes a wall with light. Wallwashers are usually recessed into or mounted on a ceiling (on a track or surface-mounted) about 3 feet from the wall, depending on the desired effect, and are particularly useful for lighting a whole wall of prints or a mixture of prints, paintings, and photographs. You can test the best distance from the wall by experimenting with a cheap, portable work light.

WATT

This is the unit that measures the rate at which electricity is consumed and which also indicates the power of a given light source. (In an electrical circuit, a watt is the amount of power being delivered as a result of the flow of current in amps multiplied by the pressure of that flow of current in volts). Every light fixture you buy should specify a maximum wattage (it is as important to have this information as it is to look for the UL mark). Watts are abbreviated as "W" on bulbs. The term is named after James Watt (1736–1819), the inventor of this measuring unit.

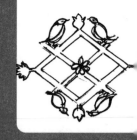

ORIENTAL AND OTHER RUGS

Though it is well as a rule, that carpets and hangings (curtains) should match, exception must always be made in favor or a really fine old Eastern rug. The tints of such rugs are too subdued, too subtly harmonized by time, to clash with any colors the room may contain....

Edith Wharton (1862–1937) and Ogden Codman (1863–1951), from *The Decoration of Houses*

Oriental rugs and carpets have been highly valued and collected in the West for hundreds of years. In the eleventh century, the crusaders brought many varieties of rugs back with them to Europe from the Middle East. Marco Polo, traveling through the East in the thirteenth century, described Konya in Anatolia (the ancient name for Asia Minor; now part of Turkey) as the town "where the most beautiful carpets in the world were woven." The use of Oriental rugs in the West has been documented for centuries in painting, where they can be found first hanging on walls or draped across tables (they were considered too precious to place on floors), and later on floors.

Beginning in the seventeenth century, new trade with the Safavid Empire (1502–1736) in Persia (now Iran) meant that many rugs from sophisticated workshops started to trickle into European and eventually American homes. And by the nineteenth century, "Oriental" rugs were being imported to Europe and America from more than twenty areas around the world, though principally from Persia, Turkey, and from nomadic tribes in Russia (including the Turkoman and Caucasus regions), Afghanistan, Bulgaria, Romania, India, Pakistan, China, and North Africa (including Morocco, Tunisia, Libya, and Egypt).

Though the rich colors and intricate patterns of Oriental rugs have made them justifiably prized for centuries in the West, and longer in the East, there are of course many other rug-making traditions of note from around the world. European and Native and South American rugs, too, are handsome and make an interesting study. Early American and English rag and needlework rugs are prized, as are the Modernist abstractions and textures produced first by members of the Bauhaus in Europe and particularly—in the case of textures—in Finland, Greece, and Ireland.

Learning how to "read" these very diverse rugs, how to discern their origins, and, in the case of the Oriental rugs, the names of the many different tribes and types of weaves, knots, and motifs can take years of experience. By providing the basic terms in use, this section will, I hope, expedite the learning process and thus be helpful for prospective buyers, regardless of the type or period of rug they intend to purchase.

AFGHAN RUGS

Made by Afghani tribesmen, these high-quality woven rugs of geometric patterns are usually considered to be part of the Turkoman or Turkman group of rugs. They include octagonal guls (stylized rose motifs) and are predominantly red in color, although that red varies in density according to the various hues used by different tribes in different areas. The attractive "golden" Afghan rugs are the usual red ones that have been washed and washed until they become a distinctive ochre-to-apricot color.

ANATOLIAN RUGS

Turkish rugs from the Anatolian region of Turkey (formerly called Asia Minor) that are often just called "Anatolians" by dealers.

ANTIQUE ORIENTAL RUGS

These are the most prized of all Oriental rugs and carpets because they are always handmade and vegetable-dyed, with particularly mellow colors derived from their age. The rarest and finest examples can show as many as five hundred knots per square inch, as opposed to two hundred knots per square inch for a good-quality modern rug. Oriental rugs from Turkey and Persia (now Iran)—made from wool, camel's hair, silk, and finely spun cotton—started being exported to Europe in the Middle Ages; they were generally considered too rare and expensive to walk on and so were displayed on walls or tables long before they were placed on floors. They are especially prized if they are thin and made of silk. There is an old Persian saying, "The richer the man, the thinner the rug." Rugs are still being produced today following all the old designs and many of them are still handmade.

ANTIQUE OCCIDENTAL RUGS

The best of these are the old antique needlework rugs like the French tapestry-woven Aubussons and old wool Savonnerie carpets and rugs, although some of the old nineteenth-century Axminster weaves are real collector pieces. Since these rugs are very rare and very expensive, it is worth noting that there are some excellent Romanian, Portuguese, and Chinese copies of old needlework designs.

AREA RUG

Simply, the term for any form of portable rug, wherever and however it has been made. Area rugs are universally popular for their adaptability; for the color, texture, and pattern they can add to an otherwise spare-looking room; for their ability to create demarcation lines between various zones in a room; and for the softness they add to an otherwise hard floor.

AUBUSSON RUGS

French rugs and carpets originally woven in the town of Aubusson from the fifteenth century. They are woven like a tapestry and therefore have no pile. Motifs are variations of floral and scroll designs.

BALUCHI RUGS

Turkestan or Turkoman tribesmen's rugs from the region between the Caspian Sea and northwest China, which includes Turkmenistan, Uzbekistan, Afghanistan, and Pakistan. Baluchi rugs have geometric designs in rust reds with dark blue, bluish mauves, and occasional touches of camel or ivory.

BERBER RUGS

Like Berber carpets, Berber rugs are characterized by a dense, looped pile made from natural undyed sheep's wool. They are available in white, cream, fawn, beige, gray, and dark brown.

BESHIR RUGS

Turkoman rugs made by Beshir tribesmen in a geometric style similar to the Baluchi and with similar coloring, although they also use some yellow and green as well as the ubiquitous red.

BOKHARA RUGS

Short pile rugs made by nomadic Turkish tribes that are a deep blood-red color, often combined with dark blue, browns, creams, and black. Patterns vary with tribes, but Bokharas are one of the best known of the Turkestan rugs. (See also *nomadic rugs*.)

BOTEHS

Traditional Islamic geometric or stylized ovaloids used for rug designs.

CARPET

In Oriental and antique carpet terms, there is often confusion about what constitutes a *carpet* and what constitutes a *rug*. Internationally speaking, a carpet can be deemed to be over 40 square feet or 4 meters square, and a rug anything that is smaller, although the terms often tend to be interchangeable. In America, however, almost all handmade pieces are called rugs and machine-made pieces carpets. People in the trade, however, generally call all rugs carpets.

CAUCASIAN RUGS

Part of Russia, the Caucasus is between the Caspian and Black Seas. Over the centuries this harsh, mountainous area has housed many different nomadic tribes from Turkey, Armenia, and Persia (now Iran), which accounts for the ancient Caucasian rug-making heritage. Designs are always recti-linear or strongly geometric with stylized birds, animals, crabs, and insects reduced to straight lines as well as medallions. Borders generally consist of stars, rosettes, and stylized running-dog patterns. Caucasian rugs include high-quality weaves from rug-producing areas like Chazi, Daghestan Gendje, Hila, Karabagh, Kazak, Kuba, Shirvan, and Sumak.

CHINESE RUGS

Though the Chinese have been making asymmetrical knotted rugs in organized workshops for over two thousand years, they did not turn it into a real industry,

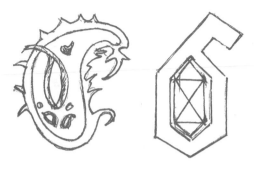

Botehs

Indian dhurrie

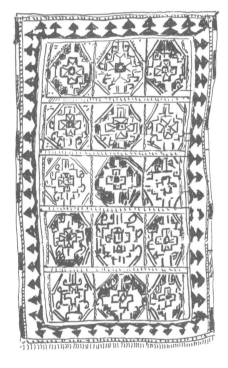

Kazak Caucasian rug

continuous designs around pillars, dragons, and flowers such as peonies, pomegranates, and the lotus. The pile is often cut or carved around the edge of a motif to give it greater emphasis.

DHURRIES

Flat woven wool rugs from India with stylized animal and geometric designs, usually in pale colors.

ETHNIC RUGS

These are produced in places as diverse as South Africa, Peru, Greece, Morocco, Ireland, the southwestern United States, Spain, Portugal, and Finland. Mostly, they fall into one of two well-known categories: dense, thick, woolen piles, such as the Finnish ryas and Greek flokatis; or the thick woolen weaves produced by the Irish, Spanish, Portuguese, and South

as it were, until the eighteenth century. In contrast to the shorter pile and mainly reddish color of Persian, Turkish, Caucasian, Turkoman, and Indian rugs, Chinese rugs make use of subtle blues, roses, yellows, peaches, and pale apricots, and have a longer pile and more give. They incorporate Buddhist and Taoist symbols as well as roundels,

 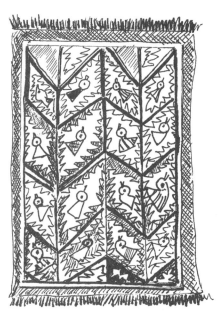

Three examples of ethnic rugs: a Greek cotton rug (above) and two
Peruvian rugs from Aycacucho, Peru (bottom).

Americans. Some other examples include the traditional cotton weaves from Morocco and Greece, along with American rag rugs, Indian dhurries, and the Navajo, New Mexican, and South American flat wool weaves.

FIELD

The "field" of a rug is its "ground," or central part, and is surrounded by a border of varying depth.

FLOORCLOTH

Good-sized squares or rectangles of heavy linen or canvas that are painted with designs, varnished, and used as rugs. If they are to be placed on a wood or hard floor they should be somehow fixed in place so that they will not be the cause of any slipping. Floorcloths have existed for centuries as an inexpensive but colorful substitute for a regular rug.

GARDEN RUGS

One of the most popular of the Persian floral-motif rugs and carpets. They are laid out in the form of stylized gardens, complete with paths, flowerbeds, streams, and pools.

GHIORDES KNOT

This knot is typically used in the manufacture of Turkish rugs. Short lengths of wool are knotted over two warp threads and then up between them. It is named after one of the major Turkish carpet-producing areas.

GULS

Traditional Islamic stylized rose motifs that are mostly octagonal and are much used in Oriental carpet designs.

HAND-KNOTTED RUGS

Good Oriental rugs and carpets, whether Islamic or Eastern, are hand-knotted and produced by knotting short lengths of wool around the warp threads of a loom. However, these

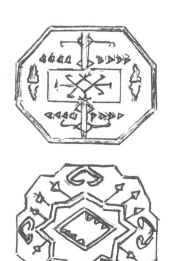

Guls

knots vary. Turkish rugs always make use of the *Ghiordes knot*. All good Persian wool rugs (although not the valuable silk ones) use the *Senneh knot* and Chinese rugs are made with an *asymmetric knot*. You can check to see whether a rug is definitely hand-knotted by parting the pile and looking to see if there are rows of knots at the base of the tufts. This is known as the "grin" test. Always examine the back as well. You should be able to trace the pattern.

HERAT

This Persian (now Iranian) carpet-making town produces what are considered to be the best of all Persian rugs. The rugs are generally identified by their medallion designs with central geometric motifs.

HERATI

Traditional Islamic geometric designs in the shape of a crossed diamond with a central stylized rose that is surrounded by stylized birds and leaves.

INDIAN RUGS

Most Indian rugs are woven in the Persian tradition, though they have a longer, somewhat coarser pile and other distinctive native characteristics. They were introduced to please the personal tastes of the various rajahs and merchants who set up workshops. Most of the Persian abstract designs were replaced with more realistic animals, flowers, and trees in lighter colors, which included the extensive use of a rosy pink color.

ISFAHAN

Another famous Persian (now Iranian) carpet or rug town that is known for its early figurative animal design rugs, often showing stylized hunting scenes.

JOSHAGAN

Persian (Iranian) rug-making town best known for its vase designs—formal floral designs with stylized vases holding plants or flowers.

KILIM, KELIM, OR KHILIM

A handwoven Oriental weft tapestry-woven rug that has no pile. Kilims are made in hugely varied designs and colors by weaving long threads in and out of the warp to cover it completely. There are still beautiful old Turkish

Herati

ones to be found. But, whether old or new, they are popular because they are generally both fairly reasonable to buy and highly decorative.

MIHRAB

The Moorish arch with pointed top is used as a design in these Persian and Turkish prayer rugs. In Turkish designs a lamp or ewer is often suspended from the arch, sometimes flanked by two pillars of wisdom. Other versions have Arabic script.

NAVAJO

These immensely attractive, strongly colored, Native American low-pile wool rugs are handwoven by the Navajo Indians in Arizona and New Mexico. Most of the prized older ones are woven in bold black, white, and gray geometric designs with red accents. Newer designs add other bright colors.

NOMADIC RUGS

These rugs are made in Persia (Iran), Turkey, the Caucasus, Turkmenistan,

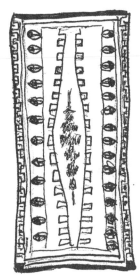
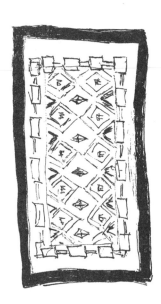

Navajo Rugs

Turkish nomadic rug

and India by nomadic tribesman as well as by village craftsmen. In many ways, they are as charming as, if not more so than, the intensely sophisticated designs woven by the master craftsmen.

NONSLIP UNDERLAYS

These are absolutely essential to use under all rugs, whether to prevent them from slipping on hard floors or to prevent them from wrinkling, or "creeping," when laid over carpet. A good choice is the slightly tacky netting that is sold and cut to size at good rug dealers.

PERSIAN (IRANIAN) RUGS

Persian rugs are believed to have been woven in much the same way for over a thousand years. However, it is hard to find anything extant earlier than the mid-fifteenth century. (A rare exception is the so-called Altei rug, which was found in southern Siberia in the grave of a warrior prince and is dated to some 500 years before Christ. Preserved deep-frozen until the 1940s, when it was found, the rug can be seen in the Hermitage Museum in St. Petersburg.) Persian rugs are almost always rectangular, or at least elongated, rather than square and woven in wool (with the exception of the highly prized silk rugs) with the *Senneh* knot. The majority of designs are based on stylized floral motifs in garden or vase designs, although there are also some figurative animal designs and geometric medallion pieces, as well as the *mihrab* prayer rugs. The Persians were actually the only Muslim people who, being mostly Shiite as opposed to Sunni

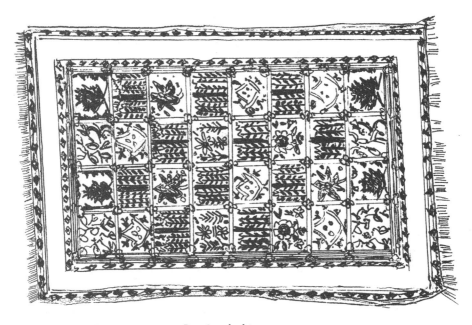

Persian baktyar rug

Muslims, were able to eschew the Koranic prohibition against the depiction of people or animals and use realistic figurative and animal designs. The coloring was and is very rich, often with a central field of crimson, indigo, or a warm golden buff, with figures in browns, greens, and yellows. Very rare rugs made before the eighteenth century are generally classified according to their designs; rugs made after the eighteenth century have always been called by the towns where they are made, such as Herat (considered to be the very best), Heriz, Joshaghan, Keshan, Qum, Shiraz, or Tabriz.

SENNEH KNOT

The knot used by Persian (Iranian) weavers—the pile yarns are tied over one warp thread and under the second.

TURKISH RUGS

Rugs from Turkey were popular in Europe long before the Persian variety. In fact, up until the eighteenth century any hand-knotted rugs or carpets, whatever their design, were called "Turkey Work." Since most of the rugs come from the Anatolia region of Turkey, they are often called "Anatolians" by dealers. They differ

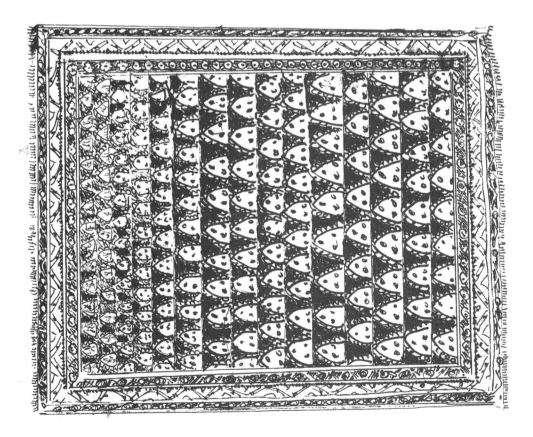

Sine Persian rug

quite sharply from Persian rugs, not just in their designs and colors, but in the special knot used called the *Ghiordes*. This knot was invented in and named after one of the leading weaving areas where the finest rugs are produced. Turkish rugs also have a somewhat longer pile than Persian rugs. Background colors are mainly red or blue, although Turkish prayer rugs are sometimes woven in the sacred color, green. Since most Turks are Sunni Muslims, they observe the Koranic prohibition against the depiction of people and animals more strictly than the Shiite Muslims. Most of their designs, therefore, are based on geometric motifs and frequently incorporate pointed prayer arches or mihrab designs at one end. Sometimes the arches are flanked by pillars of wisdom, or have holy lamps hanging from the center. The more sophisticated workshops elaborate the designs with Arabic script. The major rug-producing areas include Bergama, Ghiordes, Hereke, Kula, Kum-Kapu, Mudjur, Panderma, Ushak, and Yuruk.

TURKOMAN *OR* TURKMAN RUGS

Rugs from the great stretch of land between the Caspian Sea and northwest China. This huge area includes Turkmenistan, Uzbekistan, Afghanistan, and Pakistan and, like the Russian Caucasus, is known for the high-quality weaves of the various nomadic tribes. Turkoman rug weavers, although widely dispersed, all use a similar geometric style—usually the octagonal *gul*, or stylized rose motif—and many shades of red as their dominant color.

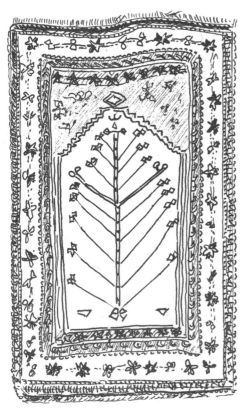

Turkish Yuruk prayer niche design

STYLES AND MOVEMENTS

What does it mean to be modern? To be modern is not a fashion. It is a state. It is necessary to understand history, and he who understands history knows how to find continuity between that which was, that which is and that which will be.

Le Corbusier (1887–1965)

Architecture, design, and decorating trends are inevitably cyclical. Old forms are continually recycled, refined, revitalized, and reinterpreted in different ways in different countries and in different centuries—and sometimes, in as quickly as decades. The ancient, therefore, can become the avant-garde with surprising regularity. There is no knowing when, and from what part of the world, some obscure motif or ancient reference may be resurrected and turned into a new fashion or transformed into a wholly different style or object.

To prove this, you have only to look carefully at old frescoes in museums that have been removed intact from archeological explorations. Or, examine furnishings in the backgrounds of Renaissance religious and eighteenth- and nineteenth-century genre paintings, as well as the illustrations in books about various periods of architecture, furniture, and interiors. You might well be surprised, if you have not observed it before, at the similarities and regurgitations of various themes throughout the centuries, dating back to the very earliest recorded times.

It is of course tempting to identify, label, and date various design styles and movements as if they all began and ended within nicely defined eras in defined geographical areas. And many dedicated Modernists act as if all styles predating the Modern movement are long since dead and buried—with the possible exception of Postmodernism, whose practitioners made much use of Classical idioms. In fact, although each period and century do appear to have their own "look," and certainly revivalism in one form or another is always with us, it is also quite possible to see, from the vantage point of the twenty-first century, that all of the various styles and movements are part of a living continuity branching off here and there and resulting in new and different strains. Given this, it is more accurate to point out that the clearly continuing vitality and interweaving of Classical architectural and design themes form more of a fertile garden than a graveyard of retired relics.

AESTHETIC MOVEMENT

A late-nineteenth-century, East-to-West, predominantly British and American movement. Though it had no counterpart in Europe, it is increasingly apparent that it had great and wide-ranging influence on decoration during the second half of the twentieth century and the beginning of the twenty-first century. In reaction to the over-crowded and over-opulent Victorian style, the emphasis was on maximum light, comfort, and informality with whites, grays, and pale, pale colors. Japanese symbols were popular motifs, as well as stylized sunflowers, peacocks, and lilies. It was inspired partly by the Queen Anne Revival and mostly by the new cult of the Japanese aesthetic, which almost certainly was first derived from the impressive collection of Japanese art and artifacts amassed by Sir Rutherford Alcock, the first British minister in Japan, that was shown at the International Exhibition in London in 1862. Another vigorous Japanese proponent was, surprisingly, William Burges (1827–1881), the neo-Medieval Gothic architect, and, not least, Arthur Lazenby Liberty, founder of his eponymous store, Liberty in Regent Street, London. This cult of the Japanese was given a further fillip by the exhibition of a rendition of the then Prince of Wales's morning room, which was decorated by the American painter James McNeill · Whistler and furnished with Anglo-Japanese pieces designed by Edward William Godwin (1833–1886). Whistler and Godwin's partnership produced many beautiful rooms, including those for Oscar Wilde in 1885. One such room in the Wilde home was decorated in various tones of white, considered hugely avant-garde and quite unthinkable only a few years before.

AMERICAN COLONIAL STYLE

A style originally developed by Europeans in their colonies, but then especially applied to, first of all, the southern states of America with adapted Renaissance and Neoclassical elements, as can be seen in so many elegant pre–Civil War mansions. After the eighteenth century the style developed in America according to personal taste. However, early American Colonial style on the eastern seaboard was based on the houses and furnishings of the much more homely late-sixteenth- and early-seventeenth-century British Commonwealth period, with a good leavening of German, Dutch, and Scandinavian folk art. This early period was manifestly a time for "making do" with simple imported furniture, primitive local work, and plain, sturdy architecture. As villages grew into towns and towns into cities the style evolved into the lovely late-eighteenth-century houses and furniture achieved when the federal government was established—thus the name Federal style. Generalized American Colonial evokes the same white clapboard and shutters, charming porticoes, and wraparound porches that the early British Colonial style evokes. But it also comprises dark painted floors, furniture, and hutches that were the contribution of German, Dutch, and Scandinavian settlers, as well as some of the most beautiful eighteenth- and nineteenth-century domestic architecture and furniture.

AMERICAN SOUTHWEST

Sometimes called Santa Fe style, it is an amalgam of Spanish and Native American influences and the American Colonial style. Hallmarks include adobe walls, rough-hewn furniture, Navajo rugs, and brightly colored Native American textile designs.

ART DECO, JAZZ MODERNE, OR ART MODERNE

A style of decorative furniture, furnishings, and architecture that flourished in Europe, America, and the antipodes from just before World War I through the 1930s. In a way, and in France especially, it had its roots in Neoclassicism, with its fluted columns, festoons, baskets of chunky fruit and flowers, inset relief panels showing Classical or allegorical themes, and its geometric emphasis. But, with the new energy engendered by the arrival of the motor car, and the emphasis on speed and power, the style started to employ symbols of the new machine age, often alongside natural motifs such as stylized waves or an idealized, muscular human body, whether male or female. Art Deco was, in fact, a kind of litmus paper style, absorbing every new fashion, interest, and discovery. It became increasingly decorative in the 1920s when it blossomed into all sorts

of other shapes carried out in exotically luxurious materials, inspired by Aztec, Egyptian, Mayan, and African art, as well as Léon Bakst's costumes and décor for the Russian ballet. The French decorator and furniture designer Jacques-Emile Ruhlmann was an outstanding exponent of the style and used tortoiseshell, ivory, lapis, shagreen, and lizard skin with abandon. André Groult, another Frenchman, was also a much-admired Deco decorator and craftsman, as was Jean Dunand, who worked in metal and lacquer as well as silver leaf. The English designer Eileen Gray, who had settled in Paris, was another significant Deco designer, although she actually prefigured Modernism and later the International style, as did Robert Mallet-Stevens, Pierre Chareau, and Jean-Michel Frank, who worked so much in the United States.

ART NOUVEAU

An architectural and furnishings style fashionable on both sides of the Atlantic from roughly the 1890s to World War I. It was known for its sinuous lines and vegetal motifs and was one of the first styles to owe virtually nothing to historical precedent, except, perhaps, for some of its rocaillelike motifs. Also, as with the Rococo style, the essence of the ideal Art Nouveau concept was to synthesize architecture, decoration, and furnishings·into one indivisible unity. The movement derived its name, at least in the United States, France, and Britain, from an innovative shop in

Paris on the Rue de Provence called Salon de l'Art Nouveau owned by Siegfried ("Samuel") Bing. Originally a dealer in Oriental art from Hamburg in Germany, he sold Modern art and objects, particularly the glass and leaded lamps by Louis Comfort Tiffany (whose work had particularly impressed him when he had visited the World's Columbian Exposition of 1893 in Chicago) and the glasswork of Emile Gallé. In other countries, the style was called by different names: *Jugendstil* in Germany, *Sezessionstil* in Austria, and *Il Liberty* or *lo stile Liberty* in Italy (the latter after Arthur Lazenby Liberty's shop in London). The first architects to create fully evolved Art Nouveau domestic interiors were the Belgian Victor Horta in Brussels and the American Louis Henry Sullivan in Chicago. Sullivan somehow managed to create curious tangles of tendrils, coral reef growths, and cabbagelike leaves within his severely functionalist buildings without any known contact with his European counterparts. Another Belgian, Henry van de Velde, created a rather more abstract version of an Art Nouveau interior for his own house outside Brussels, and Samuel Bing, who had seen it, invited Van de Velde to design four rooms for his Paris store, which evoked as much of a storm of criticism as it did enthusiasm. Other particularly distinguished exponents of the style, each with their own variations, were the Spaniard Antoní Gaudí, the Scots Charles Rennie Mackintosh and Mackay Hugh Baillie Scott; and the Viennese Secession architects Josef

Casa Batiló (1904), Barcelona, by Antoní Gaudí

Hoffmann, Joseph Maria Olbrich, and Otto Wagner. The Viennese architects preferred the unique mixture of functionalism, austerity, and elegance characteristic of the work of Charles Rennie Mackintosh over the somewhat more languid French and Belgian versions and that of the Dutch architect Hendrick Berlage.

ARTS AND CRAFTS MOVEMENT

A late-nineteenth- to early-twentieth-century movement, again popular on both sides of the Atlantic, that aimed to eschew the hitherto prevalent Historicism as well as shoddy mass-production methods and to return to the individually crafted furnishings of the past. In Britain, egalitarian movement though it was, its products were too expensive for the masses to buy. Although, ironically, companies like Liberty and Sanderson in the United Kingdom have been producing the fabric and wallpaper designs ever since. In the United Kingdom the Arts and Crafts movement was promulgated first by the architects C. R. Ashbee and W. R. Letharby, then taken up by William Morris, the poet, designer, and theorist whose name is synonymous with the movement, as well as the architect Philip Webb, who designed Morris's now famous Red House at Bexleyheath, Sussex. Other architects and designers of the movement were Charles F. A. Voysey and the cabinetmakers Ernest Grimson and the Barnsley brothers. The Red House became a symbol of the movement because Webb eschewed all references to Classicism and put his own homely spin on a mix of the asymmetrical Tudor, Elizabethan, and Restoration styles, which he thought were the last purely English architectural expressions. In the United States the movement centered around two main styles or schools: the Mission style and the Prairie School of Frank Lloyd Wright, based on his designs for outer suburban housing in Chicago. The Mission style actually originated in California when the congregation of a Franciscan mission church in San Francisco, unable to afford furniture for the church, started to make their own chairs to replace the old and battered pews. A decorator, Dora Martin, saw them and was so impressed she sent one of the simple rush-seated chairs to Joseph McHugh, a furniture manufacturer in New York City. The style also expanded to take in the heavy Native American–style furniture made under the aegis of various other missions, all of which became known collectively as Mission furniture. However, the most respected producer of the style was Gustav Stickley, who visited Europe in 1898, became a disciple of William Morris and the writer and art critic John Ruskin, and, on his return, set up the Craftsman Workshops to take up the manufacture of Mission furniture. Stickley made oak pieces with strong, straight, rectilinear lines and with rush or leather seats. The furniture became so popular it was distributed throughout the States. Stickley's magazine, *The Craftsman*, proceeded to become the mouthpiece of the American Arts and Crafts movement between 1901 and 1916. Other exponents of the style were the members of the Roycroft Community, whose founder was Elbert Hubbard, the publisher of the magazine *Philistine*. Roycroft furniture was also usually made from oak, although sometimes ash and mahogany were used. It, too, was plain, with prominent mortise-and-tenon joints and tapering legs ending in rounded feet. Frank Lloyd Wright was a founder member of the Arts and Crafts movement in Chicago, where he and other designers, who had adopted Wright's so-called Prairie School style, produced clean, simple designs deliberately suited, unlike the British Arts and Crafts products, to machine production. Wright did not share Morris's abhorrence for the machine; he only disliked machines when they were used to perform "nonmechanical" tasks, such as carving.

BAROQUE

An architecture and design style of the seventeenth and early eighteenth centuries in Europe, particularly in Italy, Spain, Germany, and Austria, as well as in France and Britain. It was based on Classicism but is characterized by an exuberant decoration of furniture and interior details and a delight in the grandeur of large-scale architecture, sweeping vistas, and a certain amount of Mannerist allusion. The term *Baroque* is thought to have been derived from a mixture of the French word *baroque*, meaning odd, curious, or bizarre, and the Portugese word *barroco*, meaning a large, irregular pearl. The Italian sculptor, architect, and painter Gian Lorenzo Bernini—who designed most of the seventeenth-century additions and alterations to St. Peter's and the Vatican in Rome, as well as the unused plans for an extension to the Louvre in Paris—was a great Baroque architect. Louis Le Vau, the main architect of Versailles for Louis XIV, is not only synonymous with Baroque architecture but also with Baroque furniture and decoration, as are Sir Christopher Wren, Nicholas Hawksmoor, Sir John Vanbrugh, and Thomas Archer in Britain. These latter architects, however, tend to be known as Baroque Classicists since their more restrained work tended to be particularly tempered by Classical elements.

BAUHAUS

The twentieth-century German school of design, founded in 1919 by Walter Gropius, based on the former Weimer School of Arts & Crafts headed by Henry van de Velde, whom Gropius was asked to succeed. On taking over Gropius reorganized and reoriented the curriculum and renamed the school *das Staatliches Bauhaus* (shortened to just the Bauhaus), declaring unequivocally that artists and craftsmen were inseparable, and that craftsmanship was the main source of creative design. He went on to advocate a balanced education in stoneworking, carpentry, metalwork, furniture-making, textile weaving, construction technique, and the theory of space, color, and design. These thoughts were not so far removed from great architects of the past, such as Donato Bramante, Louis Le Vau, and Robert Adam, who all depended on the ability of craftsmen in all specialties to realize and to perfect their ideas. However, the Bauhaus also stressed that function was as much if not more important than form, and that most ornament was extraneous. Apart from Gropius, famous alumni of the school were László Moholy-Nagy, Marcel Breuer, Paul Klee, Mies van der Rohe, and Wassily Kandinsky. The school was comparatively short lived because it had to be disbanded in the face of Nazi power in 1933, but it turned out to be the most powerful single influence in the development and general acceptance of Modern design. In 1925, the Bauhaus moved from Weimer to Dessau and the new office building that Gropius designed became a model for the contemporary "dateless" look that was the epitome of The International Style that followed.

BEAUX ARTS

The late-nineteenth-century and early-twentieth-century American equivalent of the Renaissance Revival popular in Europe and the United States at much the same time. It was named after the École des Beaux-Arts in Paris, where many of its architectural exponents were trained. With the rapid growth of wealth in the United States, numerous new mansions were built that combined modern technology and creature comforts with the appearance and details of French chateaux, Italian palazzi, and Tudor, Elizabethan, and Jacobean manor houses, all considered off-shoots of the Renaissance.

BELLE ÉPOQUE

French name for the opulent and glamorous period between the 1890s and World War I, the equivalent of the Edwardian period and the Queen Anne Revival in the United States and Britain, when, for the rich, life was supposed to have been better than it had ever been.

BIEDERMEIER

An Austrian, German, and Scandinavian decorative style, known as "the poor man's Empire," which was popular with the middle class from the 1820s to the 1840s (and again today). *Biedermeier* was actually the name for a cartoon depiction of the "common man" (as, for example, Uncle Sam.) It was, therefore, an aptly appropriated nomenclature for furniture that was not only a lighter and more attractive replacement for the more grandiose Empire style, but also considerably more affordable. Simple and graceful, Biedermeier furniture was made of mostly golden-hued wood like pearwood, maplewood, and cherry, with black-stained, or ebonylike, ornamentation. This was a matter of some importance, because the Napoleonic Wars and the Continental Blockade had pretty well impoverished most of central Europe and Scandinavia as well as depleted the supply of expensive materials. The decoration, too, was much less heavy and ornamented, and colors and patterns on walls and windows were brighter and lighter than the heavy and more imposing Empire decoration that had gone before.

BRITISH COLONIAL STYLE

A style developed in the West Indies, India, the East, Australia, and parts of Africa by British Colonials in the eighteenth and early nineteenth centuries. It was based on Georgian architecture, interiors, and furniture interpreted by indigenous craftsmen and builders in native woods and

A Biedermeier room, Palace of Capodimonte, Naples, ca. 1820

materials with adaptations to the much less temperate climate. There were also un-Georgianlike additions, such as verandas and balconies. Just the name evokes the thought of stiflingly hot weather, white-painted clapboard, handsome porticoes and pillars, louvered shutters, mosquito nets, rattan, white muslin ceiling fans, and bare polished floorboards.

BRUTALISM *OR* NEW BRUTALISM

A British term that was coined in the 1950s to describe the style used by Le Corbusier for his buildings in Marseille, France, and Chandigarh, India, as well as the style of his

followers at the time, such as Paul Rudolph and Louis Kahn in the United States; Maekawa and Kenzo Tange in Japan; Vittoriano Vigano in Milan, Italy; and Stirling & Gowan and the Smythsons in Britain. Buildings were mostly faced in rough concrete, known as *Beton Brut*, with an exaggerated emphasis on big, chunky members—a total contrast to the elegantly smooth structures of Mies van der Rohe and his followers.

BYZANTINE ARCHITECTURE AND DESIGN

The apotheosis of early Orthodox Christian art and architecture, which formed an amazingly sophisticated bridge between the achievements of imperial Rome and the considerably less civilized Middle Ages. It is fascinating because it showed a refinement and sense of luxury that was light years ahead of most of the rest of the world except for the Far East. The style developed after 330 B.C., when the Roman Emperor Constantine established his Imperial capital in the East in the city of Byzantium on the Bosphorus, which he renamed Constantinople (now Istanbul). The city remained the center of the Eastern or Greek Empire until it was sacked by the Turks in the fifteenth century. Over the centuries, the traditional Roman forms insisted on by Constantine were overlaid by Near Eastern motifs. The Classical orders were no longer observed and the already-lavish traditions of the Hellenistic and Roman worlds were mixed with the refinement, luxury, and opulence of the Orient to create a new, original, and highly sybaritic style. There are no wholly extant examples of Byzantine domestic architecture and interior design, though excavations have shown that the imperial palace in Constantinople must have been an extraordinary building, as does what is left of Byzantine buildings on the outskirts of the Byzantine Empire in, for example, Sicily, Spain, and Venice, as well as Greece. Much, too, can be learned from descriptions in contemporary literature, particularly from the tenth century. However, the Haghia Sophia, in Constantinople, built in 532–37 A.D. and designed by

Anthemius of Trallies and Isidore of Miletus, is probably the outstanding masterpiece of Byzantine ecclesiastical architecture. As it happened, one of the designers, Anthemius, was also a notable mathematician who believed that architecture was the application of geometry to solid matter. And since mathematics was considered the highest of the sciences at that time, the church was prized as much for its mathematical and intellectual qualities as for the sense of mystery created by the non-Classical play of light and dark, void and solid. "Through the harmony of its measurements it is distinguished by indescribable beauty," wrote Procopius, the Greek historian (ca. 490–ca. 562 A.D.). Little by little, symbolism began to play a greater part in Byzantine church architecture, expressed in lavish painted or mosaic decoration where numbers and even colors had a special significance. And to the Byzantine these intellectual concepts were as important as the air of mystery created by the screens and galleries dividing off the surrounding spaces from the well-lit central area.

CAROLEAN STYLE
OR RESTORATION STYLE

English Baroque architecture, design, and furniture current in the period between 1666 and 1688 in England during the reign of Charles II, and important to America because of the influence of Christopher Wren, the chief architect of the time. It is also known as the Restoration, or late Stuart period, and was the interlude between two great Palladian Revivals, the one introduced by Inigo Jones and the other reintroduced in the early eighteenth century by Colen Campbell, Lord Burlington, and William Kent. After the privations of the Commonwealth period under Oliver Cromwell, when very little new building was done because of the general lack of money (Sir Roger Verney noted in his diary, "Of all my acquaintance there is scarce an honest man that is not in a borrowing condition"), the reign of Charles II brought a whole new gusto to building and decoration. The man in the forefront of this recovery, Christopher Wren, had been deeply impressed on a visit to Paris by the high quality of French craftsmanship, which inspired him to train his own craftsmen in various skills. Thanks to the introduction of a new, harder, and quick-drying plasterwork called *stucco duro*, Elizabethan and Jacobean interiors had already attained new heights of splendor. (*Stucco duro* replaced the old Tudor mixture of lime and plaster of paris.) Wood carving under the master carver Grinling Gibbons reached unequaled standards of perfection, prompting homebuilders to concentrate on improving staircase balustrades, chimneypieces, overdoors, and paneling. Stamped leather hangings were popular, and wall and ceiling paintings started to be used, as well as portraits hung in elaborate frames. Silver-encased furniture, or silvered wood, and other decorative furniture incorporating several different woods and sometimes tortoiseshell was in demand, as were mirrors. At this time, too, the East India

Company had just started to import the Oriental painted silks, lacquerwork, and blue-and-white porcelain that would become its signature.

CHICAGO SCHOOL

The style of commercial architecture that began in 1883 with the introduction of steel framing by William Jenney (1832–1907)—with whom Louis Henry Sullivan first worked—led to the first steel-skeleton construction for skyscrapers over twelve or so floors (then called "elevator buildings"). The pioneering Holabird & Roche's Tacoma building (1887–88) had twenty-two floors and was based on a complete steel skeleton. This was quickly followed by others. Of particular note was Sullivan's Wainwright building in St. Louis, Missouri, and his Carson, Pirie and Scott Store (1899–1904) in Chicago, which was executed with unrelieved verticals and horizontals with no references to historicism, but with Art Nouveau ornament.

CHINOISERIE

European evocations of Chinese motifs—such as pagodas, cranes, wooden bridges, dragons, and exotic birds—that were highly fashionable in the late seventeenth and early eighteenth centuries and during the Rococo period. The taste for Chinese silks, porcelain, lacquerwork, and hand-painted wallpapers, as well as items from Japan and India, swept Europe and the American colonies in the seven-

Handpainted Chinese wallpaper at
Nostell Priory, ca. 1750

Chinese Chippendale breakfast table,
from the *Gentleman and Cabinet
Maker's Director*, 1754

teenth and eighteenth centuries after trade had begun with the Far East through the Dutch East India Company. The demand was so high that European companies, and later the American equivalents, started to make imitations, or as they were called, "chinoiseries."

CLASSICAL ARCHITECTURE *OR* CLASSICISM

The style based on the disciplined lines, mathematical laws of proportion, Classical orders, and ornamentation of ancient Roman and Greek architecture. Classicism was revived during the Italian Renaissance, based upon the rediscovered writings of Vitruvius, an ancient Roman architect and architectural theorist. Various forms of Classicism have woven in and out of the centuries ever since. The style is characterized by symmetry and

balance, geometric forms, clean lines, and Classical architectural details like columns, pilasters, and pediments. Recurring motifs include laurel wreaths, acanthus leaves, and anthemion (Greek honeysuckle). (See also *Neoclassicism*.)

COMMONWEALTH STYLE

Severely plain style of architecture favored in the seventeenth-century puritanical and so-called Commonwealth period in Britain and also used by the first English settlers on the East Coast of America. Mostly through necessity and partly through conviction, the settlers kept their buildings and furnishings as simple and utilitarian as possible. Their inspiration, if it could be called inspiration, was the vernacular, late-medieval architecture—with its unadorned plain interiors, whitewashed plastered walls, exposed beams, and doors made of vertical boards—still used in East Anglia, the windy East Coast of England.

CONSTRUCTIVISM

In architecture this was not so much a movement as an influential ideology that had its birth in early 1920s Russia. In brief, Constructivist architects believed in designing functionally effective buildings in a utilitarian spirit with both a respect for building materials and the knowledge of how best to use them. It was embraced by the De Stijl movement through El Lissitsky, one of its great apostles, and was absorbed by the Bauhaus and then disseminated through its teachings .

DE STIJL

Name of a group of avant-garde Dutch architects and designers founded in 1917 by the Dutch architectural theorist Theo Van Doesburg. Other members included Gerrit Rietveld and the painter Piet Mondrian, whose theories on color, line, and abstraction dominated the group, although it was also much influenced by the work of Frank Lloyd Wright in the United States. The group was named after a contemporary magazine of the same name, which simply meant "the style." The group had a significant influence on early Modernists in other countries, who much admired Rietveld's seminal Schroder House in Utrecht, with its clean-cut surfaces and metal-framed windows in continuous strips that ran up to ceilings devoid of moldings.

The group was later joined by the Russian painter, architect, and designer El Lissitsky, the apostle of Constructivism, which added another dimension to the group's philosophy.

DECONSTRUCTIVISM

Late 1980s movement based on the assumption that architecture is a language "amenable to the methods of linguistic philosophy." Philip Johnson organized a Deconstructivist exhibition at the Museum of Modern Art in New York in 1988 with designs by, among others, the Austrian group Coop Himmelblau, Peter Eisenman, Zaha Hadid, Daniel Libeskind, Rem Koolhaus's OMA (Office for Metropolitan Architecture), and Bernard Tschumi (the first, together with the linguistic philosopher, Jacques Derida, to explore the Deconstructive concept of dissociation). The exhibitors used words like disruption, dislocation, and distortion, and they were apparently not concerned with the fragmentation or the taking apart of constructions. In any event, not too many Deconstructivist structures have been built, with the exceptions of Eisenman's Wexner Center for the Visual Arts in Columbus, Ohio (1986) and Zaha Hadid's Vitra Firehouse in Weil am Rhein, Germany (1993).

DEUTSCHER WERKBUND

German movement founded in 1907 in Munich and inspired by the architect Peter Behrens, as an association between avant-garde manufacturers, architect, artists, and writers. It was similar to a slightly earlier movement, founded in Dresden in 1898, called the Deutsche Werkstatten. The laudable aim of both was to create a national art with no particular stylistic imitation, which would be based on sound production methods and the cooperation of artisan, artist, and architect. The two movements were not unlike the Arts and Crafts movement in Britain and America—apart from the fact that the German ones were rather more democratic—or Le Manufacture Royale des Maubles des Couronne (The Royal Factory for the Crown Furnishings) started by Louis XIII to concentrate France's decorative arts. (Louis XIV took over the project and amalgamated it in 1662 with the tapestry factory started by the Gobelin family and the Savonnerie carpet factory. He bought them both for the express purpose of expanding from furniture, textiles, silver- and metalwork, and woodcarving in order to create a French national art as well as a major furnishing and accessory source for his Palace of Versailles. It was directed by Charles Lebrun, the brilliant Baroque designer.) The German Werkbund, nearly 250 years later, was similarly influential, but with the vast middle classes rather than with the aristocratic elite. Their 1914 exhibition in Cologne, just before World War I, included buildings by Walter Gropius and the Belgian Modernist architect, Henry van de Velde. Its post-war experimental housing in Stuttgart in 1927 was supervised by Mies van der Rohe and included buildings by Le Corbusier and the Dutch architect Mart Stam. By that time, though, Gropius had appropriated its ideas for the Bauhaus and the Werkbund tailed to an end in 1934.

DIRECTOIRE

The style current in France in the last five years of the eighteenth century between the assassination of Louis XVI and the coup d'état of Napoleon Bonaparte. In fact, it was very little different from its forerunner, the simple and elegant Louis XVI style, but everything was produced with somewhat inferior materials because of the poverty induced by the Revolution.

EDWARDIAN

A style named after Edward VII and more or less the same period in Britain and the United States as the Belle Époque in France (between the 1890s and World War I). Designs were much lighter and airier than the Victorian decoration and building that had gone before. Sometimes known as the "age of sweetness and light," the period also encompasses the Aesthetic, Arts and Crafts, Art Nouveau, and Queen Anne Revival movements. The cozy country houses designed by Edwin Lutyens, Norman Shaw, Charles F. A. Voysey, and Philip Webb during this period were much emulated in the United States, Australia, and New Zealand.

ELIZABETHAN

The period during the reign of Elizabeth I (from 1558 to 1603). The period was one of great British prosperity, so there was an increased demand for more domestic architecture and furnishings; new houses were built throughout the country, and many of them still stand proudly. The style was idiosyncratic and somewhat muttlike in that it was largely based on Italian Renaissance forms as translated from the French and particularly Flemish versions. It was also united to the last of the late Gothic with its emphasis on very large windows with mullions and transoms, plus the adoption of the Netherlandish fashion for strap work for ceilings, with much carving and inlay. Houses were often E- or H-shaped and gables, either straight or curved as in the Netherlands, were frequent. Brick was used as well as half-timbering, and houses had dominant chimney stacks. Inside small wood panels were combined with pilasters and columns. In low-ceilinged rooms the paneling rose from the baseboards to a primitive cornice. In grander houses, an oak dado was surmounted by a molding, then paneling, and finally an entablature.

EMPIRE

Early-nineteenth-century style during the reign of Napoleon in France (1804–15) and a little later in the United States. Designs were partly derived from the Neoclassical with an emphasis on Imperial Rome, partly upon Egyptian details brought back by Napoleon's army from the Egyptian campaigns, and partly on the discoveries of the ruins at Pompeii and Herculaneum in Italy. Charles Percier and Pierre-François-Leonard Fontaine, architects and designers to the Emperor Napoleon, were chiefly responsible for both finessing the style and spreading it to a much wider audience than the upper echelons of society, who were hitherto the beneficiaries of any new design thought. They achieved this through their enormously influential, beautifully illustrated, and somewhat self-serving book *Receuil de decorations interieures*, which was published from 1801 in installments and in a single volume in 1812. In the post-Revolutionary United States, where the spirit that had produced the French Revolution was much admired (and where the French, in an effort to increase trade, had reduced tariffs), the new French style was equally embraced. The style encompassed much of the same Greek, Roman, and Egyptian motifs, with the ubiquitous appearance of the American bald eagle along with lion's-paw feet, sphinxes, and heavier mahogany furniture.

FEDERAL STYLE

American architecture and design style from the late 1780s until the early nineteenth century. It is fair to say that the Federal style in general was mainly based on the French take on Neoclassicism, although it did undoubtedly follow English precedents as well. Nevertheless, the resulting amalgam was uniquely American. Duncan Phyfe, one of the most gifted furniture designers of the period in America, certainly proved this point.

Early Federal house,
Charleston, South
Carolina, ca. 1800,
with added portico,
ca. 1850

Federal wood-framed and -clad
house, ca. 1820

Opulent Federal interior,
Charleston, South Carolina,
ca. 1816

He drew his inspirations from the French Directoire period as well as from the furniture designs of Thomas Sheraton and George Hepplewhite, and a little later from the forms of the early Empire in France as well as the early Regency in England. But the furniture he finally produced himself was subtly different and elegantly *American*. In general, the influence of the French Directoire period was especially clear in the designs of chairs and couches. Made from mahogany, their backs, sides, arms and legs were concave with saber-shaped curves. Federal rooms also reflected the abundant new choice of French wallpapers and fabrics.

GEORGIAN

The term applied to British (and American, until the Revolution) architecture and design during the reigns of George I, II, III, and IV—a long period that went from 1714 to 1830, paralleling, at its start, the Palladian Revival, and at its tail end, Neoclassicism and the Picturesque movement. The style is divided into Early, Mid, and Late Georgian, and Regency. Sometimes called "the Age of Elegance," it was certainly the golden age of British and American design in every field. Early Georgian coincided with a return to Classical ideals that was promoted by the Palladian Revival. The chief designer of this group was William Kent, who was the first English architect to design furniture specifically for houses. Mahogany replaced walnut as the basic material for furniture and the graceful Queen Anne–style furniture continued to be produced, though in a modified form. For example, the tall, hoop-backed chair was replaced by a square-backed design with straight but tapered decorated legs. By the end of the eighteenth century, the development of Georgian furniture styles depended heavily on a handful of outstanding architects and cabinet-makers. The Neoclassical style imported from France, which began around the 1760s, was in many ways personified in Britain by Robert Adam, who designed houses from the outside in and designed romantically elegant furniture with marquetry and inlays of satinwood and fruitwoods. Adam-style furniture was never very popular in America because Adam only designed for his powerful patrons and did not produce pattern books that could be copied, as did Chippendale, Hepplewhite, and Sheraton. In fact, Duncan Phyfe was so adept at reinterpreting Sheraton's ideas in his own inimitable way that American Sheraton

furniture came to be called Phyfe-style, just as the Federal period was sometimes called the Phyfe period. By the end of the Georgian era lowboys and highboys began to give way to waist-high dressers or bureaus and many more side tables and consoles.

GOTHIC

Medieval architectural and particularly ecclesiastical style from approximately 1200 to 1500, typified by the use of the pointed arch along with rib vaults,

The library at Strawberry Hill, Twickenham, near London, designed for writer Horace Walpole by Richard Bentley (completed 1754). The unique style of architecture created was internationally known as Strawberry Hill Gothic.

Fretwork for a Gothic Revival house in Connecticut

trefoils, high airy spaces, and flying buttresses. Its last phase, between the 1330s and 1530s, was known as the Perpendicular phase, as opposed to the earlier Medieval Gothic, mostly because of its much-emphasized vertical elements. Like Classicism, it is one of the great influences, weaving in and out of other centuries and styles. Much sixteenth- and seventeenth-century building work is Gothic in some detail or other. Gothic Revival (sometimes known as "Strawberry Hill Gothic" after Horace Walpole's fanciful house) started in the second part of the eighteenth century as an antidote to both the coldness and purity of Classical architecture and the excesses of the Rococo, and led to the Picturesque and Romantic movements. In the early nineteenth century, the somewhat exaggerated, perhaps rather tongue-in-cheek, Regency Gothic style appeared, often known as "Gothick." And finally the seriously academic Victorian version of Gothic surfaced in the 1840s; Pugin's facade for the British Houses of Parliament is a fine example, as are many municipal American, antipodal, and European buildings.

GREEK REVIVAL

Late-eighteenth- and early-nineteenth-century style of architecture that embraced Classical Greek models rather than Renaissance or Roman forms. It was at its height in Britain, France, and Germany in the 1790s and early 1800s and was popular in the United States from around 1820 to 1840. Doric-columned facades became practically de rigueur for official buildings as well as for handsome houses. Domestically, staircases became much lighter in form than hitherto, with splendid curves and slender stair rails. Painted, papered, and fabric-covered walls replaced paneling and were accompanied by handsome plaster cornices and marble mantelpieces.

GUSTAVIAN

Charming, late-eighteenth-century, Swedish Neoclassical style named after Gustavus III (1771–1792), who turned the Swedish court into a kind of northern Versailles. Interestingly, Sweden and Russia were the first countries to wholeheartedly take to Neoclassicism, which took longer to spread through the rest of Europe. The Gustavian version, however, was very much simpler than mainline Neoclassicism, and is typified by gray-blue painted furniture, simple checks and stripes, straw yellows, muted pinks, clear blues, pearl grays, and splendid tiled stoves.

HIGH-TECH OR HI-TECH

In design, High-Tech was a 1970s decorating and furnishing style based on the use of industrial components with a dash of early Minimalism. In architecture, High-Tech was a concept developed by the Brits Norman Foster and Richard Rogers with their Team 4 group in much the same decade, though the architectural concept has lasted a very great deal longer than the 1970s decorating style. In fact, High-Tech architects shared the beliefs of early Modernists that buildings should express a machine aesthetic and reveal the methods and materials of its construction, as well as nod to the engineering genius of late-nineteenth-century structures like Joseph Paxton's Crystal Palace in London and the

theories of Buckminster Fuller (see also *Fuller, Buckminster* in Architects, Designer, and Decorators). But High-Tech architects also favored lightweight materials and maximum flexibility of internal space, exposed structure and services together with a smooth casing or impervious skin—often of glass—and crisp, clean lines. The Centre Pompidou in Paris by Richard Rogers and Renzo Piano is an excellent example of this style of architecture. Other well-known exponents of the concept are the British Michael and Patty Hopkins and Nicholas Grimshaw.

ICONOCLASTIC MOVEMENT

Byzantine and Middle Eastern decoration based upon richly colored floral and geometric designs. It evolved as the result of an eighth-century ban by the Eastern Emperor Leo II on any sculptural or painted representations of human beings or animals. The ban was meant to discourage any possibility of pagan idolatory.

INTERNATIONAL STYLE

The name was coined by Philip Johnson (with his book of the same name written with Henry Russell Hitchcock in 1932). It describes the Modernism in architecture promulgated by Walter Gropius with the Bauhaus School in Germany and others in central Europe, and taken up in the United States and in the rest of Europe in the 1920s. Although the early Modernists were perhaps more concerned with sociological ideas and the provision of decent housing for the underpriviledged, they were also excited by the new technology and its practical as well as aesthetic possibilities, as opposed to the more purely aesthetic considerations of the International style. And in this respect it might be more accurate to say that Modernism merged in with the International style. Be that as it may, the actual Bauhaus building designed by Gropius in 1925–26 and Le Corbusier's Salvation Army hostel in Paris (1929–33) were considered to be early European examples of the International style. Early American examples were built in California by two Vienna-trained European émigrés, Rudolph Schindler, who had worked under Frank Lloyd Wright, and Richard Neutra, who had worked under Otto Wagner. The style reached its apotheosis after the end of World War II with the work of Mies van der Rohe and some of his peer group, but its precepts both for architecture and interiors (with its clean lines, simplicity, natural textures, and neutral colors) have profoundly influenced architects and designers up to the present day—even though architecturally the style degenerated somewhat in the 1960s with the slow creep of dissipated corporate Modernism.

JACOBEAN ARCHITECTURE

This follows Elizabethan architecture and incorporates the English Renaissance style of the seventeenth century with a mixture of elaborate decoration, Gothic touches, and often rather crude or ill-understood attempts at the Classical order. As in Elizabethan architecture, there are many fine examples of domestic Jacobean architecture still extant, with their mellow red brick, stone quoins, hipped roofs, dormer windows, and gables.

JAZZ MODERNE
OR ART MODERNE

(See *Art Deco*.)

LOUIS XIV

During the long reign of Louis XIV, known as "the Sun King" (1643–1715), France reached the height of aesthetic splendor. The magnificent Palace of Versailles, seat of the French court, showed off the full splendor of the Baroque style; and from Louis XIV's time to the first quarter of the nineteenth century, France was the acknowledged leader of European taste. Bottle green or crimson velvet, tawny serge or damask wall hangings, embossed leather sometimes silvered or gilded, tapestries, and carved and gilded paneling (or *boiseries*) provided the framework to rooms. Floors were covered with marble or parquetry, and with Savonnerie carpets, and there was a plethora of gilt-bronze chandeliers, wall brackets, clocks, and heavily carved furniture, all typifying the grandiose interiors of the *siècle d'or*, or golden century.

LOUIS XV

The French version of Rococo reached its height during the reign of Louis XV (1712–1774) at a time when interiors

Louis XV *lit à la Turque*

overmantel mirrors; mirrors were set over console tables; and sometimes whole walls and ceilings were lined with mirrors. In summer, sliding panels of mirror might be used to screen fireplaces, and mirrors were also used as sliding window shutters that, cunningly hidden in the paneling by day, just as cunningly disguised the windows at night. All this, including elaborately framed hanging mirrors, contributed to endless reflections. A very great number of candles were used: held in branched candelabra made of crystal and hung low in the room; mounted on candlesticks set in mirrors (called *girandoles*); or set close to other mirrors to further reflect the light. Furniture was light, often gilded, with gracefully curved legs. The curvaceous Louis XV armchairs or fauteuils, with their accommodating shape and well-rounded padding on seat, back, and arms, were—and still are—some of the most agreeable seating ever devised, as pleasing to the eye as the human frame. Fabrics followed the graceful and ornamental feel of the wall decorations. Carpets graduated from the walls to the floor and those made in the royal factory of the Savonnerie, as well as the tapestry-weave carpets from Aubusson, became as popular as Oriental rugs. People still placed chairs by their bed rather than tables, but the commode or chest of drawers or dresser replaced the old traditional lidded chests. Wallpaper started to become increasingly popular, though not in the convenient rolls that are purchased today, but in sheets. Madame de

became much more domesticated— meaning they were more attuned to day-to-day living as opposed to being the grand and formal near–stage sets that had characterized aristocratic interiors during the Baroque period. It set a style that was emulated, though not necessarily so opulently, for centuries to come. Typically, rooms would have had rounded corners; arched doors and windows; depressed arches set into walls; elaborate ceilings covered with ornamental friezes of C- and S-shaped scrolls, shell, flower, and ribbon motifs; and gilded, white- or ivory-painted paneling. Alternatively, walls might be lacquered in the new *vernis Martin*, the lacquered finish invented by the Martin brothers. Mirroring was used lavishly: large panels of mirrored glass were recessed in *boiseries* or paneling opposite tall

Pompadour, that arbiter of taste, had flock-papered walls in her luxurious dressing-room/bathroom in her Château de Chimys in the late 1750s. The most usual window treatments were "pull-up" curtains, similar to Austrian shades today, and Chinese-printed silk taffetas, known as "Pekins" and imported through the good services of the Dutch East India Company, were much prized.

LOUIS XVI

A style of architecture, design, and visual arts produced during the reign of Louis XVI (1774–93) that, in reaction to the increasing elaboration and frivolity of the that era, reintroduced simpler classical forms, and, as such, bridged the last phase of Rococo and the first phase of Neoclassicism. Characteristics of the style, however, actually emerged during the reign of Louis XVI's father. In the second half of the reign of Louis XV, the great French eighteenth-century architect Ange-Jacques Gabriel designed a perfect little Classically inspired building for Madame de Pompadour called *Le Petit Trianon*. All the major rooms—notably smaller than the then norm—were rectangular, designed for greater comfort and intimacy, and decorated in soft tones of gray, white, and pastels. (Unfortunately, Madame de Pompadour died before it was anywhere near completion.) At much the same time, Gabriel designed a suite of similar small rooms or *petits appartements* for the king at Versailles. Both sets of rooms were quite revolutionary for the time in that they

had much more restrained door cases, cornices, and paneling than the Rococo extravagances of the earlier Louis XV period, and had fine marble fireplaces surmounted by large, simple mirrors as well as simpler furniture with tapered fluted legs. The style rapidly spread to become much more the norm for elegant living in the reign of the next king, Louis XVI, and thus became known as *Le Style Louis Seize*, even though it had actually started during the reign of Louis XV, or *Louis Quinze*.

MANNERISM

During the transition between the Renaissance and the Baroque movements there was a reaction in architecture, art, and design to the restraint and discipline of the Classicism of the Renaissance, resulting in strangely attenuated figures, a deliberate upset of the Classical orders, and "grotesque" ornament in the form of griffins, birds, and insects set within cartouches connected by strap work design. The term "grotesque" did not at that time denote the supreme ugliness that we ascribe to it now, but was derived from ancient Roman decoration dug up during the Renaissance, and had its roots in the word *grotto*, or cave, presumably because of objects found underground. A good example of the style is Michelangelo's Medici Chapel and Laurentian Library at the Vatican in Rome.

MINIMALISM

In architecture and interior design, a 1970s through 1990s ongoing movement that aims at complete purity and serenity within rarified and uncluttered spaces to give a feeling of Zenlike calm. It is exemplified in the Western world by architects like John Pawson (b. 1949) in Britain, Steven Holl (b. 1947) in the United States, and Jacques Herzog (b. 1950) and Pierre de Meuron (b. 1950) in Switzerland. In Japan, of course, the style has always been a traditional aesthetic stance. It is not an easy style to maintain in the interiors of family houses or many office environments, although there is no doubting its ascetic appeal.

MISSION STYLE

(See *Arts and Crafts movement.*)

MODERNISM

This movement originated in the late nineteenth century with avant-garde theorists who embraced the technology and the idea of functionalism and eschewed surplus ornament. More importantly, the protagonists of the movement were more sociologically aware and aimed to create a new kind of architecture and urban planning appropriate to the living conditions of the time. The Austrian architects Adolph Loos and Otto Wagner were early espousers of the cause, and Wagner, in his book *Moderne Architektur* (1896), begged for a form of architecture more attuned to modern life. The movement gained momentum before the start of World War I and came to full force in the 1920s and '30s with Walter Gropius's Bauhaus School; the experimental housing in Stuttgart

shown by the Deutscher Werkbund group; and by some early work of Le Corbusier in Paris, followed by buildings in the United States by two European émigré architects trained in Vienna—Rudolph Schindler, who had also worked with Louis Henry Sullivan, and Richard Neutra (see also *International style*). The movement was rechristened the International style by Philip Johnson in 1932 and was given added impetus from the mid-1940s to the 1960s by the arrival in the United States of Walter Gropius, Marcel Breuer, and Mies Van der Rohe. However, the International style had none of the pioneering early philosophical thought of the original Modernist movement, being more concerned with form and function than social ideals.

NEOCLASSICISM

The first really international style, popular all over the Western world and the Antipodes from the latter part of

Karl Friedrich Schinkel's Neoclassical "Roman Bath" (1831–33) at Charlottenhof

A Neoclassical ceiling, ca. 1772

NORMAN ARCHITECTURE

The architecture of the Norman conquest in Britain was prevalent until the beginning of the Gothic style. It is sometimes linked with European Romanesque architecture, as in the rib vaulting of Durham cathedral. The style first emerged with the rebuilding of Westminster Abbey by Edward the Confessor around 1045, and was actually a continuation of the style used by the Normans for Mont St. Michael and the churches of Caen in Normandy. Externally, in Norman ecclesiastical architecture, there were usually two facade towers and a square-crossing tower, a design used for Canterbury Cathedral and Southwell Cathedral as well. In fact, the Normans went on to rebuild nearly every cathedral and abbey church in the country.

PALLADIAN *AND* NEO-PALLADIAN ARCHITECTURE AND DESIGN

Based upon Andrea Palladio's architecture in sixteenth-century Renaissance Italy and very influential on English seventeenth- and eighteenth-century architecture. Inigo Jones first introduced the style to England on his return from Italy in 1614, but the greater Palladian revival began in Britain in the early eighteenth century, led by Colen Campbell (who published the first volume of *Vitruvius Britannicus*, taken from the early Roman architect Vitruvius's *De Architectura*, the principal influence on Renaissance architecture) and Lord Burlington. Campbell remodeled Burlington House for Lord Burlington

the eighteenth century to the first quarter of the nineteenth. It was originally formed as a reaction to the frivolity and excesses of the Rococo movement and was the design equivalent of the eighteenth-century Age of Reason. It was based on ancient Greek and Roman forms as noted by architects visiting Italy and Greece as well as on the Classical orders, and became increasingly popular after the archeological discoveries of the ruins at Paestum, Herculaneum, and Pompeii. It segued into the Greek Revival and then tailed off into the heavier Empire style in France and America and the Regency style in Britain. By that time, it also included the influences derived from Napoleon's Egyptian campaign. Motifs from the style included the acanthus leaves of Classical architecture; lyres from Greece; lion's heads and paws, crossed spears, and laurel wreaths from Rome; and swan's necks, sphinxes, and palmettes from ancient Egypt.

from 1718 to 1719 and Mereworth Castle from 1722 to 1725, the best of the English versions of Palladio's Rotunda design. American Palladianism followed toward the middle of the eighteenth century.

PICTURESQUE MOVEMENT

Early-nineteenth-century style often called *Romanticism* as well as the "cult of the Picturesque," and defined as an aesthetic quality between the sublime and the beautiful. It was characterized in landscape gardening by wild ruggedness with rushing streams, waterfalls, apparently impenetrable woods, and so on. In architecture it took the form of haphazardly asymmetrical forms—for example, Gothic and Italianate-style country houses, and frivolous cottage ornés. In America, the same kind of picturesque building was often known as *Carpenter Gothic*. In interiors it resulted in the descent of the drawing room to the garden level, with French doors or terraces opening onto terraces and lawns. The British Regency architect and planner John Nash was a particularly strong proponent of the Picturesque, as were, toward the end of their careers, in a dramatic about-face, the great French Classicist Claude-Nicolas Ledoux and the German Karl Friedrich Schinkel.

POSTMODERNISM

This was the inevitable reaction in the 1970s to Modernism and the International style in architecture, interior design, and the arts in general.

In a way, a path to the movement had been created by the vigorous, uninhibited, antirational, antifunctionalist Pop Art. Postmodernism did not so much lead the way back to Classicism as nod to its disciplines, orders, and proportions. Leading exponents in the United States were Charles Moore and Michael Graves. It became an accepted establishment style until it degenerated into a kind of pastiche and was followed by Deconstructivism.

PRAIRIE SCHOOL

Designs by the American master architects Frank Lloyd Wright and Louis Henry Sullivan and a group of other architects and designers centered in and around Chicago from the late 1880s to the early 1900s, known as the Chicago School. The low rambling houses that seemed to grow out of the great American prairies were its chief influence, as well as the Arts and Crafts movement and that movement's American offshoot, the Mission style.

QUEEN ANNE REVIVAL

Style started around 1870 by the architects Norman Shaw, Charles F. A. Voysey, and others who were interested in reviving English vernacular architecture and who built houses with traditional English materials: red brick, tile-hung exterior walls, white-painted woodwork, and sash windows in the style of the "Wren" houses. (Actually, "Wren" houses are erroneously named since Wren, though a genius at church building, was thought to have designed very few houses himself.) Interiors

Queen Anne or Wren House in brick, 1700s

were planned to give the effect of an old house, with inglenooks, odd little rooms called "snugs," bay windows with window seats, steps up and down from rooms, and a great deal more light—hence the epithet "Sweetness and Light." This look was popular in America, but with shingles instead of tiles on the outside, and rather more open planning within. The style continued through the Edwardian period until the advent of World War I.

QUEEN ANNE STYLE

English Baroque architecture during the Queen Anne period—from about 1680 to 1714—that carried forward from the semi-Dutch style of William and Mary. Sir John Vanbrugh (Castle Howard and Blenheim) and Nicholas Hawksmoor (Easton Neston) were two designers responsible for some of the very grand stately homes of the time, but the prosperous up-and-coming middle classes preferred (and found affordable) somewhat smaller buildings such as the so-called "Wren" houses, which became quite ubiquitous, with their sensible but harmonious proportions, hipped roofs, mellow red brick, graceful sash windows, and pedimented doorways. (Wren did not actually design any houses, although it is thought that he must have sketched some patterns.) Furniture—that was both more delicate and more beautiful than the heavier, more formal pieces of the previous era—was introduced in walnut and more exotic woods, especially for elaborate marquetry. Typical pieces of the period were small, elegantly curved walnut pieces with French-style cabriole legs embellished with scallop-shell, bracket, hoof, pad, club, or claw-and-ball feet.

Queen Anne Revival, 1890s

Elaborately carved chair backs were now tall and hooped to accommodate women's extravagantly dressed hairstyles. The upholstered wing chair was introduced around 1700 and this was followed by the settee. The Queen Anne style reached America just after the Queen's death in 1714 and remained in fashion right up until 1755–60. Mahogany started to be used more and more, although walnut, maple, and pine continued to be popular. Cabriole legs with claw-and-ball feet or rounded pads replaced straight legs and became a predominant feature of furniture design.

RÉGENCE

The last years of Louis XIV's reign turned out to be a somber sunset for the monarch known as the Sun King. Financial worries and the deaths of leading members of the royal family, including the king's son and heir, made Versailles a gloomy place, and much of the court drifted away to the lighter pleasures to be found in the Parisian salons of fashion leaders like the Duchesse de Maine and the king's

nephew, the Duc d'Orleans. The latter became the regent after Louis XIV's death, pending the majority of the new heir, the future Louis XV, who was the old monarch's young grandson as well as the Duke's nephew, and thus gave the name to this transitional style. During this *Régence* period the oppressively grand atmosphere of the former court at Versailles, with its emphasis on display and ceremony, gave way to a new desire for informality, intimacy, comfort, and elegance.

REGENCY

The British equivalent of the French and American Empire styles but somewhat lighter and more relaxed. Interestingly, although the period heralded the easy, comfortable, and eclectic interiors of today, it was regarded with some scorn from the end of the nineteenth century to the late 1930s and not really prized until the 1950s. Its name is taken from the time when the Prince of Wales (later George IV) became regent (1811–20) for his apparently demented though actually

Design for a Regency writing table
in the new Egyptian taste
(from George Smith's
Household Furniture, 1808)

Two Regency chair backs: one in the
Picturesque style, ca. 1800–50 (left) and
the other in the Gothic (tracery) style,
ca. 1800–50 (right).

sick father, George III (who "lost," as they say, the American colonies). But the style was in sway from the 1780s to 1830. It, therefore, ranged architecturally from the later Neoclassical Greek Revival years, to a much more lighthearted Gothic style, and on to the fantasies of the Picturesque and the vaguely Hindu exotica of the Prince's Brighton Pavilion. Moreover, the great English country house started to become less important as smaller houses and villas found favor. Indoors, the taste for the Grecian aesthetic manifested itself in plainer surfaces, a reduction or complete absence of relief ornamentation—with a resulting emphasis on painted decoration—and much simpler rooms. The most famous English furniture designer of the time was Thomas Hope, whose influential *Household Furniture and Interior Decoration* included French Empire- and Directoire-style pieces. Many of the same Greco-Roman and Egyptian motifs used in the Regency style— the swan's necks, griffins, caryatids, winged sphinxes, and so on—were very much the signature of the French and American Empire styles. At the same time, the Grecian couch was introduced. Since, unlike most furniture hitherto, it was not necessarily designed to be set up against a wall, it started a more casual approach to furniture arrangement, as did the new sofa tables, set in front of sofas for writing or reading (rather than behind, which is more customary today), and the occasional tables used for card-playing or as a focus for conversational groups. Furniture was moved much more into the center of a room and around the fireplace. The development of the villa and the changes in furniture arrangement, though seemingly slight in themselves, constituted a quite significant design revolution.

RENAISSANCE

This began in the early fifteenth century in Italy, or *quattrocentro* as it was called, and was to Italy what the extraordinarily creative fifth century B.C. was to Greece, or what the enlightened eighteenth century was to Europe and America. The Renaissance was a time of immense discovery, invention, and social evolution as well as a re-evaluation of the arts, architecture, sciences, and humanities—all of which had an enormous and far-reaching influence first in Italy and then over the rest of Europe. The comparative peace after centuries of bitter rivalry and warring meant that the great Italian families were able to turn their attention to domestic building instead of wanton destruction, to being patrons of the arts instead of marauding warlords. Interestingly, as more and more was discovered about the universe and its workings, so the civilized Italians of the time began to revel in the discovery of their Classical past, and particularly the scale and variety of its architecture. New buildings reflected this fascination with the Classical age and the powerful contemporary princes: Lorenzo de'Medici (1449–1492), who made his city, Florence, the center of learning and patronage; and Federico da Montefeltro (1422–1482), who created a spectacular palace in Urbino (started as early as 1450), were as able as scholars as they were as soldiers and leaders. Moreover, they collected antiquities with the same enthusiasm that they showed for commissioning contem-porary painters and sculptors. As unfortified palaces and splendid country villas sprang up around Rome and Florence and in the Veneto near Venice, so painters, sculptors, stonemasons, ceramicists, metal-workers and master cabinet-makers began for the first time to create items for domestic as well as for ecclesiastical settings. The building, decorating, and furnishing of fine houses and the collection of sumptuous rugs, tapestries, furniture, and works of art became an absorbing occupation among the rich. The dome that Filippo Brunelleschi (1377–1446) designed for the cathedral in Florence (1420–61) was hailed as the first great achievement of the new architecture—and one that rivaled or even surpassed ancient Roman architecture. But neither Brunelleschi, nor any other architect of the period, attempted to reproduce the domestic interiors of the Classical past for the simple reason that they had no idea what those interiors had looked like. Descriptions of ancient interiors were occasionally to be found in books, as in the works of Pliny the Elder (23–79 A.D.) or in the *De Architectura* of Vitruvius, an architect of the first century A.D. But not until the eighteenth century discoveries of the well-preserved remains of Pompeii and Herculaneum (buried by the eruption of Vesuvius in 79 A.D., which buried Pliny the Elder in the process) did designers have a chance to look at Roman domestic interiors, the main basis of Neoclassicism. Nevertheless, Brunelleschi's contrasting white or pale blond plastered wall surfaces with their gray stone moldings and details, together with his application of antique motifs such as pediments over doorways, laid the foundation for the revival of Classical architecture in Europe and eventually America. And it was Brunelleschi, who in association with Leone Battista Alberti, established certain rules of perspective and proportion that even today dictate the standards by which we judge a room.

RENAISSANCE REVIVAL

Also known as neo-Renaissance, this was a much-favored style on both sides of the Atlantic in the latter part of the nineteenth century, when the newly rich wanted to display their wealth and consequent buying power. Its heavy forms and elaborate decoration were actually taken from the Baroque period as well as the Renaissance and were designed more to impress than for comfort.

RESTORATION

(See *Carolean Style*.)

ROCOCO

The light and comparatively frivolous early-eighteenth-century style introduced during the reign of Louis XV, which finally laid to rest the heaviness and pomposity of the Baroque. The style was first and foremost a style of interiors and more particularly of elaborate *boiseries* or paneling, and beautiful ceilings. The ebulliently carved *boiseries* with their asymmetric, somewhat abstract shell-like forms and many C- and S-forms were painted in light pastel colors, and there was an emphasis on mirrors reflecting mirrors lit by candles and stunningly elaborate parquetry floors. Flowers, monkeys, branches, whole trees, and chinoiserie were all motifs used by the style, which spread all over Europe and was especially espoused in Germany and Austria. French Rococo architecture was known for its grace and delicacy, although in England and America the style was mostly used in interiors. Rococo had a popular revival in the late nineteenth century, when it was particularly taken up in the United States. (See also *Louis XV*.)

ROCOCO REVIVAL

Also known as neo-Rococo or just plain "Louis Revival," this curvilinear, rather florid nineteenth-century style started in Britain, where French taste was once again vastly admired, in spite of the somewhat short-lived chauvinism instigated by the Napoleonic Wars. It was popular, too, in France during the reign of Louis-Philippe (1830–48), where it was known as *Le Style Pompadour*, in an acknowledgment to the great taste and influence of Louis XV's famous mistress. The revival spread to Germany during the second half of the century, and from there to the United States, where it was much extolled by contemporary arbiters of taste like Edith Wharton and Ogden Codman.

SHAKER

A style loosely based on the simple, functional interiors of the Shaker sect

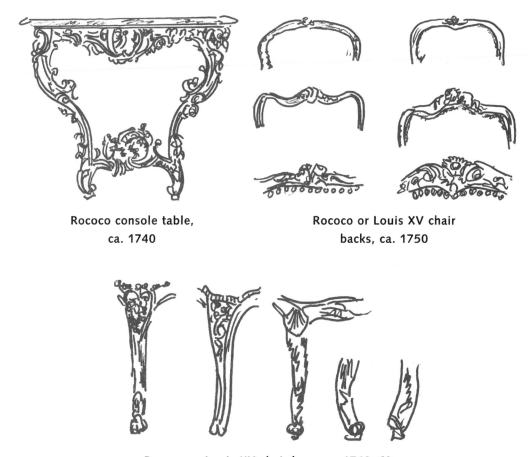

Rococo console table,
ca. 1740

Rococo or Louis XV chair
backs, ca. 1750

Rococo or Louis XV chair legs, ca. 1740–60

founded in 1774 but at its most populous in the United States in the first half of the nineteenth century. The Shakers were best known for their beautifully crafted, clean-lined, simple wood furniture, much of it built-in; their stacking oval boxes with dovetail joints; and their practical habit of hanging chairs, brooms, mirrors, and baskets on peg rails around the room to keep floors clear. They held that "beauty rests on utility"—a philosophy that was in many ways a precursor to the late-nineteenth

and early-twentieth-century doctrine of Functionalism, and the tenet of the American pioneer Modernist Louis Henry Sullivan that "form follows function."

TUDOR

The style current during the reigns of the English Tudor monarchs up to the Elizabethan period of Elizabeth I (1558–1603), which roughly covered the first half of the sixteenth century. At the beginning of the period, late

Gothic forms still predominated, but they were slowly diffused by the gradual introduction of ideas from Renaissance Italy arriving via France and Flanders. Decorative plasterwork, or "pargetting," which was very often richly colored, covered the ceiling with motifs of Tudor roses, scrolls, cartouches, and French fleurs-de-lis. Walls were generally paneled, and the center or "field" of each panel was often carved with a linenfold design. Furniture was still heavy and made of oak, but more pieces for more functions were being introduced.

VICTORIAN

The umbrella title given to the period of Queen Victoria's reign in Britain from 1837 to 1901, though the name was given to most nineteenth-century design in English-speaking countries all over the world. The long period actually included a mixture of nostalgic Revivalist styles, like neo-Baroque, neo-Gothic, neo-Renaissance, and neo-Rococo, as well as a reaction to all this historicism, as manifested in the Arts and Crafts movement, the Aesthetic movement, the Queen Anne Revival, the Vienna Secession, and Art Nouveau. Nevertheless, when most people hear the term "Victorian," they immediately conjure up visions of somber, dark, or richly colored rooms, with layers of heavy draperies over window glass filtered by lace curtains, floors covered by "Turkey" rugs or carpets, and almost every surface cluttered with miscellaneous *objets,* from stuffed birds or fish or small animals in glass domes or cases to decorative glass, pieces of porcelain, bits of silver, and boxes of every size and description. Grand pianos might sport fringed cloths to hide their legs since unclothed legs of any description, human or otherwise, were considered somewhat *risqué*, and then there would be the near-obligatory "garniture" of at least three to five elaborate vases on the mantelpiece. There are two significant points worth noting here. One is that with the benefit of hindsight, and the earliest uses of photography, we can look back and discern all the different movements and styles that took place in the course of a century. And the other is that the "Victorian" look is actually the look of the long middle period of Victoria's widowhood, and more importantly, the look of the rising middle classes, who wanted to show the world that they were solid, prosperous citizens—so the more objects, collections, furniture, rugs, and general clutter of possessions that they had, the better.

VIENNA SECESSION

Avant-garde Viennese movement founded by Josef Hoffmann and Joseph Maria Olbrich in 1897. It promulgated stark geometric or cubist buildings with interiors devoid of ornament such as cornices and moldings. In many ways these buildings were the precursors of today's standardized mass-produced housing.

A Victorian chair back
with carved panels,
ca. 1800–50

A Victorian chair back
with barley-sugar twist
turning, ca. 1800–50

A buttoned-leather
Victorian chair back,
ca. 1800–50

WIENER WERKSTÄTTE

The group (founded in 1903) of talented Viennese architects and designers who were determined Modernists and reformers in the early twentieth century. Their aim, like that of William Morris, was to develop more unity between architecture, crafts, and the machine. They were also somewhat influenced by the work of Charles Rennie Mackintosh, whose furniture and sketches had been included in the Eighth Exhibition of the Vienna Secession in 1900. The group was headed by Josef Hoffmann (1870–1956).

WILLIAM AND MARY

The anglicized Baroque Transitional style practiced in the late seventeenth century in Britain and then in North America. It was named after the joint reign in Britain of the Dutch William III (1689–1702) and his English wife, Mary II (1689–1694). It was a less-flamboyant style than the Carolean (or Restoration) period that preceded it, and a precursor of the splendid early-eighteenth-century Queen Anne style. It was also the time of the great English architect Sir Christopher Wren. William brought to England a team of Dutch craftsmen as well as skilled Huguenot craftsmen, such as Daniel Marot, who had fled France after Louis XIV revoked the Edict of Nantes. This injected a whole new vigor into English craftsmanship. By 1690, French-style chairs with upholstered backs and seats had replaced the cane-paneled chair so popular in the Restoration period. Lacquered furniture was much in demand, and when supplies from the Far East began to run out, they were replaced with the native "Japanned" finishes. Other new pieces of furniture were writing desks, tea tables, and bookcases. William and Mary also promulgated their taste for the blue-and-white porcelain being shipped from China by the Dutch East India Company and the Dutch blue-and-white delftware. The style—complete with blue-and-white porcelain, imported goods from the Far East, and a taste for what became known as "Wren" houses—became very popular in America just before the beginning of the eighteenth century, where it lasted long after the monarchs (who had given their name to the style) had both died. One of the most interesting developments in furniture, particularly in America, was the highboy, or tall chest of drawers, which had five or six tiers of drawers on a six-legged stand. The stand on its own with one tier of drawers was called a lowboy. Walnut was used on both sides of the Atlantic to make much lighter furniture than the heavy early oak pieces.

WINDOWS
AND WINDOW
TREATMENTS

*The shape, size, and spacing of window openings are vital
elements of architectural design. They spell out rhythms
like passages of music…. They may march across the face
of a building in a lively manner like the allegro movement of a symphony, or they may adopt a cool, reflective
disposition which might be described as andante….
Windows may be small and secretive, defensive, serene,
inviting, confident, or hesitant. They are the eyes of a
house and reflect its spirit. They abound in subtle and
delightful details and you can ruin all of these things
with one crass or careless act of modernization.*

Hugh Lander, from *The House Restorer's Guide*

In a construction age in which the use of glass is ubiquitous and, by prior standards, extravagant, it is hard to think of a time when window openings were not only uncommon (they let in too much cold and moisture), but when windows *without* glass were the norm. Yet in medieval times, glass was extremely rare. Window openings were usually closed with shutters or bits of parchment or wood or reed lattices, letting in little of the light and air that are now so important to us.

By the fourteenth century, glass was occasionally used to form the top, fixed portion of a casement window, though the rest of the window opening was still protected with shutters, lattice, or trellis. Even in the late fifteenth century, when most larger houses had glass windows, the precious glass was designed so that it could be removed and reinstalled in another house when necessary. Sash windows, the other main window type, are thought to have been developed in Holland during the seventeenth century and, from there, to have spread to Britain, the British and Dutch colonies, and North America.

Since then, windows have consistently given more character to the facade of a house than any other element. In grand eighteenth- and nineteenth-century houses with a classical leaning, splendid columns, pediments, door cases, and even statues may compete for our attention, but in the vast majority of buildings it is the fenestration—the shape, size, and spacing of windows—that we notice first. Thus, though it may seem the right decision to enlarge or replace a window when standing inside a room, the effect on the exterior should always be considered first.

The *dressing* of windows is equally important. We use curtains, shades, shutters, and other window dressings to decorate a room, provide privacy, modulate light during the day, and add visual and, in cooler climates, physical warmth at night. This brings me to the whole question of curtain nomenclature. What the Europeans call *curtains* used to be known in America as *drapes* or *draperies*, or even as old-fashioned *hangings*. What Americans called *curtains* are what the Europeans used to call *nets*, *glass curtains*, or *sheers*, or similar light curtains meant to partially conceal while filtering light. Many interior designers and decorators, however, seem to feel that the term *drapes* or *draperies* is a little déclassé. Since each of these terms comes up in this section, I've tried to address this confusion as clearly as possible. And, of course not wanting to be thought déclassé myself, have come down firmly on the side of *curtains*.

ARCHED WINDOWS

If you possess elegantly arched windows it is a shame to hide them with curtain headings. A rounded—or pointed, depending on the shape of the arch—track or rod can be installed to follow the line of an arch. Curtains can then be hung from this fixed track or rod, though they will have to meet in the middle and be held back on either side with tie-backs. Alternatively, a rod may be fixed across the window below the semicircular portion, covering the window or windows below (as in, for example, the case of a Palladian or Venetian window). Then either leave the semicircular arched part bare, or if you want to keep out the light, fill it with a fixed, shaped shade or fan-shaped curtain. Balloon, Austrian, and various types of pull-up shades can also be hung from a curved or arched rod, but the top part must be stationary and kept flat within the arch itself.

AUSTRIAN SHADES

Gently-ruched shades that were first popular in the eighteenth century and had a resurgence in the last part of the twentieth century. Austrian shades have rows of vertical shirring and can be raised and lowered by cords threaded through rings that are attached to the back of the shade, underneath the lining at regular intervals. The shade is fixed to a batten or to an Austrian shade track fixed to the top of the window frame or just above it. Screw eyes are attached to the underside of the batten or track for the cords to pass though. The cords are

Austrian or festoon shades

then plaited together and knotted to hang at one side and be maneuvered when necessary.

BALLOON SHADES

Shades with deep inverted pleats that create a billowing balloonlike appearance if they are made in a sufficiently lightweight fabric. Balloon shades are formed by attaching special ring tapes in vertical lines to the back of the shade. Each line of rings is threaded with a cord attached to the lower ring. The top of the shade is attached to a wooden batten or an Austrian shade track (the same track used for Austrian shades) with the cords knotted together in the same way. Tailored balloon shades are generally made of heavier fabric and in much the same way, except that the cording is omitted from the sides, allowing the fabric to droop at the edges.

BAY AND BOW WINDOWS

Styles of windows that project outward—bays being more angled and bows being more rounded—and that create window recesses that are generally considered to be an asset in a room, though they often cause problems if there are window seats or radiators underneath them. One solution for dressing these windows is to install shades or blinds with or without permanently looped-back side or "dress" curtains.

BLACKOUT LINING

A light-blocking fabric that comes in a variety of thicknesses and colors and is essential for anyone who does not want to be disturbed by light. This special blackout lining works well for both curtains and shades and will make any fabric look more opaque. An alternative is Milium, a thermal fabric that blocks out light (although not quite as well as blackout lining) and also provides insulation.

BLINDS

English term for shades. In the United States the term is most often used to describe matchstick, bamboo, or Venetian blinds.

CAFÉ CURTAINS

A short curtain hung from a rod suspended halfway across a window as in some French cafés. This sort of curtaining is sometimes hung in a double tier and is useful treatment for windows that open inward or face directly onto a street, since the tier system allows privacy with a minimal loss of light.

CASEMENT CURTAINS

A light or translucent fabric with pockets or casings at either end for expandable spring pressure curtain rods, adjustable rods, or simply stretch wires that are fixed straight to the inside of the window frame.

CASEMENT WINDOW

A window suspended on side hinges that enables it to be opened inward or outward as opposed to sash windows, which are pushed up and down. European casement windows open inward as opposed to those in the United States, United Kingdom, and the antipodes, which open outward. Inwardly opening windows need to be taken into consideration when choosing window coverings, especially if you ever want windows open and coverings or shades down at the same time. Always fix headings well above such windows if you can, and hang curtains well wide of the windows, or fix shades, blinds, or appropriately named casement curtains right on the windows with a uniting top treatment. Alternatively, hang a curtain on a nineteenth-century-style portiére rod that swivels so that the curtain opens with the door. Otherwise you will just have to bear a bump in the curtains if you want them drawn when you are also aerating the room.

Regular casement window

Full-length casement window

**A circular or
oeil-de-boeuf window**

CIRCULAR WINDOW

Often called an *oeil de boeuf* (literally, "bull's eye") window, this is best left bare, perhaps with the frame painted a color that contrasts with the walls so that it looks a little like a painting frame—or you could replace clear glass with etched, stained, or painted glass.

CLERESTORY WINDOW

A window placed near the top of a wall. The term *clerestory* or *clearstory* originally referred to the upper story of a church that is above the aisle roofs and is pierced by windows. But nowadays *clerestory* windows can, rightly or wrongly, refer to long and narrow horizontal slits normally referred to as *ranch windows*. The best treatments for clerestory windows are shades or blinds of some sort, if you definitely want them covered; the same goes for ranch windows, unless they are very shallow, in which case they are best used as display areas for a collection of this and that, or two or three single-stem vases or plants.

CORNER WINDOW

Formed by two windows at right angles to each other in a corner, this window can be dressed with either shades or blinds fixed in the recesses or with curtains that are fixed to a right-angled track overlapping the ends of the two windows. An alternative treatment is to install glass shelves—lit from above or below, or both, by small recessed spots—which can hold plants or glass or ceramic collections. In this way, glass shelves let light in during the day but at the same time provide some privacy, depending on the number of objects placed on the shelves. When lit at night the shelves are very decorative.

CORNICE

A piece of straight, carved, or shaped wood that can also be fabric covered or decoratively painted and fixed over a window treatment, either to finish it off neatly or to hide any hardware or strip lighting that has been placed behind it for effect. (See also *lambrequin*, *pelmet*, or *valance*.)

CURTAINS

There is always some confusion in the English language about this term. In the United States, a *curtain* originally meant a stationary window covering, such as a casement curtain—that is, a headed and hemmed length of translucent fabric attached to a rod or wire and used to soften the window frame. In Europe, the United Kingdom, and the antipodes, *curtains*, in simple terms, means suspended wide widths of headed fabric that can be pulled backward and forward across a window. However, many Americans now also use the term for what they formerly called *drapes* or *draperies*.

CURTAIN RODS, POLES, AND TRACKS

There is a big choice from the flat-faced rod intended to be used with curtains with a case heading or a rod pocket (which hides the rod), to a whole range of brass, wood, nickel, chrome, and plastic rods or poles with matching rings, clips, leather hoops, or fabric tabs. Nondescript poles can look very attractive if covered in a sheath of fabric matching the curtains or drapes. Alternatively, a pole with a concealed traverse mechanism can be used, in which case rings are attached to sliders for ease of drawing to and fro. If the curtain or drapery heading, valance, cornice will hide the drawing mechanism, a conventional traverse rod is used. These rods come in various styles, including double rods for both curtains or drapes and valance, curved and angled styles for bay and bow windows, and flexible, bendable varieties for arched windows. Some can be fixed to the ceiling instead of the wall above the window, or the window frame, to make windows seem longer.

DORMER

A window in a vertical structure that projects from a sloping roof. *Dormer* is the name for both the window and the structure in which the window is set. Roller or Roman shades are a good idea here, because dormer windows, jutting out from roofs, never have any wall space to speak of on either side of the frame. An alternative is to run hinged, slim rods through casings sewn into the

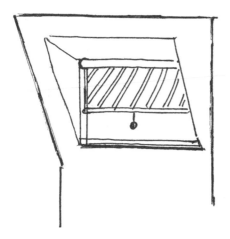

**Roller shade for
dormer window**

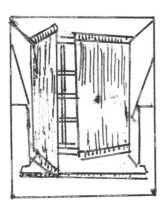

**Short curtains attached to casement
rods on a dormer window**

top of a pair of short curtains, so that both rod and curtains can be swung back during the day.

DOUBLE-HUNG SASH
OR WINDOW

Two sliding, framed, glass sections forming a standard window controlled at the sides by pulleys and

weights. One section is lowered from the top, the other is pushed up from the bottom.

DRAPES OR DRAPERIES

Originally, the American word for curtains in the English or European sense, drapes are basically headed window coverings that can be pulled across, or let down, to hide a window. They are normally suspended from a track or pole. (See also *curtains*.)

DRESS CURTAINS

Not meant to be pulled or drawn, dress curtains are used simply to soften the sides or edges of a window. Also called *side curtains*.

FANLIGHT

(See *fanlight* in Architectural, Building, and Decorating Terms.)

FESTOON SHADES

Another type of pull-up shade that functions similarly to Austrian shades and pull-up shades.

FINIAL

In window treatment parlance, the term refers to the decorative end of a curtain rod. It can be made of wood, iron, brass, nickel, glass, or stainless steel depending upon taste, style, and budget.

FRENCH WINDOWS
OR FRENCH DOORS

These are casement windows that extend to the floor and that most often appear in pairs, as double-hinged doors of framed glass. Many French windows or doors open inward, as do French casement windows, which can create a problem if you want them open when curtains or drapes are drawn. (See *casement window* for window treatment suggestions.)

FRINGE

In window treatments, the decorative edging or trim with twisted threads or loops and tassels used to give a finishing touch to elaborate curtains, pelmets, or tie-backs.

HEADING

The treatment of the top of curtains, drapes, or some shades, which may be in the form of gathers, smocking, pleats, scallops, shirring, or tabs. The heading chosen determines the style of the treatment and will affect the way curtains or drapes hang. Many headings are decorative in their own right and are meant to be paired with decorative poles. Traditionally, *pleated headings* (pinch pleats, French or goblet pleats, Flemish pleats, box pleats, and cartridge and pencil pleats) were made by hand; for a shortcut use heading tapes, which will achieve various looks rather more quickly, though not necessarily more elegantly. With *fixed headings* the curtains or drapes are permanently joined at the center top. The sides are then held back by tie- or hold-backs at any level, and are simply released to close them. Such fixed headings are invariably graceful treatments, but are best used either in rooms that have an abundance of light, and can therefore afford to lose a little, or at night.

BOX PLEATS: It is possible to buy box-pleat heading tapes to form these elegant, crisp-looking headings.

CARTRIDGE AND PENCIL PLEATS: The former are small round pleats, stiffened with rolls of cartridge paper to maintain their shapes. Each pleat should take up about 2 inches (5 cm) of fabric, with small spaces between pleats. Pencil pleats are smaller variations of cartridge pleats, simply placed closer together to form a more casual and gathered effect. Again, it is possible to buy heading tapes for such pleats.

EYELET HEADING: Jumbo eyelets or grommets are inserted along the top edge of a curtain, which is then folded accordion-style to take a pole slotted through the eyelets. Clear plastic poles look good this way.

FLEMISH PLEATS: An attractive heading that needs to be permanently fixed and handsewn. Basically, pleats are bound or trimmed at the base of the heading with a handsewn cord that is sometimes twisted into decorative knots. Alternatively, cord is sometimes placed right across the base of all the pleats. In this case the cord should be attached to every third pleat so that it (the cord) falls in loops between each pleat.

FRENCH OR GOBLET PLEATS: These are made in much the same way as pinch pleats, except that the three pleats are not stitched in place along the entire length of the curtain but simply secured at the base of the fold. The pleats are either kept quite small, as in regular flat French pleats, or are made a little larger and then stuffed with tissue paper or interlining to give them a goblet shape (thus the name *goblet pleats*). The goblets can then be accentuated by adding a contrast binding or lining.

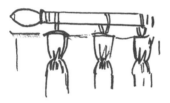

Example of a goblet heading

GATHERED HEADING: This is a good casual heading and can be achieved either with a special heading tape or by forming a casing or rod pocket stitched at the top of the curtain or drape, through which a curtain rod can be slipped. Since each curtain should be at least twice as wide as the length of the rod, this automatically produces a gathered effect. If the casing or rod pocket is positioned slightly down from the folded top edge of the curtain or drape, the edge will stand up above the rod.

PINCH PLEATS: One of the most commonly used of all headings. They allow fabric to form in precise folds that can

fixed in place with heading tapes. If they are handsewn, the right number of pleats and spaces must be worked out to fit neatly into the given space. A single tuck made at regular intervals is then divided into triple pleats. The heading is fixed to either a conventional or decorative rod by pin hooks attached to the back of each pleat.

SCALLOPED HEADING: The upper edge of the curtain or drapery is cut in a series of down-pointing curves and backed with a matching facing. Curtain rings can then be attached to the gaps between the scallops and slipped over a narrow curtain rod. With this type of heading, the curtain needs to be only a little wider than the rod in order to display the scallops. If you want the curtains to look fuller, form a pinch pleat between each scallop.

SHIRRED HEADING: Permanently gathered top achieved by drawing up material along two or more parallel lines of stitching, or, more simply, over cords or thin rods that have been threaded through casings or rod pockets.

SMOCKED HEADING: This will always make a room look splendidly detailed and cared for, but even if you use a special "smocking type" to give a smocked outline, the actual smocking still has to be handstitched. If the whole heading is to be handstitched, plot out the smocking design on paper first, before transferring it to the top of the curtain or drapery. Smocked headings always look better fixed.

TAB HEADING: Basically, these headings are made from a series of tabs attached to the top of the curtains or drapes, or sometimes integrated into the curtains themselves, which are then looped over decorative curtain rods. Tabs, of whatever chosen size or shape, can be made of the same fabric as the curtains or of a contrasting fabric, or outlined with a contrasting trim. Both ends of each tab can be stitched to the curtain like a loop, or just one end can be stitched and the other buttoned.

HOLD-BACK

A decorative brass, bronze, or wood (which can be silvered or gilded) device to be screwed into a wall at the desired level to hold back curtains or drapes. Sometimes they are just open hoops of metal, sometimes rosettes on long stems.

HOURGLASS CURTAIN

A curtain stretched between two rods, fixed at the top and bottom of a window, and tied in the middle to show a triangle-shaped portion of the window at each side. To cover the window, the tie is simply removed.

INTERLINING

Interlining, which is typically a quilted or stuffed cotton fabric, is inserted between the lining fabric and curtain or drape fabric. Unless you are aiming for a breezy, floaty look, curtains and drapes will always hang much better and look that much more luxurious if they are interlined. Interlining also provides insulation. A really luxurious and professional-looking effect will be obtained on lined and interlined curtains or drapes if an extra strip of interlining is rolled lengthwise and invisibly handstitched inside each leading edge to form subtle padding.

ITALIAN STRINGING

This is another way to hold back curtains or drapes with fixed headings. A diagonal line of rings is sewn into the back of the curtains at a point about a fifth of the way down the outside edge and about one-third of the way down the leading edge. Cord is then run through these rings (or, if it is just a one-curtain window, along a batten fixed at the top). Pulling on the cords at the side pulls the curtains aside as in a puppet theater. Releasing the cords closes the curtains. Because the curtains are looped high, more light is let in with this method. If you would like the curtains permanently swept gracefully up, you can always install a shade behind to be let down at night. Also called *reefing*.

LACE CURTAINS

Just that. They were much used as undercurtains in Victorian and nineteenth-century houses in general, and still are by anyone who wants to achieve that sort of look.

LAMBREQUIN

In window treatments, similar to a shaped cornice but made to reach down the sides of a window, sometimes to the floor, to make a window look

An elaborate French lambrequin,
ca. 1850–60

more distinguished. (See also *cornice*, *pelmet*, and *valance*.)

LEADED LIGHTS

Small panes of glass set in lead cames or frames, to form a window; much used until the eighteenth century, and later used in copies of old houses.

LEADING EDGE

The inner edges (facing each other when curtains are drawn) of a curtain. They are often bound, trimmed, or bordered.

LIGHTS

The professional term for window glass.

LININGS

Curtains should always be lined (and if possible interlined), with the exception, of course, of deliberately thin fabrics meant to filter light rather than block it out. Lining protects the main fabric from the ravages of sun, dust, and pollution, encloses hems and raw edges, and, if carefully chosen, can provide an interesting contrast when the curtains are caught or flicked back—although contrasting half-linings superimposed on the actual lining can be used for that effect as well. Good linings also make curtains look better from the outside, and it is usually a good idea to use the same lining material for all windows so that there is a pleasing uniformity both by day and night. (See also *interlining*.)

MATCHSTICK BLINDS

A blind composed of slim pieces of wood sewn tightly together with thread. Matchstick blinds are generally rolled up and held in place with cords, although sometimes they are sold with spring mechanisms like roller shades. They can be left natural or spray painted.

MINI BLINDS

A smaller, thinner, finer version of Venetian blinds or shades. (See example on the next page.)

PALLADIAN WINDOW

(See *Palladian window* in Architectural, Building, and Decorating Terms.)

Mini blinds in an arched studio window (the top section in the arch is fixed)

PELMET

An English term for a *valance*, usually made of fabric, but it can also be wood, covered or painted, and shaped or plain. (See also *cornice*, *lambrequin*, and *valance*.)

Antique gilded wood pelmet

PICTURE WINDOWS
OR **WALLS OF GLASS**

These are useful for obtaining maximum daylight but hard to treat for night unless, in a generally hot climate, an outside yard or area garden is subtly lit, or you live in a high apartment in a well-lit city. Otherwise, few people enjoy looking at what essentially, from the inside, will be great big black holes. A series of Roman or roller shades, vertical louvers, or suspended chains (as used in the famous Four Seasons Restaurant in the Seagram's Building in New York City) or other varieties of commercially made shades are often the best solution. Or you could hang a single, dramatically looped-back curtain or drape at a picture window, depending upon the style of the room.

PIVOT WINDOW

Pivot windows, which turn this way and that from a central pivot control, are difficult to treat when they are open. If you require privacy, mount lightweight or sheer curtains on the window itself. If windows pivot horizontally, attach slim rods to the inner frames and install café curtains. For vertically pivoting windows, fix portiere rods that will hinge outward complete with curtains, or casement curtains, made by slipping expandable spring-pressure curtain rods, adjustable curtain rods, or stretch wires through narrow casings at the top and bottom of a lightweight curtain and attaching it to the frame.

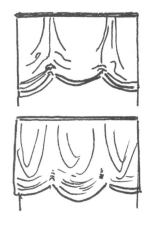

Pull-up shades

PULL-UP CURTAINS *OR* SHADES

These were much used in the eighteenth and nineteenth centuries for long windows. They look somewhat like balloon or Austrian shades, but they are made to lower right to the floor, at which point they look like long continuous panels of fabric.

PLEATED SHADES
OR CELLULAR SHADES

Permanently or accordion-pleated fabric shades gently diffuse light. Cellular shades are made with double layers of pleated fabric to produce small air cells that insulate against cold. Both types are factory made and available in a great number of finishes and colors.

RANCH WINDOW

A modern window that is wide but annoyingly shallow and placed higher up the wall than normal casement or double hung or sash windows. Their high position is supposed to make furniture placement easier but in fact they are difficult to treat with any grace and can be something of a fire hazard, since they restrict egress. They are also called strip windows.

REVERSE SHADES

These are fixed at the bottom of a window. They can have a spring mechanism like reverse rollers, or if the fabric is light and easily rolled, they can simply be supplied with a pair of cords and screw eyes.

ROLLER SHADES

The earliest form of shades, they were originally called *Holland blinds* because Holland was the name of the highly glazed, finely woven, cream or green linen with which they were always made. Today, they can be made of any appropriate-weight fabric that can be wound around a roller and that can be stiffened or laminated, or from a solid-colored fabric that can be painted or stenciled. Controls are either from spring or cog mechanisms.

ROMAN SHADES

These are flat when pulled down, with no extra fullness across the width. They draw up in neat horizontal pleats. These are formed by stitching in a series of slim battens at the back of the fabric in parallel lines in casings or pockets, with a slightly heavier batten or slim metal rod at the bottom to help them hang well. The fabric can be edged, bordered, or inset bordered, or the bottom edge can be beaded, fringed, shaped, corded, or tabbed over a slim rod or pole. They can either be hung by themselves or given a valance, pelmet, cornice, or lambrequin. Any shade that is wider than 5 feet is hard to pull up properly. Very wide windows will need two or three narrower shades fixed side by side.

Interior view of a sash window
with twenty-four panes, c. 1764

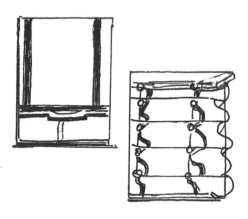

Roman shade with inset border (left).
Back of Roman shade (right).

Exterior view of a sash window
with "six over six" panes

SASH WINDOW

A double-hung window with sashes (frames) to hold the glazing (glass). The window slides up and down in vertical grooves and is moved by a pulley system.

SHEERS

Curtains made of transparent, or nearly transparent, fabric. They are more useful for filtering light than for privacy since, although they obscure windows by day, they become very see-through with artificial internal light at night.

SIDE CURTAINS

(See *dress curtains*.)

SKYLIGHT

An opening in a roof that is most often protected with toughened glass and that is designed to admit more light to an upper room. Most skylight manufacturers now sell specially fitted Venetian blinds to go with their skylights. Alternatively, casement curtains can be used or, if you have relatively easy access to the skylight, then roller, Venetian, or mini blinds can be held against the wall with a cup hook, though the latter is a less satisfactory solution than fitted blinds or casement curtains.

SWAG AND TAILS

A somewhat grand, mainly nineteenth-century curtain treatment that consists of what looks like an extra length of fabric draped in a half-moon shape across the top of the window—*the swag*—with either end falling in careful folds down the sides—*the tails*. In fact, the tails are usually pleated and sewed onto the swag separately. However, there are less-complicated ways of achieving much the same effect by, for example, casually winding a hemmed and perhaps edged or fringed length of fabric around a pole so that the ends hang down over the curtains or sides

A simple form of swag and tails

A swag and tail or cascade, ca. 1825–30

of the windows, or by attaching a length of fabric to either end of a pole so that it drapes over the curtains like a shawl. In any event, it is necessary to have high ceilings and a large traditional room to carry off such a treatment.

TIE-BACK

If you do not want curtains or drapes hanging straight to the floor when pulled aside, you can loop them back with tie-backs. Usually used in pairs, tie-backs are made in different shapes from stiffened matching or contrasting fabric or interlined tubes of fabric, or heavy cords, and are attached to the walls at either side of a window with rings and hooks. The usual height to position the hooks is two-thirds of the way down the window, but of course they can be placed wherever you think the resulting swoops of fabric will look most effective. Contrast lining, or half-lining, looks very good when held back by tie-backs.

VALANCE

Valances give a decorative finish to curtains or drapes and sometimes shades as well as hide the hardware of the less-decorative headings. Straight and shaped valances can be lined with buckram and given a soft flannel interlining concealed by the lining, or they can be pleated by hand or by using

A shaped and fabric-covered valance

a heading tape. A valance can either be attached to a shelf that either sits above the curtain or drapery rod or has the rod fixed to its underside, or it can be attached to the panels of fabric themselves with a decorative pole. (See also *cornice*, *pelmet*, and *lambrequin*.)

VERTICAL BLINDS

These are made from threaded-together slats or louvers that can be angled to admit or close out light, and are vertical so that they can be drawn from side to side and are thus practical for patio, veranda, or French doors. When fully closed, and if made from strips of linen, they look like large panels of fabric. Slats are usually made either from the stiffened strips of linen, or of vinyl or aluminum.

VENETIAN BLINDS

These are like slatted or louvered vertical blinds, but are horizontal and have narrower slats. They can be made in vinyl, aluminum, stiffened fabrics, or wood.

VENETIAN WINDOW

(See *venetian window* in Architectural, Building, and Decorating Terms.)

WOVEN WOOD SHADES
OR WOVEN WOOD BLINDS

Horizontal slats of wood woven together with different weavings of yarn. They are constructed similar to Roman shades—that is, they are pulled up in horizontal folds—but are sometimes made to be vertical.

WOODS FOR FURNITURE AND FLOORS

A culture is no better than its woods.

W. H. Auden (1907–1973), from *Bucolics*

From the advent of the earliest woodworking tools made in the ancient world, wood has been a staple—and stable—material for flooring and furniture. Of course, particularly for floors, sometimes other grander and harder materials—such as marble and stone, slate and travertine, and limestone and sandstone—have been favored by those who could afford them. Other, more affordable alternatives to wood flooring include bricks, clay and ceramic tiles, polished concrete, and, since the twentieth century, rubber, linoleum, and vinyl. Practically speaking, however, compared with very hard stone or tiled floors, wood has more "give" and is thus easier on the feet. Nonetheless, wood floors, too, like other hard flooring, are often covered with rugs to soften them, and when deemed out of fashion, they have been covered by wall-to-wall carpet. Particularly since the twentieth century, furniture, too, has been made from alternative materials, including plastics, steel, leather, chrome, and glass. Nevertheless, wood has generally remained the key component for flooring and furniture, whether used unadorned, polished, lacquered, painted, turned into parquetry, or, particularly in the case of furniture, carved, gilded, or inlaid. Wood is certainly longer lasting than cheaper materials and, for furniture, is capable of being conjured into endless permutations.

International trade and shipping—since the Age of Exploration, during the subsequent centuries of British and European colonization, and up until the present day—greatly increased the accessibility and taste for exotic woods. In fact, the demand was so great that by the eighteenth century, as Geoffrey Beard has pointed out in his excellent book *The National Trust Book of English Furniture*, "No furniture maker could advance his business without maintaining and using a wide range of woods, both indigenous and exotic."

Today, due to over lumbering or other commercial or environmental reasons, some woods have become endangered. As a result, manufacturers of furniture and an increasing number of individual craftspeople and woodworkers are more skilled at staining and graining readily available woods to simulate finer and rarer species. Nevertheless, there is still an extraordinary choice of woods from all over the world to be procured for floors and furniture, as well as many sources for old and recycled woods for floors. The choice is so large that it is useful to have some knowledge of the color, graining, and figuring of all this exotica and of what woods are best used for what purposes.

ACACIA

Hard, durable wood with brownish markings that ranges from a light brown to a kind of reddish green. It looks a little like the American locust wood, and in the eighteenth century it was used as a substitute for the rarer tulipwood, particularly for inlays and bandings.

ACAJOU OR ACAJOU MOUCHETE

French term for *mahogany*. The mouchete variety is very fine quality with a slightly wavy grain and small darkish spots; it was much used for tables, commodes, cabinets, and other smaller pieces during the reign of Louis XVI.

ALDER

Pale wood with occasional curled fig-uring (meaning, a wood's markings). In the eighteenth century it was used for country furniture and often for the rails of some types of Windsor chairs.

AMBOYNA

Light golden-brown West Indian wood with a tight "bird's eye" figuring, used as a veneer and as decorative banding. It is sometimes confused with African thuya wood.

APPLEWOOD

Hard, heavy, close-grained wood of a light reddish-brown color. It was much used in the seventeenth century as a veneer and an inlay and later, in America, for country furniture. It is also one of the sweetest-smelling firewoods.

ASH

Grayish white wood with light brown veining that, although hard, is often attacked by worms. It was mostly used for cheaper country chairs and the seats of Windsor chairs, as well as for drawer linings. Some Georgian pieces have a decorative veneer of ash culled from specially polled trees.

ASPEN

A silky, light-colored, slightly striped American wood rather like the European white poplar. It has a natural sheen.

AVODIRE

Blond, lustrous African wood with brown vertical streaks used for contemporary cabinetwork and for veneers.

BASSWOOD

Light-colored wood from the northern United States and Canada. It does not warp easily and is used for crossbanding in plywood panels as well as for carving.

BAYWOOD

This is also called *Honduras mahogany* although it is lighter than Cuban or Spanish mahogany and is much used for veneers.

BEECH

Light-brown soft (but not softwood) wood that resembles both birch and maple. It has a speckled grain and is subject to worm attacks. It was often used as a substitute for walnut and particularly for the stained or painted cane-back chairs of the seventeenth century. Since it was one of the cheapest woods available, late Georgian painted chairs were often made of beech. It was also used very frequently, as it still is, for carcase work, and as rocker supports and bent chair backs, as well as for bed frames.

BENGE

Hard, rich, brown African wood with dark markings.

BIRCH

Some figured cuts closely resemble the much more expensive satinwood, for which it was sometimes used as a substitute from the end of the eighteenth century. It was mostly used for chair making and for cheaper country furniture, as well as for door trims and floors.

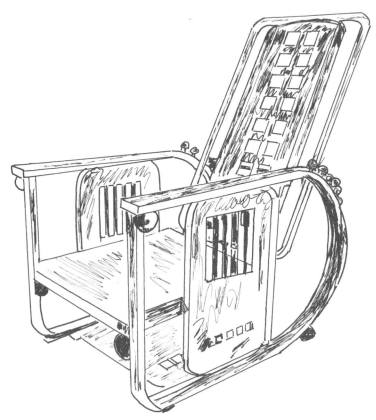

Josef Hoffmann's beechwood Sitzmaschine ("Machine for Sitting"), designed 1904, stained to look like cherry

BIRD'S-EYE MAPLE

Curly-grained, "blistered" veneer, made from maple wood. (See also *maple*.)

BLACKWOOD

Native to Australia and Tasmania. It is very similar to acacia and can be used similarly for veneers and banding.

BOXWOOD

Hard yellowish wood with a fine grain. It was used from the sixteenth century for the inlay for oak and walnut, and in the eighteenth century for border lines on satinwood furniture.

BRAZILWOOD

Reddish, strongly marked wood that is very similar to mahogany. In the seventeenth century it was used as an inlay, but not much thereafter.

BURL

A term for a growth found in the root of a tree (or bole). It is sliced for veneers so that the underdeveloped buds and pith centers integral to the growth form "eyelike" pits or a "knotted" effect. This burl appears in walnut and myrtle, among other woods.

CALAMANDER

Brown-mottled, fine-grained wood streaked with black from Sri Lanka (formerly Ceylon). Popular through the second half of the eighteenth century for bandings and veneers.

CEDAR

A light, reddish-brown, rather soft wood used from about 1750 for drawer linings, boxes, chests (the insides and out), and wardrobes. It was and is much valued for its moth- and insect-repelling qualities.

CHERRY

Close-grained, hard, reddish wood used for smaller early furniture as well as for some seventeenth-century inlays. Quite often used for chests of drawers, and small side and bedside tables, from the nineteenth century onward. When it ages it looks like mahogany.

CHESTNUT

Whitish horse chestnut is used for small drawer linings and, when figured, as a veneer. *Sweet chestnut* tends to be a more reddish-brown red. It was used a lot in the seventeenth century for carved chairs because it sometimes resembled walnut. Both varieties were also used for late-eighteenth-century veneers since they somewhat, like birch, resembled the highly prized satinwood.

COROMANDEL

Wood from the Coromandel Coast often described as "streaked ebony." The Chinese used it for much-prized screens as well as for occasional tables. It was also used as a veneer and as banding in the eighteenth century.

CYPRESS

Moth- and worm-repelling wood originally from Persia (now Iran) and the Levant, but also native to America. It has been used for furniture since earliest times, and especially for chests and cupboards where clothes and linens were to be stored.

DEAL

Name for *southern yellow pine* in the United States, *northern soft pine* in Canada, and *Scotch fir* in the United Kingdom. It is predominantly used for carcase work; for plain, simple furniture; and for wainscoting.

EBONY

Extremely hard, close-grained wood used as an early inlay and for turned woods. In the early nineteenth century, especially for Biedermeier furniture, pearwood was stained black to imitate ebony. Today, although expensive, it is used to make handsome staircases and furniture.

ELM

Hard, tough wood that takes stain and polish well, though it is liable to warp, and is receptive to worms. It was usually used for the seats of Windsor chairs and for country furniture. *Burr elm* was used as a veneer. Elm disease has made it rare in Europe.

FIGURE OR FIGURING

The markings or grain of a wood.

Writing cabinet veneered with "oyster" princewood (another name for kingwood), ca. 1675

HARDWOOD

As opposed to softwood, or wood from conifers. Hardwood is really the lumber obtained from broad-leafed and deciduous trees such as oak, maple, beech, walnut, sycamore, and mahogany. Since it is porous, it is not truly hard.

HAREWOOD

Actually a sycamore veneer, sometimes called *silverwood* because it stains a silvery-gray color. It was popular for banding for eighteenth-century furniture and is still used for cabinetwork.

HICKORY

Tough North American wood not unlike walnut.

HOLLY

Hard white Native American and European wood with almost no grain. It has been used an inlay from the sixteenth century until today, as well as for marquetry furniture, stringing, and banding. It takes stain easily, but browns with age and exposure to too much sun.

KILN-DRIED LUMBER

(See *kiln-dried lumber* in Architectural, Building, and Decorating Terms.)

KINGWOOD

Brazilian wood, also a native of Sumatra, not unlike rosewood, but lighter and with more contrasting markings. In the late seventeenth century it was sometimes used as a veneer. In the late eighteenth century it was often used both as a veneer and for crossbanded borders, as it still can be. Also known as "oyster" princewood.

KNOTTY PINE

Pinewood that shows a good many darkish oval shapes formed by the knots in the wood. When the wood is pickled or whitened, as it often is for paneling, the knots become exaggerated.

LABURNUM

Southern European and British yellowish wood with brown streaking that is still used. It was used in parquetry floors and for early furniture, as well as for "oystershell" decoration for the fronts of cabinet doors and drawer fronts in the William and Mary and Queen Anne periods (oystershell decoration is achieved by cutting transverse slices through a gnarled bough of both laburnum and walnut to form a particularly decorative veneer).

LACEWOOD

Decorative, lacy veneer wood from Australia.

LIGNUM VITAE

Hard, dark-brown West Indian wood streaked with black, used both as a veneer and for turned furniture in the seventeenth century by the Dutch and the Flemish as well as for linen chests and cupboards. Introduced to Europe in the sixteenth century for its medicinal properties, its name means "wood of life."

LIME OR LINDEN

Soft, close-grained, whitish-yellow British wood, though the American *basswood* is sometimes called *linden* as well. It has been beloved by carvers since Grinling Gibbons's (see also *Carolean style* in Styles and Movements) day in the seventeenth century to the present time.

LIMED OAK

The silvery-gray finish given to oak to give it a frosted appearance and to accentuate the grain. It was particularly popular in the 1930s. Much the same treatment—a white filler or paint rubbed into the grain and then wiped off—can be given to several woods, and is a handsome treatment for floorboards. All woods treated this way should always be sealed after the process.

MAHOGANY

A handsome, reddish wood with an attractive grain. It has been popular for furniture since the eighteenth century, polishes well, and is worm resistant. It is available in wide widths as well as long lengths and comes from Africa, Cuba, Central and South America, and Spain (one of the best). *Honduras mahogany* is a paler yellowish-rose to golden-brown color. *Madeira mahogany*, sometimes called "canary wood" (after the Canary Islands) is a light, yellowish-brown

MAPLE

Hard, light-colored wood that is straight-grained and not unlike birch. It is much-used for interior finishes and was used in the seventeenth and eighteenth centuries for marquetry and veneer.

MYRTLE BURL

Native of the western United States producing attractively figured blonde to golden wood used mostly for cabinet-work, veneers, and inlay. (See also *burl*.)

OAK

One of the first woods used for furniture, carving, paneling, and floorboards. It is hard, durable, and sturdy, in either a slightly reddish or whitish color, and was generally seasoned in water. *English, Scandinavian*, and *French oaks* are rather finer grained than *American oaks*. Both types need to be filled before taking a stain because they are porous. It is generally "plain sawed," that is to say, sawed parallel with the diameter of the trunk. *Bog oak*—oak preserved in peat bogs—turns almost black and was used as an inlay together with holly during the age of early oak furniture

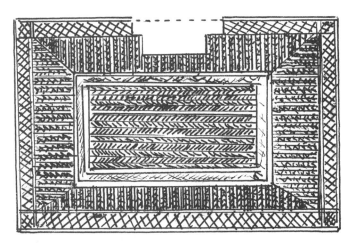

A mahogany and oak floor

in the sixteenth and early seventeenth centuries. Whiter, softer clapboard was originally American oak.

OLIVE

Hard, greenish-yellow wood with black spots and veining that is a little like walnut, English ash, and yew. It was much used in the late seventeenth and eighteenth centuries for parquetry floors and is often used for inlays. It takes polish extremely well.

ORIENTAL WOOD

Hard, tough Australian wood with a pinkish cast and distinctive streaks. It is also called *Australian laurel, Australian walnut,* and *Oriental walnut.*

OYSTER GRAIN

Walnut-wood veneer, popular for furniture in the Queen Anne period, so figured to resemble the inside of an oyster shell.

PADAUK

Southeast Asian tree with a reddish wood which, in texture, resembles rosewood. It was imported into Europe after 1730 and was mostly, but rarely, used for solid wood furniture.

PARQUET FLOOR

Strips of wood—sometimes of different colors—inlaid to form different floor designs. (See also *parquet flooring* in Flooring.)

PARTRIDGE WOOD

Streaked red-and-brown Brazilian wood that resembles a partridge's feathers. It was used both as an inlay in the seventeenth century and a veneer in the eighteenth.

PEAR

Yellowy or pinkish-brown dense wood with almost no figuring and a slight resemblance to boxwood. It is sometimes used for carving and for fine

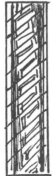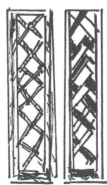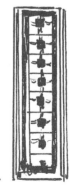

Parquet borders combining cherry, rosewood, maple, thuya wood, walnut, and mahogany, ca. 1900

cabinetwork, and was also used for early country furniture as well as for inlays. For the latter it was occasionally stained to simulate ebony.

PECAN

United States and Australian wood from the hickory family that, logically, since the nuts are similar, looks like walnut. Pecan and walnut are sometimes used in conjunction with each other on furniture.

PINE

American pine, a softwood, has an interesting grain, is easy to work with, and is popular for furniture as well as for many interior finishes. *White pine* is a softwood of little interest used for structural purposes and generally painted rather than stained. *Yellow pine*, also a softwood, is tougher and often used for floors, doors, and trims. Again, it is mostly painted rather than stained. It is often used for country furniture. (See also *deal*.)

PICKLED PINE

Like limed oak, this rub-off paint finish gives a whitish-grayish finish or whitish rubbed look to pine panels and furniture, and accentuates the grain and knots.

PLANE

A whitish, close-grained wood derived from the English sycamore tree. It was used in the eighteenth century for veneers and inlays and in country furniture as a substitute for beech and a base for painted chairs.

PLUM

Hard, heavy yellow to reddish-brown wood used both for turned legs and for inlays up until the eighteenth century.

PLYWOOD

Panels of wood with a thick, semiporous core and thin laminated layers of veneer layered to either side with the grain of the veneer running perpendicular to the grain of the core. The top layer is a veneer that runs parallel to the core, so that all tensions are pulling in different directions to ensure great strength. It is much used in construction.

PURPLE WOOD OR VIOLET WOOD

Hard, heavy Brazilian wood with a purplish cast that turns brown when exposed to air. It is not unlike rosewood. It was used from the late eighteenth century for veneers, and sometimes for banding on satinwood.

ROSETTA WOOD

Red-colored wood with dramatic black graining widely used by Spanish and Indian craftsmen in South America during the seventeenth and eighteenth centuries, although it came from the East Indies. It was also used as decorative panels on some early American chests.

ROSEWOOD

This comes from both Brazil and India, is marked with dark streaks, has an even grain, and veers from a light hazel to a rich, warm, rosy brown. It is actually called rosewood because it smells like roses when it is cut. It was used from the sixteenth century on as a veneer and for banding and from the early nineteenth century as a solid. It also makes very handsome floorboards.

SABICU

Hard-wearing Cuban wood used as a substitute for mahogany.

SANDALWOOD

Yellowish close-grained wood grown on East Indian and Pacific Islands. It is rarely used for furniture but often for intricately carved doors, boxes, and ornamental objects. It also has a quite distinctive smell, which is often used for incense.

SAPELE

Another substitute for mahogany from Africa, but harder and more evenly striped.

SATINWOOD

A great favorite for furniture in the eighteenth century, when its lustrous pale yellow was much used for veneers and inlays, as well as for solid pieces of furniture. It was also used a background for the painted medallions fashionable at the time. It was forced to give way to a trend for rosewood during the first twenty years of the nineteenth century, but came back into favor soon after and has remained a popular wood ever since. The West Indian or Guianan variety was introduced around 1760 and the East Indian type in 1780. The latter becomes cloudier when polished.

SNAKEWOOD

Dark-brown spotted red wood sometimes used as an inlay in the seventeenth century, then as a veneer in the late eighteenth century.

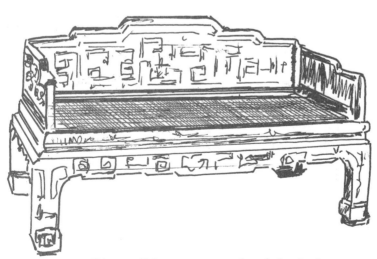

Chinese Ch'uang rosewood and chestnut
couch, late eighteenth to early nineteenth century

SYCAMORE

Sometimes called *harewood*. A white, fine-grained wood that resembles plane wood and polishes very well. It was a favorite inlay for the floral marquetry work of the late seventeenth century, and has been used for veneers ever since. When stained with oxide of iron, it takes on a delicate greenish-gray color.

TEAK

Tough light-brown wood that grows darker as it ages. It is native to India, Burma, Java, and the Malay Peninsula, and much valued in tropical countries because of its imperviousness to insects, heat, fungus, and rot. For these reasons it is a favorite wood for outdoor furniture.

THUYA WOOD

North African reddish-brown or golden-brown wood with a bird's-eye pattern. It was used from earliest times by the ancient Greeks and Chinese, and has been used for cabinetwork through-out history and was occasionally used in the eighteenth century as a veneer.

TULIP WOOD

Yellowish-brown wood with reddish stripes from Brazil. It was much used during the Empire and Regency periods for crossbanding.

WALNUT

Another early wood, the *European variety* was in use since the Tudor period, and both the ordinary *English*

Early-nineteenth-century
Polish armchair made
of thuya veneer

variety and the *black walnut* were being grown in England from the second half of the seventeenth century, although the latter was more prized. It was also grown throughout Asia, Africa, and America, although *American walnut* has a somewhat coarser grain, making it very good for floorboards. It produces a large range of different markings depending on the slicing method used. *Burr walnut* is particularly finely figured.

WENGE

African wood popular today for wood countertops, window frames, and shelves.

WILLOW

This was often dyed black and used as a substitute for ebony in the seventeenth, eighteenth, and nineteenth centuries.

BIBLIOGRAPHY

Author's Note: Books consulted both for reference and for illustrations are listed under section headings. Some, of a more general nature, appear in several sections. Several of the books from my own library are now out of print but, since they are classics in the field, they can usually be found without too much difficulty in the architectural and design sections of secondhand bookstores.

ARCHITECTS, DESIGNERS, AND DECORATORS AND STYLES AND MOVEMENTS

Abercrombie, Stanley. *A Century of Interior Design: 1900 to 2000*. New York: Rizzoli, 2003.

The American Renaissance, 1876–1917. New York: The Brooklyn Museum and Pantheon Books, 1979.

Beard, Geoffrey. *Craftsmen and Interior Decoration in England, 1660–1820*. London: Bloomsbury Books, 1986.

Beard, Geoffrey. *The Work of Robert Adam*. Edinburgh and London: John Bartholomew & Son Ltd., 1978.

Boulti, Rinato. *Art Nouveau*. London: Cassel, 1987.

Chadanet, Sylvie. *Tous les Styles du Louis XIII à l'Art Deco*. Paris: Elina/Sofedis, 1973.

Fleming, John, Hugh Honour, and Nikolaus Pevsner. *The Penguin*

Dictionary of Architecture and Landscape Architecture, 5th edition. London: Penguin Books, 1999.

Fowler, John, and John Cornforth. *English Decoration in the 18th Century*. London: Barrie & Jenkins, 1986.

Gilliatt, Mary. *Period Style*. New York: Little, Brown & Company, 1990.

Gore, Alan, and Ann Gore. *The History of English Interiors*. London: Phaidon, 1991.

Heyer, Paul. *Architects on Architecture*. New York: Walker & Co., 1966.

Kidson, Peter (Part I) and Peter Murry (Part II). *A History of English Architecture*. London: George G. Harrap & Co., 1967.

McCorquodale, Charles. *A History of the Interior*. New York: Vendome Press, 1983.

Miller, Judith. *Influential Styles*. New York: Watson-Guptill Publications, 2003.

Norwich, John Julius, gen. ed. *Great Architecture of the World*. New York: Random House, 1975.

Palladio, Andrea. *The Four Books of Architecture*. New York: Dover Publications Inc., 1965.

Pegler, Martin M. *The Dictionary of Interior Design*. New York: Fairchild Publications, 2001.

Pevsner, Nikolaus. *Studies in Art, Architecture and Design*. London: Thames & Hudson, 1968.

Pignatti, Terisio. *The Age of Rococo*. London: Cassell, 1984.

Praz, Mario. *An Illustrated History of Interior Decoration, from Pompeii to Art Nouveau*. London: Thames & Hudson, 1982. (First published as *La filosofia dell'arredemento*; first English edition, Thames and Hudson, London, 1964.)

Seidler, Harry. *The Grand Tour: Travelling the World with an Architect's Eye*. Köln: Taschen, 2003.

Smith, G. E. Kidder. *The New Architecture of Europe*. London: Prentice Hall International, 1962.

Smith, G. E. Kidder. *A Pictorial History of Architecture in America*, 2 vols. New York: American Heritage Publishing and W.W. Norton & Co., Inc., 1976.

Spencer, Robin. *The Aesthetic Movement*. London: Studio Vista/Dutton Paperback, 1972.

Thornton, Peter. *Authentic Décor, The Domestic Interior 1620–1920*. New York: Viking Penguin Inc., 1984.

Thornton, Peter. *The Italian Renaissance Interior 1400–1600*. New York: Harry N. Abrams Inc., 1991.

Varnedoe, Kirk. *Vienna 1900, Art, Architecture and Design*. New York: The Museum of Modern Art, 1986.

Watkin, David. *A History of Western Architecture*. London: Lawrence King Publishing, 1986.

Whitford, Frank. *Bauhaus*. London: Thames & Hudson, 1984.

Wrenn, Tony P. and Elizabeth D. Mulloy. *America's Forgotten Architecture*. Washington, D.C. and New York: The National Trust for Historic Preservation and Pantheon Books, 1976.

Yarwood, Doreen. *English Interiors: A Pictorial Guide and Glossary*. Cambridge, England: Lutterworth Press, 1983.

ARCHITECTURAL, BUILDING, AND DECORATING TERMS

Calloway, Stephen, ed. *The Elements of Style*. London: Mitchell Beazley, 1991.

Fleming, John, Hugh Honour, and Nikolaus Pevsner. *The Penguin Dictionary of Architecture and Landscape Architecture*. London: Penguin Books, 1999.

Gilliatt, Mary. *Great Renovations and Restorations*. New York: Watson-Guptill Publications, 2003.

Lander, Hugh. *The House Restorer's Guide*. London: David & Charles, 1986.

Lawrence, Richard Russell and Teresa Chris. *The Period House: Style, Detail, and Decoration, 1774–1914*. London: Weidenfeld and Nicolson, 1996.

FABRIC AND WALLPAPER

Cooke, Jr., Edward S., ed. *Upholstery in America and Europe from the Seventeenth Century to World War I*. New York: W.W. Norton/A Barra Foundation Book, 1987.

A Dictionary of Textile Terms. New York: Dan River Inc., 1971

Hoskins, Leslie, ed. *The Papered Wall, History, Pattern, Technique*. New York: Harry N. Abrams, Inc., 1994.

Nylander, Jane C. *Fabrics for Historic Buildings*. Washington, D.C.: The Preservation Press/National Trust for Historic Renovation, 1983.

Phillips, Barty. *Fabrics and Wallpapers*. New York: Bulfinch, 1991.

Zaczec, Iain. *The Essential William Morris*. London: Parragon, 1999.

Saunders, Gill. *Wallpaper in Interior Decoration*. New York: Watson-Guptill Publications, 2002.

FLOORING

Calloway, Stephen, ed. *The Elements of Style*. London: Mitchell Beasley, 1991.

Gilliatt, Mary. *Mary Gilliatt's Interior Design Course*. New York: Watson-Guptill Publications, 2002

Gilliatt, Mary. *The Decorating Book*. London: Penguin Books, Ltd., 1981.

Lot, Jane. *Floors and Flooring*. The Habitat Home Decorator. London: Conran Octopus, 1985.

Whiton, Sherril. *Interior Design and Decoration*. New York: J. B. Lippincott Company, 1974.

COLOR, PAINTS, VARNISHES, AND DECORATIVE FINISHES

Davidson, Alex. *Interior Affairs: The Decorative Arts in Paintwork*. New York: Sterling Publishing Company, Inc., 1991.

Fastnedge, Ralph. *English Furniture Styles from 1500 to 1830*. London: Penguin Books, 1955. (Note: Included here for its marvelous recipes for gilding, lacquering, and japanning.)

Gilliatt, Mary. *The Mary Gilliatt Book of Color*. New York: Little, Brown & Company, 1985.

Hunt, Belinda. *Decorative Paint Finishes*. London: Ebury Press, 1987.

Kaufman, Donald, and Taffy Dahl. *Color: Natural Palettes for Painted Rooms*. New York: Clarkson Potter, 1992.

Sloan, Annie, and Kate Gwynn. *Color in Decoration*. New York: Little, Brown & Company, 1980.

FURNITURE AND UPHOLSTERY

Bates, Elizabeth Bidwell, and Jonathan L. Fairbanks. *American Furniture, 1620 to the Present*. New York: Richard Marek Publishers, 1981.

Beard, Geoffrey. *The National Trust Book of English Furniture*. London: Viking, 1985.

Cooke, Jr., Edward S., ed. *Upholstery in America and Europe from the Seventeenth Century to the Present*. New York: W.W. Norton/A Barra Foundation Book, 1987.

Fastnedge, Ralph. *English Furniture Styles from 1500–1830*. London: Penguin Books, 1961.

The Late Georgian Period, 1760–1810. London: The Connoisseur, 1956.

Moody, Ella. *Modern Furniture*. New York: Dutton Vista Pictureback, 1966.

Pictorial Dictionary of British 19th Century Furniture Design. Woodbridge, England: Antique Collectors' Club, 1977.

Sheraton, Thomas. *The Cabinet-Maker and Upholsterer's Drawing Book*. New York: Dover Publications, Inc., 1972.

Taylor, V. J. *The Antique Furniture Trail*. London: David & Charles, 1989.

Ward-Jackson, Peter. *English Furniture Designs of the Eighteenth Century*. London: Victoria & Albert Museum, 1984.

GLASS AND CERAMICS

Art & Design in Europe and America 1800–1900 at the Victoria & Albert Museum. London: Herbert, 1987.

Battie, David, ed. *Sotheby's Concise Encyclopedia of Porcelain*. London: Conran Octopus, 1990.

Charleston, Robert J., ed. *World Ceramics*. London: Paul Hamlyn, 1968.

LIGHTING

Gilliatt, Mary, and Douglas Baker. *Lighting Your Home: A Practical Guide*. New York: Arrow, 1980.

Gilliatt, Mary. *Mary Gilliatt's Interior Design Course*. New York: Watson-Guptill Publications, 2002.

Sudjic, Deyan. *The Lighting Book: A Complete Guide to Lighting Your Home*. London: Mitchell Beazley, 1985.

ORIENTAL AND OTHER RUGS

Bosly, Caroline. *Rugs to Riches: An Insider's Guide to Oriental Rugs*. New York: Pantheon Books, 1980.

O'Bannon, George. *Oriental Rug: The Collector's Guide to Selecting, Identifying, and Enjoying New and Antique Oriental Rugs*. Philadelphia: Courage Books, 1995.

WINDOWS AND WINDOW TREATMENTS

Calloway, Stephen, ed. *The Elements of Style*. London: Mitchell Beazley, 1991.

Fleming, John, Hugh Honour, and Nikolaus Pevsner. *The Penguin Dictionary of Architecture and Landscape Architecture*, 5th edition. London: Penguin Books, 1999.

Hoppen, Stephanie. *The New Curtain Book: Master Classes with Today's Top Designers*. New York: Bullfinch, 2003.

Lander, Hugh. *The House Restorers' Guide*. London: David & Charles, 1988.

WOODS FOR FURNITURE AND FLOORS

Beard, Geoffrey. *The National Trust Book of English Furniture*. London: Penguin Books, 1985. (Note: Included here for its exceptionally fine glossary on woods.)

Calloway, Stephen, ed. *The Elements of Style*. London: Mitchell Beazley, 1991.

Pegler, Martin. *The Dictionary of Interior Design*. New York: Fairchild Publications, 2001.

INDEX

NOTE: **Bold** page references signify main headings in this dictionary. *Italic* references signify illustrations. Plain page references signify other mentions.